FASTBALL JOHN

FASTBALL JOHN

John D'Acquisto
Dave Jordan

INSTREAM BOOKS

NEW YORK

Instream Books

FASTBALL JOHN. Copyright © 2015 by JF D'Acquisto/Dave Jordan. All
Right Reserved. Printed in the Unted States. For information, address 750
Lexington Avenue, New York, NY 10022

www.instreamsports.com

The Library of Congress Cataloging-in-Publication Data is available
upon request.

2015 by John F. D'Acquisto & Dave Jordan

ISBN-13: 978-0692750278 (paperback)

ISBN-10 0692750274 (e-book)

Second Edition: June 2017

10 9 8 7 6 5 4 3 2 1

For Mom and Dad

The following is a work of non-fiction. While some of the identities have been changed to respect the privacy of certain non-public friends, loved ones and associates I've met along the way, the events, the intimacies, the circumstances and the outcomes you are about to experience are all true.

For better and for worse...

Contents

Foreword

No period in baseball history was more tumultuous than the one that stretched from the beginning of the 1970s and into the early 1980s. It was an era in which drab wool-blend uniforms were replaced by eye-popping, form-fitting polyester, and pristinely manicured grass playing surfaces were muscled out by budget-friendly Astroturf; a time where players felt free to fly their freak flags on the field, and fans felt entitled to express themselves by invading it. The antiquated Reserve Clause that bound players to their teams in perpetuity was finally done away with in 1976, allowing players to play out their options and take their services elsewhere, usually for a lot more money than they were previously earning. Not coincidentally, the 1970s and early 80s also saw the game nearly go completely off the rails on three separate occasions, thanks to work stoppages resulting from increasingly heated battles between the MLB team owners and the Marvin Miller-led Players Association.

It's also an era that syncs up almost exactly with John D'Acquisto's professional playing career. When the San Francisco Giants picked him in the first round of the 1970 June Amateur Draft, he was a good-looking high school grad out of San Diego with a live arm and the burning desire to use it on a major league diamond. By the time he hung up his cleats in 1983, he was a well-traveled veteran who'd pitched for six different major league teams and eight different minor league ones, played under some of the era's most iconic owners and managers, rubbed shoulders with (or pitched against) some of the greatest players of his day, and selflessly served as a player rep during one of the nastiest labor disputes in MLB history — an endeavor that probably did his career no favors.

John D'Acquisto saw some shit, in other words; and in this enormously entertaining book you're about to dig into, he shares his view from the mound, the dugout and the clubhouse. There's no shortage of off-the-field color in here, either: Dalliances with "Baseball Annies," long-distance drag races with teammates, inadvertent business dealings with mobsters, soul-crushing negotiations with agents and owners — it's all part of the Fastball John story. Music plays a big part in the story, as well. Like so many children of the original rock and roll era, John grew up with at least one ear constantly cocked towards the nearest AM radio, and he remained tuned in through all the musical changes of the 1970s. The Carpenters, the Eagles, Jefferson Starship, Diana Ross, and Blondie are some of the 70s artists who appear as part of this book's "soundtrack," serving as Greek choruses to John's narration, or as triggers for memories that have long lay dormant. It's part of what makes this book such a fantastically evocative trip back in time.

Unless you followed baseball religiously during the 1970s, it's entirely possible that you're unfamiliar with John D'Acquisto's name and career. After The Sporting News named him the National League's Rookie Pitcher of the Year for 1974, injuries and an inability to consistently control his fearsome heater kept him from fully living up to his potential; he never made an All-Star team (though he came close in 1978), and the closest he ever came to post-season glory was pitching for the Montreal Expos during the last two months of their ultimately unsuccessful bid to capture the 1980 NL East flag.

Don't let John's lack of superstar credentials or Hall of Fame-worthy accomplishments dissuade you from reading his story, however. For my money, this is the best book ever written about what it was like to be a "Baseball everyman" in the major leagues amid the craziness of the 1970s. Fastball John puts you in the shoes of a player talented enough to be in the bigs, but not other-worldly enough to consistently guarantee himself a place on the roster. It communicates the confusion of being traded to another team in the middle of the night, and captures the heartbreak of watching the managers you love get fired. It brings to life the brutal grind of a 162-game season, and illustrates why a stint with a minor league team in Hawaii might sometimes be preferable to pitching for a no-hope major league squad. It also vividly renders the loneliness of life on the road, the anxiety of dealing with contract negotiations, and the difficulty of finding your place in the world once your playing career comes to an end.

For all of that, though, Fastball John is anything but a bummer. It's an uproarious tale told with wit, humor and honesty, and it reads as if you were sitting across the table from the man himself while sharing a nice chianti and a pot of linguini fra diavolo. Is that Fleetwood Mac's Rumours I hear? 'Scuse me while I go turn up the stereo...

— **Dan Epstein**

author of *Big Hair and Plastic Grass: A Funky Ride Through Baseball and America in the Swinging '70s.*

San Diego: December, 1995

The first thing I heard was the screeching of their tires puncturing the tranquility of a Sunday afternoon. Unmarked cars rarely traveled 40 miles per hour down my quiet, residential street with such an immediacy and desire to let my neighbors know something was about to go down.

What could be so urgent?

As I emptied the garbage in front of my driveway, three men, one suited, two in plain clothes, jumped out of their vehicle, stepped quickly over and into my face.

"Are you John D'Acquisto?" one of them asked, "We're with the Secret Service. You're under arrest for securities fraud."

I was dumbfounded. My wife Michelle rushed out the front door.

"What's going on?" she said, worry rising in her voice.

"What are you talking about?" I said, as they tried to twirl my six-foot, two-inch frame, curling handcuffs across my wrists.

"You know damn well why we're here," one of the plain-clothes men said with a snide tone, as he looked up into my eyes.

"Watch the arm," I demanded, as if by instinct, as I was led into the back of the car, gently pushing me headfirst down into the vehicle. *No Miranda rights reading.*

"Johnny, what's the matter?" Michelle shrieked, approaching the car.

"Stay back, ma'am," one of the agents scolded my wife.

"Call Tom and Allan," I told her from the back seat.

Driving away, I saw my son John-Paul staring out from the window, by the dining room curtain, the same questions running through his mind as mine. *"What the hell is going on here? Why are they treating me like this? I'm not a criminal."* As I shook with worry and concern, passing the many San Diego landmarks of my childhood, I never for the life of me considered that the man who was known for striking out the side in the big leagues would be mired in one humiliating inning for the next seven years...

The Draft

Throughout my life, the music playing in the car set the tone for my day. Upbeat tempo, rockin' tunes, the mellow stuff, really anything that would get me in the mood. From my earliest days, I would hear a song on the radio and I would drift into the world of its lyrics and melody.

My mother drove me to the Mike Marrow Little League field in May of 1958. I was seven years old, and it seemed like The Everly Brothers were the only singers on the airwaves at that time. We stopped off at the complex on my way home from a Cub Scout meeting to see my brother Fred's game. Dad was the coach for Fred's team and also manicured the fields. Mom would work the concession stands with the other mothers, like Mary Nettles, who was also a league coordinator, mother to Graig and Jimmy, two boys among the shining youth baseball stars of the community. That day I was worried about building my car for the upcoming pinewood derby, but all I had to do was step onto the gravel of the little league parking lot and I would dream about Baseball and playing on Fred's team.

The memories of these times are rich with color, strikeouts in saturated hues. Snapshots of my friends running the bases lay stashed in the sharp, Kodachrome photo albums of my mind. All the kids before me on this San Diego little league diamond wore buzzed flattops. Maybe one or two blond-haired kids were the first I saw to sport the emerging surfer kid hairstyle.

I so wanted to be in a baseball uniform, Fred's uniform, definitely not my Cub Scout blues, but rather stirrups and high-stretching socks. My brother was a hero to me growing up. Unlike many siblings in the world, Fred always brought me along with him, regardless of whether his friends were annoyed by my presence. Truth be told, I just wanted to be with both of my idols; My Dad and Fred.

During the game, a batter hit a foul pop over the backstop and into the stands. As I retrieved the ball, the umpire motioned for me to toss it his way. It wasn't much action, but this was a chance to show my stuff. I ran around the dugout opening, into foul territory on the field, wound up and whipped it back at him. The ump didn't make a big deal catching my throw without a glove, but he did shake the sting from his hands, and glance quickly over at me, before handing it to the catcher. I loved seeing that expression on his face, the *"That wasn't just any old throw"* leer he gave me. Not exactly a splash, but the best statement a six-year old wannabe player could make.

That was also the last day I ever wore a Cub Scout uniform.

* * * * *

We lived in North Park, a small, secluded suburb of San Diego. There wasn't a lot of traffic in our one-way-in, one-way-out type of neighborhood. We were neither rich nor poor. Our modest ranch house sat among other track homes in a newly constructed San Diego suburb. All the parents knew each other and looked out for the children as if they were their own. Suburban San Diego was a special place. Definitely isolated from the rest of the world. My parents were second-generation Sicilians. My mother, Frances Piraino, was the fourth of six children. My dad, Fred D'Acquisto, Sr., moved from Milwaukee to San Diego and lived with his aunt and uncle.

Mention the word Sicilian and the term *"mob"* or Mafioso comes to mind. However, my parents were the Italian version of Ozzie and Harriet. Mom and Dad were conventionally ethical, moral and hard-working people who loved their children to death. They corrected us for bad behavior, for good old-fashioned discipline was an integral part of our lives. They never hit us. Intimidation was king in our house - the paddle or wooden spoon was flashed before our eyes in times of childhood mayhem, but never utilized.

To be sure, I always did as I was told.

* * * * *

From ages 9 to 11, I played for every Little League All-Star team. Threw a lot of no-hit games. I don't think I ever lost during that time. Became known for the velocity of my pitches.

During one afternoon in the summer of 1962, I had just hit a home run into the Pony League ball field about 300 feet away. The game started late, so we needed to wrap up before sundown. I had already struck out 13. Last batter stepped to the plate. I went into my windup; the batter knew he hadn't a chance against me.

Three pitches. Game over. No-hitter.

After my teammates surrounded me in celebration and the traditional goodwill handshakes with the opposition, I ran off the field to Mom and Dad. As a five-foot, eight-inch 11-year old, jumping right into their arms was no small act.

"Mom, I threw a no-hitter!" were the first words out of my mouth.

I was so happy to share this with them. My dad, a man of few words, greeted me with the smile of a father who was proud but used to games like this -- it was my fourth no-hitter that year. As we celebrated the win, an unfamiliar gentleman in a beige jacket and khaki pants approached us. He seemed serious, yet carried a polite demeanor.

"Mr. D'Acquisto," he said to my father, "My name is Bob O'Regan. Can I talk to you for a moment?"

Dad nodded and walked over to Mr. O'Regan. Mom brought me to the concession stand to allow them some privacy, and then went back to helping the other mothers behind the grill. As I stood against the wooden walk-up of the canteen enjoying a cherry snow cone, I watched Dad chat with Mr. O'Regan. I blocked out all the ambient sounds of sizzling fries, kids begging moms for Italian ices, and a couple of other games in various states of play.

The conversation seemed serious. Mr. O'Regan handed Dad a business card, as well as a small sheet to fill out. They shook hands and Dad joined us at the snack bar.

"Who was that, Pop?" I asked, snow cone spilling down my cheeks. Dad mussed my hair and grinned.

"Don't talk with your mouth full," Dad laughed. He watched O'Regan walk away, not certain what to make of him.

* * * * *

My dad's meeting with Mr. O'Regan had bugged me all weekend long. The following night, my baby sister Jeannette was sleeping on Mom's shoulder as Dad read the evening newspaper beside her. I sat on the floor against the couch watching Walt Disney on our black-and-white television, still wondering what that man at the ball field wanted.

"Pop," I finally asked, Tinkerbell whisking across the TV screen as the show's credits rolled behind me, "Who was--"

"It's 8:30, Johnny." Dad cut me off softly, folding his newspaper. "Time for bed." I sighed, dropped my head, walked over and gave him a kiss goodnight. For some reason, Dad wasn't telling me. After awhile, I stopped asking.

Once Mom kissed me goodnight and left the bedroom, I snuck my new transistor radio under the covers, and Vin Scully would deliver my play-by-play bedtime story; sometimes a flashlight and notebook to keep score. I loved listening to Sandy Koufax and Don Drysdale battle the league's best pitchers, especially Juan Marichal and Bob Gibson. I was awed by Marichal's graceful motion when I watched him on the Saturday Game of the Week, but nobody messed with Gibby.

These were my baseball role models.

* * * * *

When I reached 13, I could stand up on the surfboard. Fred used to drive me in his 1949 army surplus, olive green Chevy coupe, three-speed stick with green interior, searching for the coolest waves up and down the coast. We listened to the Beach Boys, same as everyone. "*I Get Around*" would blast through Fred's scratchy radio at nine in the morning heading to the beach, playing that song just a touch louder than the others, our boards across the back of the car. It was all suntan oil and ocean mist.

All day long we would talk about our ballgames, hang out with the other kids, and ride waves. Skip Frey, the legendary surfer, was around every now and then handing out tips and surfing pointers. The music in our transistor radio fizzled as the batteries wore down. Surfing with Fred every day that summer was magical.

Coming home from the beach, our car would drive through the early evening afterglow as buses filled with young men rode beside us preparing to leave for Vietnam. The Naval shipyard, the government's portal to combat for these boys, was basically my backyard. This was the point of departure where the new recruits would literally ship out to Asia. My eyes would meet theirs, vehicle-to-vehicle and I never knew how to respond properly. Didn't salute, didn't wave – just gave them attention for a slight moment, letting them know they were on my mind as America's future motored down the road.

It was 1965 and The Byrds jangled their way onto the car radio as the California sun began to set on my childhood. Five years and counting before I was eligible for service. In the eyes of Uncle Sam, I was on the clock.

* * * * *

San Diego was one of the largest military ports in the country. It wasn't like this Midwestern farm town where the boys went off to war and it was out of your mind. Signs were everywhere during those years; grabbing Bonusburgers and onion rings at Jack in the Box with friends, young men with luggage and their families having final meals before shipping out; world-weary, uniformed veterans sitting at the Woolworth's lunch counter, drinking coffee, alone; on my first date at the local pizza place, the soldiers streamed in and out, some stayed for a slice, others carrying pies while we sat listening to The Monkees from the jukebox. It wasn't another pleasant valley Sunday in North Park if I wasn't face to face with the constant reminders of war.

Baseball was the best distraction for me during this time. Sitting around the family room one early afternoon that summer, Dad was antsy as we were watching the Saturday Game of the Week, like he was waiting to surprise me.

"C'mon, let's go to the ballpark," he said, dropping the newspaper,

"Go back?" I asked him, "I had a game this morning."

Dad smiled and shook his head.

"The ballpark."

* * * * *

Dad took me to a *"Padres"* game. I had seen the Dodgers a few times before at Chavez Ravine. This was certainly not that experience, but still enjoyable. Of course, the Padres *Major League* franchise was still three years away. This was their inaugural season as the AAA affiliate for the Philadelphia Phillies, after being home to the Cincinnati Reds' minor league club for much of the early '60s. The small organization had been in town since 1936 and playing in Westgate Park, about 25 minutes from our house. We probably attended 10 or 15 games every year. Great way to spend an afternoon. Made it even better that Dad seemed to know everyone at the park. He introduced me to Eddie Leishman, the general manager of the San Diego Padres, who took us on a tour of the clubhouse. Walking through the small press box, we met John Bowman, the PA announcer. Very cool glimpsing the other side of a professional baseball team. As we left the clubhouse, Mr. Leishman shook our hands, then pulled Dad aside.

"Ya know, we could use a batboy for the next couple weeks. Would Johnny be interested in helpin' out?" Dad turned to me with an amused look, asking my permission with a shrug.

"Would I?" I exclaimed, "That'd be super!"

"I'll make all the arrangements," Eddie replied excitedly, cupping his hands together, "You can start tomorrow. Enjoy the game."

The following day, the clubhouse attendant at the time, Ray Peralta, brought me around the lockers and the dugout. I met Padres coach Whitey Wietelmann, who gladly showed me the bat rack, instructed me on how to take all the pine tar, weighted bats and rosin bags to the on-deck circle, which foul balls to fetch on our side of the field, which players were approachable and those best left alone.

So many of the guys treated me like a teammate during those two weeks. I had met Padres players before at little league banquets and after games at Westgate Park, you know, guys like Sammy Ellis gave me pitching tips back when the team was affiliated with the Reds, but it was nothing like the exposure I received here. Bo Belinsky was among the veterans trying to work their way back into the bigs. Dallas Green, too. Among the younger players, I met Grant Jackson, Gary Sutherland, Rick Wise, a young pitcher named John Morris. So many pitching lessons, my head was spinning. I kept quiet most of the time, only speaking when spoken to, basically doing as I was told. More important, the experience molded me and provided the confidence I would hold once I got to high school. I was already throwing 80 MPH. You think over-sized freshmen would intimidate me now?

* * * * *

That fall, I began the ninth grade at St. Augustine High School in San Diego. I had a number of friends at the school when I arrived, and not just among the students. John Bowman, the Padres PA announcer, was my English teacher. Bill Whitaker, one of the founders of the little league, was the baseball coach. Tuition wasn't cheap, even back then, but Dad worked odd-jobs at the school to help with costs. Young ballplayers with big-league aspirations wanted to play for Coach Whitaker, not just because he was a smart instructor and knew how to handle teenage kids, but he also "bird-dogged" for a number of major league franchises throughout his life. If you performed well at St. Augs, someone important in the majors was going to know about it. You see, that's the other thing about scouting in those years. It wasn't enough to dominate on the field – someone important had to know that the tree fell in the forest and made one helluva sound. I pitched a number of outstanding games as a freshman, so well I was asked to start against Clairemont High School in a pivotal summer league tournament. The game was a big deal. About six or seven big league scouts were watching in the stands. For me? Nah, they came because of our star player, a kid named John Wathan. He had an excellent profile, smart base running, excellent at-bats, plus power. Wathan was everything an organization wanted in a ballplayer.

The scouts in attendance that day received quite a bonus. I struck out 14 batters, mostly older kids. From that day forward, the seats for my starts were never empty. There were no radar guns back then for this level of competition, but they knew what they were watching.

"Big league scouts came to the game, Pop," I said, as we stood at the counter of the local pizza place waiting for a pie. Dad just smiled, paying for our take-out and thanking the cashier. "I never had scouts watching me before." Dad didn't laugh a whole lot, but whenever I brought up scouts it really cracked him up. I was never privy to this little inside joke brewing in his head, but I knew it was there.

* * * * *

Sophomore Year I played both varsity football and baseball for St. Augustine. Offensive Guard and Defensive End in a 4-3 set. Roving linebacker, too. The coaches said I had a knack for smelling a play and filling a hole. I weighed 225 lbs by 1967. Bench-pressing 470. Dad loved football and loved watching me play. Also named MVP for the season in Baseball.

Pitchers at that time weren't supposed to be lifting weights, but this was about football. The coaches had me pegged initially at Quarterback, but said I threw too hard for the receivers. Actually, I loved playing defense. One afternoon, I was working out at Leo Stern's Gym in North Park. A new trainer was hired. Gene Fisher, a Green Beret, became my constant companion at the gym, conditioning me for the football games. Gene had just returned from Vietnam with an honorable discharge. He went the extra mile for me, checking my nutritional intake in addition to the pure weight training. Sometimes, after we finished working out, I would ask Gene about the war.

"I was shot in the lung," Gene replied reluctantly. He didn't like talking about it, but with every day passing that President Johnson hadn't brought us home, it became a weight on my conscience. "You don't wanna hear what I saw, 'cause it's some of the most horrible things you could ever imagine."

After a few of those sessions, Gene opened up about his time in Vietnam, the images that kept him awake at night, the shocking sights his mind would never allow him to erase.

"We'd be sleeping on the side of the road in ditches," Gene said one day after a workout, "There was a kid assigned watch over our platoon. He fell asleep. We woke up and there was VC all around us. We didn't even know they were there. They looked down into the ditch and we ambushed 'em. Shot our way right outta there. Don't know how we got away but it was real bloody. Pretty soon, some of the smarter platoons caught on to what the VC was doing, you know, hiding in bushes, camouflaging themselves, and started ambushing in the same fashion. That's how we survived. God, I don't wish that stuff on anybody."

"Ya think we'll still be there in three years?" I asked him. Gene thought for a moment, then reached for the barbells.

"Let's get ready for the game this weekend," Gene said with a smile, "Think about what ya can control in life. Not what ya can't. You'll drive yourself crazy. Believe me."

* * * * *

"The Mail" started flowing in the fall of 1968, the beginning of my junior year. Not *that* letter, but queries from schools around the country. As I flip through the mental highlights of my football and baseball games, the recap in my mind plays like a sports movie montage. September was full of opening-night tackles, sacks, the game-winning fumble recovery and three letters from Division One California colleges; October brought the changing colors of school recruiters trying to get Dad's attention on the sidelines at halftime; November led to more tackles, more sacks and 35 more letters from universities. The December holiday season presented a Christmas card from Notre Dame in the mailbox as I stepped through the front door only to find a rep from Stanford sipping coffee with Mom and Dad in our living room;16-strikeout baseball games sprang from March as well as Arizona State birddogs ogling me from behind the backstop. April saw a no-hitter, 40 more letters, and UC-Berkeley on the phone with Coach Whittaker asking about my intentions as I passed the athletic office; and May, she brought me the greatest gift of all...USC wanted to talk.

Our final tally had me collecting 144 letters just for football alone. 100 for baseball. UC-Berkeley, Stanford, Notre Dame, Wyoming, Texas/Austin, University of Arizona, Arizona State, the University of Southern California. Every day it was the same words from my football coach, Joe DiTomaso, or Coach Whitaker. I'd walk into the athletic office and it was, *"Johnny, we got five more letters today. If you and your folks need help with anything, I'm here."*

It wasn't like today, when talented, savvy teens understand their worth in the marketplace at a young age. I never really considered how "valuable" my abilities were. I was just a good kid, brought up by kind, loving parents. My folks wouldn't have tolerated any outlandish attitude, especially my mother. My father wouldn't allow me to get too headstrong from all the accolades. I was taught to respect the elders in my life -- my mother, my father, my coach -- and I lived by that code. The other side of this, to be fair, was that my parents never looked at me like a meal ticket. Same with my coaches. I recognize that not every young talented athlete had that experience. I was very lucky.

In the following spring of 1969, I started a game against our rival, Santana High School. The Sultans' hotshot lefty, a big, blond kid named Terry Forster, was on the mound. Forster had Major League mechanics at the age of 16. Simply watching him taught me a thing or two. I really wanted to beat Forster, not for any malicious reasons, but because he was so damn good. Heck, the whole team was stocked. Another tough lefty on their squad was Kyle Hypes. Hypes wasn't a power pitcher like Forster or myself, but boy could he deal. Amazing curveball.

Terry and I dueled for seven innings, tossing bean after bean. I ended up on the winning end of our 2-1 joust, but everyone there knew Terry would be wearing a big league uniform sooner rather than later. The ride home with my Dad was like a World Series celebration, in my mind. I beat Terry Forster!

We entered the house ready to share the good news with Mom. I walked in to see Walter Cronkite reporting the escalating fatalities in Vietnam.

My service time was now only 12 months away.

* * * * *

Senior Year, 1969. In football, I'd been named All-American. One night dining with Dad at Anthony's Fish Grotto, a popular restaurant in town, we ran into Sid Gilman, head coach for the Chargers in the NFL. Gilman congratulated me and told my father he wanted the Chargers to draft me when I came out of school. Dad, standing beside me, could barely contain his pride. That was the implication – I was going to college.

With all the cross-winds regarding my future, Dad wanted me to talk to Mr. Bowman, who by now bird-dogged for USC. Just about everyone wanted me to be a Trojan. Notre Dame was still recruiting me heavily for football only. Sure, they didn't care about me pitching, which was a concern, but for one night, I dreamed of wearing the legendary gold and blue. I loved football; really, *really* loved it. Baseball, though? Baseball was just easy. At this point, every night, the conversation was about college football.

I asked my Dad, "What should I do?" He immediately shook his head.

"Johnny, it's your decision. I can't help ya with this."

"Dad, I need some advice."

"Ask the coach. This stuff could change your life. I'm not gonna be the one to lead ya down the wrong road. Go talk to Mr. Bowman, he's your counselor." Dad never pointed me in either direction, but if it was his call, he preferred football, and more important, college.

Mr. Bowman explained USC's pitch to me.

"The school doesn't offer four-year scholarships, but they do offer two years for each sport. You'll be getting a two-year for football and a two-year for baseball, because they want you for both sports. You need to sign that, because that's worth a lot of money to you, son."

Besides Rod Dedeaux, the legendary baseball coach, besides the Hall of Fame caliber football stars and college players that called the L.A. Coliseum home, it was less than three hours away from San Diego. Close enough but far enough. Baseball may have had more longevity compared to the NFL, but man, USC. Even in 1969, it was still *USC*!

"You have two options," Mr. Bowman added. "USC is an excellent institution. You'll do great up there and make lifelong friends. Then there's professional baseball. They like you. You're a good kid and you throw 100 MPH. You'll be in the big leagues in three years or so. Whichever road you wanna take, you're gonna be successful."

I didn't think twice. I signed the letter of intent.

The school invited me to campus for a weekend visit. I was sponsored by Frank Alfono, a kid from my town who was attending the school. As I joined the rest of the group in the gymnasium, who do I see on the tour as well? *Terry Forster!* I slapped him five and chatted for a bit as we walked around campus.

"So what are ya gonna do?" I asked him. Terry looked around at the buildings and grounds with great appreciation.

"This is all pretty cool," Terry nodded, "But I always wanted to be a *bonus baby.*"**[1] That was the terminology of the time. When a big league team would draft you in the first or second round, the bonus was generally at least $5,000. We reasoned that you could always go to college. But being a bonus baby…that was something special.

It turned out to be a great weekend. Walking onto the grass of the L.A. Coliseum was definitely an a-ha moment for every football recruit on that tour. What Terry said stuck with me, though.

Sure would be nice to be a bonus baby.

Soon as I got home, I sat down for a long talk with Dad in front of the TV. Before getting up from the couch to go to bed, he told me one last thing.

---

[1] **The actual "Bonus Rule" ended with the creation of the first-year player draft in June 1965. Word didn't travel as fast back then, as you could imagine. Besides, we all just dug the term.*

"Don't forget, if ya end up goin' to school in Los Angeles, you'll be spending more time with the football program than baseball. That's what John McKay told me."

Dad had a chat with the Trojans' coach. That also stuck with me as my final baseball season at St. Augustine began a few months later.

I made it clear to Coach Whitaker and everyone in the athletic office that I was a baseball player first. It was around February 1970 when a lot of men fully aware of this knowledge began knocking on our front door. Not colleges.

Major league scouts.

Back then, it wasn't easy to track a prospect, especially me. We weren't listed in the phone book. They found us anyway. My coach was telling them where we lived. The doorbell rang frequently.

"Is John home?" they would ask Mom and Dad. *"May we talk to him?"*

Big league teams would interview you, just as recruiters would discuss the merits of their college.

"How do ya feel about playing professional baseball?" "How do ya feel about living in Atlanta, Georgia?" Questions like that.

The Braves were really coming on hard and so were the Detroit Tigers. Atlanta had just won the new National League Western Division the previous season and the Tigers, well, they were the World Champion Detroit Tigers from 1968, the Tigers of Denny McLain and World Series hero Mickey Lolich. My draft stock continued to rise. In the end, the Braves and Tigers were among clubs like the Dodgers, Yankees, the Seattle Pilots and a host of others who checked in on me.

Two other teams stood apart from the pack.

Eddie Leishman was by now the General Manager of the now-*Major League* San Diego Padres. Buzzie Bavasi was president and C. Arnolt Smith, the previous owner of the minor league club, had secured the franchise for our town. The Padres would be one of the four expansion teams and 1969 was their maiden season. Considering Mr. Leishman's friendship with Dad as well as his knowledge of all my success on the high school mound, I truly thought I would be a Padre.

There was a lot to choose from in terms of local talent: Me, Terry, Kyle Hypes and, of course, Steve Dunning was finishing his final year at Stanford. *Everybody* wanted Steve. The Padres organization also adored this kid named Mike Ivie. Big strong, catcher from Decatur, Ga. Based on what I heard, Padres management wanted to grab one of us with the first pick in the draft and then hope the other would fall to the second round.

I enjoyed a super year on the mound for St. Augustine. Couldn't get off the field without a scout introducing himself to me or my folks. Two days in particular stick out in my mind.

We were battling with our arch rivals Santana again. Once again, I toed the rubber against Terry Forster. This game had real-life implications outside of the victory – we brought about 10 scouts between us. As I was tossing warm-up throws, I looked over at Terry with a *"Can you believe this"* grin on my face. Terry smiled and nodded back. He was the worthy opponent and boy did we battle. A rerun of the previous match-up – chucking heat, frame after frame. Three up three down, three up three down. In the end, I may have come out with the victory, but it didn't matter. Neither of us made a mistake and we both knew it. As the teams shook hands, I reached out to Terry and our smiles told each other this game would get us drafted.

Two weeks later, we faced Patrick Henry High. I felt pretty strong going in and my instincts weren't wrong. The backstop at their school was smallish, sort of like the cage at a softball field. Mound was well-groomed. My parents were there. A few other scouts showed up. None of them could match the aura of one person in particular.

I noticed this older gentleman standing behind the backstop. Tall like a ballplayer, dark glasses and a sport jacket. This was the last man in America who wore a fedora. Something told me I *really* wanted to impress this guy. I motioned to my catcher that serious heat was coming. I threw the warm-up as fast as anything I ever tossed before. That ball went past my catcher, over the umpire's shoulder and was stopped cold by the chain-linked fence. The umpire removed his mask.

"That ball had to be over 100 mph," he gasped.

The man in the fedora stared me down, removed his glasses and approached the umpire from behind the cage. As the ump tried to remove the ball from the chain-link fence, the man in the fedora offered help. He couldn't do it, either, first using his fingers, then his pipe. Nothing worked. Finally, Coach Whitaker dislodged the ball with a fungo bat.

"May I have that ball," the man in the fedora asked.

"Pardon me," the umpire replied. He didn't know who the man was, but assumed he was important, shrugged and tossed it over to him.

"I need something to show 'em back in San Francisco," the man in the fedora said. "My name is Carl Hubbell."

"Carl Hubbell," Coach Whitaker said with wonder in his voice. "The Carl Hubbell?"

"That's right," Hubbell said. "I'm the head of player development for the Giants."

"It's an honor to meet you, Mr. Hubbell." Coach Whitaker said as he quickly waved my father and me over to join them. "This is the boy's dad. We're very honored to have you here."

Mr. Hubbell turned to my father.

"I'm here to see your son," he said. "We're thinking about drafting him. That boy can throw. Can you sign this ball so I can bring some proof of what I saw?" My father never reached for a pen so fast.

Carl Hubbell stayed to watch the rest of the game. I pitched with such adrenaline going through my body. Patrick Henry High School couldn't do anything with my stuff. If the chain-link grease mark on the ball wasn't proof enough, I ended the game with my second no-hitter of the season. These were the only moments during the spring of 1970 when my mind wasn't thinking about The Draft. It was baseball that served as my true distraction.

* * * * *

Off the field, my attention turned to the calendar, my birthday, and the home mailbox. Just waiting for that letter from the military. My social life was pretty much school and sports, but I still found a little time for girls. I had been going steady with this girl for over two years, a cute cheerleader, who was terribly excited for our senior prom. About a week before, Coach Whittaker called me into his office.

"Johnny, ya need to do something for me," he said, with all seriousness in the world.

"Anything, Coach," I replied, wondering if this had something to do with my college or professional future.

"It's about Terri," he continued, "Her boyfriend just broke up with her and you know the prom's coming up in a week."

"Yeaahhh…"

"Well son, ya need to take her to the prom."

Now Terri was coach's daughter, his pride and joy, the apple of his eye and a lifelong friend of mine in town. We were born in the same room at San Diego Hospital, one day apart, along with my catcher Chris Kinsel. The three of us always shared that special bond. Any other girl, I would have flat-out refused – I was going steady. Any other man, I wouldn't have even considered the request.

"Coach," I said, watching my words, "This is a lot of pressure on me. I have a-"

"-I know ya have a girlfriend, she's there at every game-"

"It's my girl, I already asked her to go -"

"Cancel it."

"But, Coach-"

"Johnny? Johnny? Can I count on you?"

* * * * *

Prom night arrived. I drove up to the house in my tuxedo, the corsage riding shotgun beside me in Dad's burgundy Chevy Impala. I got out and rang the bell. My date's father answered and without saying a word, opened the door to reveal this adorable ray of sunshine in heels. She was standing there waiting for me. It really felt like a magical moment as she walked toward me, all harmonies and harpsichords, like something out of an Association song. One of my most cherished high school memories.

"Hey Johnny," she smiled.

"Hi, Terri," I smiled back. "You look great."

"Take care of her now," Terri's father said sternly.

"You bet, Coach," I replied as we walked toward my car.

I always did what I was told.

It was much more than that, though. Terri asked why the sudden interest.

"Did my Dad put you up to this?" Terri inquired on the phone two days before the prom.

"This is how it's supposed to be," I replied tenderly, "We came into this world together. We're graduating together, too. Still wanna go?"

"I'd love to," Terri replied, choking up a bit on the other end.

I'd love to say the conversation with my girlfriend was this pleasant. It wasn't. She wasn't my girlfriend for much longer, either.

I drove Terri and some friends on the big night. Stopping at a light, we passed yet another bus full of young men preparing to enter the naval shipyards. I couldn't get away from the almost-constant reminder of getting my number picked.

We entered the community center with a gloom hovering over our prom. No band, just a couple of kids spinning records. Store-bought, papier-mâché decorations hung from the walls across the room. Balloons everywhere. We sipped punch, had a laugh or two, but me and the fellas couldn't get past what awaited us right after graduation.

Where the hell was I going? USC? San Francisco? Saigon? Where would my life be in six months?

Terri and I swayed to the music, trying to enjoy the night, but in my head, I was three hours away at the L.A. Coliseum, 600 miles north at Candlestick Park with Willie Mays, Willie McCovey, Juan Marichal and all the stars of the San Francisco Giants. Then I was 7,500 miles away in the jungles of Vietnam. My mind was everywhere except in that community center with the class of 1970. I'd see other buddies dancing with their best girl or best option for a prom date, and our concerned eyes would meet. Some would shrug. Some would turn away as if to say, "*Not now*," that we would have time soon enough to figure this all out, or not.

* * * * *

Graduation came and with it the dread of waking up and finding a letter from the draft board sitting on the kitchen counter. I sweated out every single day. A week later at breakfast, the phone rang in my kitchen. Dad answered. There was a lot of nodding; a few "uh-huhs," but no words explained who was on the other end of the receiver. Only the sparkle in Dad's eyes indicated good news.

"Tomorrow? Ok, we'll be there. 'Bye now."

Dad hung up the phone.

"What was that all about?" I asked through a spoonful of Corn Flakes.

"That was Mr. Leishman from the Padres. He wants ya to come down and throw for 'em."

Dad wasn't one for dramatic pauses, but he took a moment to continue speaking.

"Johnny, this is gettin' serious."

I looked out the window and the mailman drove by and stopped at our walk. Nothing could be as serious as what could lay in his pouch.

* * * * *

Tomorrow came. Not one word was said in the car. I tried turning on the radio to hear some Jimi Hendrix or Crosby, Stills & Nash to calm me down. Dad turned the dial to this easy listening station that played acts like Henry Mancini all the time. He was just as nervous as I was.

We drove through a San Diego that was exiting the '60s. Ours was a sheltered, quiet, fishing town. Now there were new buildings and new freeways, shopping centers and a new baseball franchise. My whole world was evolving that spring.

We made our way down Friars Road. The Padres gate attendant sent us to players' parking. He told Dad that the team was expecting us. No fancy cars in the players' parking lot. By looking at their choice of automobiles, it seemed like they were just regular guys.

"Ya ok?" Dad asked me.

"Not really," I laughed nervously, "This is it. They're all here, Pop."

My Dad calmly reached into his wallet, pulled out a business card and handed it to me. "Remember that man from the ball field when you were a kid?"

"Robert O'Regan, New York Mets," the card said.

"They've always been here, Johnny. They've been watching ya since you were 12. They already know what ya can do. If this--"

He nodded to my right. I looked over and saw a Major League Baseball stadium.

"If this is what ya really wanna do," Dad said, "They're in there waiting for ya."

I smiled at him, nodded, and we got out of the car.

Dad and I walked through the entrance into this dungeon of the stadium and met the guard at the restricted area. He led us down this sparse hallway, past the Chargers' clubhouse that housed San Diego's football players during the NFL season, and toward the Padres' clubhouse door. As my Dad turned the knob to my future, I inhaled the faint smell of cigarettes. Dad threw me a smile when he opened up the door. It was like I walked into a bar. The thick smoke smacked us right in the face.

Cito Gaston. Nate Colbert. Downtown Ollie Brown. Al Ferrera. All cracking jokes, half-dressed, playing cards, listening to music, preparing for the day's game against the Dodgers. I was dumbfounded.

"Far out," I said under my breath.

Ray Peralta, the Padres clubhouse man, approached us. He was carrying some laundry.

"You must be John and Fred," Ray said.

Padres manager Preston Gomez walked past us. This was such a trip. All the players I watched on TV were right next to me.

"Here's your uniform," Ray said, handing me some clothes. "Try it on."

I laughed as Ray pointed to an empty locker.

"Go get dressed over there. Here's your hat, belt, stirrups -- everything ya need."

"Whoa."

I buttoned up the 1970 San Diego Padres jersey, then looked over and saw a couple tears streaming down my father's cheeks. Only, he was laughing.

"If I didn't see it with my own eyes, I wouldn't have believed it. My son is going to be a San Diego Padre."

"It ain't happenin' yet, Pop."

At this moment, catcher Chris Cannizzaro approached us, holding a brand new baseball.

"You and me, kid, we're goin' down to the bullpen and you're gonna throw."

Cannizzaro was the first all-star of the Padres franchise and a popular player in town. He took me down to the bullpen area, beside the stands. I toed the rubber, wound up, and the first pitch hit Cannizzaro right on the toe. He started playfully cursing me out. From the stands, my Dad started laughing.

"You sure you wanna do this?"

It was a joke, obviously, and once I settled down, the next five pitches were strikes. Pop. Pop. Pop. Pop. Pop. Cannizzaro removed the mitt and shook the sting out of his hand.

"Jeez, kid, you're killing me."

It may have been the greatest compliment someone outside my family ever paid me. Even the team's promising young pitcher, Clay Kirby, came over, giving me tips on how to grip the curveball and talking about life in the big leagues. Dreamed how cool it would be to pitch alongside my hometown team's ace. Clay represented the youth and promise of baseball in San Diego, one of the most beloved players on that team. Everyone felt Clay Kirby was ready to become a star pitcher and carry the ballclub to the first division, and judging by the confident smirk he wore on his face, so did Clay Kirby. At this stage, he was *everything* I wanted to be in baseball. The All-American Boy.

Afterward, Cannizzaro introduced me and my Dad to Preston Gomez. My father spoke fluent Spanish and had a pleasant bilingual conversation with Gomez, who would turn to me throughout, politely smiling and nodding.

On the ride home, Dad said, "Mr. Gomez really liked you. He wants ya here."

"I'd love to play here in town," I replied, "But this team's kinda bad. They lost 100 games last year."

"If you get drafted by 'em, ya gotta play here."

"Yeah, I know, but maybe I go to school and get drafted by a better team in four years."

"Johnny, ya know how it works, right?"

"Yeah, I know how it works."

"Well, it's your decision."

I really wanted San Fran. Juan Marichal was my idol. I wore no. 27 in high school specifically because of Marichal. Still, it was the greatest day of my life, a day made even better when the mail showed up with nothing addressed to me.

* * * * *

Three days later, no one went to work. No one went surfing or goofing around with friends. No one went to the market. I knew where Terry Forster was, where Steve Dunning was. I knew where Kyle Hypes was. The June 1970 Amateur Draft had arrived. There was no sports channel, no Internet, no Keith Law-types handicapping the Top 100 prospects in America. Media coverage of the draft was all but non-existent. As for us, we were just high school and college kids sitting in our living rooms, waiting for the phone to ring.

The San Diego Padres had the first pick. We thought this would either be wrapped up early or there would be lots of waiting.

We got a call in the early morning. San Diego had just selected Mike Ivie with the first pick in the draft. My parents were sad. I was relieved, actually. The Padres said they were hoping I would fall to the second round. Then they would most definitely select me. At that moment, in our hearts we all knew I wouldn't be a Padre. My mother, especially. She had remained quiet all these years, but now that decisions were to be made, Mom took command of the D'Acquisto draft room.

"It would've been nice if you got to play at home," she sighed.

"Yeah," I replied, "I just hope I get drafted."

A little while later, the phone rang again. We had no idea who was on the other side of the ring. Remember, this was before cell phones or Caller ID. Turned out to be a buddy who heard that Steve Dunning was selected by the Indians with the second pick in the draft. I was happy for Steve, nervous about falling from the first round.

Mom looked up at the clock in our kitchen and collected herself.

"Johnny, you're late for the doctor," Mom directed, rushing me out the door. "I'll let you know if I hear anything." I grabbed the car keys and headed out through the kitchen.

"Johnny," Mom reassured me as opened the back door, "Won't be long now. Good things will come." She had confidence I wouldn't be on the board by the second round. I smiled and left the house.

While I was in the examination room with the doctor, the draft continued. The Atlanta Braves, who had the 21st pick in the draft, had asked me to undergo a physical. Had a strong hunch I was headed to Georgia if I made it past number 20. As the doctor checked my reflexes, catcher Barry Foote's household got a call from the Montreal Expos that he had been picked third. The Brewers would call fellow amateur backstop Darrell Porter, telling him he was fourth. Others came off the board.

The office nurse entered the room after a slight knock.

"John," she asked, not sure of my name, "I think your mother's on the phone." I grabbed my pants off the examination table and stepped quickly into the doctor's office and reached for the receiver.

"Johnny," Mom said excitedly, though it might as well have been Scott McKenzie on the other end of the line.

I was going to San Francisco.

I couldn't have been happier. We had extended family in the Bay Area, so it was nearly a perfect fit.

When I got back home, I spoke with Joe Henderson, the Giants' San Diego area scout, who had left his number to speak with me about the good news. Joe's son Kenny attended Clairemont High School in town and was the current starting left fielder for the Giants. "We just drafted you number one, seventeenth in the nation."

"Nation?" I asked, "Not just California?" I didn't know any better.

"In the nation. And we'll be seeing you tomorrow, so get some sleep, if ya can."

Of course, I couldn't get any sleep. Just stayed up, thinking of visiting Alcatraz, riding trolley cars, pitching against the Dodgers, every other San Fran-related tourist cliché you could conjure. Later that night, Mom came into my room, turned out my light and gave me a sweet, soft kiss.

"Now let's see what they offer you," my agent said coldly. My mother, my consigliere. My Tom Hagen. My Scott Boras.

My mother would be running the negotiation. I agreed.

I always did what I was told.

* * * * *

Joe Henderson brought George Genovese, the Giants' regional head scout, to our house the following morning. Talking contract as soon as they sat down. Polite, but all business.

"We would like to offer you a $20,000 bonus," Joe said, as if this was the most generous gift in the world. Mom wouldn't budge.

"He's worth more than that," she replied.

Mom and the Giants executives went back and forth for about an hour. Finally, Mom stood up.

"My son's had a long year. I'm sending him on vacation with his cousin to Hawaii. Let's talk when he comes back." The next day, I hopped on a plane with my cousin for a week in Honolulu.

It *was* a long year and I looked forward to the scuba diving, snorkeling and surfing. No baseball, which may have been a problem since I was set to start the North-South High School All-Star game at the Big A in Anaheim immediately upon my return. I was not nearly as prepared as I should've been, especially since Rod Dedeaux, USC's baseball coach, was also in attendance. As I reached the hotel where I was staying with Mom and Dad, we found Joe Henderson and George Genovese waiting for me in the lobby. Again, polite gentlemen, but driving hard bargains. They offered me $27,000. I nodded my head.

"Here's what I want," I began, as if repeating Mom's grocery list to the butcher, "I want to go to college, but I also wanna play ball. I want a four-year college education, paid for by the team, whenever I ask for it."

Joe and George turned to each other, sighed and nodded, "Okay, we'll come back to you."

The next day, I pitched in the game, didn't expect to do real well and didn't. Threw the ball hard but walked the yard a bit and left the game early. As the players stepped into the dugouts to leave, Rod Dedeaux approached me on the field.

"You didn't do real well today, Tiger."

He was right. I was awful.

"I know Coach McKay wants you to play football for him. We're gonna have to wait and see on you pitching for us for now. Of course, you can try out for the team."

"Try out for the team," I replied, as he started walking away. "Wait a second coach, I signed a letter of intent. Two years football, two years baseball. That's what the school said-"

"That's what the school said, that's not what I said-"

"But I have a letter of intent-"

"Ok, Tiger," Dedeaux assured me, "Let me know what you wanna do. We'll talk later in the week."

Maybe Dedeaux spoke too soon or was too honest too soon. Lucky for me Joe Henderson and George Genovese – who were staying with my folks on the field about 100 feet away from me– didn't hear any of this conversation. As I walked over to them a bit dejected, the two scouts handed me a contract.

"We got ya everything ya wanted," Henderson smiled, "Cash, college paid for, everything. We got a deal?" I grabbed for that pen so fast. I was a San Francisco Giant.

Mom and Dad couldn't have been happier. We enjoyed a celebratory Italian dinner soon as we returned to San Diego. It was the greatest day of my life.

And then we came home. The letter was sitting alone on the kitchen table, commanding all of our attention.

It was my Induction notice. My Selective Service Lottery Number was *two*.

I was going to Vietnam.

* * * * *

The following morning, Mom sent me for a pre-induction physical. I was absolutely distraught over this, as my worst fears came to fruition. The orthopedic surgeon examined me. After a battery of tests and x-rays, the doctor said I had a degenerative hip condition – Fred suffered a similar medical condition that ultimately kept him out of flight school. Apparently, it *was* genetic. Sitting in the examination room, the doctor handed me my x-rays. "This is a potential disaster," he said, "Bring these with you to the recruiting office."

"What does this mean?" I asked, petrified of the answer.

"I dunno, Johnny. For one thing, you can forget about football. You should be all right playing baseball. For how long, who knows? These things just don't go away. As far as combat goes, we'll see what Uncle Sam says." No football meant no more USC, especially after Coach Dedeaux wavered on my baseball scholarship. Most likely meant no scholarships anywhere.

* * * * *

It's June 1970. Just one month earlier, a Hall of Fame player representing my dream ball club indicated that his team would select me with their first pick. Now I was riding on a bus from San Diego to the army induction office in Los Angeles alongside a collection of fresh-faced young men just like myself. The driver parked on a street corner. Some women in mini-skirts and colored sunglasses passed us; others in long, paisley dresses walked by, their heads eagerly cocked with sympathy, peering at us through the bus windows as if we were museum exhibits.

After years of looking over my shoulder at what seemed like the inevitable, I was finally here. I had been assured by the wisest people I knew that I would be in major leagues by the next presidential election.

Fresh from high school, I had just experienced the greatest month of my life. Yet on this day, the most successful GM in history, Uncle Sam, had at last gotten his man.

There were some of the saddest faces I had ever seen riding with me, helplessly hoping that their lives would be intact at the end of this process. I know I was. One stop away from being one of those young kids heading into the naval shipyards preparing for war.

We got off the bus and marched slowly into the recruitment office. Some boys accepted their fate with grace, with honor and did as they were told. Others tried pulling tricks. One guy wanted to get out on a 51-50 and wore girl's panties when we were instructed to strip down to t-shirts and boxers. Didn't work. The sergeant on duty went into detail about the physical we were about to undergo. It was almost like a four-inning game that could determine the rest of my life.

First they checked my eyes, examined them closely. "*Accepted,*" they said. I passed the vision test. Next, the doctor examined my heart and lungs.

"*All clear,*" he said. They ran blood work on me. While results wouldn't come back for awhile, they didn't see anything out of the ordinary and I moved on.

Finally, I met with Dr. Robert Kerlan, an orthopedic surgeon who examined the recruits. I handed Dr. Kerlan my x-rays. He studied them carefully, than examined me himself. I said to myself, *if this doctor gives me a clean bill of health, I will be the best soldier this army has ever seen. Make my parents and country proud of me. I have been a winner at every level of my life and I wasn't about to stop here.*

"Johnny, it looks like you have you a potential case of sclerosis," Dr.Kerlan said. "Do you play any sports?"

"I play baseball and football."

Dr. Kerlan handed me my x-rays back. "You can never play football ever again. One awkward tackle and your hip will be destroyed. Best case. Come back in six months and we'll see if your hip improves."

Induction denied.

I got home that night, went to bed but couldn't fall asleep. It was a clear evening, and from my bedroom, I could see the Naval Shipyards. It was all so close to me, to my house and my upbringing. All the pain and sorrow of sailors and soldiers potentially losing their lives half a world away. I saw it in the eyes of the boys at the recruitment office and for a few hours on that day, looking at the examination room mirror, I saw it in myself.

* * * * *

Read in the paper a few days later that Steve Dunning went straight to the big leagues, starting a game for the Indians. Found out that Kyle Hypes from Santana High School was also drafted by the Giants and would be joining me on the rookie club in Montana. Terry Forster ended up being picked in the second round by the Chicago White Sox.

After a week of lying around the house decompressing from the stressful events of those 10 days, I was ready to head to Great Falls, Montana for Giants' Rookie League. That morning, I came into the kitchen and found Fred's bags were packed as well, as he sat at the table wolfing down breakfast.

"Where's he going?" I asked Mom.

"Your brother's going with you," she replied, handing me a plate of eggs and toast. I was actually excited.

"Really?" I replied, "You're comin'?"

"Yup," Fred said, after swallowing his food.

"You're still my baby boy. Just until you get settled in up there."

I nodded, sat down and had my final breakfast as a civilian.

* * * * *

As we pulled our bags from the Impala at the San Diego airport, Mom saw Fred and me off with kisses and hugs.

"You be good now," Mom warned me.

"Everything's gonna be fine," Fred assured her, "I'll be there."

Mom looked at Fred, then back at me.

"You just concentrate on baseball."

"I'll be ok, Mom," I said as I kissed her goodbye and headed toward the airport entrance.

Fred cracked up as we walked toward the gate. I wasn't in on the joke.

"What?"

"The girls were pretty hot stuff in the Air Force," Fred replied, shaking his head, "But you're a ballplayer now. Yoooou got no idea, do you?"

"What?" I really didn't. Fred just laughed as we boarded the flight for Montana, rookie league and the beginning of my baseball career.

I grew up in a community whose elders sheltered us by design, from the darkest impulses of humanity's deepest chasms, a good kid eight months behind the culture, as the '70's were about to begin for me. Soon I would realize I had some serious catching up to do.

Rainy Days & Mondays

"Johnny, wake the hell up," screamed my catcher Chuck Erickson, "Where's your head??!? You're walkin' the ballpark!"

I was standing there on the mound in a daze, as both Chuck and my manager, Harvey Koepf, scolded me loudly as we found ourselves down 6-0 in the first inning.

"C'mon, Johnny," Harvey said, "Get your stuff over the plate. Throw strikes."

"I got it, Skip-"

"'Cuz if I take you out now, you're still gonna go throw in the bullpen to get work in. Might as well just throw strikes here."

"Yeah, stop jerking around, Johnny," my catcher came back at me, "This ain't San Diego-"

"I said I got it, just gimme the ball," I snap-caught Chuck's toss.

No doubt about it, I was spilling batters all over the bases. Where were all these walks coming from? I was 0-3 in my first five starts for the Great Falls Giants. Never experienced this kind of failure, much less this kind of wildness. There were a couple games where I simply zoned out from all the walks, like my right arm threw on auto-pitcher, low and away, low and away. Sure, it was rookie league, but I faced some serious talents. Al Cowens. Dan Briggs. Paul Dade. Pete LaCock. Morris Nettles was a singles hitter who could fly. That's just the guys who would eventually make it to the bigs. Where were all these walks coming from? Out of 207 players that would wear uniforms in the 1970 Pioneer League, just 21 of them would ever undress in a major league clubhouse. Still it was by far the most competitive atmosphere I ever entered as a player.

Where were all these walks coming from!!??!?

* * * * *

Fred and I got off the Pacific Southwest Airlines flight from San Diego to Great Falls three weeks earlier. As wonderful a brother as he is, you never needed to give Fred an excuse to be up in the air. Still was very cool of him to join me on the trip and get settled in my new career. We stepped through the gate, grabbed our stuff at the baggage claim and looked at each other.

"Now what?" Fred asked me.

"Go to the ballpark, I guess," I shrugged, walking toward the exit lugging our bags, "Cab driver should know where it's located. Small enough town, right?"

We arrived at the park soon after. Calling it a stadium might have been a bit generous – Centene Stadium seated barely 4000 people. The ballpark was owned by the town and also housed the local high school teams during the spring. We made our way into the clubhouse and met my new manager, Harvey Koepf. Looking back now, I couldn't have asked for a better rookie skipper – minor league lifer, knew the league backward and forward, he was also from the Bay Area (Half Moon Bay, to be exact) and had the instructional mentality – Harvey was a teacher in the offseason - the kind of teacher who was strict, but got it. The league structure fit right in for Harvey since the Pioneer League ran from the beginning of June until almost the end of August, about the time Harvey had to return home and teach school in September.

Upon arriving at the park, I was immediately scooped up by some of my new teammates and given two uniforms - one road uni, one away version. I was assigned a locker where I stashed my equipment, my high school shoes and glove. Not a whole lot to leave in there at first.

Afterward, Harvey sent Fred and me to an apartment complex. Felt like what I assumed college dorms resembled - smallish, three-bedroom with a kitchen, barely a bathroom and a common area. Fred gave the place the once over.

"You're in the army now, kid," he joked. My salary was $500 a month, plus some meal money. Mom took care of my finances, got my bonus in the right hands. A few minutes later, my buddy from home, Kyle Hypes, swung by our room.

"Johnny," he greeted me and Fred by slapping five, "Welcome to Montana, man."

"Thanks," I replied, looking around the place. "Sure ain't San Diego."

"Nah," Kyle laughed, scanning the apartment along with Fred and me, "Most of the pitchers bunk together here. I'm staying with Butch Metzger, You're uhhh… you're with Steve Ferrea, Steve Tener, Bill Bates and Ricky Schroder. Douggie Capilla is in your room, too."

"Sounds good," I replied.

"Tough league from what I hear. I'm gonna go get my stuff and head down to the ballpark - see you over there."

"Yeah, I'll see ya in a couple hours."

After Fred moved my belongings into the apartment, we returned to Centene. I walked onto the ball field where my teammates were soft-tossing and jogged across the grass. From the outfield, I watched Harvey approach Fred, who was leaning against the cage. Suddenly I noticed Fred nodding as he bolted into the dugout. Few minutes later Fred was running toward us in uniform, shagging flies. My brother was tracking down every ball in the vicinity, diving catches, sliding catches, Fred was an amazing athlete in his own right. We all took batting practice and you should've seen Fred. Man, could he rake. No lazy fly balls, no weak grounders. Laser beam line drives, whistling, opposite-field dingers, sonic-boom level cracks off the bat. Soon, Harvey walked over to me.

"Johnny, why isn't Freddie playing organized ball?"

"He should be, right," I said, in the middle of soft-tossing. Harvey nodded, mouthing *"Yeah"* as he walked back to the clubhouse. I called out to Fred, who jogged over to join us in the outfield. Some of the other guys gave Fred kudos for his hitting prowess.

"You really impressed the skipper," I told him, tapping his shoulder playfully.

"Just havin' fun," Fred replied with smile and shrug, "Taught ya everything ya know." After all the meetings with recruiters, I recognized impressed managers, coaches, and executives when I saw them. Harvey had that look, the look that said, *"I might be able to use this guy."* I imagined for a few moments how great it would be for the D'Acquisto Brothers to light up the Pioneer League. Sure enough, once we entered the clubhouse to change, we heard from Harvey.

"Fred," my manager called out, "Can you come'ere a minute?" I joined the two of them in Harvey's office.

"You looked pretty good out there," Harvey said to Fred, "I can sign you right now. This is the rookie league, though. I need you to answer one question. How old are you?"

Fred paused for a moment, turning to me. Harvey looked over and saw my face as well, and frowned. There wasn't going to be a D'Acquisto duo on the roster.

"I'm 23," Fred said, not exactly sad, but he knew what that meant.

"That's too bad," Harvey replied, "I just wish you were 20. You swing the bat really well."

As we left Harvey's office, Fred looked back at Harvey.

"Hey Coach? Thanks for thinkin' of me that way." Harvey smiled and shrugged.

"You bet."

As Fred and I stepped over to my locker, I turned and saw Harvey through the window of his office, shrugging as he ripped up what looked to be a contract. Freddie came so close.

* * * * *

"This is it, Johnny," Fred said as I walked with him to the airport curb.

"Thanks for coming out here with me."

"I'm always up for a free plane ride."

Fred hugged me with a back slap and picked up his bags.

"You're on your own now, man. Stay out of trouble. And don't let the chicks mess up your brain."

"Hey," I called out to Fred before he entered the airport, "Why didn't you just tell him you were 20?"

Fred paused, considered it, then smiled. "We're D'Acquistos. We're not liars."

I stood there for a moment watching Fred almost study the airport, the landscape he loved so much.

* * * * *

More walks. More runs. I barely lasted three innings before Harvey replaced me.

"Johnny, you're not off to a good start here," Harvey explained. He wasn't the manager that yelled, but he wasn't the players' manager, either. He had caring eyes and a voice that demanded respect. "Not everyone here is goin' to the majors. But a lot of 'em are sittin' on your fastball, and it hasn't been as fast as we were told, either, and your high velocity stuff is going all over the place. You gotta throw strikes or you won't be here much longer."

"I'll do better, Skip," I assured him.

"I'm serious, Johnny. The Giants will release you if you don't get better. Now go to bed, get some rest."

As I lay on my bed the night before my next start against the Twin Falls Cowboys, I could hear giggling through the walls of the apartment next door. Not just the loud laughs of my goofy teammates. *Giggles.* You know what that means. They were having fun and they weren't alone. *"Woodstock"* was playing loudly on the stereo and here I was brooding over my awful start, my awful season and the fear of facing my family at the airport back home, disappointed yet supportive when they'd greet me, knowing I'd been released.

I wanted to hang out with some girls. *I'm the number one pick,* I thought to myself, *I can beat these guys. I can beat all these guys. This ends tomorrow. "*

* * * * *

I only heard cheers and the bark of the umpire blue when I pitched that next start.

There would be barely any ground balls. Barely any cans of corn. Barely any double plays.

Mark Mengo? Down on three pitches. *Jack Pierce?* Struck out twice. *Rod Gilbreath?* Struck him out twice, too. I would trot back to the dugout after punching out the Cowboys, striking out the side as Harvey would glance over and grin, slapping me on the leg as I stepped down into the dugout.

I threw six innings of no-hit, no-run baseball. My first professional victory.

We won the game easily, but I never, ever felt this great before. I didn't feel like a professional, but an elite professional, like a special ballplayer, worthy of the number one draft pick designation.

I was stardust, I was golden and I got myself back to the garden of my organization's good graces.

Later that night, a bunch of us found ourselves at this bar called The Pizza Hut recapping the night's performances.

Great tunes played on the jukebox beside the well-worn dart board. A watering hole filled with locals who didn't have much use for a bunch of ballplayers. Most of the state drinking ages in America were 21 back in 1970 and wouldn't begin to be lowered until the following year when the voting age was reduced to 18 years old. Sometimes we were turned away; sometimes not. This night we were lucky. Kyle and I found ourselves with slightly older cuties. After a few rounds of Coors, we asked the girls to come back to Kyle's apartment, and they agreed quickly. Just as they did the night before, Kyle turned on his small stereo. One of the girls shut off the light and just as the action began, there was a harsh knock at the door.

"You boys in there?" It was Harvey. The look on Kyle's face was priceless.

"Shit, bed checks."

"Can I come in?" Harvey asked forcefully.

"Get in the closet," we whispered to the girls, who kept snickering and stumbling through the darkness as they felt for a doorknob.

"Come in," Kyle and I said off-key and sloppily. Harvey entered the apartment. He knew the deal. He almost laughed at our clumsy attempt to con him. A manager with ten years in the minor leagues? He could barely hold his angry grin, as if counting down the moments before the girls' giggles gave us away. Sure enough....

"Open the door," Harvey said. Kyle sighed as the girls came out, giggling even louder.

"Sorry," they both staggered their way out of our apartment.

"Skip, I dunno how they got in there," Kyle pleaded, knowing how ridiculous it sounded but feeling the need to say something.

"Kyle, make sure those girls get home safe. And if you're not back here soon, don't bother coming to the park tomorrow." Harvey knew Kyle was a good kid that would do what he was told. Me, too. As Kyle left, Harvey turned to me.

"I'm sorry, Skip," I stuttered out an apology, "I just wanted to, you know, have a, it's been tough-"

"Johnny, don't miss anymore bed checks. No more guests that don't need cups."

"Yessir." Then he sat down on the couch for a moment.

"You really pitched great tonight. I asked you to improve, I didn't ask for a major-league performance.

"Thanks."

"The organization wants my recommendations for the Arizona Fall League."

"I'm goin' to Phoenix," I asked excitedly.

"Johnny, if the front office listens to me, you'll be in spring training with the Giants. You're this close to being a great major league pitcher. You're not gonna have any trouble finding girls like that, but you're gonna catch a whole lotta trouble if you don't find an off-speed pitch."

I finished up my year in Great Falls with a record of 2-5 in 12 games. Pitched 55 innings with 84 strikeouts and 74 walks. I went to the Arizona Instructional League trying to figure out where all these walks were coming from.

* * * * *

Once again I found myself on a baseball road trip with Fred headed to Phoenix, Arizona at the end of September 1970 to play in the San Francisco Giants Fall Instructional League. I walked into the clubhouse. I had my own locker with four uniforms – two home, two away - three bats, plus a Wilson glove and shoe contract.

I rapidly placed myself in a good position by not allowing any runs in my first three starts. Performed well in this league, providing a glimpse of my billing as one of the top prospects in the San Francisco Giants organization. Maybe *the* top.

After my third start in the instructional league, one of the coaches approached me at my locker.

"Charlie wants to see you." I entered Giants' manager Charlie Fox's office, who was sifting through paperwork, a cold can of Budweiser on his desk. Charlie had spoken to my folks when I signed, assuring them that the organization would take care of me.

"Johnny, have a seat," he said, dropping the files as he made eye contact. "You're impressing a lot of people here. Looks like ya blew off the early jitters from your first few starts in Great Falls. Ya got the best fastball this side of Sam McDowell. Dunno if you're ready for us next year, but I dunno if you're not, either. So you'll be with us in February for spring training. How's that sound?"

I was so excited.

"I can't wait," I stuttered.

Charlie stood up and shook my hand. He made me feel not just like simply another player, not simply a special player, not even a player vital to the hopes of the Giants' future. Charlie made me feel like family.

"Enjoy the holidays with Mom and Dad, give 'em my best and we'll see ya in the spring."

* * * * *

The Giants of the mid-1960s were among only a handful of teams in baseball history with six Hall of Famers on the same roster. That was 1965 - Mays, McCovey, Marichal, Orlando Cepeda, Gaylord Perry and Warren Spahn's final season. Cepeda was hurt most of the year. What a collection of guys I played with in spring training, '71, just six years later, as most of the nucleus remained intact. While stepping through the Padres' dugout the previous June, I felt a sense of grown men doing their jobs and enjoying their lives, but from the moment I entered the Giants' clubhouse that February in Casa Grande, Arizona, it was as if I entered the Psychedelic Shack.

Temptations music blasting from wall to wall. America's sports superhero Willie Mays holding court as rookies surrounded him in awe, his youthful baseball ward Bobby Bonds right beside him, along with good friend Jimmie Hart. Willie and Bobby were inseparable. Talking, strategizing, laughing, eating, drinking. They were the very best of friends. Juan Marichal, my personal idol, in the corner gently twisting a rookie's arm back and forth, explaining pitching theory. Willie McCovey bopping to the music as he sat in a chair next to his locker. *"Stretch"* (or *"Mac"* as we really called him), was one of the coolest dudes in the clubhouse – the judge for the team's Kangaroo Court, always had a pearly-white smile at the ready, but don't let that fool you. Mac didn't take crap from anyone. None of them did. Not even our catcher, All-Star backstop Dick Dietz, who was the union representative for the ball club. It was a team of leaders, of teachers, of winners. While baseball historians often cite the 1971 Pittsburgh Pirates and their all-black starting lineup, our clubhouse had more than its share of soul.

One field general behind the plate, three players we knew were headed to the Hall of Fame, and the one everybody believed was on his way. With a caring manager in Charlie Fox that watched over us all.

I was 19 years old, my first spring training game. We were facing the Chicago Cubs, a veteran ballclub with a number of future Hall of Famers of their own and tons of talent on their end of the field, led by a manager in Leo Durocher who would use any advantage to beat you. Crowd of maybe 1500 fans. My nerves got the best of me in the first inning and then came the walks. I gave free passes to Glenn Beckert and Don Kessinger, my first two batters. I managed to fan Billy Williams and then Ron Santo stepped to the plate. Beckert stole third. Now I was rattled, especially with Beckert's dancing outside the base line. I couldn't focus on Santo. I should've just ignored Beckert because Santo had a great eye and knew how to work out a walk. I just couldn't do it, though. With every pitch, Beckert made stomping sounds. Someone may have even yelled, "He's goin'."

I calmed myself.

I toed the rubber.

Set.

"He's goin'!!"

I stopped.

Balk.

Beckert clapped obnoxiously loud as he trotted home. The Cubs dugout laughed their ass off and pointed at me. I was pretty embarrassed. They wouldn't stop. *"Muley"* (Dick Dietz' nickname) called time and jogged out to the mound.

"You all right, kid?" he asked me. I nodded as the Cubs continued busting my chops from their side of the field. McCovey joined us from first base.

"What'sa matter?" Mac demanded to know.

"They're bustin' his balls," Muley answered, nodding to the Cubs dugout.

"You don't take that shit, Rook," McCovey said to me, his back to the plate, rolling his eyes at Santo.

"Put that mother fucker on his ass."

Muley flashed a knowing smirk, slapped me on the rear and went back behind the plate.

I gulped for a moment. "You want me to hit Ron Santo?"

McCovey whispered to me once more before retreating to first base.

"Do it."

I always did what I was told.

My next pitch was a 96-MPH heater stuck right in his rib cage. Santo fell like a ton of bricks. Muley stood up above him, grinning as he tossed me back the ball. The laughter coming from the Cubs dugout stopped instantly. I fanned the next two guys up, glaring across the field as I walked off the mound.

Took my time heading back to the bench as Mays came up behind me, slapping me on the shoulder as he jogged in from the outfield. Marichal chuckled knowingly as I stepped down into the dugout, reached over, rubbing his hand over my cap like I was a little boy done good. Charlie Fox had no expression as he leaned in, whispering, *"Finally, I got a young pitcher like you."* McCovey came by. *"That's the shit I'm talkin' about."* I felt like a teenage gangster getting congratulated by the mob for my first caper. As I walked across the dugout to grab a drink of water, someone gently kicked my leg to get my attention. I turned to find Bobby Bonds winking his approval.

"Nice goin', Rook," Bobby said calmly with a slow smirk.

I pitched a fair amount of games that spring, reasonably well with a lights-out fastball and a curve that still needed a whole lot of seasoning. The Giants sent me to play in "A" Ball, the Decatur Commodores of the Midwest League, a division stocked with even better hitters and pitchers than Great Falls. I only played a few weeks that March with Mays, Mac, Marichal and Bobby before the badass 1971 San Francisco Giants took the National League West by storm, but I knew one day I would soon return to spend my summers chillin' in the Psychedelic Shack.

* * * * *

Decatur, Illionis was the soybean capital of the world, along with a corn crop that was second to none. Truly the heartland of the United States. My manager was Frank Funk, a fine major league hurler in his own right for the Washington Senators and the Cleveland Indians during the 1960s. Frank had a strong reputation of working with young pitchers. When I arrived at minor league camp, Frank pulled me aside.

"Johnny, the organization is happy with your work in Phoenix," Frank said, sitting me down on a dugout bench, "You're here for one reason and one reason only. Ya need a major league slider to go along with your fastball, and I'm gonna teach ya how to throw it. Just stay out of trouble, focus on baseball and not all that other stuff, and you'll do good."

Frank knew all the fine points of the game and really looked after me like an involved uncle. In addition to teaching me how to throw a slider, Frank helped me with my change up as well, which was a sinking fastball choked in the back of my hand utilizing the same arm speed as my heater.

I was throwing in the bullpen one morning when Frank came over to observe my work.

"Your fastball's great, but even the backup infielders can sit on your fastball," he said, gesturing to my catcher to toss him the ball, "You're gonna need this. See, here are the two rails on the baseball. Place your middle finger on one of the rails facing towards the outside. Look at the U shape of the ball - the bottom of the U faces to your right. You ever throw a football before, fingers across the laces? Imagine you gotta throw it like a football. Make sure your release point begins at the middle of the plate – your ball should break about six inches."

I followed his directions – at first my brain was processing his words like a Betty Crocker cookbook recipe – but soon it became second nature. After about 10 pitches, the ball spun somewhat. We were getting there.

"Good, now throw it harder," Frank instructed. With a touch more velocity, the ball broke effortlessly.

"I think I got it," I said to him.

"Johnny, if you can get control of this pitch, your strikeouts are gonna go through the roof."

We didn't always win in Decatur, but Frank was on the money. My strikeouts increased. Baseball wasn't the hard part here. It would be the life lessons.

* * * * *

There wasn't a whole lot to do in the Midwest League. Towns like Appleton, Cedar Rapids, Waterloo, Quincy didn't exactly showcase a top-tier nightlife. There were still a few states where the drinking age remained at 21. Most nights, the older players would sneak the young guys in. We drank quite a bit in the motel room or our apartments, but we had more than our share of nights out. There were pockets of talent on our roster. Had a major-league prospect at shortstop in a guy named Larry Milbourne, an impressive hitter whose inconsistent glovework got him moved to second base by the 10th game in the season. Butch Metzger came up with me to A ball. I felt like I was in for some hard-luck during the season, but also that my strikeout pitch wouldn't let me down.

There were some heady expectations for the ballclub as well as my performance. The Decatur Commoodores had finished in third place the previous year, but the team lost two of their better hitters in an outfielder named Gary Thomasson and my Instructional League roommate, Steve Ontiveros. Frank slated me to start opening day against Burlington, the Oakland A's affiliate. We didn't know what to expect from them, but their hurler Glenn Abbott had an impressive season in rookie ball, winning eight games in 14 starts. Wasn't going to be easy, but I was ready to turn my back on that awful 2-5 debut at Great Falls and ignore the butterflies.

Of course, those butterflies had their say in my performance. I gave up eight runs in four innings opening day, capped off by a two-run blast by this flashy outfielder named Dan Ford. He ignored my fastball and just waited for the off-speed stuff and took it for a ride. Not an auspicious beginning for me by any means.

It was about a week later where I began to appreciate life in the minor leagues, both on and off the field. We traveled to Danville for a Monday night game, facing off against the Milwaukee Brewers A ball team and closest club distance-wise to Decatur. I had a no-hitter going through six innings, double-digits in strikeouts – much like in Great Falls, I had that sense that this would be my turning point toward minor league stardom. After Danville's shortstop Pedro Garcia got on first due to an infield error, I was up against this kid named Gorman Thomas. Tall, burly power-hitter. He could jack it a country mile or go down on strikes trying. I felt I could blow it right by him. Tonight was my night. I checked Garcia at first, delivered and Gorman just smoked it right over the fence in left-center. No-hitter gone. Tie broken. My heart, too. I left the park by myself upset that I let the team down, in addition to taking my record to 0-2. Didn't really want any company.

"Hey,hey Pitch?" someone yelled over to me in a gruff voice. I glanced over to see Gorman heading toward me with another player.

"Yeah," I replied, wondering what this guy who ruined my night wanted.

"Pitched a hellvua game, man," Gorman said, his hand extended to slap some five.

"Thanks," I shrugged, returning the gesture lifelessly. Gorman nodded to the lanky dude standing next to him.

"This is Travers. We're headin' over to the bar. What the hell ya doin tonight?"

"I dunno. Probably grab a bucket of fried chicken and watch friggin' Hee Haw." Gorman just over-laughed.

"That's stupid. There's a couple joints around here. Hang out with us." Travers beckoned, mouthing "C'mon." They both walked away, as if assuming I would follow.

"But I'm not 21," I argued softly.

"Me neither," Gorman barked without looking back. It would turn out to be a long, fun night with my new friends.

* * * * *

You wouldn't find very many "Baseball Annies" in Decatur, or any of the other towns of the Midwest League, but of course, girls were out there. We met a lot of them in different towns, but the lesson that Gorman taught me here was that if you weren't a total jerk, you ended up having buddies everywhere. We fought for every edge on the field, but when the final out was registered, we would pal around like high school chums. There would be nights we played against each other where Travers and Gorman would shoot me a signal from across the diamond during the game to meet up outside the ballpark after the final pitch. Hung out a few times with a hotshot righthanded starter on the Appleton Foxes team, the White Sox affiliate, this kid from Colorado named Rich "Goss" Gossage, a strapping, strong thrower who had a fastball nearly as powerful as mine, only he had superior command of his other pitches as well. We had a couple things in common besides the ability to throw triple-digit gas. I mentioned Terry Forster, my old competitor in San Diego high school circles, who accelerated faster through the minor leagues than all of us. Goss was a ton of fun to hang out with. Bucky Dent was also there and would go around after dark with him, too.

The night out with Travers and Gorman was just what I needed. I felt at home in the league. I stopped trying to impress anyone, and when that happened, I pitched four complete games in a row, a three-hitter against Cedar Rapids, got my revenge against Burlington, 12 strikeouts, (including seven in a row,) and a 5-0 whitewash of Quad Cities, where I fanned 16 batters. I was turning heads and getting respect as one of the top pitchers in all of A ball. My consistency could've been better in the month of June – a shutout here, a CG loss there, but I was learning the entire time.

My manager was right about one thing. There *were* girls everywhere, mostly college girls from Illinois-Champaign, but alongside the town's fair share of nice locals. We were all only 19,20,21 years old, what did we know about life? There were a lot of guys who ran into trouble with women on the road, but sometimes they would just throw themselves at you. I managed to (*mostly*) dodge those girls, but then there were the more subtle ones, the ones with substance. After gutting out a road victory against Danville one evening in late June, I was running around town with Travers and Stormin' Gorman. I felt great about winning a game without my best stuff – seven-plus innings, only two strikeouts – and Gorman blasted another two dingers – we were all feeling pretty good about ourselves. After leaving the guys, I finished up at a bar across the street from my motel, just one last chance to see what's what for the night. This wasn't a common thing for me, but in the early AM hours, few places were carding and I was still pumped up about the win. Two women sitting at the bar caught my attention. One was named Katie, a cheery hostess at a hotel restaurant in Danville. Very pretty girl, dirty blond hair, hazel eyes, trim figure, and a pleasant, mid-western demeanor. Her friend struck up a conversation with me and the three of us chatted for about an hour until the friend gave a knowing goodbye nod to both of us. The bar had just about emptied out. The jukebox played Carpenters most of the time we were there. Hanging out with the guys like Goss, Bucky, Travers and Gorman, that felt like we were classmates in a close-knit boys' high school. Almost everyone on the team was single. Talking to the coaches and managers certainly felt like grownups were in the room. Talking with Katie was like my first one-on-one adult conversation. She was taking classes at the local college, had her own thoughts about politics. Didn't remember the last time I even thought about President Nixon – maybe when he threw out the first ball during a Senators game a couple years back.

"We're closin' up," the old bartender reminded us, pointing to his watch. We completely lost track of the night. As Karen Carpenter belted out yet another hit from that summer, Katie drew her stool closer to mine. It was right here when I realized one of the most exciting elements of life – that window in time between a woman communicating that she wants to spend the night with you and the moment you actually kiss. It could be five minutes, it could be an hour, could be a walk across the street, could be a cab ride, that interval of anticipation is what being alive is all about.

Carpenters would be our soundtrack for the rest of the night and well past sunrise.

* * * * *

My confidence grew and grew as the summer days passed us by. Even a 2-1 complete game loss against Glenn Abbott, Dan Ford (who hit yet another homer off me) and the Burlington team couldn't deter me. My next two starts would also be complete games, especially as I took a no-hitter into the ninth inning against Qunicy, an 11-inning three-hit shutout. I was starting to see Katie often during homestands. I was flattered that she would make the 90-minute trips just to spend time with me. As I was leaving the ballpark with Katie at my side the next night in Danville, my manager yelled to grab my attention. I excused myself from Katie and ran back into the clubhouse.

"Hey Romeo, save your strength," Frank said, "You've been selected to the Midwest League All-Star Team. Ya might be the starting pitcher for the Northern Division."

"Far out," I said, genuinely surprised. Frank didn't look up from his notebook.

"Be at the ballpark early tomorrow. Don't get lost."

"Thanks, Skip," I rushed, heading out of the clubhouse.

"Hey," Frank called over, finally giving me a knowing look, "Don't get lost."

I got lost in Katie's eyes for the next few hours, but when the Decatur sunrise woke me the next morning, Frank's words sunk in.

I made the All-Star team. Of course, I was used to extra accolades in Little League and High School, but it wasn't like this.

45 years out, words can't capture the feeling in my heart standing on the baseline right before the game. And you know what? So many of my friends would be there, too. Goss. My teammate Larry Milbourne. My Burlinglton rivals Glenn Abbott and Dan Ford. Other talented guys like Paul Dade, Bobby Forsch, Hector Cruz, and "Will" Campbell. We were a stacked All-Star squad. Funny thing, the Midwest League didn't field two rosters from each division. The All-Stars played against the best first-half team in the league, which was Danville, so even Gorman and Travers came along for the ride. Lining up for those opening ceremonies, having our names called out over the loud speaker, alongside Goss and Abbott, alongside a great hitter like Dan Ford, across the field from my pals, catching Katie beaming at me from the stands, in that precious, 4500-seat capacity sandbox that was Danville Stadium, with those milky floodnights shining upon us, hell, it felt like the only place in the universe and we were the stars of the baseball galaxy.

Goss ended up starting the game, and he shut Danville down for the first two innings as we grabbed an early 1-0 lead. I came on in the third and man, I could feel the excitement in that small stadium – maybe a bit too much. I gave up a quick run on two singles and a stolen base, allowing Danville to tie it up. The stalemate didn't last as Dan Ford came up and in what seemed like every time I faced the guy, he blasted a moonshot home run. I even got in the offensive mix of the inning with an RBI single. I pitched two more shut-down innings and they didn't score the rest of the game. We beat Danville 4-1, but the only true outcome that mattered was that me and my friends on both sides of the field were all going somewhere.

My good fortune continued as I pitched four complete games in a row at the beginning of July, up until running into Gorman and Danville – Travers had his turn at glory, shutting us down 5-0. It almost seemed like each of us had our own special moments to shine that year.

* * * * *

I won my 10th game in early August against Appleton. I may have been leading everyone in strikeouts, but man, Goss was unhittable. 12-1 to that point in the season, tops in the league. Even though my team came out with the victory, when the game was over, Goss was pumped up to hang out.

"Hey, 'D?" Goss called over to me after the game, "Ya comin'?"

"Where we goin'?" I yelled back.

Goss shrugged.

"I dunno. Ya comin'?"

"Yeah, sure." Then I heard her voice.

"Johnny?" she called out to me. I looked up into the stands and found Katie standing there. Goss gave me a knowing grin as he stepped into the Foxes' dugout.

"See ya later, man."

I walked over to the railing of the fence. "Didn't know you were in town."

Katie shrugged and smiled. "I got the weekend off and thought I'd surprise you."

It was a surprise, a surprise that drove over two hours to reveal itself. I was too polite to blow her off and go hang out with Goss, and she was gorgeous. Katie had a girlfriend who managed the desk at one of the hotels in Appleton and got us a large suite for the night. Even with a raise for making the All-Star team, I spent a little more of my $700 per month salary than I would've liked, but I enjoyed Katie's company, singing songs to each other from the jukebox, dancing in honky-tonk bars. She was low-maintenance, light and breezy, easy to talk to. I was beginning to fall pretty hard for Katie, and not minding the three or four more times she would show up unannounced at games in Danville (especially when I was with the guys *and* other girls) and in Decatur.

I faced the best players A-Ball had to offer. My fastball had a little extra something, as well as the improvements on the slider Frank Funk taught me. Barely anyone touched my stuff. I couldn't believe the success I was experiencing. I was getting a lot of attention in Decatur, from kids in the stands, fans on the street, women in the pizza places and at the ballpark, from Katie. Especially from Katie.

Things got awkward for me when one early evening I was slated to start against Danville. Clouds filled the skies. Was a very good chance we wouldn't get the game in and I didn't feel as bad about it as I should've. About 10 minutes after the umpire suspended the game, I was heading out of the clubhouse for a night with Katie. Before leaving I heard a voice, *"Where ya goin'?"* Frank was behind me.

"It's a rainout….*butttt* I'll stick around if you need me here."

Frank just stared at me, and while he was not happy, he simply shook his head.

"No no, you go on and do what ya gotta do."

"You sure?"

"Yeah, you'll start tomorrow. Be here early."

I ran off to meet Katie, have a bite to eat at the restaurant where she worked (which helped because I was getting paid five dollars a day in meal money) then back at her place to listen to records. It was a wonderful night, but I got Frank's point loud and clear. My head was still on the field but it was clear my affections were somewhat sidetracked. I needed guidance from an impartial observer.

I struck up a friendship during the season with one of the players on Quad Cities, Ken Medlock. After pitching another long game against them, a bunch of us from both teams went to the county fair in town the next day. Ken was one of the smarter players in the league and someone I really respected.

"You still seeing that girl?" he asked me as we walked past the prize pigs. Man, those animals attracted almost as many fans as some of our ballgames, I could barely hear Ken over the cheers.

"What?"

"The girl? Remember the blond who just showed up out of nowhere in the parking lot?"

"Oh, Katie, yeah, she's a cutie."

"She's falling for ya. Be careful."

"Awww, we're just havin' a few laughs, that's all."

"You ain't gonna be here next year. I'm just sayin'."

As Ken walked over to an amusements stand and knocked down some empty soda cans, he definitely had me thinking. I was falling for Katie pretty hard. This wasn't just a couple teenagers having fun, someone to be with when the games were cancelled.

She was driving all around the Midwest to meet up with me. We went fishing together a couple times, real date stuff. There were a lot of jokes about young minor leaguers swinging at the first pitch they saw. I was still just 19 and we only had a couple weeks left in the season. I would most likely be back in California next year. I gazed around the county fair and thought about Katie. One of my first relationships. Really substantial – in the minor leagues, where are you gonna find substantial? Then I paid attention to the families running throughout the fairgrounds. Dads with sons and daughters. Moms wiping mustard off their children's faces. Parents chasing wild kids around to exhaustion. Did I really need all this commitment stuff at this point in my life?

After 12 complete games (and one 15-inning effort, if you can believe that), it took me three starts to notch my 11th victory. Frank called me into his office before we took the field against the Wisconsin Rapids team. We discussed my previous start, another tough loss against Burlington, another home run given up to Dan Ford. I thought I was in for a stern talking-to, but it was a kind discussion filled with constructive criticism and warm advice. We only had a couple weeks left in the season where the team would finish 54-70. With my 244 Ks, I broke the single-season strikeout record Vida Blue set a few years earlier with 179. Ultimately, I would go on to lead the league in complete games, innings pitched, and strikeouts. Also led the league in walks. Still couldn't kick that new habit.

I hadn't heard from Katie in a few days. Didn't make much of an effort to reach out to her, either.

"Ya almost got that slider down," Frank said, "You're gettin' the curve. You could use a little more work on it. The organization is sending ya back to the instructional league in Phoenix this fall. We'll work more on the slider in a few weeks."

"Ya got it, Skip. Thanks for everything this year."

"You're a good kid." I shook Frank's hand and left his office, but not before he got my attention one more time.

"Johnny," Frank said, like the wise uncle he was to me that summer, "Go home." I knew what he meant, just nodded and left his office.

That Monday night, I pitched one of my best games of the season, striking out 11 batters against Quincy. After my final inning of work, I glanced into the stands. I think I saw Katie, leaning over, politely trying to grab my attention. I stopped on the top step. I didn't have a phone, but I was able to call her at the restaurant if I really wanted to track her down. I could've made sure that was Katie sitting out there and not just some other girl waving to a player, but there's no doubt in my mind, we would've ended up together that night, listening to Carpenters until the sun came up, maybe the next night, and maybe the night after that, maybe making plans for the off-season, flight schedules, Christmas together in San Diego, Mom making sure there was an extra gift under the tree. In the end, I did what basically every person I respected in baseball suggested I do.

I kept walking into the dugout and through the clubhouse. Then I went home.

Alone.

* * * * *

I really began enjoying the life of a professional baseball player. There's competition, but you make friends that will last a lifetime. You meet young girls that want to hang out – sometimes for the night, sometimes for much longer. At age 19, you don't always read the signs properly, and when you get stuck, you don't always make the right call. The girls are really cute, flirtatious and tons of fun. It gets serious when they allow themselves to be vulnerable at this stage of *your* life. For a lot of guys, the situation ends pretty badly. For the rest of us, they just end.

That's the thing about the maturation process for a ballplayer that makes it easy for them to walk away from relationships, to move forward from the Rainy Day romances of the minor leagues.

It's that thing that makes you one of those exceptional players, a clutch player, *a gamer*, how to enter the clubhouse after a tough outing like it never happened. It's what makes fans and ex-jock color commentators praise your make up, how you play the game the right way. You learn how to shrug off a loss.

Brandy

Does anyone know what time it is?

The triumphant horns section of the Chicago album blaring from the tape deck of my Z28 Camaro kept asking, as I motored down Interstate 8 over the border at Yuma, entering Arizona, en route to Casa Grande for my second major league spring training.

The 1971 Giants clinched a spot in the post-season for the first time in nearly a decade, coming within two games of the World Series. The ballclub had finished in second place for five straight seasons from 1965 to 1970, and yet, going into 1972, there were yellow flags everywhere. The other teams in the NL Western Division improved – the Reds got faster with Joe Morgan; the Astros got stronger with Lee May; the Dodgers pitching staff improved with Tommy John and their lineup seemingly fortified with the great Frank Robinson. Everyone felt the Giants backed into the division crown in 1971, and yet we traded away one of the mainstays of the rotation in Gaylord Perry. Why? More about performance in the stands than on the field.

San Francisco developed serious attendance issues; regardless of the team's success, ticket sales had dwindled from seventh in the league in 1967 to dead last by the spring of 1972. Longtime Giants owner Horace Stoneham was experiencing serious financial difficulties – unlike other owners in baseball, the Giants were his sole source of income. Even before free agency, before Messersmith-McNally, how do you pay five potential Hall of Famers when you're counting less than a million fans coming through the turnstiles?

The answer is you don't.

During the Winter Meetings of 1971, Stoneham made a move. He traded Perry along with shortstop Frank Duffy to the Cleveland Indians for southpaw Sam McDowell. Sudden Sam had a dream season as late as 1970, striking out over 300 batters, an All-Star four years in a row – a player that simply needed a change of scenery, Stoneham thought. Sure, Perry and McDowell made the about same salary, but Perry was due for a big raise. Marichal was already making $125,000 per. One of them had to go.

I arrived at the Giants' spring training just in time for a simmering of labor troubles that had been bubbling below the surface among the players. After suiting up in the clubhouse, I stepped out of the dugout and onto the practice field. I was still in the phase of my career where the first day of spring training, that first moment the crack of sunlight hits your face is like a six year-old child's first time seeing the Magic Kingdom at Disneyland. All wide-eyed awe, wonder with a touch of fantasy.

I walked across the diamond to find this older gentleman in rolled-up shirt sleeves and loosened tie lecturing my teammates right on the edge of the infield behind second base. Mays, Marichal, McCovey surrounded by most of the roster. Some guys were standing, other sat on the grass, arms over knees like high school freshmen at basketball practice. First time I had ever seen my idols, my heroes looking up at another man, listening obediently. The Major League Baseball Players Association leader Marvin Miller gave the speech. Right beside him was his assistant, Dick Moss – they were the Players Union's version of the M&M boys. Marvin spoke about why a potential work stoppage was necessary, why we needed to be concerned about our future and the future for the players that come after us. If not, then why even have a union, Marvin reasoned. He asked for questions. I raised my hand.

"How is this gonna affect our families and insurance later on?" I asked.

"How old are you, John?" were the first words Marvin Miller ever said to me. I was in shock.

"20," I chuckled nervously. Still stunned. "You know my name?" Remember, this was before last names on the backs of uniforms.

"I know everyone's name," he smiled, a smile you needed to take seriously as his eyes met every player one by one. "You're all important to me."

I was hooked right then and there. So were many of my teammates, too. Dick Dietz, our team's union rep, clapped the loudest of all every time Marvin finished speaking.

"John, you're just breaking in," Marvin continued. "What's gonna happen if you don't play four years in the major leagues?"

I shrugged, willing to listen without having any idea where this was leading.

"If you don't play four years, you don't get vested in the pension plan. That's what we're trying to do. Get you guys in the pension and benefits plan, get you something – it might not be a lot, but it's enough to supplement income when you do retire, to supplement your social security or your next job. You'll have enough to survive. "

So many issues in the air, so many questions. Could I really make this ballclub? Was I ready? If I did travel north to San Francisco with the ball club, would I be stuck in the bullpen? Would there be a players' strike? Was I ready? Would a work stoppage destroy the very fabric of my profession? Are the fans ready to accept their heroes on picket lines?

Was I ready?

* * * * *

Charlie's instincts were spot-on. I was overpowering that spring. Sure the hitters were rusty and didn't condition anywhere near the level of the modern athlete, but only a few of them were able to keep up with my fastball. While it seemed that the front of the rotation would be Juan and Sam, the last two spots were still up in the air. Charlie was leaning toward Steve Stone as his number three. Jim Barr may have been kept in the pen, along with lefty Ronny Bryant, who Charlie wasn't 100% sure could handle the load of starting.

The tenor of spring was overshadowed by the threat of the strike. I still couldn't understand how I would make the team with the all these veterans in camp. A few weeks before the Giants were set to break for opening day, I met Charlie out on the practice field at Casa Grande. Standing with him was Frank Funk, my manager in Decatur.

"Let's take a walk, Johnny," Charlie said, leading me down the baseline with Frank beside him.

"I want to bring ya north with the club," Charlie continued, staring out toward the outfield fence, "Frank thinks your curveball isn't quite there-"

"Ya throw the ball real good," Frank said, more reassuringly than contradicting his boss, "Real good-"

"Really good, Johnny," Charlie agreed, "I think good enough to be in the majors on Opening Day. I want ya with me, but I gotta listen to my coaches. *"Davvy"* (Jim Davenport, the manager of the Phoenix Giants, our AAA team) wants you down there, the organization thinks you should spend the year in Amarillo (our AA team in Texas). We're sending you to Fresno – high A."

This sounded like a demotion in many ways.

"Ok," I responded respectfully, but yet not understanding fully, "Still A-Ball?"

"You're gonna be with Frank another year. He did a real good job with ya last year. We want ya to continue to develop under him. Frank's so good with young pitchers and the two of ya have a good relationship. You'll do good there. But that's not all. If I need ya, you're only a couple hours away from San Francisco."

Marichal. Sudden Sam. Steve Stone. Jim Barr and Ronny Bryant.

Why would Charlie need me so close to the ballclub with that pitching staff?

Later that night, I would have a better idea what was weighing so heavily on Charlie's mind.

* * * * *

I walked into the dinner room of the camp – there was a poker tournament going on with the guys. Some were playing, others just hanging out. The camp was within close walking distance to the hotel where the veteran players stayed. Sly and The Family Stone reverberated from the speakers throughout the room. No one was dancing to the music, but it was a groovy scene. A card game was happening at a table in the corner of the room. Willie, Mac, Bobby, Jimmie Hart, Juan, Tito Fuentes, our excitable second baseman and Sudden Sam were in the midst of seven-card stud. Mac was dealing, sitting out a hand, leaning over, coaching Marichal with his selection. It was more for fun than money, so you had guys at the tables who generally weren't card players. There were some rookies in the room – Garry Maddox next to Steve Ontiveros chatting at another table. I loved my roommates in Great Falls, hanging out with Goss, Gorman and Katie last season in Decatur, but this was a whole different....well, you know.

"Hey Rook," Bobby called over, nodding to the cooler sitting on a spare table, "Grab me a beer, will ya?" As I passed a Bud to our starting right fielder, Bobby winked his appreciation.

"Nice throwin' today, kid," he grinned, as he took a sip, "You might just make it."

"I know I don't want to face him," Willie Mays interjected, his eyes fixated on his hand.

"Hell no," McCovey laughed, dealing the cards around the table.

"Hey Rookie," added Sam McDowell, reaching into his checkered pants pocket, "Here's my room key. Go upstairs and grab me a bottle of vodka. Room 807. We're running low down here."

I'm a rookie, he's Sam McDowell, probably a future Hall of Famer, there wasn't a question.

"You got it," I answered, taking his key to fetch his request.

As I entered Sam's room moments later, I saw worn suits folded on the bed, uniform pants and jerseys dangling off a desk chair, couple emptied suitcases and travel bags.

And 25 bottles of Smirnoff lined up in boxes and all along the wall ledge.

One on top of the other, like the warehouse for a small local distributor, more alcohol than a single human being could ever drink in a lifetime, let alone six weeks in Phoenix. From one end of the wall to the other – double stacked. I snickered a little bit, reached into a box for a bottle and returned to the dinner room.

"Here ya go," I said, handing Sam his bottle, upon returning to the dinner room.

"Thanks, kid," Sam nodded, then proceeded to unscrew the cap, not even using a glass and poured half of it down his throat. Immediately. His chug seemed to last five minutes. Every conversation, every bull session in the room stopped on a dime. The card players stopped tossing dollar bills into the middle of the table. Tito Fuentes' eyes bugged out. McCovey's skeptical, arched eyebrow looked like it was caught in suspended animation. Mays had this blank glare on his face. Bobby, too. Everyone watched in silence, the only sound you heard was Sly and the Family Stone narrating the background as Sam downed a half a bottle of Smirnoff. Then he placed it on the table, wiped his lips, looked around at his teammates and said matter of factly, *"Deal the cards,"* like it was the most obvious next step in the world.

Everyone, still in shock, remained motionless until Mac unleashed his hefty laugh out loud, shaking his head as he tossed the cards to his teammates.

Right then and there, I had a hunch of what concerned Charlie about the pitching staff for 1972.

* * * * *

The labor vote came back about a week later – it was nearly unanimous. There would be the first baseball players' strike in history. The fans reaction was almost uniformly siding with the owners. The first 10 days for the 1972 season would be cancelled. Charlie didn't think the strike would last very long – either the players or the owners, someone was gonna break quickly. In the end, Marvin got the union exactly what they needed. Inclusion in the pension plan, expanded payments and binding arbitration for player contract disputes. It was a major victory for the Union...but a major loss for the ballclub and a Giants player I admired greatly.

Dick Dietz was our representative at the time of the Major League Baseball players strike that spring. He was also coming off two incredible seasons, most certainly an All-Star caliber backstop. Muley made the mistake of crossing management during the labor negotiations. When the players returned to the field in April of 1972, Dietz was gone. Stoneham didn't even trade poor Muley; he placed him on waivers. The hated Dodgers didn't think twice, scooping Dietz off the waiver wire almost immediately. There was talk about some *"clerical error"* in the Giants' front office, but we all knew the truth. Dietz was let go for his attitude during the negotiations. First week in the season, Dietz broke his finger and was done by June. Purchased by Atlanta the following spring, 1973 would be his final season. His OBP in 191 plate appearances was .474 alongside a .295 batting average. After being released by the Braves in the spring of 1974, Dick Dietz couldn't find a job. Such a smart, sure-handed receiver, made a fireballer like me look like a control pitcher. A shame what happened to him. You could've easily found at least five teams that could've used 'ol Muley. He was 32 and out of the majors. Blackballed. One of the more reprehensible labor-related stories in league history.

He also wouldn't be the last Giants player to go in early 1972.

One month later, Stoneham cut more payroll, albeit in the classiest manner possible. It's an oft-told story, but basically Willie Mays wanted security and Stoneham's financial situation was anything but. So by sending Mays, the face of the franchise, back to New York, Stoneham created a heartwarming Baseball tale *and* cut over $150,000 from the payroll. I was sad that I wouldn't get a chance to be regular-season teammates with Mays, but hopefully I would be there to play with future Hall-of-Famers like Marichal, McCovey and Bobby Bonds. For my present circumstances, none of it mattered to me, though. I was already in my car by the time opening day rolled around, listening to Led Zeppelin, heading up Interstate 5.

I was going to California.

* * * * *

The Fresno Giants played in the California League, which was known to be a hitters' paradise. Our home park was Euless Field, been around for decades, nice infield, patchy outfield grass. Very spacious, though. Perfect park for me. I felt I would have no problems there. I had been so confident of my success. Sitting with Frank Funk in his office before the start of the season, I let him know how much faith I had in myself to dominate at this level. Was thrilled Frank was still my manager. It was as if you were bumped up a grade in school and your favorite teacher came along with you.

"I think I'm gonna win 20 this year," I told him.

"You don't need to win 20, Johnny," Frank lectured me, "Ya just need a second pitch. And a third. Your fastball's already there, everyone knows that, but what happens when you're two times around the order and Clemente has you timed? Maybe ya blow it by him or maybe he smashes it right-center and empties the bases. Ya got a nice slider, but your curveball isn't ready. That's why you're here and not going to San Francisco."

"I did really well in spring training, right?"

"Yeah, against guys who haven't picked up a bat in five months. You're gonna need to change speeds when Johnny Bench is in playing shape and Pete Rose is leading off first bugging the hell outta ya. One of these days you're gonna need a change-up, too. Any pitcher can blow by the bottom of the order, but what about Lee May? What about Nate Colbert? What about Stargell? And the walks still bother me. You can only spend so much time sitting around the strike zone before the hitters figure you out."

Frank went about teaching me the advanced points of the slider. We were out on the field before games with Joey Martin, one of our catchers, where Frank would break down the movement, the motion, the follow-through for the slider.

"You're still throwing it wrong," Frank would say, "Twist your hands this way, not that."

"It feels like a curveball," I replied, out of frustration.

"It's like a curveball, but it's not. Here, lemme show you. Ya need to keep your arm on the right side of the catcher, release the ball once your arm is across the plate."

Again and again, I would twist and turn, until after four-five lessons, the pitch started breaking. Frank gingerly led me through the lessons. As I figured out the pitch, you could see the look of satisfaction on Frank's face, like a sculptor who began to recognize the slab of clay before him.

"Johnny," Frank smiled, "Now ya got a slider. A major league slider."

I started using the slider more in ballgames, mixing my pitches, changing speeds. The hitters couldn't sit on the heat not knowing what was coming next. What was coming next was a lot more smiles on Frank's face.

I won my first start in overpowering fashion 6-1. Struck out 11, walked a few – still had yet to figure out the wildness I picked up in Great Falls – but we were winning. We had a great lineup. Skip James was our power source at first base – seemed like he hit a dinger every other game. Another great hitter we had was a guy named Gordy Carter, a smart outfielder who came from USC. I became good friends with Gordy – he was always talking about his little brother, a high-school kid named Gary who was on the verge of being drafted. Gordy said Gary was either gonna play organized ball or going to UCLA for football. Always made a joke about Gary going to college at his rival school. Gary was on the Giants' draft radar, but the team always seemed to draft pitchers with their top choices – San Fran grabbed Bob Knepper with their second pick in '72..

Skip James lived next-door to me at an apartment complex in Fresno. The Giants tended to draft intelligent players, and Skip was no exception. A college kid from the University of Kansas, Skip seemed much, much older than his 22 years. Rookie league and most of low A-ball was filled with high school kids away from home for the first time. I came to realize the low-minors was less like college and more like boarding school, especially with so many players living in rooming houses. High A ball was different, as guys like Skip were a bit more worldly than the rest of us. It was also the first time I ever had a teammate that possessed true, real-world experience.

Skip was married.

Barbara was Skip's wife, also 22. Even though they had what seemed to be a mature relationship, they were like college kids playing house. It was Barefoot in the Ballpark, if that makes any sense. Some of us received signing bonuses, but that was untouchable money, especially in my case. Mom never let me even look at the bonus money. It was just $700 a month, plus meal money, which was still only like $5 a day, not a whole lot of dough after taxes. I would drive over to the ballpark with Skip most days; Barbara would come by later to watch Skip. She would beam when Skip kissed her goodbye before running out onto the field for the National Anthem. They were less a married couple than loving, affectionate life partners. When we had a homestand, sometimes the three of us would get dinner together, which was basically a pizza. There was a lot of pizza in the minors, with the occasional hamburger when you wanted to splurge. Money was tight, though. As the season wore on, there were a few nights where Skip and I would come home from the ballpark after a rough day starving for something special.

"Hey Johnny?" Skip called to me as I was opening my apartment door, "I'm tired of pizza. Wanna go in on dinner? Barb's the best cook in the world."

"Yeah," I nodded, "Good idea."

"Let's treat ourselves tonight. I wanna have chicken."

I reached into my pocket, counted up the coins and one dollar bills with Skip and pooled our 10 bucks for a real meal.

Barb would run out to the grocery store, whip us up a home-cooked cornish game hen with some scrumptious sides out of the can that we'd wash down with cheap wine when there were a couple bucks left over. The three of us would sit there, listen to some Chicago on their modest stereo system, I'd just watch Skip and Barb finish each other's sentences, coloring the other's world. It made me think of Katie, that this was what real love must look and feel like. The day-to-day. It's the most beautiful thing on the planet, I would think to myself as I walked back into my apartment. Then the phone would ring.

"Johnny, we're at the pizza place," Tammy said loudly from what sounded like a payphone, "C'mon out."

And soon I was in my car to meet Tammy, this classic, upbeat, barely 22-year old California blond, her friends and a couple of my teammates for a late-night snack. Oh yeah, and her roommate…also named Tammy.

* * * * *

The mall was a relatively new concept in 1972. The mom-and-pop shoe store, clothier and even neighborhood hobby shop were rapidly being replaced all over America by these sprawling concrete slabs where families and teenagers could go and get their sneakers, their leisure suits and blouses, their records in one place. I was always fascinated by the malls back then – was also a spot where I could grab a cheap meal. Tammy worked in the mall with her roommate of the same name. *Tammy Blond* was petite, light hair with an animated personality, a pronounced Southern California accent and a far-out figure. She possessed the kind of alluring posture where she leaned while standing still. Her roommate, *Tammy Brown*, a bit taller, attractive brunette with hazel eyes, always wearing this unusual demeanor of rebellion and responsibility all at once. Tammy Brown oozed confidence. Being with them, both slightly older than me, I always felt safe, and I never felt cooler.

I met The Tammys one afternoon while searching the stacks of albums at the mall record store. The debut LP for the band America was playing on the speakers through the ceiling. Tammy Blond approached me – we talked about the band's soft harmonies – she compared them to Crosby, Stills, Nash & Young, one of my favorites. The conversation came pretty easy between the three of us, especially after they revealed that they frequented the Fresno Giants games. The girls loved hanging around the ballpark while not sorting through records during their work breaks at the mall. We often met up for beers at the local pizza place after games. I was still under 21 at the time, so we didn't crawl through the bars much, but we enjoyed ourselves. I would talk with Tammy Blond about the differences between Fresno and San Diego, how much I liked playing in the California sunshine versus the corn fields of Decatur. Always talked about music. One night, one of my teammates had a little too much to drink at the pizza place and began to make his presence known.

"I think it's time to get outta here," I suggested.

"Why don't we go back to our pad?" Tammy Blond offered, catching my attention with a dead serious smile, "We got beer."

"Yeah, let's grab a pie and split," Tammy Brown chimed in, nodding to the waitress.

Besides the obvious, this made perfect sense. Keeping us off the road and out of trouble was the smart move. The quickest way to get flagged by the organization as a troubled player was getting thrown in the local drunk tank with a DWI violaton. How could you handle the pressures of big league cities if you couldn't stay out of harm's way in Anytown, U.S.A.?

The Tammys were always playing records at their apartment when all of us were over there. Must have been an impromptu party after the pizza place at least once every homestand. Carole King seemed like the patron saint of the women I knew in the minor leagues during those years. They all felt the earth move. The smallish, four-room flat was scented with cheap beer, carbonation and cigarette smoke, but it was glorious. The women of Fresno possessed a certain agency about how they dictated their lives; no judgments and no regrets, and there was more free agency going on in 1972 than you could shake a stick at. One word describes nights like this, once everyone left me behind with The Tammys as the two of them dead-bolted the front door, slowly turning toward me sitting on their well-worn couch, mischevious smiles on their faces.

Joy.

* * * * *

A month later, we played a scrimmage against the Giants up in San Francisco at Candlestick Park and I was brought into the office with Frank Funk to update Charlie Fox on my progress. Sure, he could read my success from the box scores and scouting reports, but Charlie wanted to hear it straight from my manager.

"Let Johnny stay with us," Charlie said, "You did a great job with him, Frank. We'll take it from here."

"I could do that, Charlie," Frank replied, "But..."

"But what?"

"I dunno. Something tells me he's needs more time."

"He's won 11 games already."

"I know. I just think it's too soon."

Charlie could've made every acceptable excuse for me to finish the year in San Francisco, but he trusted Frank's instincts and let me return to High A and complete my year, which suited me fine. Truth be told, going to Candlestick was more like a college sophomore coming home for Christmas break. Was nice to see the family, but I wasn't done with school yet. Nor did I want to be. I was having a blast.

I returned to Fresno, dropped off my gear at the apartment, then swung by the pizza place. Sure enough, the guys were there with The Tammys.

I woke up the next morning at Tammys' apartment after another party. It was about nine AM, the girls were already awake, already listening to records, percolating the coffee on the ancient stove. I wasn't at all a heavy drinker, just stuck to beer, but I had a throbbing headache the morning after. I grabbed a hot mug and sat beside an open window to take in some fresh air. The Tammys were bouncing around, getting ready for work, humming a song from some Broadway musical that caught fire in a nation running through the early innings of the Human Potential Movement. Me, too, I guess, as I found tranquility with where I was at that point in the season. The slider was breaking, my heater was snapping at 98-99 MPH well into the late innings. I was once again an All-Star pitcher, and it just seemed as though every start gave me more and more confidence:

July 9th: went the distance against Modesto en route to a 5-1 victory. Smacked a dinger, too. *Day by Day.*

July 15th: fanned 10 against Reno for my ninth straight victory. *Day by Day.*

July 26th: another complete game – this time against San Jose. Another 150 pitches. Another victory – my 11th in a row. *Day by Day.*

My winning streak ultimately ran my record to 15-3. The one ballclub in particular that got me excited to compete against was Bakersfield. I just loved that rivalry and not just because it was the Dodgers' affiliate, but the other great pitcher in the league was their ace Rick Nitz. We were battling for the lead in victories. He was an outstanding pitcher. Curve, slider, great change-up, excellent control *and* a good fastball 90+. Amazing control spotting his heater. We had some classic battles. This was the type of pitcher I would be facing when I got to the big leagues. Down in the minors, you had rivalries, but just like with Terry Forster in high school, we all had the same goal – get to the majors. We faced each other two times, each winning a game, improving our records, but more important, our reputations.

The losses occured as seldom as cicada sightings. Wins were like sunrise to me in 1972 – they were just supposed to happen. The Tammys were a trememdous support system. Tammy Blond gave me extra attention after losses when we were alone hanging out in her apartment, mainly because they were so infrequent. Words of encouragement as we lay there in the wee hours as Carole King wove this amazing tapestry of lyrics and melody on the turntable in the corner of her bedroom.

"There's always tomorrow, *amIrite*?" she'd softly remind me as if it was all one word.

"I dunno. I pitch again in three days. I dunno what's gonna happen." Tammy Blond would shrug off my own dejected attitude, just bunch her head into her shoulder and keep the optimism in front of me.

"Then it'll be tomorrow before you know it, *amIrite*?" It was 86 and sunny every day in Tammy Blond's world. Made me feel good to know that people like that existed.

* * * * *

I finished 1972 with a 17-6 record, second in the league to Rick in victories, but led everyone in strikeouts with 245. It was pretty clear I would never throw another pitch in Fresno, maybe not even the minor leagues. After our final game, I helped Skip and Barbara pack their stuff and watched them drive away into the off-season. The connection between the two of them, their love and commitment to one another stayed with me for a long time. Even that night's pizza and booze fest at The Tammys was something of a bittersweet soiree.

It would be the last nightfall I would ever spend in Fresno, a going-away party of sorts, but for that final evening, the music was groovin' and the cigarette smoke floated around us as The Tammys blissfully crooned "*Brandy*" in tune with the record. I *really* enjoyed myself with her, but the feeling of longing for a bond like Skip and Barbara, it was a confusing time for me. The isolation of the road will do that to you. Did I want the picket fence, the loving wife, kids, coaching some little league? Did I just want to get after it? I was turning 21 soon, and had no idea what was right for me. In my heart, I just didn't want to be alone.

Late into the night, Tammy Blond, dressed in her trendy headband and blue jeans, double-fisting bottles of Coors, softly bobbed and weaved through the partygoers in that small apartment and sidled up to me with an affectionate hip-check.

"Ya feelin' gud?" she asked with an eager grin. I slowly bobbed in tune with the music, smiled back, hugged her shoulder and kissed her forehead as Tammy handed me another round.

Take It Easy

Johnny, *whaddya doin'?*" my manager Jim *"Davvy"* Davenport huffed at me, standing on the mound next to my catcher Richie Sauget as Skip jogged in from first base, the 98-degree dry heat much more intense than the ninth inning of the game I was pitching, "Ya got a four-run lead and you're walkin' the ballpark. We should be outta here by now."

"I'm just messin' around with the screwball," I replied coolly.

"Let's wrap this up and go home, huh?" Davvy stepped back toward the dugout, but not before I added another comment.

"Don't worry," I heckled, "The beers will still be cold." Davvy whipped around as Richie and Skip enjoyed a laugh as well.

"Don't be a smart ass," Davvy snapped as a smile crawled across his face, "Just get this kid out, will ya? I wanna go, we got people waiting for us." I nodded back with a smirk as Richie slapped me on the ass with his mitt and jogged toward home plate.

That was AAA Phoenix, 1973.

* * * * *

"Charlie wants to see you," the Giants clubhouse manager Mike Murphy told me as I entered the spring training facility that February.

"Thanks, Mike," I replied, whom I remembered from my previous two spring trainings in Casa Grande. After dropping my gear off at my assigned locker, I entered Charlie Fox's office, where he greeted me with a hug.

"How's Mom and Dad?" Charlie asked me. I nodded my reply as he offered me a chair in front of his desk.

"Ya ready to come north with us or what?" he asked pointedly.

"Sure, I guess."

"Whaddya mean, ya guess?" Charlie laughed, "Ya rather be in AAA?"

"I'll be there soon, Skip. I just don't wanna go and, you know….stink."

"Ya not gonna stink, Johnny-"

"I know, but….."

Charlie laughed incredulously. "If need ya, I'm calling ya up. You're my number six starter and ya haven't even thrown a ball off the mound yet."

"I'll do whatever you want me to do, but a spot starter-"

"You're not gonna be a spot starter-"

"Ya know what I mean-"

"Look, the organization has you slated for AAA, but if ya do well this month, you're comin' with me. And that's it. Go get ready. I'll see ya out on the field."

Once I left Charlie's office, I walked past Juan Marichal, who was sitting in front of his locker.

"Hey, Juanito, what's goin' on?" Marichal asked, nodding toward Charlie's office.

"Nothin', you know, just stuff."

Juan laughed. He knew the deal. "What's goin' on?"

"Charlie wants me to come north with the ballclub."

"And you coming, no?"

Here we go with the players now, I thought to myself. I've been in the car for five hours. Can I at least go take a leak before they pack me up again?

"Of course I wanna come. Just don't wanna screw up, that's all. Trying to be smart about it. What do you think?"

Juan didn't always possess the clearest English, but no one spoke more common sense to me about pitching.

"I think you ready, they think you ready, but *you gotta* think you ready. You got best arm of all of us. But pitching is not just here, but up here and in here, too. You gotta make sure your head and your heart are good, too, not just your arm," as Juan gently shook my right elbow.

* * * * *

Spring Training felt different without Willie Mays in camp. Our captain and signature star was gone, but it opened the floodgates for guys like Garry Maddox and another rookie, Gary Matthews. Of course, Bonds was still here, sort of grabbing the mantle of team leader. It was just a spectacularly talented outfield. Some people in the media thought that Maddox dogged it a little, but they weren't paying attention. Maddox was tall, thin and his long strides in center made it appear as though he wasn't hustling. Maddox ran a 9.4 400, Matthews ran a 9.5. Bobby, of course, ran a 9.3. With an outfield like that and with Willie's enthusiastic embrace of New York, fans today would be shocked how quick people forgot about Mays back then.

One of the sadder observations was watching the decline of another of Bobby's close friends on the club, Jimmie Hart. Known on the baseball card as Jim Ray Hart, he had been the power-hitting third baseman for years, until his knees blew out in the late '60's. He had tried to come back many times from his injuries, but also he had serious stage fright. Jimmie did *whatever he could* to get himself out on the field. A very proud man, but nerves got to him often. This is an ailment not discussed much in big league circles or the newspapers, but it's more prevalent than you might think. Jimmie would be wearing a Yankee uniform by the end of April.

Donny Carrithers was another unfortunate story. He had some of the best stuff I'd ever seen – his slider was harder than his fastball and there was only one other similar pitcher in that sense - Bob Gibson. Gibby threw harder with his slider than he did with his heater – he threw 90 with his fastball – 93 with the slider. Unheard of. Problem with Carrithers was that his very best stuff was always left in the bullpen. Had a little stage fright once he got on the mound. He came to the big leagues as a starter, but ended up in the long relief role for the Giants. Ultimately, he was shipped to Montreal and enjoyed a couple nice seasons coming out of the pen. There were many stories like Donny's that gave me pause about getting to the majors too quickly.

It was a spring training like the other two I had attended, a little more confidence, a little more control of my off-speed stuff, my curve and slider were breaking the way I wanted. Still was walking more than I should've, but I kept the ball in the park. I handled major league hitters well. Often times, I felt ready. I got along great with Jim Davenport, the former Giants player managing AAA Phoenix. I'll admit my status as a number-one pick allowed me greater face time with the managers. My parents drove down from San Diego to watch me pitch. They often mingled with the other coaches' wives and families. Charlie would come over and talk with them. My folks also got to know Betty, Davvy's wife. With only a few weeks left in spring training, I still had not been cut. One afternoon, I went golfing with Davvy at the Scottsdale Country Club, just the two of us.

"You're stayin' with me, Johnny," Davvy said while we were on the 10th hole after a quick bite to eat. Davvy had a pretty solid drive and like a ballplayer admiring his home run, he would pause and watch his ball sail through the sky for that extra moment.

"Better than Amarillo," I replied, stepping over to the tee.

"Nope, you're stayin' with me and you're gonna start opening day."

"Is that okay with Charlie?"

"Fuck him," Davvy remarked, waving his hand at the suggestion, "You need one more year." Davvy and Charlie would bicker like relatives – they'd bark at each other but deep down, you knew they cared for one another very much.

"He really wants me to come north, but you know I'll do whatever-" Davvy gave me the look that said, *"I'm done with this topic."*

"We'll talk to Charlie tomorrow."

* * * * *

"Ya made the team, Johnny. You're comin' with us," Charlie said, while Davvy and I sat in his office.

"Ok," I replied.

"Fuck, no," Davvy interjected, "You ain't bringin' him up."

Charlie was having none of it.

"You're AAA. I'm the big club. I say he comes. He's ready, we know he's ready-"

"He ain't ready, he's a kid, for Christsakes. He's 21 years old-"

"There's a lot of fuckin' 21 year-olds doin' just fine-"

"What about Garibaldi? What about Rich Robertson? We brought them up too early. We're still trying to fix Carrithers-"

"We had no choice, they were bonus babies, college guys-"

"And that didn't work. He's three years out of high school-"

"Ah, fuck you." Davvy turned to me.

"Johnny, what do you wanna do?" I was like a ping-pong ball going back and forth between the two of them.

"Look, I just wanna do whatever the organization-" Charlie cut me off.

"What do you wanna do, Johnny?"

Planes versus buses. Hotels versus motels. Stadiums versus ballparks. Hometown papers versus *media.*

"I wanna pitch for the San Francisco Giants…." Charlie threw Davvy a *"Told you so,"* look, but I wasn't finished talking.

"….When I'm ready. Charlie, I can't wait to play for you, but you already got Juan, Bradley, Bryant. What about Barr? What about Sam? Willoughby's having a great spring, too. Is there even a spot for me?"

"Charlie, the kid has never been a reliever and he's never been a spot starter. C'mon."

Charlie sighed, but one of the things I loved about Charlie was that he always placed logic and reason before his ego.

"Davvy, if you fuck this up, I'm gonna come down there and kick your ass. It's on my head if something happens to this kid." Then Charlie looked over at me and stood up. "You, I'll see ya in September. Enjoy your fuckin' vacation."

* * * * *

I know what you're thinking. Why would I choose, or better yet, *prefer*, to stay in the minors just a little while longer? Good question. I'm not gonna lie to you, I didn't mind it in the minors. I mean, sure Bert Blyleven was in another world as a 21-year-old in '72 and Don Gullett pitched well for the NL champion Cincinnati Reds, but I had never experienced failure in baseball, my first month at Great Falls the lone exception. That stood out in my mind during this time – I felt like I let everyone down when I went 2-5 those early days in organized ball. The last thing in the world I wanted to do was get lit up on the major league stage and have to come back to Phoenix with a 1-6 record, an ERA north of seven and suddenly I'm no longer the best arm in the organization, just another pitcher who couldn't get guys out in the bigs. I enjoyed two seasons of being the big dog on the staff, the main attraction of the ballclub. It would be interesting to see whether I was right to take it slow, versus other teams who were eager to get their draft picks and golden boys onto the major-league rubber ASAP. Maybe I was scared, maybe I felt so comfortable working with Davvy that I just wanted to stay a little longer in the cocoon. Big fish in a small pond? Probably, but I felt like a rock star traveling to these small ponds up and down the West Coast, and I was hopping from pad to pad.

* * * * *

Sunday, April 8th, 1973. I was reading the local morning paper, the Arizona Republic. Front page article of the business section showed a blueprint for *"The New Phoenix,"* no longer this one-road in, one road-out mini-city. 31-story skyscrapers, a completed freeway, four-star hotels to be built across from the Phoenix Civic Center. The longest street in the area, Scottsdale Road, ended in dirt and gravel out by the canal – there was nothing past the canal. The only major thoroughfare that existed was Highway 10 and that was a federal road. Van Buren took you into the capital – just one building. That was all about to change. It seemed as though the city was growing up as quickly as I was.

I rented a three-bedroom apartment at an exclusive complex in Scottsdale. Our favorite watering hole was Mabel Murphy's – super pub grub, music, dancing. Another cool spot was The Red Barn, within walking distance from our place, so no need to get behind the wheel when we were plastered. Everything was calculated for our well-being, with as little risk to us as possible, since we were assets of the Giants organization, though that didn't always stop us from being 21-year-old idiots every so often. A great group of guys - Gary Thomasson, *"Twiggy"* Hartenstein, Eddie Figueroa, to name a few. We tore up the town, especially after the final out. Chasin' it like crazy. None of us had a ton of dough, but hey, it was Phoenix, really didn't need it.

Steve Ontiveros, who had bunked with me at the Instructional League during the two previous winters, was my roomie once again. He was one of the organization's prized hitters. The Giants drafted him a year ahead of me as a third baseman, but after 32 errors at the hot corner, they found a spot for him in right field. Man, could Onti rake – hit .321 in '71, had some pop, walked 102 times – the team loved Onti's ability to get on base. Great eye – knew the strike zone as well as any hitter I played with to that point. He would be given every chance to rise to the big club just like me. As soon as Onti finished moving his stuff into the apartment, he walked out of his room and clapped his hands once.

"So where we drinkin'?" he asked me. Right then and there, I knew we'd be pals.

Skip James also came up to Phoenix with us. He had a great season alongside me in Fresno, hitting 32 dingers. The problem for him was that Skip had a number of guys in his way at first base in San Francisco – Mac was still there, Kingman, Ed Goodson as well. I didn't know what was gonna happen to Skip and Barb. Phoenix Municipal wasn't like Ueless Stadium in Fresno at all. Much bigger park, the wind blew in from right field. Even for the PCL league, well-known to inflate hitters' stats, for a lefty-swinger like Skip, it was extremely frustrating. Skip hit for average, a decent average, but that wasn't good enough for the Giants organization. For me, as much as I sympathized with the guys in the lineup, well, Charlie was right. Some days it did feel like a vacation.

I enjoyed playing in Phoenix, Municipal Stadium; the park always drew a good crowd for minor-league ball, always around 1200 or so. We won our first game of the season in easy fashion against our rivals, the Tucson Toros, 9-1. I went the distance, striking out 10. The Turos were the AAA affiliate for the Oakland

A's. There were serious hitters on that team, not just guys like my old foil Dan Ford and Phil Garner. They had a catcher named Tim Hosley who had power, hit for average and was able to work the count on me. Other solid players like this guy Jose Morales who could just flat-out hit and major league vets working their way back like Jay Johnstone. All things considered, though, I felt it was easy to pitch against the hitters of the Pacific Coast League. I think a lot of that had to do with pitching in a bigger ball park than Fresno. The other thing was I pitched differently to up-and-coming players than ex-big leaguers proving they were still capable of performing in the majors. Where I might try to blow it by a youngster like Manny Trillo, you know, just throwing it hard, harder, hardest, I knew I had to be smarter, crafty with an intelligent hitter like Jay Johnstone, who had already faced Seaver, Gibson and Sutton. On this day, the stacked Tucson Toros lineup really couldn't touch me, and as soon as we returned into the clubhouse after the game, I heard Onti bellow out, *"Hey 'D (that was my nickname in Phoenix), Cattlemen's Steaks tonight!?!?!"*

"Count me in, Roomie!" Onti started pointing around the clubhouse to whoever was paying attention, "Steaks? Steaks? Steaks?" While Onti was generally a quiet guy, he got really fired up when we won. Great guy to have on the bench during those celebratory moments. So me, Onti, Skip James and Charlie Williams, another pitcher on the staff, went to Cattlemen's Steakhouse for a great piece of meat and cold beers. This sort of became our thing when I pitched. When we won, Onti would yell *"Steaks!"* in the clubhouse, and we'd head over to the Cattlemen's - very cowboy, very rustic. Lots of boots and jeans everywhere.

I ate steak after my first three starts. *This was getting too easy*, I thought to myself. That third night with the boys digging into a medium-rare prime rib and mashed potatoes, I wondered if I should've gone with Charlie, that perhaps I was selling my talents and my organization short by lounging in AAA. Then this gaggle of twenty-something beauties sauntered through the door and sat down across the room.

Nope, I think I'm good for a little while longer, I answered in my head, paying the check for the table, standing up from our spot to retrieve some after-dinner drinks and general mayhem at The Red Barn. We walked through that bar like we were walking onto a yacht.

God, Phoenix was a great place to play ball.

* * * * *

So I proceeded to *lose* my next five starts. The league was pretty competitive and I lost focus a bit after my three-game winning streak, taking it all a bit too lightly. We faced the Tacoma Twins, Minnesota's AAA affiliate, in the second game of a double-header. A lot of power on that team – fellow San Diegan Jimmy Nettles was there, Eric Soderholm, Rick Renick, Tommy Kelly, a monster masher named Craig Kusick and this older dude named Chuck Manuel. "Country" had been in the Twins' system for about a decade, stuck on the Bloomington-Tacoma shuttle between AAA and the big club. A West Virginia guy, everybody loved Country, his accent and down-home demeanor. Could drink with the best of us. I started the second game of the double-header. I was a little frustrated, but felt good after my warm-ups. Before running out to the mound, Davvy pulled me aside.

"Stop fuckin' around, Johnny," he said softly but authoritatively, "*Mr. Stoneham's here.*"

"Where?" I replied, scanning the stands behind the backstop to see if I could locate where the Giants' owner was sitting.

"I dunno, he's just in the ballpark somewhere. Let's get a win, huh?"

"I know. I'll get it done." This response didn't soothe Davvy.

"Yeah, don't think Charlie's not watchin', either. Don't embarrass me."

"I said I got it." I pitched carefully to experienced major-leaguers like Nettles and the younger players with good eyes like their catcher Glenn Borgmann, Tommy Kelly and of course, their big guy Kusick. I mowed them down, striking out 13. I walked out for the sixth inning, glanced to the scoreboard and realized, *Holy shit. I'm throwing a no-hitter.* I didn't allow myself to get nervous, especially since this was the second of a minor-league twin bill, which traditionally only lasted seven innings. I retired the first two batters quickly and then Nettles came to the plate. We weren't all that close personally, but we knew of one other coming from the same home town. After blowing a couple heaters by him, I tried to sneak a curve in there, but it hung just a little too much, and Nettles smashed a hard grounder to first. Skip knocked it down but bobbled it as well, just missed beating Nettles to the bag in time. It was only the third Twins' base runner I allowed all game. The official scorer charged Skip with an error. I struck out the next batter to end the inning. Three outs left. I returned to the dugout itching to finish this off.

The seventh inning came and I managed to retire the first two batters easily. Up to the plate steps Country. Six-foot-four inches, imposing lefty swinger. I just needed one more out and I had to go through Chuck Manuel. He must've fought off five or six fastballs.

He was timing me – a dead fastball hitter. I took a chance. I set. I wound up. I threw an off-speed pitch that caught him by surprise.

Right down the middle.

Strike three.

No-hitter.

My teammates mauled me on the mound, celebrating the achievement, a group effort and most important....

Steaks.

Couple hours later, me, Onti and Skip James were pounding ribeyes and an endless pour of cold beer at Cattlemen's when we had a visitor approach our table.

"You pussies only drink that watered-down shit." It was "Country" Chuck Manuel.

"Heyyyyyy," I replied, genuinely happy to see him and have him join us as Onti grabbed a chair from the neighboring table for Chuck to sit down. Our managers frowned upon players fraternizing on the field, but all bets were off after the final out. And everyone loved him. Country slapped backs, exchanged friendly nods and looked around for a glass as the waiter approached our tables.

"Another couple pitchers please," I told our server as I looked across at Country, "Some tequila shots, too." Everyone agreed, with a raucous *"Yeahhh"* coming from our group.

"That's more like it," chimed in Country, as Onti poured him a tall one.

This was as calm as the night would get.

Four hours later, we found ourselves at The Red Barn. Still more beer, more tequila shots. Rowdy evening that ended with us standing on tables singing The National Anthem. We even got Skip, who usually went right home to Barb, to stay out the whole night. Finally, it was closing time. I didn't have very far to drive, which was a good thing, because I was pretty intoxicated, but Country had no way to get back to his hotel. It was thoughtless, it was irresponsible, it was wrong, but of course, I drove what seemed like half the Phoenix Giants roster plus six-foot-four Charlie Manuel in my cramped, four-seat Camaro back to the Sands Motel where the Tacoma Twins stayed.

Backwards.

To this day, I can't believe we weren't pulled over. I drove backwards down Van Buren Road. Country, who was at least 6-7 years older than all of us, was drunk but still the voice of reason, as I turned my head around, driving 25 miles an hour staring through the back windshield.

"What the fuck y'all doin?" Chuck screamed, "Gonna get us killed-"

"Shut-up, Country," I slurred, "I'm concentrating!"

"You tell 'em, 'D," Onti shouted, "Take his ass all the way home! Show this bastard what the Giants are really about!"

We finally arrived at the Sands. Charlie got out, drunk and a bit shaken up.

"You, you sons of bitches are crazy," Charlie said, staggering to his motel entrance.

"Oh, Country, don't say that," I slurred back, "Didn't ya have fun?"

"Fuckin' Country," Onti cried out heartily. Charlie was just shaking his head. He wouldn't even face us.

"I love you guys, but y'all crazy." We drove off, drunkenly saying good-bye to Country.

There was more than our fair share of drinking and driving that year. After a spring training game against the Angels in Palm Springs a few months earlier, I grabbed some dinner with another young pitcher, Bruce Heinbechner. Born and bred in California just like me, *"Heinie"* was a fun-loving kid who owned this gorgeous 1966 Porsche 912 coupe, red with black interior. Heinie had no problem getting that machine up to 100 down Interstate 10. Later on that night, we met up at a bar with a few of our respective teammates. Some cocktails and mingling with the ladies later, I got Heinie's attention at the bar.

"I'm gonna get going," I said.

"What are ya talkin' about," he replied, "The night's just startin'."

"Onti's leavin', he's my ride-"

"Nah, stay a little longer. I'll drop ya off."

I shrugged and hung around until closing. We got into Heinie's Porsche and he showed off the car's power, gunning it down the main strip of Palm Springs. We were driving way too fast for the road, but I'd be lying if I said I didn't fall in love with the Porsche right then and there. I knew somewhere down the line, I would own one. We reached the Ramada a few minutes later. Bruce wasn't flat-out drunk, but there was a little buzz in the air.

"You all right?" I asked him, "You can crash with us if ya want."

"I'll be fine. We're only right down the road anyway."

"Thanks for the lift, man," I said as I shut the door.

"See ya later, alligator," Heinie said, peeling out and screeching away.

Drinking and driving was fairly common among ballplayers back then. Fairly common. We were all talented, agile, young men with elite reaction time.

We never thought anything tragic would happen.

* * * * *

I was named to my third straight minor league All-Star team, which paid me a nice $1200 bonus, in addition to the $1000 extra the club owed me for the no-hitter. By the beginning of August, I was sporting a 13-10 record, once again among the league leaders in complete games, wins and strikeouts. The whole season felt like an extended Eagles tune. As a nation in 1973, we were just beginning to emerge from the ugly hangover of late 60's-early 70's tragedy and sense of emotional despair. In many ways, the songs of the Glenn Frey and Don Henley-led group were like our musical Gatorade – especially in Phoenix. So many girls in flat-bed Fords seemingly on every corner. We lost, we won, and in my heart, I knew I would never be playing there again. The intensity wasn't where it should've been. After awhile, as much as I loved life in the minor leagues, I was starting to get a bit antsy. I was stuck in a slump trying to get my 15th win of the season. I had lost three straight and now we were on the road against the Albuquerque Dukes at Sports Stadium, where the ball traveled so well it practically had its own passport. I didn't have my good stuff from the get-go.

"How ya doin'?" Davvy asked me as I came into the dugout after the third inning.

"I'll go nine."

"He hasn't thrown a curveball all game," Richie, my catcher chimed in.

Jerry Crider, a 30-something relief pitcher on the downside of his career, was sitting around us listening to our dialogue.

"You should be throwing your curve more," Jerry interjected.

"What's that?" I said, a bit irritated he was butting in.

"You're gonna be gone in a month-"

"How the hell do you know-"

Jerry gave me the *"Of course, they're gonna call you up"* face. To be fair, Jerry had been offering me advice on improving my curveball throughout the season. Maybe he wanted to see the fruits of his labor blossom. Or maybe he was a bored veteran busting balls.

"You'll only be facing these kinda guys once or twice in the batting order in the bigs. You need to throw more off-speed stuff. C'mon, 'D, I wanna see how far they can hit your curveball."

I nodded and went back to the mound. I faced Tom Tischinski, a 29-year old catcher who hadn't been in the majors since 1971. I started him off with gas on the first two pitches. On a 1-1 count, I did as I was told and threw the curve, which hung up there too long and I think that ball is still flying. Well over the scoreboard in left. I was so pissed, absolutely furious - I allowed another guy to get on base before Rick Auerbach also took me downtown for his first and *only* dinger of the season. Davvy yanked me after that.

"You satisfied, asshole?" I said to Jerry, sitting down beside him after I left the game. Jerry just laughed his ass off.

"Don't you ever fuckin' tell me how to pitch my game," I snarled at him, "Put my game in jeopardy for your entertainment? Fuck you."

"I'm just trying to help," Jerry giggled, palms up, mock surrendering.

Even if he was having fun at my expense, Jerry was right inadvertently; the end of my potential and the time to move along was just about here. Things wouldn't get much better as I would discover the moment I walked through the door of our motel later that night.

* * * * *

"I got called up," Onti said, rushing to pack his bags, "I gotta be at Candlestick tomorrow." Onti did everything possible in the minors. He was crushing the ball at Phoenix, batting .357 with 84 RBIs in 472 plate appearances. He was ready for the majors. Where he was gonna play with that outfield was anyone's guess. Were they really gonna give him third base?

"That's great, man," I replied and slapped him five, "Gonna miss ya."

Of course I was thrilled for Onti, but I was losing a solid teammate, a helpful roommate and the best drinking buddy in the league. Also probably my best friend on the team. Never had someone so close to me on the ballclub get called up that early in the season.

"Oh, come on. You know you'll be with me in a month."

"Maybe, I dunno." Onti picked up two of his bags and made his way toward the door. I grabbed one and walked with him to the cab outside the motel.

"I'll tell ya what ya should do," Onti said, stepping into the car, "You better ask for a raise. And go get the bonus money they owe ya."

"Yeah."

I closed the taxi door for Onti, as he rolled down the window.

"If I don't see ya, I'll see ya." I nodded and watched Steve Ontiveros go to the majors. This feeling of loss, like a classmate moving up a grade without me, was a true wake-up call.

* * * * *

Three weeks later, it was close to the end of the minor league season, where specific players at AAA start to wonder when and if they will get called into the manager's office and get *"the call."* I gave them an outstanding season at Phoenix – won 16 games for a 70-73 ballclub, 185 Ks, four shutouts, threw a no-hitter, made the All-Star team– it was a very good year. I was making $950/month. At this time of the season, you had guys going into the general manager's office seeking raises and performance bonuses. I spent the morning at the mall, milling through albums in the record store, taking my mind off the conversation I wanted to have with the front office of the Phoenix Giants. That afternoon, I went to see Rosy Ryan – he ran the club – and kindly asked for a bump up to $1250. We negotiated our own contracts then - there were no agents handling such matters at the time – just 21-year old me.

"I ain't givin' ya any raise, Johnny," he responded. Rosy was a crusty, elderly man with a kind heart, in his late 70's, great guy, but I was just trying to get a little more gin in my jeans, business was business. We went back and forth for a good 30 minutes. "Fine," I nodded coldly and got out of my chair.

"Where ya goin'? We're not done yet," Rosy beckoned to the seat in front of his desk.

"Home," I said, "I'm done. Almost end of the season anyway. I'm gonna go take a rest." Started packing as soon as I walked into my apartment.

Ethan Blackaby, the general manager for the Phoenix Giants, was knocking on my door shortly after I arrived home. Ethan helped pack my things, trying to dissuade me the entire time.

"You can't just go home like this." I wouldn't budge.

"I want my raise." Ethan sighed and shook his head. "Lemme see what I can do," and looked around the living room for a phone. No need, since it rang as soon as he reached for it on the coffee table.

"I got good news and bad news," Rosy barked on the other line.

"C'mon, Rosy, don't play games," I replied, "What's the deal?"

"Ya got your raise. We're giving you $2500/month plus those incentive bonuses ya keep bitchin' about."

"Thanks."

"Ya just gotta go to San Francisco to get it. You've been called up. Your ticket's waitin' for ya at the airport. Go hop on a plane. Now."

I said nothing.

"Ya there, kid?"

A pause.

"Yeah."

"Ya got the call, Johnny. Go prove yourself." I hung up the phone.

"What'd he say?" Ethan asked, but I just stared at him for a moment, as my mind let Rosy's words sink in.

No more Red Barn. No more golf games with Davvy. No more peaceful easy feelings.

The rest of my life was taking off in less than three hours.

Ground Control

"*Good Afternoon ladies and gentlemen, this is your captain speaking. We are preparing for departure, non-stop to San Francisco. The weather is 64 degrees with a slight gust of wind. The time of our trip should be approximately one hour and 55 minutes. We expect a relatively easy ride and on schedule. The stewardess has just turned on the no-smoking sign, so please fasten your seat belts. We hope you enjoyed your visit to Phoenix and thank you again for flying Hughes Air West.*"

Lift off.

I was floating in a tin can, far above the world. I'd been observing all the carcasses of young phenom pitchers spread throughout the major league pitching mounds of 1973. The Texas Rangers' number one draft pick, high school senior David Clyde, got smacked around after a victorious debut. College star Eddie Bane went straight to the majors with the Twins and was getting tattooed all over the place. The Phillies' 19-year old first-rounder Larry Christenson broke camp with the big club in April and was back in the minors by May. Even my old A ball buddy Goss, who was now answering to the major-league ready moniker "*Goose*," ended up back in AAA Iowa by mid-season suffering from bouts of wildness with the White Sox. With the expectations of my manager, Charlie Fox, my organization, the San Francisco Giants, my parents, the fans that paid close attention, the media, I had no choice but to perform. Sometimes there's an odd comfort in that space between potential and having to execute to everyone's projections. People look at you differently in that space, they treat you differently in that space, waiting for the payoff of their expectations. David Bowie's prescient lyrics resonated with me that summer, especially as I prepared to land at San Francisco International Airport. You think your spaceship knows which way to go, but what if something's wrong? No one can hear your fear on the mound, especially not in Riverfront Stadium with the bases full and Johnny Bench at the plate in front of 39,000 screaming fans.

* * * * *

My brother flew down from San Diego to grab my car and the rest of my stuff from the apartment. Upon arriving at SFO, I went straight to the Holiday Inn South San Francisco near the airport. As the doors slid open, I found my manager standing in the lobby, waiting for me like a father picking up his son from college. He greeted me with a handshake that led into a hug.

"Grab a shower and change," Charlie said, in what seemed like a whirlwind of a moment, "We're having dinner at Bertolucci's Restaurant."

Not all managers spend their off-days waiting in hotel lobbies for their rookie to arrive, but the relationship I had with Charlie was special. Charlie Fox was Irish, but he grew up amid a heavily Italian neighborhood in Brooklyn. He understood me. I was *his* guy – he pushed for me to get to the majors, fighting with management who didn't want to rush me. Frank Funk, Davy, Carl Hubbell - they all argued for patience with my development.

Bertolucci's of San Francisco had been around since the late '20s – still there today – and had some of the best Antipasti this Italian kid had ever enjoyed. Coming from a household where I knew my way around anything Parmigianino, that's saying something. Once the server placed our steaming entrees on the red and white-checkered tablecloth, Charlie poured me another glass of wine.

"You know you're starting the second game of the doubleheader tomorrow," Charlie mentioned casually.

"Tomorrow," I asked. I could hardly breathe as I proceeded to polish off a half a bottle of red thanks to Charlie's bottomless glass rule that settled my nerves from over-heating.

"Tomorrow. You ready?"

"I think so."

"I told all the reporters you're wild."

"Why would you do that?"

"The Braves have the best home-run hitters in baseball. Ya think I want Aaron straight up, waiting on your fastball? Fuck 'em. Let those bastards wake up tomorrow reading about how you got no control of your 100 MPH heater. Put that in their heads before they dig in against ya."

I was so excited by the call up to the big club, all these inside baseball conversations, I didn't know what to do with myself, but Charlie kept me at ease. Every manager – I would say every person in the business world who has the authority to hire and fire – has that one young guy or gal with whom they possess paternal pride, joy and hope to see them develop properly, sometimes to the extent where they perceive them as family. You need those people behind you, but you also need a gimmick. Mine just happened to be triple-digit gas with movement. Charlie was that figure to me. We must've finished at least two bottles of wine at that meal. What better way to prepare for my first big league start.

* * * * *

Candlestick Park was a monstrosity of a stadium. Built next to Hunters Point on the bay in San Francisco, alongside Section 8 housing, the place was consistently cold, dark, dingy and windy, not to mention (much like many teams at the time) going through its *"Hey, Astroturf is a great idea"* phase. Sure, it was much more impressive than Municipal back in Phoenix, but it's nothing like the classy facility that is AT&T Park. The 'Stick was a dungeon, but on September 2nd, 1973, it was the Eighth Wonder of the World to me. I hadn't been back since the exhibition game for Class A Fresno the year before. Walking through the grass, across those baselines, those numerous auburn seats in the stands, one after the other, just as you would see in the photo background on baseball cards, your adrenaline kicks in. I couldn't control it. For the exhibition, we weren't even allowed to suit up in the visitors' clubhouse – we were given the 49ers' locker room, so this was my first time actually stepping into the Giants' private domain.

I glided through the clubhouse, taking in the greetings of all my new teammates, but not by their full names, not by the surnames listed in the box score, but their baseball fraternity names, in what seemed to be surreal slo-mo:

There was Mac and his deep, smooth voice (*"Heh-heh, how's it goin', kid?"*); Tito in his gleeful accent (*"JAHN-NEEE!!!"*); "Spei" and his chipper Bay Area accent, (*"Heyyyy"*); "Goody" (*"Welcome to the big leagues"*); "Sweet Matt" (*"Mah man"*); "Arlo" (*"What's new, John"*);"The Bear" (*"Yo"*); my buddy "Onti" (arms extended with an "*I told ya*" expression on his face); "Horsehead" ("*Good to see ya, John*"); "Knuckie" ("*Hey D*"); "BB" ("*Hiya Rook*"); and the man who gave me my first nickname, one of the funniest men I met in the game, my catcher, Dave Rader, also known as "*Radar.*"

"*There he is. Fastball Johnny D has finally landed.*"

Clubhouse manager Mike Murphy brought me to my locker on the left-hand side of the room; he sat me next to 20-game winner Ron Bryant and that legendary, life-size teddy bear he kept for good luck. One by one, they all walked over; it was all "*Do ya need anything?*" "*Do you need a place to stay?*" "*Can I get ya anything?*" Never before had I felt so welcomed anywhere outside of the home where I grew up. In retrospect, with all that was happening off-the-field with the organization, I was blown away by everyone's congeniality. Soon the beat reporters surrounded my locker, firing questions at me, one after the other, basically asking me about the new shirt I was wearing and how I made the grade. Few other questions about my wildness, as Charlie predicted, or perhaps orchestrated. After the final inquiries from the guys at the San Francisco Chronicle, we were 50 minutes from first pitch of the second game.

It was time. I placed the cap on my head as an official San Francisco Giant and exited the clubhouse capsule.

One of the points Charlie made to me at dinner the night before was that so long as everything went as expected, I would be a mainstay in the rotation in 1974. Question was, who had to go? There was the bulldog Tom Bradley, who would make 35 starts in '73; Jim Barr, for whom the organization still held extremely high hopes. Sam McDowell was long gone. Of course, Ron Bryant was considered an emerging star with his 20-9 record to that point in the season, plus he was only 25, barely making $25,000. The process of elimination and Baseball economics made it clear that I would be replacing the one of the starters in this four-man rotation, the one who happened to be making $135,000 a year, one of the highest-paid players in the game. On a money-losing ballclub. Who was 35 years old. A fan-favorite, an immortal in the midst of a 1-5 skid that would extend to 2-9 over the remainder of the season.

Someone named Marichal.

My mentor.

Business was business.

Juan had pitched for the Giants since 1960, was beloved in the community, the ballpark and the clubhouse, especially the clubhouse, a nine-time All-Star on a team once full of them. This was the September of his career, had lost 4-5 MPH off his fastball, plus with the financial issues of the organization, everyone knew this would most likely be his final month in San Francisco. Giants owner Horace Stoneham was still having financial issues. Major League Baseball had to take over the club just to keep the spotlights in the scoreboard bright, but the league kept it quiet, because they didn't want to embarrass such a storied owner. In the end, the league went to a select group of financiers and informed them the ballclub was for sale.

I walked down the dark tunnel leading to the field. Don McMahon, the pitching coach the team re-activated in June due to a bullpen crisis, who by the way, was also our short man outta the pen (talk about getting two employees for one salary), was tossing BP. Don, a 17-year vet, went 4-0 in '73 with an ERA under a buck and a half, a sub-1 WHIP. For my Sabermetrically-inclined friends, that's a 1.3 WAR for three months work, at age 43. He was ready to go at any time, could still throw that cutter right in your kitchen. How do you like that? Oh yeah, and he threw BP every day, too. Never tightened up, either.

I was stepping through the door of a whole new world. The butterflies in my stomach were floating in a most peculiar way.

Once in the dugout, Marichal called me over. He started the opener of the twin bill, went seven, didn't get the decision in a 10-inning game we ended up winning. He wasn't the same Hall of Fame–caliber superstar at this point. With the lost velocity, the hitters could see him clearer and started going the opposite way on him. He tried mixing things up with his screwball and that didn't work, either. He was losing ground fast.

All this going on in his career, yet Juan still took me under his wing.

"How do you pitch to these guys?" I asked him. I never heard someone laugh so loud. The Braves' lineup in '73 was daunting, to say the least. Hank Aaron chasing Ruth; Darrell Evans having what may have been his greatest season, in a career full of them. Dusty Baker also had a breakout year. Even Mike Lum ended up hitting 16 home runs. There really wasn't much to discuss.

"How you pitch them?" Juan laughed, "What you gonna do? They all hit home runs. The fucking second baseman has 30 home runs!! There's no way to pitch them. You pitch around people – make 'em hit breaking stuff." Then he said something I never heard a pitcher or coach say to me before.

"Pitch backwards."

"Pitch backwards, what does that mean?"

"Use secondary stuff first, use your fastball to get 'em out. Off-speed breaking ball, off-speed slider – make 'em come off the front foot." He got up from the bench, a slap on the back, gave me a hug. He was so supportive.

"Just get the ball over the plate," Marichal said, as he made his way down the stairs into the hallway leading to the clubhouse, "Don't try to place it."

Charlie entered the dugout as I was stepping onto the field. He pulled me aside, with a shit-eating grin on his face.

"Remember what I said last night," Charlie paused, then nodded over at the Braves dugout, "First warm up pitch...make sure you hit the backstop. They know how hard you throw." So I got to the mound, toed the rubber and I let that mother rip, 98 MPH over my catcher's head and straight to the backstop. I heard a random *"Oh shit,"* here, a *"Jesus"* there, coming from the Braves' side of the diamond. Exactly the reaction Charlie wanted. Our starting catcher for the second game of the doubleheader was *"The Sheik,"* Mike Sadek, who came running out to the mound.

"You ok?"

"Don't worry, Charlie told me to do that."

"Yeah, I kinda figured. But you all right?"

"Little nervous, but I'm ok." How could I be ok? My legs were shaking. Sadek knew, too. The good catchers always knew.

"Just settle in. You'll be fine." Then Mike went over the signs. "One is the fastball, two's the curve, three is the slider," Mike said, very matter of fact. "Do you have a change?"

"No sir, I do not," I replied, nervous as hell.

"Don't call me Sir, call me Mikey."

"Ok, Mikey, I don't have a change-up."

"Then let's go with one, two and three, ok? And don't try to throw it where I'm asking you to throw it, just set your sights in the middle of my crotch and let it go."

Marichal told me starting the second game of a double header wasn't easy because it was just a long day sitting in the cold at Candlestick. Today was different, though. I was so excited it didn't really matter to me if I was throwing an exhibition at the North Pole against Santa Claus and a lineup full of elves. I managed to get through the first inning with a walk and two strikeouts. The second inning was a different story. Found myself in a bases-loaded, one-out jam, but thankfully, it was at the bottom of the order. I struck out Carl Morton, the opposing pitcher. Ralph Garr, the Braves leadoff hitter and one of the fastest men I ever faced, came to bat. Speier jogged over from shortstop.

"Garr's a free-swinger," Spei told me, glove at his face, "Don't give him anything to hit."

At Spei's suggestion, I kept the ball out of the strike zone and Garr chased, managing a weak fly out to end the inning. Spei always had tips on nearly every batter in the lineup – couple times a game he would run in and give me relevant information I didn't possess.

I wasn't overly concerned about being taken out of the game. Charlie didn't necessarily have a quick hook, but he did possess a good sense of whether you were fried or not. Charlie could tell by your eyes and body language. When you would return to the dugout, he would look over. The first couple of innings, I walked confidently off the mound and once I sat on the bench, Charlie turned to me. I offered him a slight smile with a cocky nod and wink. By the third inning, the wink was gone.

The late summer Phoenix nights were 90 degrees if you were lucky. San Fran was an icy 36-degree wind chill factor on this night. I wore my football parka, warm-up jacket and thermals – couldn't grip the ball until I started breaking a sweat. As I sat down after the first inning, Marichal approached me.

"You cold?" he asked. I half shook my head. He knew I was freezing. He called one of the batboys and pointed at me. "Sauna." I was walked into the clubhouse and handed a transistor radio. I sat in there fully-clothed between innings with the radio to hear how many outs there were before returning to the dugout. It wasn't a 60 feet, 6 inches walk, either, I'll tell you that much. I felt so touched how Marichal watched over me as he did. One of the most generous guys I ever met in the game. He showed me many tricks of the trade, how to act, how to conduct yourself as a ballplayer and as a local celebrity.

At the end of the third, Charlie walked over.

"How ya doin'?" I had my head down.

"I'm OK," I shrugged. Charlie didn't want to hear my shrug. He wanted *"I'm great, I just made a couple of bad mistakes, and I'll be fine."* He didn't hear that. By the top of the fourth, the cocky smile was gone, too. Got back out there, enjoying a 4-0 lead, but my nerves got the best of me. Gave up three singles, walked two runners in, Charlie had seen enough.

"You're done, aren't you?" Charlie asked as he reached for the ball in my hand. My legs were still shaking. This wasn't the 6800 fans in Phoenix anymore – 20,000 plus. "That's enough for you today."

We ended up winning in a laugher, 11-3, sweeping the doubleheader, but the Bravos would have their revenge a week later down at the Launching Pad, Fulton County Stadium in Atlanta. The Braves lit up Marichal in the first inning, Charlie walked over to me on the bench. "Juan's not doin' too good, I need ya to go to the bullpen and start throwing. Now. It's your work day, anyway." I entered the game in the third, struck out three and didn't give up any free passes, but the vision that remains with me from that day was Juan walking off the mound in the first inning, realizing that September means different things to different people.

Great to be on the winning side for the first game I pitched, but nothing like the sense of victory I would experience the day after my debut.

* * * * *

Before I arrived in the '73 season, the Giants were in first place for all of May until the Dodgers had taken over the division lead by the middle of June. Mac and the outfielders carried the ballclub all season, keeping us relevant in the race. Bobby took his hot first half right to the 1973 All-Star Game in Kansas City, representing the ballclub (along with starting shortstop Chris Speier.) Man, did he put on a show, going 2-for-2 with a long home run, receiving the game MVP award for his efforts.

The Dodgers held a pretty comfortable lead all summer until the Reds made a push in late August. We hung in there as well, and Bobby led the team the entire way. By the time I joined the club right before the September post-season eligibility cutoff, the first thing I noticed was that Bobby was always in the manager's office with Charlie after the game, having drinks, dissecting the team's performance. Bobby hung out so often in there you would've thought he and Charlie shared a desk. He was truly becoming our spiritual leader, and he hated, I mean *hated*, the Dodgers, hated them this year especially for taking the division lead from us. Bobby wasn't at all a vengeful person from what I saw, but there was no doubt he wanted retribution.

L.A. had lost three in a row to Houston and let the surging Reds come within a game of first place. This would be a pivotal win for them but we wanted to hand it to the Dodgers something awful. Didn't quite begin as we planned. The Dodgers had already been leading 3-1 when they busted the game open with five runs, chasing our starting pitcher Tom Bradley and reliever Donny Carrithers. We were down 8-1 by the sixth inning. A few minutes after my teammates piled into the dugout, I looked over to the tunnel leading to the clubhouse. Smoke was coming from behind the runway wall, floating onto the field. Whenever the team was behind, Bobby would go through a couple Winston cigarettes between innings down there, he was so wound up about losing. He couldn't take it – it got him so frustrated. Today, he was especially annoyed. No, scratch that – he was pissed, marching through the dugout, declaring *"We're not losing today,"* to all of us, *"Not today."*

We went quietly in the bottom of the fifth and Bobby kept smoking. Tommy John really had our number early on. He punched out Bobby on a called strike three in the sixth inning; Bobby walked back to the dugout, calmly placed his bat in the rack and went for another smoke. He was furious. Soon small pockets of the tepid 15,000 some-odd fans in attendance started making their way toward the exits.

Tommy John ran into trouble when he faced the middle of our order the following inning. Matthews and Mac both reached base on singles. Speier hit a clutch double that plated Gary. John countered with back-to-back strikeouts. Dave Rader, who was a pretty good hitter himself, singled to center, bringing home McCovey and Speier. After giving up another base hit, Dodgers manager Walter Alston brought in Pete Richert to face Bonds. Bobby was so jacked up, I was expecting either a monster homer or a strikeout. Bonds sent Richert's pitch into left for a ground rule double, scoring Rader, we were back in it, only down by three runs. The fans stopped leaving. A Tito Fuentes single brought home two more and it was suddenly a one-run game.

Charlie brought in Coach McMahon to face the Dodgers 2-3-4 hitters and Don continued his hot pitching, retiring them 1-2-3. Richert struck out the side in the bottom of the eighth. McMahon finished the ninth without allowing any baserunners, a fantastic job of keeping us in the ballgame.

Going into our half of ninth, we were very concerned no one would be able to touch Richert. Bobby was in the runway cooling his heels with another Winston, the smoke filling out the other side of the dugout. Then Richert started off the inning with a walk to Gary Thomasson. Dave Rader went up to bunt, squared and perfectly placed it between home plate and the mound, Richert raced to the ball, fired to second, but Thomasson just beat the throw. The smallish crowd's demeanor began to build into an optimistic cheering section. I looked over, the smoke was gone, and Bobby moved through the dugout, toward the bat rack, bearing the determined grin of a man on a mission. Mike Sadek, the rookie catcher, pinch hit for McMahon, bunted as well, a beauty down the third base line, Ken McMullen charged, turned and quickly threw to second. Dave Rader just beat the throw. Bases loaded – no outs. The fans were going absolutely batshit.

Alston appeared totally shell-shocked at this chain of events; there was a hint of mope in his walk to the mound to remove Richert, as he motioned for the left-hander, Jim Brewer, one of the five or six best relievers in the game. Nastiest screwball you ever saw. I watched Bobby in the on-deck circle swinging his bat slowly, staring, studying and sizing up Brewer. The 37 year-old reliever finished his warm-ups, the crowd screamed as the P.A. announcer called Bobby's name and the human walk-up song strutted to the plate. I felt like a fan just like everyone in the stands.

Brewer, the southpaw, set, wound up and delivered a screwball. Bobby swung right through it, as if expecting the gas. The crowd noise ignored strike one, the stadium hum stoked Bobby, while trying to distract Brewer as he caught the toss from Joe Ferguson behind the plate. Bobby wasn't deterred. As locked-in a dude at the plate as I had ever witnessed. This was his game, he had spent too much time in the dugout angry, too many days and months stewing about losing the division lead, to let this aging, all-star pitcher define the day. Brewer set, Bonds squared, Brewer let the ball go, Bonds guessed screwball...

Bonds guessed right.

Monster shot to deep left. The joyous buzz of the crowd escalated as the ball sailed further across the dusky San Francisco sky. Dodgers' outfielder Bill Buckner went back, back, back, looked up...

Grand Slam.

Giants win 11-8.

Heartbreaker.

It was the most badass display I had ever experienced in baseball. Fans celebrating with pitchers in the bullpen, throwing popcorn, Cracker Jacks, seat cushions tossed across the stands, light debris flying onto the field. Bonds circled the bases with a rhythmic jog, the triumphant hero. It was glorious pandemonium.

The 1973 Dodgers never recovered, went on to lose another five straight as the Reds blew right past them.

After the game, Bobby emerged from Charlie's office into the clubhouse celebration, raising his glass to all of us, telling everyone he could find, players, coaches, beat reporters, *"We're still in this, too. Don't count out the Giants."* We were all engaging in bravado and smack talk about us making the playoffs ourselves, overtaking both the Dodgers and the Reds, but that was just joyous chatter on the back of an implausible victory, and Bobby was the loudest voice in the room. Mac was still there, Marichal was still there, but it was clear. Bobby Bonds was the spiritual core of the San Francisco Giants, for which Charlie Fox took no issue.

For now.

* * * * *

While Juan was so great to me, I still felt the stress of my teams' projections throughout that September to have an outstanding 1974. Whenever I walked by Charlie Fox in the clubhouse that first month, he was telling anyone beside him at that moment – another player, a coach, a beat guy – that I was the golden boy of the franchise. It was an enormous weight on my psyche. I made two more relief appearances until I was passing Charlie's office one evening after a loss to Cincinnati. It was by now a familiar sight; my manager enjoying post-game cocktails with our star, Bobby Bonds. Charlie had this way about him; not so much a players' manager in the doormat sense, but he treated his players like men. He held extra reverence for Bobby and Bobby felt very comfortable in the manager's office. Very comfortable.

"Hey Johnny?" Charlie called out as I stepped by his doorway.

"Hi, Skip," I said, nodding hello to Bobby as well, who sat on the other side of Charlie's desk, still in half uniform, his feet up on the chair beside him.

"Hey, Rook. We gotta get ya out there again."

"You're pitching the second game of the doubleheader on Friday against the Padres," Charlie smiled, "Be ready."

If I was thrilled to be starting any game in the majors, it was against my hometown team, where all my friends and family would be watching on KCST, channel 39.

* * * * *

Unfortunately, only the first game of the doubleheader was televised. Mom, Dad, Fred and everyone else would have to settle for KOGO, 600 on your AM dial, to hear their son go up against another local rookie by the name of Randy Jones, who came to San Diego in June after lighting the AA baseball world on fire, with an 8-1 record, along with a 2.01 ERA. Both Southern California boys, head to head. I had never met the 22-year old golden brown-haired kid, but this game was important to both of us.

My teammates staked me to a 3-0 lead, as Maddox and Matthews hit run-scoring singles and Spei added a double. Outside of Padres hero Nate Colbert tattooing a fastball over the left-center field fence off me, I cruised – struck out seven in the first three innings, gave up only four hits the whole game. We beat the Padres easily 7-2 for my first complete game victory – 11 strikeouts.

Afterward, I was interviewed by Jerry Coleman in the Padres' dugout, as the broadcast hookups for the visiting ballclub were on the other side of the field. I had never met the man before, but he had my background down cold; San Diego roots, my High School pitching record, stats from my minor league seasons, how the Padres wanted to draft me in 1970, everything. A smooth, pleasant interview, as if he prepared all day. It was a very classy touch, interviewing me literally for my friends and family back home. As soon as the interview ended, Jerry dropped the microphone and extended his hand.

"Welcome to the big leagues, Johnny," Jerry said warmly, "You pitched well today." I must have repeated those nine words in my head over and over and over that night. After returning to the clubhouse, I ran straight to the phone.

"Mom, mom," I said, like that little boy with all the cherry snow cone on his face, "Can you believe it?"

"Johnny," my mother replied, "We're all so proud of you."

That night, I entered Scoma's Seafood restaurant in the Wharf area of San Francisco. Rick Scoma himself came out to congratulate me on the victory. Patrons got up from their tables and introduced themselves. Well-dressed children asked for my autograph. As I left Scoma's, full of cabernet and shrimp, I gazed across the bay toward Sausalito, then solemnly upward at the late night's sky, lit by the lights of the Golden Gate Bridge, there was no doubt in my mind.

The stars looked very different today.

* * * * *

The Giants finished the season 88-74, 11 games behind the Reds and Dodgers, nearly 20 games better than the previous year, and actually only two games worse than the division-winning ballclub of '71. Still, there were serious issues the organization had to deal with. Attendance at Candlestick Park was once again among the worst in the league, under one million for the third straight year. Payroll needed to be cut. This mindset led to the team trading Willie McCovey, one of the most beloved players, to the San Diego Padres for another pitcher, Mike Caldwell. His '73 season was considered a disappointment at the time, but through today's lens, .420 OBP, 105 walks, 160 OPS+, it was a great year. He actually crushed it against southpaws - .324 in 160 plate appearances. Hit well above .300 at The 'Stick. The team would say Mac just couldn't stay healthy enough to play 150 games any longer. They would say they felt they had enough coverage at first base between Dave Kingman, Eddie Goodson and possibly my old friend Skip James, who was still stuck in Phoenix.

Nope.

It was just a money thing. The team wasn't done with the plastic surgery of our franchise faces. On December 7th, 1973, the Giants finally sold Marichal to the Red Sox. When I heard this news, I knew it was for real. They were virtually unloading every high salaried player on the roster. All this hysteria going on in my mind could barely be soothed by the holiday season.

* * * * *

It was weekend dinner at my folks' house, December 1973. My younger cousins sat in the family room watching the end of Mr. *Magoo's Christmas Carol*. I had been home for a few weeks waiting to receive my 1974 contract in the mail. So many thoughts moving through my mind. What's the contract gonna look like? How am I going to handle all this? The team had me slotted in the rotation even before spring training. What if I flop down in Phoenix next March? I threw fine in September, but there were no guarantees. I glanced over into the dining room, finding my Mom, Frances, chatting with her sisters, plates of clams and mussels in Italian sauce up and down the extended leaf of the dining room table.

Her sister Lu must've told her a very funny story that made her generate this boisterous yet graceful laugh. Mom looked over at me on the couch. Her sweet laugh became a concerned smile. She didn't even have to get up from her chair. I stepped behind my uncles' chairs in the dining room toward the kitchen. Mom soon followed.

"Johnny?" Mom asked me, "What's the matter?"

"I dunno," I shrugged, sipping a can of RC Cola, "Haven't got my contract yet. Thinking about next year in San Francisco, just some stuff."

"You got nothin' to worry about," she assured me, rubbing my shoulder, "You did good this year. All those strikeouts." Mom wasn't a stage parent or anything, but she knew my important stats. Like any good agent. "The team's gonna take care of you."

The phone rang in the middle of our conversation. One of my high school buddies called asking to meet up. Mom nodded to the door. "Go out with your friends. Stop worrying." I left the house as the kids were beginning to fall asleep in front of the Andy Williams Christmas special.

It was still a couple weeks away from Christmas Day; not like today where holiday music hijacks the radio the moment Walmart opens its doors on Black Friday. Songs like Ringo Starr's

"Photograph" were played constantly on AM radio up until noon on Christmas Eve.

I drove around the holiday lights-strewn suburban streets of San Diego toward Balboa Park to see the incredible Christmas presentation. Balboa Park was lit all the way down to the Laurel Street Bridge on one side and the amphitheater on the other. They had everything going on. Every tree was decorated. Nativity scenes illuminated the drive. Growing up in San Diego, it was a big family event to ride through Balboa Park and see the Christmas display. Coming back in 1973 a (sort of) grownup, it meant even more. Vietnam was ending, and we were thousands of miles away from the bubbling pot of Watergate. The dark clouds were dissipating just a little bit. The mood in our little piece of the world was improving. We'd go listen to the choir sing holiday standards at the amphitheater, where this life-size Santa Claus sleigh with actual reindeer sat right out in front. With live animals, real donkeys, camels, everything – the zoo was located up the street from the park. It was pretty cool. Always made me feel better.

After this beautiful diversion, I ended up at Bully's East – this was our hangout. It had only been open for a couple years at that time, but me and my high school buddies felt most welcome there. They had a little room in the back called *"The Saints Room,"* where all the fellas who attended my high school, St. Augustine's, used to hang out and pound a few. The owner of Bully's had been an alumnus of Saints himself, sort of took us under his wing, looked after us, looked after me. I have no clue what's it's like for a phenom of drinking age today to want to go out with his friends and get a couple pops. I hope young athletes have a local place or hangout where the owner has known him and his family for years and has him under his watchful eye. Millionaire draft picks today have to deal with such crazy issues in the world that I never even had to consider. Bloggers looking to report your every move to sports gossip websites. Camera phones.

The red light is always on, boys.

* * * * *

Couple days later, still no word from the Giants. Hadn't yet to receive my contract for 1974. By league mandate, a major league contract had to be in my hands by December 16th. If not, I was considered a free agent or worse – released. Mom just said, "Son, come on. You don't think they're gonna give you a raise?"

"I only played for a month, they don't have to gimme a raise-"

Mom had this ESP-like sense of the world, an amazing intuition about things. The best gut for important decisions of any person I ever met.

"No," she said, "You'll get something. If it's not what you want, you send it back, and if you don't wanna do that, I'll talk to them."

Finally the doorbell rang early the next day. "Johnny," Mom yelled for me from the front door. I ran over from the den, like Christmas morning, expecting a bike or train set under the tree. It was even better.

"He won't let me sign for it," Mom smiled. It was a certified letter from the Giants. My contract had arrived. I quickly gave my signature and opened the large envelope.

No Scrooge story here, which surprised me because of the club's financial woes. The organization offered me a $10,000 raise off my rookie salary of $12,500. I was elated – this was over $120,000 in today's money adjusted for inflation. I also found a separate letter attached from Charlie, basically outlining the organization's expectations of me for the coming season. Off-season exercises, preferred weight for me to maintain while at home, a small host of line items. At the bottom of the typed letter was handwriting:

Get ready to eat a lot of San Fran's best Italian food. Gonna be a great year, Johnny.

-Charlie

"What do you think?" I asked Mom, as I folded up Charlie's personal note.

"Sign it and send it back," she nodded, like I just uttered the silliest question in the world. "It's a lot of money, a lot more than everyone you know makes."

"But what does that compare to? I mean, probably means I'm gonna get the starting job, right, and all the starters make over $35,000-"

Mom shut me up with a smile as she grabbed my face gently and kissed me on the cheek.

"Just sign it, Johnny," she said, walking away. Mom was right, of course.

I quickly signed it and sent it back.

The next day, I received a call that the San Francisco Giants gave me clearance to work out with the Padres players at San Diego Stadium for the upcoming year. I arrived at the ballpark, walked into the weight room where I found my opponent from my first victory.

"Hey Bud," Randy Jones greeted me, "Heard ya might be stoppin' by."

"John D'Acquisto, nice to meet ya," I replied, extending my hand.

"Shit, I know who you are," Randy laughed, "Whipped my ass last September."

"You still had a good year."

"Wasn't bad. Get yourself together and c'mon outside. There's someone I want ya to meet."

I walked out onto the field, where Randy introduced me to Padres' catcher Freddie Kendall and an older man who was twisting his wrist with a baseball.

"Hey Roger?" Randy called out, "D'Acquisto's here. Johnny, this is Roger Craig, the best damn pitching coach in baseball."

Roger laughed and nodded as he shook my hand. "How's it goin, John?"

"Nice to meet you, Mr. Craig." Roger really found this funny.

"Ha-ha, c'mon, kid."

"Yeah, Johnny's one of those nice Catholic San Diego boys-"

"Call me Roger."

I knew a little bit about Roger. An old Brooklyn Dodger and original New York Met, he was a very well-regarded pitching coach in baseball circles. I was actually curious what insights he could offer. I still wasn't sure about the rules with all this mingling of teams working out together.

"Maybe you could help me with my change-up."

"I don't see anyone here," Roger smiled and he went into the finer points of his master class on the off-speed pitch. I couldn't believe that our direct competition would be so open and willing to instruct me and allow me to hang around. I would begin workouts the week after the holiday.

* * * * *

Christmas Eve was always a huge party in my house. Not only was it the day before the holiday, it's also my birthday. At least a couple dozen family members over every year. A lot of bumping into each other passing through the dining room, arms raised with beer bottles trying to make space on the plastic-slip covered couch in the living room. The whole extended D'Acquisto clan would celebrate Christmas Eve and my birthday at our house. My brother would go get the dining room table extension leaf to accommodate all the grownups and of course, the kids were eating in the kitchen. Aunts stepping into the dining room with an assortment of desserts. My middle-school aged sister was busy filling the cannolis on the kitchen table. I walked into the house with two arms filled with presents from Buffums, the high-end department store in town, sort of the '70s Southern California version of Nordstrom. Dad would come in with all sorts of seafood – lobster, oysters, mussels, clams, crab, and Red snapper for the base and then prepare his specialty, cioppino, an Italian fish stew that was just to die for. All the kids would open some presents in the family room with the TV volume on low and the Christmas music drowning our conversations. Time would fly by and the clock on the dining room wall chimed, reminding us it was midnight. My birthday had past, but Christmas had arrived. The kids were asleep around the tree hoping to wait out Santa's arrival. I don't know how we fit 40+ people into basically a three-bedroom ranch. My uncles would stay up into the early hours playing poker and drinking VO and Seven while my aunts would be wrapping the last of the presents. These are the snapshots I hold close to my heart on my favorite day of the year, and as I looked over the smiles and delight on the faces of my family, I observed the presents everyone received. Mom got a necklace from Dad. My nephews got G.I. Joe dolls and Rock 'em, Sock 'em Robots. My sister Jeannette got earrings. I couldn't help but think about the gifts my teammates back in San Francisco received this year. Onti got a sweet taste of major league baseball for the first time and more than a fighter's chance to start. Mac got a one-way ticket to San Diego to tutor another young phenom – this time a talented outfielder named Dave Winfield as well as the opportunity to hit home runs in a canyon of a stadium. My mentor Juan Marichal received an all-expense paid trip to learn the tendencies of another 175 hitters in a bandbox called Fenway at the age of 35. Bobby Bonds got 24 players to lead; The Young Giants were all his now. Charlie finally got his pitcher. And as for me, through the new undershirts, the socks, smart slacks and other sundry items Mom bought me that I would never get for myself, I realized the one incredible gift I received that first day I stepped into the clubhouse back in early September.

I got a name.

Fastball John…commencing countdown, engines on to 1974.

Bobby

Baseball America wasn't a thing yet. Most fans (outside of those located in minor league towns) barely knew of your existence until you joined the team. The 1974 season outlooks written for newspapers and magazines wouldn't be published for a few more months. Looking back, I found a baseball annual for '74 that included remarks like, *"Rookie John D'Acquisto will definitely be in the rotation,"* or *"D'Acquisto has a great fastball and curve...he can be a big pitcher for the Giants."*

To read quotes like that in the papers was daunting, but at least it wasn't in my face every single day.

Spring training, 1974 was more about working out and getting game-ready than any real concern about making the big club. Charlie had called my house a few weeks before we arrived in Casa Grande in addition to the letter. He was very excited for my success in the rotation. Charlie was my number one advocate in the organization and had been pushing for me to make the team since 1972. Now it was time for me to pay off on expectations. The rotation in Charlie's mind was to be Ron Bryant (who ended up leading the league in victories with 24 the year before), Tom Bradley, me, Mike Caldwell and Jim Barr as the number five starter and long man. Of course, these things don't always work out as planned. Pitchers and catchers' workouts had begun relatively easy until about a week into full camp, I laid down a bunt and severely pulled my quad running to first base during an intra-squad game. Charlie ran out on the field to check me out.

"I'm fine, Skip," I replied, showing as little pain as possible. In reality, it was excruciating. I pitched another two innings, but Charlie took all the pre-cautions with me. I sat for about a week before I began playing Cactus League games in Phoenix. Thank God this didn't occur at the end of spring rather than late February. The papers had me listed as "*ill*." It was the quad.

About three weeks later, the ballclub bussed us to Palm Springs to take on the Angels. The California club had been rocked by the death of my buddy Bruce Heinbechner. Heinie, who was 23 years old, smashed his Porsche one night after being out with a few of the guys. Bruce ended up crossing a divider on Highway 11 about 500 yards from the Gene Autry Motel where the Angels bunked during spring training. The details of Heinie's death – they were as gruesome as you could possibly imagine – ended drinking and driving for most of the young guys, me especially. Basically stopped any kind of carousing for the rest of spring training. Any type of fun we had during the remainder of that month happened on hotel grounds, which probably allowed a major blow to the Giants starting staff to occur that spring.

I entered the training facility at Palm Springs Stadium one morning and saw our near-Cy Young ace of the staff in a half-body cast. I grabbed Don McMahon, our pitching coach, who was walking by.

"What the hell happened last night?" I asked him.

"We were at the pool area at the Ramada," Donny told me in his Brooklyn accent, "You know, everyone's still a little shaken because of the kid dying, so they're acting like assholes in and out of the pool, this one on the diving board, that one splashing like an idiot in the shallow end. Ronny tries to slide down like he's Pete Rose, next thing you know, the dumb shit slips off the slide, scrapes his body against the coping of the pool and splits his side open. All cut up. Screaming in pain. Ambulance came and everything. It was a big, bloody, fuckin' mess."

"Jesus." In the end, thankfully, it wasn't as bad as we thought, but our number one starter was definitely beginning the year on the disabled list. The only issue that concerned us that morning was Ronny's well-being, but soon I realized I was no longer one of Charlie's luxuries to develop slowly over the course of the season. I was now the San Francisco Giants' number two starter. I had no choice but to produce results.

With Gary "*Sweet Matt*" Matthews, National League Rookie of the Year in 1973, finally over his contract holdout, and Garry Maddox continuing to improve, Bobby, the last superstar left on the ballclub after the off-season salary purge, was ready to mold the team in his own image. He took on more the form of a headliner act than anything else. As every TV promotional teaser for the 1974 season would say, we were now Bobby Bonds and the San Francisco Giants.

It was time for us to boogie down to the Bay Area for the regular season.

* * * * *

"Owww," I cried out, sitting beside Gary Matthews' locker as he jabbed at my head with his oversized comb in early April 1974, "That hurts!"

"Damn," Gary complained, "Sit still, 'D!"

"How much longer's this gonna take?" Gary insisted I try teasing out my hair, which was naturally curly to begin with. A few painful moments later, he tapped me on the shoulder and nodded to the mirror in his locker.

"Check it out, kid," Gary smiled, proud of his work.

At first I didn't know what to make of my new curls. Wasn't salon quality but there was potential there.

"I dunno, you think it looks good?"

"Nah, that shit's outta sight, man," Gary said, "That's your new look. That's Fastball Johnny D. There, keep the pick."

It would be many years before I wore my hair straight again.

* * * * *

The clubhouse in '74 was for the most part harmonious, even if there were a few cliques. Bobby had his own group, usually playing cards on the team plane with Maddox and Matthews. We were the "*Young Giants*," as the PR department labeled us. Our play-by-play man Al Michaels enjoyed giving us nicknames. He was the first person who called me "*Johnny D.*" We were all respectful of one another, tolerating (if not always embracing) each other's cultures, tastes in food and drink, music especially. There were more than a few team-building events, golf tournaments, fishing trips where nearly the entire roster came aboard. The room was this fabulous, multicultural mix tape of personalities. As our unofficial leader, Bobby played an enormous part in creating this environment. I spent a fair amount of time in the clubhouse with Bonds that year, just not the one you might think.

Some of my most cherished memories of 1974 have nothing to do with wins, losses or rookie awards. I was shagging fly balls in right field before a home game in early April when this spunky, excitable 10-year old kid in jeans and a long-sleeved baseball shirt came out to join me with his glove. He didn't ask to play; just stood there watching. I finally turned to him and said, "Barry, would you like to catch a few?" He just nodded, stepped over like it was nothing and started flagging down flies. We would do this together at least once a week for the entire season. By the end of the year, Barry envisioned himself as our center fielder, running down flies with a youthful grace, precocious positioning through the afternoon glare, catching, stepping and throwing, pretending he was nailing Lou Brock at the plate.

Barry was at the ballpark all the time. He sat in the dugout with us during games. He wasn't the bat boy, but he wasn't the mascot, either. He was part of the team. In a time where white players and black players still sat separately on the bench, Barry would talk and mingle with everyone. We all loved having him around, playing tag with Maddox and Matthews in the outfield before games, celebrating in the clubhouse with us after victories. See, that's the thing people who aren't from the Bay Area fail to understand why local fans defend Barry Bonds so feverishly. We watched Barry grow up, watched him run around the 'Stick with his other brother, Bobby Jr. The crowds were so small, they felt intimate. The Giants drew barely 510,000 total for the season, easily the worst in baseball. There was no one at the ballpark so everyone who was there often times knew each other. You saw the same fans again and again. They would all watch Barry roaming the field, Bobby's boys dashing across the Astroturf during batting practice. Barry knew all the vendors' names. Fans would walk by and say hi to Barry and Pat, his Mom, Bobby's wife, eating ice cream and hot dogs at the concession stands, or observe Bobby give Pat and their kids a kiss in the stands before games. Barry Bonds wasn't just the son of a Giant icon, not just a Giant icon himself.

Barry's family. And right or wrong, regardless of everything that has come to pass, you defend family to the death.

These are my favorite scenes from 1974. The offstage drama was another story altogether.

* * * * *

Major League Baseball had stepped in and continued to provide financing for the Giants as Stoneham's money situation worsened. Charlie and Bobby were not getting along. Charlie was under pressure to build off our third place finish. Bobby felt the Young Giants were his team, his responsibility. As Willie had a voice in running the ballclub, Bobby felt he was next in queue, a San Francisco birthright of sorts.

This was a huge legacy that Bobby carried around in his head. He was the superstar puzzle on the back of every All-Star baseball card in 1974. Much like the kids who collected in vain but couldn't find all the pieces, to me Bobby was almost complete, but *something* was off, something not quite in place. I would see Bobby outside the clubhouse door kissing Pat and their kids goodbye in the hallway, the look of contentment vanishing the moment they walked around the corner. His inner peace came from Pat and his children. I joked with him once about how Barry said he's gonna be the best player in history, better than everyone else, even his Daddy. Bobby would crack up, laughing as he puffed through another Winston. "*Yeah*," he chuckled, his eyes wide with pride for his son, "*I love that boy.*" Affectionate father and husband, great leader, great teammate, still I could never uncover that missing piece that would make Bobby Bonds, the person, whole.

Toward the end of May, I hit a rough patch, losing five straight starts after winning my first two. The Dodgers came to town, and lit up Ron Bryant (who re-joined the ballclub on April 16th) with six runs in the first inning. By the time the middle of the second rolled around, Charlie, staring at a 6-0 deficit, nudged me on the shoulder and nodded to the bullpen in right field.

"Johnny, go get some work in," Charlie said, "I may be throwing you in this game soon."

"You got it, Skip," I replied, grabbing my glove. I ran out to warm up and next thing I know I'm on the mound with runners on 1st and 2nd, down 8-0. Over the course of 3 2/3, I struck out eight and gave up a lone hit. I did my part to give us a chance to get back in this thing. After striking out the side in the top of the fifth, Bobby emerged from the runaway, dashed out his Winston with his spikes on the dugout ground, walked over, threw his arm around my neck, and gathered the ball club. "Enough of this shit, guys," Bobby said, "Rook's pitchin' his heart out and we're lettin' them come into our yard and treat us like this? We need to win this game. We did this last year, we can do it again." We made a valiant comeback, but '74 wasn't '73. We ended up losing 9-5. No more heartbreakers.

The post-game cocktail parties Charlie and Bobby had enjoyed for years became less and less frequent. Their relationship deteriorated quickly. A couple weeks later, I walked into Charlie's office after the Cubs whipped me around for five runs and seven hits in five innings, dropping us below .500 for the first time that season. Charlie was sitting at his desk, staring at a bottle of Johnny Walker with a puzzled expression on his face. He sighed with a "hmm." then looked toward me.

"Hi, John."

"Sorry about the game, Skip."

"Eh, team was sloppy out there, it's gonna happen. Just throw strikes, stay within yourself. It'll come." We didn't talk much, but sometimes when you let the boss down, you just want that level of reassurance that everything's ok on his end. Charlie gave me that, sort of, as I got up to leave.

"You haven't been in here, have you?"

"You don't have any tequila in there, so it can't be me." Charlie half-smiled.

"Yeah, I know. That's what I was afraid of. 'Nite, Johnny."

* * * * *

About a week later, we were at the airport waiting for our flight to Pittsburgh, when Bobby approached me in the executive club for the charter passengers. He was carrying a paper bag.

"Hey, Rook?" he said quietly, "Bring this on for me, will ya?" I looked in the bag, sorted through about a half-dozen airplane bottles of Johnny Walker and Jack Daniels. I was a rookie, I didn't ask any questions. I always did what I was told.

"Sure, no problem, BB," I replied, grabbing the bag as the stewardess announced it was time to board the plane. A few moments later, I passed Charlie, who was sitting up front. He smiled at me for a moment, then glanced at the bag. He knew the moment his eyes caught mine. He excused himself from Joey

Amalfitano, one of our coaches sitting beside him and called me over to the flight attendant's food prep station.

"Who's is that?" Charlie asked pointedly.

"Just some stuff for the flight." Charlie asked *"lemme see"* with his fingers and sifted through the small bag.

"There's no tequila in here," Charlie said, finding nothing but hard whiskey and vodka.

"Who's is this?" he asked again.

"Just thought I'd try some..." I fumbled my words as Charlie gently took the bag from my hands.

"You're a good teammate, Johnny," Charlie fumed as he folded up the bag, "Go sit down."

As I stepped toward the back of the plane, I grabbed my seat next to Onti. I looked over at the front and watched as Bobby was the last player to enter the cabin. Charlie stopped him and they walked to the stewardess' station. Judging from Bobby's contained grimace, it wasn't a pleasant conversation. Bobby eventually came by me. I felt awful putting Bobby in that situation.

"Hey man, I'm sorry," I pleaded, but Bobby just tapped me on the shoulder reassuringly.

"It's ok, Rook, we're cool, we're cool," with the forced smile of an older brother trying to calm his younger sibling as he took his seat a few rows behind me.

The post-game chats in Charlie's office with Bobby continued for the next couple of weeks, only they weren't the friendly, open visits between manager and team leader, but rather closed-door shouting matches. The ballclub was now a few games below .500

and quickly falling from contention in the National League West. Charlie always enjoyed a close relationship with management, but the front office had expected us to be competing with the Dodgers and Reds. He also didn't count on another prominent voice in the organization possessing an equal level of influence.

One evening after a game, I went upstairs in the stadium to the marketing department to discuss my promotional duties – coordinating shopping center openings, sporting goods store signings, that sort of thing. I walked in the direction of Horace Stoneham's office. The San Francisco Giants owner was 72 years old now, getting along in age, but still remained close not just to the coaching staff and the manager, but certain players as well. I approached the owner's doorway and heard loud laughter coming from the room. As I passed by, I saw Mr. Stoneham standing beside his desk, with a jovial grin on his face.

Pouring Bobby another drink, who was sitting down across from him, in what appeared to be the middle of a very funny story.

My manager, my Godfather in the organization, was in deep, *deep* trouble.

Sundown

We lost four of our next six games. We needed a win badly. I needed to pick up Charlie. Sometimes the players pick each other up when they're going through rough patches. Sometimes the players' pick up their manager if they love him, and I adored Charlie. We were stuck in fifth place, three games below .500. We had already beat Bob Gibson once this year, couple weeks back. This would be my first professional start opposing a Hall of Fame pitcher. Being a hurler that relied on his heat, obviously Gibby was one of my idols, the arm extension of his motion, the power thrust from his hips through his legs. Gibby was the mentor I never met, until tonight. I was ready to not merely show him what I could do, but what I learned from watching him. I was getting Charlie this win with every fiber of my being.

We made a small push in the top of the first, as Gibby found himself in an early first and third, two-out jam, thanks to a sweet single to left by Ed Goodson. Gibby managed to get out of it, though. I could see the look on Eddie's face returning to the dugout at the end of the inning. He felt tonight would be our night.

I had Rader behind the plate. He liked to psyche me up when he was back there. "*C'mon, Nolie, show me what cha got,*" he'd bark out during warm-ups. He called me Nolie, obviously after Nolan

Ryan because of my fastball. "You want the gas? Ok." I threw a 100-MPH strike, then asked, "How's that?" "That's OK," Rader yelled over half-heartedly, removing his glove, then shaking out his left hand, before running to the dugout to add a batting glove and a small sponge to increase the padding.

Lou Brock, who had a magical 1974 by eventually setting the single-season stolen base record, started things off with a double to right field. Next up was Ted Sizemore, a dependable hitter who had a great eye at the plate. Didn't hit .300 a lot, but always seemed to be on base when I played against him. History wasn't wrong here, as I walked him. Bake McBride came up and hit a rocket grounder to Chris Speier, who wheeled to Goodson at third to nail the lead runner. Speier saved my hide again by capturing a Ted *"Simba"* Simmons grounder over second base to force out McBride, but not enough to finish off the double play. I really wanted that double play. Would've gotten us out of the inning. It's nobody's fault – Speier made another great stab, it just wasn't there – doesn't mean I wasn't upset. Remember, I'm only 22, not all of us have poise at that age, which unfortunately is the one thing you need when a guy like Joe Torre steps to the plate. A great, smart batter who knew how to just jump all over the mistakes of a young pitcher, and he did just that. Single to left field – Sizemore scored, Simba to second.

This upset me. If Gibby straightened himself out, even at the age of 38, some days he only needed one run. Time to stop the bleeding. Here comes Jose Cruz. A talented player from a talented family – his brother Hector at the time was crushing the ball at AAA – still hadn't established himself. *I'm just gonna blow it by him and get us back to the dugout*, I thought to myself. Dave called for the gas, I wound up, threw and Cruz just destroyed it, sending my 96 MPH heater way back in the right-field seats. Three-run blast. 4-0 Cards.

Of course, I looked over and saw action in our bullpen. I'm rattled now. *"Shit shit shit shit shit!!"* is blaring in my mind. Tom Heintzelman came to the plate – of course, I walked him. *"I'm never getting out of this inning,"* I worried to myself. Rader trotted out to the mound.

"You ok, Nolie?" he asked with concern.

"Yeah," I nodded, but that means nothing. What happened next meant the world to me. I saw Charlie Williams sit down from throwing. The action stopped.

"Really, you ok?" Rader asks again, not seemingly to notice the unoccupied bullpen mound.

I looked into the dugout – my eyes found Charlie's. His arms are folded – no expression, just a nod. It's your game now.

"Yeah, yeah, I'm fine now." Rader nodded and headed back behind the plate. With everything happening to the club, with Charlie's job in jeopardy, a lesser man would've pulled my ass out of the game. Maybe even a smarter tactician. With his job on the line, my manager left me in there. No deck chairs re-positioned on this Titanic. Charlie Fox was my teacher – he wanted to see me learn life the hard way. No net. He was going down with me. I didn't even focus on Heintzelman at first, just Mike Tyson at the plate. Couple pitches and a soft fly ball to Maddox out in center and the inning was over. I stepped slowly toward the dugout, looked over to Charlie, who flashed the hint of a grin. I returned the affection. As the players followed me in, Bobby tapped me on the fanny, quickly whispering, *"We got ya, Rook."* Soon, he commanded the players, clapping his hands, *"C'mon, let get some runs for Johnny!"* As I walked to the bat rack, obviously I felt bad about the score, but something inside me shook it off, like it never happened.

Speier took Bobby's lead and singled to right to start off the second inning. After a Chris Arnold fly out, Rader shot a line-drive single to right as well. First and second and I came up. I was never the best bunter and this plate appearance was no exception. Gibby struck me out quickly – two outs. Bonds strutted by me and gave me that look again, what Speier, Rader and even Arnold knew: Gibby was hittable today. Bonds entered the batter's box, dug in against Gibson. I turned around to get a cup of water and next thing you knew, the crowd went quiet.

Bobby did it again. Three-run shot over the left-center field fence. 4-3 Cards. Bobby was a man of his word. He picked me up.

Returning to the dugout, we all congratulated Bobby, though I held his hand a second longer and looked into his eyes, offering wordless appreciation. Time for me to support *his* efforts.

Gibson is the first batter for St. Louis in the bottom of the second. I thought to myself, *"Let me just get through the pitcher's spot and focus on everyone else."* I figured a brilliant pitcher like Gibby would be looking for my heat and would be swinging away. Gibby was no slouch at the plate, either – he hit five dingers through 106 plate appearances in '72 at the age of 36. You extrapolate that to 600 at-bats, you're looking at a 30-HR guy. "Gonna throw him a curveball – no way he's expecting that." I wound up, I threw and my pitch whizzed right past Gibby's face!

"Oh my God," I shrieked in my mind, *"You just dusted Bob Gibson! What the hell are you doing? You're a fuckin' dead man now."* My number two broke the wrong way. Under no circumstances did I mean to throw at Gibby. Had no reason to – he's doesn't know that, though. To him, his opponent just launched a 90-MPH missile at his brain. I couldn't walk over and apologize – no one does that

and certainly not in 1974. Wouldn't have mattered. I'm sure Gibby was unhappy about the Bonds dinger, this certainly didn't help. I managed to strike him out, but Gibby glared at me as he made his way back to the dugout. Concern about retaliation was irrelevant. It was just gonna happen. I tried to shrug it off, but wanted to make sure my curve was on. Didn't use it on Brock, the next hitter.

Lou tagged me for a double down the right-field line and then came Sizemore. *"Gonna have to use the curve and try to trick him"* I was thinking, *"Or at least maybe jam him – he most likely wouldn't take me out of the park."* I tried to keep the ball down and away, but that pesky Sizemore got his bat on the pitch, smacking it to right field. Bobby ran it down, but Lou felt it was time to test Bonds' arm. BB made the catch, Lou took off, bookin' toward third, Bobby wheeled and delivered the throw, Brock slid, Chris Arnold caught the ball.....Brock out at third. Bobby saved my ass once again.

Gibby stepped out of the dugout for the top of the third. I was thinkin' he's definitely putting Maddox on the ground just as I did him, but he didn't. Maddox started us going with an opposite-field single. Goodson stepped in and Maddox took off – hit and run! – as Eddie smacked a screaming liner to right-center. Maddox rounded third, but Goodson was stopped at second trying to stretch it into a double. Gary Thomasson and Speier again reached base with singles. Chris Arnold hit into an inning-ending double play to bail out Gibby. Didn't matter, though. With Maddox scoring, tie game at 4. Gibby and I went back to zero.

Bake McBride reached on a walk to start off the bottom of the third. I remember bearing down, with the confidence of a tie game, also realizing that Bobby couldn't do the pitching for me, too. Ted Simmons came up. I tried to hold Bake on first, but he was, in his rookie season, one of the fastest guys in the game, and proved it with a stolen base. I concentrated on Simmons, a catcher who used his deep knowledge of the strike zone as a batter to great success. Not here, though. I blew it right by him. Torre was up again. This was the type of situation where Torre always drove the runner home. No fat fastballs for Torre. Maybe one high heater to set him up. Rader called for high heat; ball. Now nothing but junk. Curve-slider-off-speed. *Torre's expecting the heat,* I thought to myself. Nope. One more number two. I threw the curve and it broke right in the zone. Strike three. Torre caught looking. Now it's Cruz. He hurt me bad last time. *I won't let that happen again,* I thought to myself. Rader had me keep the ball outside and away. Cruz managed to tap a slow grounder past me down the first base line – I trotted quickly toward the bag just like you always see in the first workouts of spring training. The ball careened off Goodson's glove, Tito Fuentes ran it down, soft tossed to me at first, and we got Cruz by a step. Inning over, but the game was really about to begin.

After Rader grounded out to third, it was time for me to face Gibby in the batter's box. You know what's comin', I know what's comin', every freakin' fan in the park knows what comin', Simba behind the plate knows what's comin', Gibby most definitely knows what's comin' next as his heel sits against the rubber. Let me put it this way…

Gibby cracked my helmet.

Thankfully my head wasn't in it, as I had bailed out and fell to the ground from the moment he released his pitch. I could see the hint of a grin on Simba's face as he returned the ball to Gibson. Next pitch? Same thing. Waayyy up and waaay in. I just kept digging in – I wasn't showing any fear. Idol, mentor, the heck with all that. I simply nodded and waited for his heat, because he was gonna try and blow it by me. I dug in, Gibby set and delivered a blazing fastball. I swung and smacked it right back at him, the ball whizzed past his ear, up the middle and into center field for a single. Let me tell you about Bob Gibson.

The man never flinched as the ball passed him. He sure as hell didn't love giving up a hit to the opposing pitcher – a rookie, no less – but he did what hall of fame-caliber pitchers do: he went back to business, getting Bonds and Tito Fuentes to offer up cans of corn to end the inning.

I threw away all that nostalgia and affection for the man. It was on now.

Next frame, I had complete command – Heintzelman, groundout. Mike Tyson, soft fly to right. Gibby stepped to the plate. You know it – dropped his ass again with a high and tight heater, then struck him out with a 98 MPH fastball right in the zone. Art Williams, the home plate umpire, to his credit, didn't throw out any warnings to us or the opposing dugouts. The man just let us play hardball, and we gave the fans their money's worth and then some. Gibby came back in the top of the fifth with a renewed vigor, striking out two while only allowing yet another single to Goodson. Bottom of the fifth, I got three soft groundouts, especially one from Brock, who I was convinced had me figured out. Gibby made easy work of Arnold and Rader and then it was my turn at bat. Yes, he threw at me again. Yes, I dug back in. Then Gibby tried to get cute by tossing nothing but sliders, one after the other and I didn't chase. I worked out a walk against Gibby, which made him even angrier. Once I reached first base, Torre's standing there with this amused look on his face. He's enjoying this show as much as everyone in the park. I remembered Bobby talking to a few of us in the dugout in between innings.

"Johnny, you get on again, Gibby's gonna be so pissed, he's gonna balk your ass to second," Bobby laughed in between cigarette puffs.

I smiled, and took a walking lead off the bag. Torre gave me this smug glance that said, *"What do you think you're doing,"* as he moved over to hold me on. Suddenly, don't know if it was a player, a fan, someone yelled "He's going!" Gibby flinched and Art Williams stopped play and pointed out to the mound.

"Balk," Williams yelled and I trotted to second.

Man, was Gibby furious, humiliated and just royally pissed, throwing me a look that said, *"You're gonna pay for that, Rookie."* Of course, Gibby settled down and got Bobby to pop to the catcher to get out of the inning.

Next inning, Simmons, Torre, Jose Cruz – fly out, groundout, lineout – 1-2-3 and we came out for the top of the seventh. Tito slapped a single to center off Gibby and then proceeded to steal second. He struck out Maddox and then in the ultimate show of respect, Gibby intentionally walked Goodson. This is the mark of a brilliant pitcher. Eddie Goodson was still merely a good, young player and by no means an all-star, but Gibby recognized that the kid saw something, some glitch, some edge that was allowing him to beat Gibby in every at-bat. He then got Thomasson to fly out and a soft grounder from Speier and the Cards were out of the inning.

I had my game going now. Heintzelman, Tyson, Gibby – fly out, groundout, fly out. We were up at bat again, going into the eighth inning, still tied at 4.

I returned to the dugout, figuring my night was over. Gave them seven innings, close game, *I'm headed to the showers if we build any kind of lead,* is what I was thinking. Gary Matthews, Kingman,

Bruce Miller, all ready to pinch-hit. Charlie slowly leaned over to me on the bench, nodding to the helmet rack. *"Grab a bat."* Nothing else, just grab a bat. That told me, as much as Charlie needed this win to keep his job, that he wanted me to steer this amazing game to its conclusion. *The balls on this guy,* I thought to myself. Sure enough, a single by Chris Arnold. Rader popped a shallow flyball into center, not enough for Brock to catch it and just enough to get Arnold over to third. I walked to the plate with Charlie's fate in my hands. I know Gibby wanted to dust me just one more time, but not in this situation. I squared to bunt and fouled it off. I squared again; fouled it off again. *I should swing away,* I thought to myself. I looked to the third-base coach, Ozzie Virgil. The signs said bunt. I squared again; I bunted. Foul. Strike three. Charlie's plan backfired, but he simply half-shrugged a *"No big deal"* my way as I returned to the dugout, clapping out a *"Let's go"* as Bobby dug in at the plate. Bonds grounded to third – Reitz gloved it, his only thought was home – fired to Simmons - Arnold nailed at the plate. Two outs, first and second. Here comes Tito Fuentes. Gibby set and delivered, Tito smacked a line-drive single to left- center. Rader scored, Bobby to third, Tito advanced to second on the throw home. We took the lead 5-4. Gibby clamped it down, fanning Maddox to get out of the inning, but now we had the lead and I was still firing away.

The bottom of the eighth was nothing for me – Brock, Sizemore, McBride – groundout, groundout, fly out. 1-2-3. I never felt as alive as I did walking back to the dugout. And never respected another pitcher more than seeing Gibby come out for the ninth. 14 hits and Gibby stayed in the game – Red Schoendienst stepped out of the dugout and approached the mound but Gibby stopped him with a simple shake of the head. Not this game, not tonight. Gibby wasn't coming out of this game.

Goodson was the first batter up for us and flied out to left. Thomasson and Speier flew out softly to center and right as well. Gibby did his job in this inning. He may have given up 14 hits and stayed in the game, but he finished us off in the ninth and gave his batters a chance to win it against me.

I was simply exhausted at this stage, but Charlie had faith I could finish the game, even though he had the pen going just in case. I managed to get Simmons on a fly to Maddox in center. One down, two to go. Torre stepped in. He knew my heater was flat at this point, and Torre just sat on my curve, which is what I threw him. It was also lifeless and he smacked it up the middle for a single. Jose Cruz, the batter that took me deep in the first, was due up. Charlie stepped out of the dugout and signaled for the veteran left-hander Steve Barber. This would only be Barber's fifth game with the Giants. He won 20 with the Orioles when I was 11 years old, a very good starter back in the early '60s. I understood. Charlie gave me as much love and support as possible, but he needed to nail down the win. I handed Charlie the ball, and he slapped me on the fanny.

"Thanks," he muttered, but he looked me in the eye when he said it. I wasn't concerned about losing this game for my record – I just wanted Charlie to get a win and save his job.

The Cardinals' manager Red Schoendienst countered with pinch-hitting veteran Jim Hickman, another player on the verge of being released. Hickman once hit 30 home runs in a season, but at 37, was primarily a bench player at this stage. You wanna talk about the drama of the game, this was a moment. Charlie needed a win. Hickman needed a hit. Barber needed a save. Any outcome against their needs could have very easily resulted in termination for one of these men. Barber dealt a pesky slider and Hickman popped a weak fly to Goodson at first. Out number two, and Hickman trotted calmly back down into the Cards' dugout. Reggie Smith thought he had the night off when he got called on to hit for Heintzelman. Barber got him to fly to Bobby in right. We won a hard-fought game. Charlie got a stay of execution. Barber got a chance to continue his career, albeit on a week-by-week basis. Charlie shook my hand and grabbed my shoulder as we went out to the mound to greet Rader and Barber.

It would be the last time the Giants congratulated Steve Barber after a victory. He appeared in 11 more games for us before getting his release in August. Hickman would be let go by the Cardinals less than a month later.

As for me, the winner of the toughest game I ever pitched, I let the Cardinals' reporters know how I was feeling. Beat guys were all like *"Gibby pitched a good game. You beat one of the best pitchers of all time."*

"Enjoyed it," I replied, *"Learned a lot, too."* Mostly the St. Louis press. I beat their best. Sure Lynn McGlothen was having a great season in '74, but Gibby was still the ace of the staff.

"How many times were you on your back?" one of the writers asked. I chuckled, "Well, ask Gibby how many times he was on his back." The writers laughed, wrote quickly and in that moment, I said to myself, *Son of a bitch. All of these guys have known Gibby for at least a decade. You know this is getting right back to him 15 minutes from now.* "It was a great game, though," I added. It was no use. I opened my mouth. Thank you, St. Louis Dispatch.

* * * * *

There was a passageway in Busch Stadium from the clubhouse that allowed players to leave the ballpark without getting swarmed by fans and autograph seekers. I usually loved that part of the game, but tonight I just wanted peace and quiet. The hallway led to an elevator and as the doors opened, I realized for the first time in my life that God likes to laugh.

Gibby's standing there in his suit. Alone. And he's still pissed.

Now remember, Gibby was on the verge of reaching 3000 strikeouts at this point, making him only the second pitcher in baseball history to attain that mark. A career ERA under three. One of the proudest athletes to ever put on the uniform, and his '74 record stood at 3-8 after losing to me. Just like most players of the day, Gibby wasn't a guy with $30 million in the bank. He was still singing for his supper just like the rest of us. Losing to me, a first-year player, giving up 14 hits, including a single and walk *and balking the opposing pitcher*, was to him, humiliating. I stepped onto the elevator. Quiet as can be. I was on the right side – he was on the left. I barely muttered *"Hi"* as the doors slowly closed. He replied the same. I tried breaking the awkward silence.

"Nice game, man."

"Fuck you."

Now, I don't care who you are, no one says that to me.

"What'd you just say," I turned to him.

"Fuck you, Rookie," he nodded, like I was nothing.

"Well, fuck you, too, ya old fart," I shot back, getting closer. Instantly, Gibby pushed me back and we went at it. I wrestled Gibby to the ground like a linebacker in a football game, then he slammed me down on the floor. I managed to get him pinned against the side of the elevator with all the brute strength I had, more grabbing than trying to land punches - we really didn't want to hurt each other. The elevator doors opened. My teammates are there waiting for me as Gibby and I were rolling against the panels in the elevator, the doors opening and banging back and forth against our legs. Randy Moffitt, one of the Giants' relief pitchers, came in and broke it up.

"Johnny, get off," Randy yelled, pulling me off Gibby, who got to his feet and pointed his finger in my face as the closing elevator doors ended the confrontation.

"I'll see your ass next week," he warned me chillingly.

"Yeah, I'll see you too," I yelled back. Not the most witty comeback, but hey, I was 22, and out of my mind furious, agitated – not the time for clever repartee. Moffitt calmed me down.

"Hey, hey, Johnny, it's ok," Randy said softly.

"I'm gonna get that son of a bitch," I fumed. "Fuck me?"

"Johnny, you already got 'em. You beat Bob Gibson." Moff calmed me down.

"Yeah," I nodded, "Yeah, I sure did."

"C'mon, let's go get a beer." My post-game show with Gibby notwithstanding, I managed to get Charlie a stay of execution. We continued on the road to L.A. and San Diego, where the amazingly durable reliever Mike Marshall and the surging Dodgers would sweep our three-game set. I left the final game in the seventh with two runners on and a slim 3-1 lead, which L.A. won on a walk-off in the ninth. Three more losses to the lowly Padres and the teams' spirit was all but gone. It would be up to me again to protect my father figure and keep him in the manager's office.

* * * * *

The team was hovering around .500, but not making much traction in the division. Charlie had always been something of a players' manager, but now he was constantly feuding with Bobby. Finally, on June 27th, I went up against my buddy Randy Jones down in San Diego. Pitched one of my best outings of the year, complete game, gave up six hits, two runs, struck out five, walked one. Bobby played great, 3 for 5, including a triple and a 3-run homer. He seemed like his old self. Charlie greeted me on the field, shook my hand and once my teammates drifted away, he whispered in my ear.

"*I'm done,*" Charlie said.

"What?" I replied, half-distracted, nodding at teammates, half–listening with the ambient crowd noise, "Whaddya mean you're done?"

"I'm no longer your manager. I was fired tonight. Thanks for letting me go out a winner. Glad it was you on the mound." Charlie jogged toward the dugout. I walked briskly behind him, trying to get his attention.

"How, how could they do that?"

"Johnny, it's baseball," he shrugged, stepping away, and as the crowd of 11,295 made their way for the exits, so did Charlie Fox.

Once I got through the tunnel and into the clubhouse, I kept looking for Charlie, as we always talked at length after my starts. Couldn't find him. I passed by Bobby, who was enjoying a cigarette and a beer at his locker. Bobby extended his hand.

"Good game, kid," Bobby said, slapping five.

"You too, man." I nodded, agreeing somewhat.

"Yeah, I felt relaxed tonight."

"You know what happened?" I asked pointedly. Bobby's words stopped me. "Yeah," he nodded with a polite coldness, "Yeah, I know."

That's all Bobby needed to say.

Just like that, my mentor, my father figure in baseball was gone. It felt like a professional hit to my heart. No one looked after me in baseball like Charlie, and Bobby was like an older brother, so I knew not to get between them. It wasn't like Bobby was this petulant employee disobeying his owner. Bobby was a very powerful voice in the organization. You could almost consider him head salesman for the company, and sometimes in the corporate world when a standoff comes down between an upper-level executive and a revenue-generating employee, sales wins. And I know that Bobby respected Charlie. This was only business.

"You're daddy's gone now, Rook," Bobby said, "You'll get over it. We all do."

I got dressed quickly – didn't even wait for the official announcement and went to my Mom's house, which is where I stayed when I was in town to play the Padres. I loved my team, loved my manager to tears, loved the guys, but it was so obvious that the ballclub I dreamed of playing for was all but dismantled. Bobby was left, as well as Speier, Kingman and Jim Barr. Ron Bryant was having an awful time pitching after the Spring Training pool incident. Tito Fuentes was still around, but having a bad season. I had never been through a manager firing. The cherry had been popped.

* * * * *

Wes Westrum was named manager for the San Francisco Giants. A former catcher, he had previously led the New York Mets for a couple of seasons back in the '60s. Seemed more like a consensus, interim choice than any pointed new direction for the ballclub. Wes was an affable sort, truly nice man, but you never thought any great insight or strategy was coming from him. In another indication that the league had a hand in ballclub affairs, Westrum was drinking buddies with Chub Feeney, president of the National League.

I missed Gibby and the Cardinals once we returned to Candlestick a week later. I pitched against my fellow rookie Bob Forsch and beat him. The team proceeded to go 20-24 over our next 40 games – win one, lose two, win two, lose three – barely treading water. Speier was our lone representative at the All-Star game in Pittsburgh, his third in a row. Jim Barr and Caldwell were enjoying nice seasons. I was 9-10 by the middle of August – some nice performances, but when the other team had my number, they really had it. Westrum didn't provide much leadership, but the open-door policy to the manager's office was reinstated, and Bobby availed himself of the spare chair after games, sharing cocktails and discussing the ballclub with Wes. Bobby was firmly back in charge.

* * * * *

Thursday, August 15th, as we were sitting on the United charter preparing for our next series, McMahon handed out the stat sheet on our opponent. Who's hurt, who's hitting, basically a primer preparing us for the matchups.

"Just get it over the plate and try not to walk so many people" was their directive to me specifically every game. I was never involved in any scouting strategy – there was no *"Pitch Aaron this way, and remember Schmidt has a good eye,"* no, for me it was *"They have to hit*

your fastball." Was that the smart way to go? I dunno, but that was my command.

Oftentimes, the starting players sat in first class as they handed out the stat sheets to certain guys on the charter. The catchers would get them as well. Some guys would head to the back of the plane and play cards, but tonight, class was in session.

Regarding my pitching, location was the only thing we discussed. "If my ball is up, I'm gonna start throwing sinkers, I want the ball on the ground." They knew there would be more ground balls. If I had my heater locating properly, I'd be throwing more cutters and rising fastballs. Speier, who was almost as much a leader on the club as Bobby, would lean in and say to me, "Just throw strikes, Johnny. That's all ya gotta do."

Speier and Tito, our double-play combo, would strategize mid-flight.

"If Johnny's fastball is on," Spei would say, "They're gonna be hitting behind it, so there'll be a lot more grounders to the opposite field." Looking back and forth between me and Tito, Spei would continue, "I'll be shading more to second base against guys like McBride and Ted Simmons (a switch-hitter who hit lefty against me) with Johnny on the mound. Tito, you shade more on guys like Torre and Sizemore (right-handed hitters). They won't be able to get around on Johnny's heater. I'll coordinate with Bobby and make sure the outfielders are positioned properly."

Speier was captain of the infield and gave signs to everyone on defense. He would position himself a bit more toward second base and Tito toward the 3-4 hole – toward first base. Thumb up behind Spei's ear – that was the sign to shade in a certain spot.

None of this would matter to me once I looked down at the matchup sheet.

Game #2: B. Gibson vs. J. D'Acquisto.

Duel at dusk.

* * * * *

Gibby was 6-10 at this stage, improved his ERA a bit, but this was not at all where a pitcher of his class wanted to be. Today had the feel of a heavyweight boxing match. To be honest, coming into this game, in my mind I was the favorite here. That's how I felt driving in the cab heading to the Marriott across the street from Busch Stadium, Gordon Lightfoot chiming in from the radio. That's how I felt when I entered the clubhouse the day of the start.

Rader approached me as I got dressed in my locker.

"You ready for this today?"

I was never this confident before a start. "He's on his back every single time. And I'm not letting him up."

Rader was one of the goofiest fellas I ever played with, but his nutty demeanor never betrayed a fierce competitor. He laughed at my brazen cockiness. "Ha! He's probably gonna take *your* head off."

"I don't give a shit. I'm ready for it. Don't worry about me. Worry about yourself. He knows you're calling all these damn pitches." Rader stopped laughing, considering my point.

"I didn't think of that........shit." Rader grabbed his catching gear and walked toward the tunnel. Lucky for him, Ken Rudolph got the start. Then it seemed like a steady stream of well wishers.

Mike Caldwell strolled over, a huge wad of tobacco in his cheek.

"Ready, man?" he asked in that heavy North-Carolina accent.

"Yeah, I'm fine," I repeated, "We're gonna be ok today."

"Ya better be." Another concerned slap on the shoulder.

"He better be, too. Mine hurts more than his." I was trying to convince the guys in the clubhouse how not scared I was. Maybe myself included. If you could read my mind, you'd see a 22-year old kid who felt nervous as hell, but I knew, if I showed some courage, I would come out on top.

* * * * *

I didn't know what a game with playoff implications felt like. 28,723 showed up for the rematch. Not the biggest Friday night home crowd of the season for the Cardinals, but it was pretty close.

Once I entered the dugout, the bench went dead silent. Nobody wanted to say anything to me, not Rader, not my coaches. I glanced across the field and saw Gibby talking to Torre, looking my way. Could've been nothing, could've been everything. I still used that for fuel. I was gonna beat them both. I was gonna blow it past Torre, a former NL MVP, one of the smartest players in the game. He was going down on strikes every time. Gibby was gonna lose again. The hero would be me. I'm the one who would walk away like a movie star. Before stepping onto the field for the pre-game warm-ups, I got another hand on my shoulder, this one from Don McMahon, our pitching coach. Before the words even got out of his mouth – I didn't know who it was – I turned swiftly but not enough to make a scene. "Yes, I'm ready." Don was stunned slightly because this was not like me, but also pleased at the fire.

"Well, go get 'em," Don smiled.

"Sorry, Don," I apologized quickly. Don shook off the offense, gave me a fatherly nod and a slap on the fanny, dismissing any issue.

"Go get 'em, Johnny."

Gibson vs. D'Acquisto. Enter Number Two.

In the first inning, Tito Fuentes reached third on a one-out triple, but Gibby got both Maddox and Matthews to both ground out to Ken Reitz at third to get out of the inning with no runs on the board. When I got to the mound, I was fired up like never before. I started my warm-ups with fireball after fireball. After four pitches, Rudolph removed his glove again.

"Go get your batting glove," I smirked, jab-catching his toss. My intensity wouldn't let me down. Brock, who owned me in the first game, watched a called strike three whizz right past him. Sizemore, that pesky number two hitter, blew it right by him. Reggie Smith, one of the greatest players *not* in the Hall of Fame, fought off some of my heat before grounding to second to end the inning.

Gibby brought it himself as well, three fly ball outs to get us back on the field. I pounded my catcher's glove with intense velocity, challenging Torre with my fastball. He probably wasn't smirking at me before the game, but then I didn't care. I allowed my mind to play some tricks on my adrenaline. Torre couldn't touch me. Down on strikes. Jose Cruz touched me for a fly ball again, but this one didn't leave the park. Simba Simmons grounded to second to end the inning.

Here's the part where the heartaches come. Ken Rudolph started off the top of the third with a single to left. I'm supposed to bunt him over so Bobby, our leadoff hitter, can get him home. *"How's it gonna happen,"* I asked myself, *"Will he take my legs out from under me? Will it be 86 MPH right to my teeth as I square to bunt? Will he show mercy with a Love Tap curveball in the ass?"* Yeah, I was nervous. Hell, I was downright scared, but this is what you think about in the big leagues. I approached the batter's box, Simba said nothing, just raised his eyebrows at me quickly, just to let me know something's coming. Or not – wouldn't that be a great psyche out?

There was no psyche out. Gibby wasn't that kinda guy. He looked me right in the eye, set up, wound up, I squared to bunt, right under my chin, I went right down.

I didn't get hit, didn't suffer a brain injury, didn't die. Now I was mad. Look over to Ozzie Virgil at third, begging for a swing away sign – nope, the bunt's still on. I was a little rattled, my squares and efforts were just awful. Gibby had me in his clutches. I ended up fouling my third strike bunt. Out. I walked back to the dugout – Bobby gave me the *"I'll take care of this,"* look on his face. He just got under a Gibby fastball for a hard single to left. Wasn't enough, though. Gibby closed out Tito and Maddox to end the inning.

It went back and forth like this all night long. I would get up, get decked by Gibby. Gibby would come to plate, I'd drop his ass and – here's the weird part – he'd get up and smile at me, almost a prideful, *"You're catching on quick, Rookie"* kinda smile. Unlike many heavyweight bouts, this game lived up to the hype in my mind.

I walked Sizemore, the first Cardinals' base runner, but was soon erased on a Reggie Smith double play. We would get one or two guys on each inning, but Gibby would settle down and keep us off the board. I struck out Torre again and Cruz as well in the fifth inning, but then Simmons, who had a catcher's perspective even when he was hitting, an uncanny ability to figure out what I was about to throw, got the first hit off me in the fifth. Kenny Reitz then hit into a force out at second to end the inning.

We had a real chance to score in the sixth. Second and third with one away, but then Rudolph lined out to center, not enough to score Goodson from third and then I came up. I had the knowledge that Gibby wasn't gonna try to drop me and come close – the last thing he needed to do was load the bases for Bobby. He had to get me out. During the first game, he tried to get me to go fishing for the slider and ended up walking me. He knew he couldn't do that, either. *He has to come with the heat*, I thought. I wasn't there to bunt. I was swinging away. No more head-hunting. No more gamesmanship. Pitcher vs. hitter. Just baseball. Simba set the sign. Gibby wound up, he threw, I swung-

Fouled off his best fastball. Just didn't time it well. Here we go again – sets, throws…

Now he got me with the slider. 0-2. I remember thinking to myself, *"This son-of-a-bitch thinks he can get me with the slider. He's not getting me with that slider again."* I have to help my own cause, because it's looking like one run will decide it. Gibby set, I dug in, waiting for that waste pitch…that never came. Knees locked with heat right down the plate. Strike three. Inning over. As Gibby slowly stepped off the mound, I thought he was strutting like a peacock, making this obnoxious winking face as he crossed the third base line. It was a walk by design, but much different than what my 22-year old mind assumed.

The bottom of the sixth brought a Mike Tyson foul fly out and then Gibby came to bat. Again, with that face, again with that strut. I came close with my first delivery, brushing him back slightly. He just made that face and dug in again. Then I said to myself, *"All right, Gibby, you want my best. Here's my best."* I threw him a 97 MPH heater. Swing and a miss. I gave him a taste of his own medicine, I was gonna make him chase a slider. He chased it all right – stepped into the slider and popped it into right field. Had to tip my cap to the old man. Brock came to the plate – I had no interest in holding Gibby on. He wasn't going anywhere, barely took a lead off the bag. A force out at second, Gibby barely ran. I know pitchers in the seventh inning generally conserve their energy, but not only did he dog it to second, he could've read the Sunday New York Times from cover to cover in the time it took him to return to the dugout. Something else was going on here. I held Brock close, he didn't get a good jump off me and Kenny Rudolph threw a perfect strike to Tito at second to nail Brock.

I sat down for the top of the seventh and Gibby slowly walked to the mound. I had never seen a pitcher take such a leisurely time warming up. Vaguely remember Cardinals manager Red Schoendienst on the top step of the dugout as if he was about to come out on the field. I noticed Gibby, hands on his knees, standing on the side of the mound, simply raise his head, and shake it slowly to ol' Red. The manager stayed in the dugout. What a warrior.

The seventh inning went by in a flash – three up, three down, three up, three down, of course ending properly with me blowing it by Torre for his third K of the game. I remember jogging off the mound, thinking to myself, *"Man, 'ol Torre's going home with four strikeouts,"* or as they say today, the old "golden sombrero." I was getting a bit fatigued, but I wasn't going anywhere until one of us scored a run.

Top eight started with Matthews getting on from a Mike Tyson error with Ed Goodson, who owned Gibby in the first game, now up at bat. Gary took a reasonable lead off Gibby, but the hit and run didn't work and Matthews was punched out at second, Simba to Tyson. Eddie smacked a Gibby fastball toward the warning track in center for an out. Now the guys were starting to time Gibby a bit, who didn't have much left in the tank. Chris Speier took Gibby's next offering into the seats in left field for the first run of the game. Great, I felt this was all I would need. I have a two-hitter going with eight strikeouts. While I'm picturing what next inning will look like, Gibby got Bruce Miller to fly out to right. Time for me to lock this baby down.

Bottom of the eighth, that dinger from the first game was a forgotten moment in my mind as I struck Jose Cruz out looking. I pitched around Simba because he knew me like he's my catcher and I ended up walking him. I always wondered if Schoendienst was trying to out-think me by sending another catcher up to hit, having the brilliant Tim McCarver bat for Ken Reitz. Jim Dwyer was on the bench, the .292-hitting Bake McBride was on-deck. In any case, McCarver hit into a force out at second that we couldn't double up. McBride hit for Tyson and fouled out. Two hits over eight innings and nine strikeouts. I was gonna beat Gibby again.

Wes our manager felt so confident he had me come up in the 9th inning with a runner on first. Forget insurance runs, right? Forget that I threw about 130 pitches, right? What do I care? I'm beating Bob Gibson. I grounded into a force out, but here comes Bobby to save the day again. Gibby gave it all he had, but Bonds smashed a gapper to center – I ran faster than ever before thinking, this was an easy triple – but then Jose Cruz ran it down for the out – only problem was I'm all the way between second and third. Double play. Huge mistake.

We go to the ninth and I was absolutely winded.

That sprint around second took all the energy out of my body and I had to pitch one more inning. First Red finally removed Gibby from of the game, pinch-hitting him with Jim Dwyer, a young hitter who knew the strike zone pretty well. Dwyer worked out a walk on me, only my third of the game. I turned around and saw Sosa warming up in the pen. Wes was not Charlie – if this was Charlie, it would've been my game to lose. Not Wes. We didn't have the relationship there. I started thinking, "*If Brock gets on base, I'm out of the game. That's it.*" I tried to cool my nerves against Lou, who hit pretty well in the few at-bats against me. The slow-footed Dwyer wasn't going anywhere at first. I wound up, I delivered, and Brock delivered, too, pulling a single to right, Dwyer to third.

Shit.

Here comes Wes. At this point, I was thinking, *not only no shutout for me, no complete game and possibly a loss.*

I walked off the mound and the great St. Louis crowd gave me some scattered applause for the game I pitched. In came Sosa.

First and second, nobody out. Sosa dealt to Sizemore, fly ball to center, Maddox tracked it down, threw it in. Dwyer, who's slow afoot, didn't test. I'm sitting on the edge of the bench. "*We got one out now, we can do this.*" Reggie Smith came to the plate. In the middle of Sosa's windup, *Brock takes off for second!!!* He stole safely. Second and third, one out. Wes had Sosa intentionally walk Smith. Based loaded. Of course, you know who came up to the plate.

That's right: Torre. At 33, Joe really wasn't the same player he had been even three years earlier. Regardless, smart players (as long as their skills have not completely eroded) can still get the job done. Remember, Torre was an all-star catcher up until 1970 – he still knew how to analyze a pitcher's weakness. Sosa never saw this coming. He tried to blow one by the hitter and Torre just lashed a line drive to center. Dwyer scored. The speedy Brock scored, of course.

Game over. I lost. This was the first time I ever felt like a game was taken away from me. I looked out and saw Gibby strut his strut and make that face coming out of the dugout to congratulate his buddy Torre for winning the game for him.

Again, the beat guys came around. "One of the best," I said. What else was I gonna say? They all rushed me – I was icing my sore arm while having a beer at my locker.

I was crushed. My only consolation was hearing later that the Cardinals manager said some nice things about me to the Associated Press.

"*I've never seen anybody throw better than him this season,*" Scheondienst said about me. I never heard such glossy comments in the midst of defeat. Torre chimed in.

"*Just getting up and not having to face that other guy (me) felt good,*" Torre said. Even my enemy, Gibby spoke up graciously in victory.

"*He had a great fastball,*" Bob Gibson said after the game, "*He was great.*" You wanna talk about great? After the game, Simba told the Associated Press reporters that Gibby was suffering from a painful knee injury. "*He doesn't tell people how bad his knee hurts, but you just know it does,*" Simmons said, "*It's not something you talk about. I don't even like to think how's he's hurting.*"

Let me just say, never before in competitive sports and never again, would a man compliment me with his passion and risk injury to compete against me the way Bob Gibson did in those two games. Another thing about the games? They both finished in under 2 ½ hours.

As I made my way through the tunnel, I found Wes pouring drinks for him and Bobby.

"Pitched your heart out, Rook," I heard Bobby yell out of the office. If anything, Bobby always made sure to show his immediate appreciation for my work. He was a great leader in that sense. The problem was I didn't know if his leadership would be appreciated outside of Westrum's office for much longer.

Bobby

While not having the best year to begin with, Bobby hit .261 in the first half. With Charlie out of the picture and off his back, Bobby still barely batted .250 after the all-star break, hitting .247 in August and then falling to .222 in September. As word began to leak out that the team still had yet to nail down new ownership, Bobby's performance continued to erode. Whispers around the team were that interim management would try to move Bobby. I couldn't believe what I was hearing. The club finished the season 72-90, the teams' worst record in nearly 30 years. But still, how could they trade Bobby?

He wore the pressure to perform on his face. Especially with the beat reporters. Bobby was weary of the same questions asked of him over and over. *"Why aren't your numbers higher?" "What seems to be the problem?" "Do you think you'll be here next season?"* They would make snide remarks when Bobby wasn't available to comment on a loss, a strikeout or a missed opportunity to drive in the winning run. Where last season it was nothing but accolades, now Bobby was getting queries about his inability to come through in the clutch, and audible whispers and speculation about his bad year. It didn't matter to the reporters that Barry was sitting in my locker right across the clubhouse and could hear every sarcastic remark, every snide comment, see every eye-roll. Barry didn't just listen to what the reporters said about his dad. He studied them all, observed how they acted when things weren't going Bobby's way. There were more than a few times where I would lean in to Barry, *"C'mon, let's go get a soda,"* and lead him out of the clubhouse for some fresh air. Barry would look back and witness the media's daily interrogation of his father.

September also brought the annual year-end callups, and one in particular would have a profound effect on my life, for better and for worse.

* * * * *

Almost a year to the day of Bobby's walk-off grand slam, we were back in L.A. Ronny Bryant still had not righted himself, sitting at a record of 3-13. After spotting us two runs in the first inning off a Tom Paciorek throwing error in left field, Bryant gave up three walks and a single – to be fair, there was also a passed ball and a Bruce Miller error at third to give the Dodgers a 3-2 lead. Wes had seen enough. He brought in the rookie.

Not me.

The one they called The Count.

John Montefusco was another great pitching prospect the Giants' organization had scouted, signed and developed, this one coming from the poorly manicured fields of a community college in Lincroft, New Jersey. Count wasn't even drafted – he was signed as an amateur free agent, not a highly-regarded, top pick like many of us. Knowing he wasn't given such a lofty signing bonus that guys like me and others received motivated him in addition to his innate confidence, and Count had a ton of confidence on the field. He had been at AAA Phoenix just six hours ago when he got the call to be at Dodger Stadium for the game. He was just itching for a moment like this. I was cocky, but Count…. wow. Strutting out to the mound, ready for a fight, ready for his close-up on the major league stage.

After inducing a Paciorek groundout which scored Garvey, Count proceeded to fan Steve Yeager and pitcher Doug Rau to get us out of the inning and keep us only two runs behind. When Count returned to the dugout, he was amped up.

"Fuck these guys," Count bragged, "We're gonna win this game." There was no Bobby leading the charge on this day. It was all Count, the rookie. L.A.'s starter didn't have it, either, walking our catcher Ken Rudolph, Count and then Bobby before Gary Matthews took a curveball over the left-center field wall for a grand slam to put us back in front and knocking Rau out of the game.

Count had a shaky second inning, surrendering two singles and a walk to load the bases before inducing a Ron Cey groundout to end the inning.

The following frame, Rudolph got hit with a pitch and Radar went in to run for him. Count turned to us and winked, all the confidence in the world. Couple pitches later, Count took a Charlie Hough fastball over the fence – his first major league hit, first major league home run, on the way to his first major league victory. Once inside the clubhouse, Count made his presence felt with the beat guys immediately.

"I hate the Dodgers," Count said into the mikes and tape recrorders, "I knew that guy wasn't gonna throw me a knuckleball. I was guessing fastball all the way and I hit it."

The reporters loved him instantly. The Giants had another star pitcher on the staff. In the midst of the post-game celebration,

Bobby was nowhere to be found. It felt as if we were in the midst of a transition; the badass, boogie-down Giants of Willie/Mac/Marichal and Bobby were evolving into the Young Giants of Count, Gary Matthews and Johnny D. I wasn't complaining, but this wasn't the Bay Area ballclub I signed up for. It wasn't just in San Fran where this was happening. Transition was in the air all over the game that off-season.

1974, to me, seemed like the year in baseball when the last collection of players from the *"Black & White TV"* era were changing teams for a final big-league hurrah or leaving the game altogether. During that off-season, Aaron would return to Milwaukee. Billy Williams went to Oakland chasing post-season glory. The Tigers cut Norm Cash in August and Al Kaline retired. Minnesota Twins icon Harmon Killebrew was politely released by the team. This was also pre-free agency, with the Catfish Hunter/Finley controversy in its early stages.

Bobby finished the season batting .256 with 21 homers and 71 RBIs. 1972 hadn't been much better for him and possibly worse, but now Bonds had to carry a club without McCovey and Willie leading the way. It was also the last time I saw little Barry, who was less and less a presence in the clubhouse that final month.

* * * * *

It was close to a week after the 1974 World Series had ended when the news hit the papers. I'd like to say I remember where I was when I found out the Giants traded Bonds to the Yankees on October 22nd, 1974, but the fact is I can't and the reason for that is it wasn't the shock to me that it was to everyone else. The rumors were persistent in the clubhouse for weeks. I could have been driving in the car and heard it on the radio, maybe read it a day later in the paper. News traveled a lot slower back then. Remember, there was only the Today Show on in the mornings in 1974, no real local A.M. TV news. What shocked me, if anything, was the All-Star who came to San Francisco in the deal.

In many ways, Bobby Murcer and Bobby Bonds were kindred spirits, both dragging legacies attached to their backs that they couldn't possibly uphold. What bothered me more about BB being traded was that – jeez, we traded the most talented player in the game – everyone's on the table now. Me, Barr, Kingman, Tito, Speier, Maddox – everyone has a price on their head. Maybe I was being naïve, but again, I'm only 22 at this point. Goodbye Yellow Brick Road indeed.

I wasn't wrong, either. Over the course of the next six months of 1975, Dave Kingman was sold to the Mets, on the advice of Willie Mays for $150,000. Tito Fuentes was sent to San Diego for Derrel Thomas. The contract for the retired Ronny Bryant would be shipped to St. Louis for Larry Herndon, which actually turned out to be a nice little swap. Garry Maddox was sent to Philly for Willie Montanez. Ed Goodson, a former number-one draft pick, owner of one of the sweetest swings you would ever see before his career-killing injury, was quietly delivered to the Atlanta Braves.

One of the saddest photos ever taken of Murcer exists on his 1975 *TOPPS* baseball card. Yes, the Giants' insignia and colors are airbrushed all over him, but this could not be a better metaphor describing Murcer's reaction to coming to San Fran. Bobby wrapped himself up in the legacy of Pinstripes. You see it in his face on this card. The backdrop is fascinating. Sure, he's wearing the Giants orange and black, but his spirit would always be located in the house that Ruth built. His heart was broken. I almost wonder if the *TOPPS* card designers back on the East Coast at the time were making a statement of some sort with their choice of photo and background.

This isn't just opinion, either. After the team bus stopped at the hotel in Los Angeles for the Giants' first true road trip in 1975, most of the young guys went out on the town. As I stepped off the bus, Bobby gently grabbed my arm and said, "C'mon, Johnny, let's get dinner." We enjoyed a couple of steaks, a bottle of wine and then finished up at a nearby bar for a nightcap. Bobby went into all the pressures he had to deal with following Mickey Mantle. "Mickey was the most terrific athlete I ever saw," Bobby told me that night, "And that's in the mid '60's. I never hung around him with Yogi, Whitey and the fellas. If he didn't go out and about as much as he did, he could've been the greatest player of all time."

Murcer talked about New York all night, its many attractions and many more distractions. "To Mickey's credit," Bobby continued, "As much as he went out, he always did *what he had to do* to get on that field. He was a true ballplayer." Bobby wasn't a heavy drinker at all but tonight it really hit him where he was. Nursing a whiskey, Bobby opened his heart to me. All this talk of Mickey, the Bronx and the Yankees really got to Bobby.

"John, I still can't believe I'm not in New York," Murcer said between sips of our final scotch that night, "And I'll give you everything I have in me. But I don't wanna be here. I am a New York Yankee. I'll always be a New York Yankee." And it's not even that he hated San Francisco – he got along great with the fans and reporters – everyone loved Murcer, one of the classiest men I ever met in baseball. He just never saw himself as anything but a Yankee. And what a gamer he was on the field for us. Bobby certainly held up his end of the bargain. He always hit with men on base. Turns out the deep numbers prove this as well. Murcer drove in 20 percent of his inherited runners in 1975, not only the best mark of his career, which included his three or four brilliant seasons with the Yankees, but was also the best in Baseball in '75, slightly better than Fred Lynn in his amazing rookie year, slightly better than Jim Rice, better than Reggie, Boomer Scott, Rusty Staub, Schmidt, Bull Luzinski, everyone. Murcer got the runners home.

Murcer was the Giants' lone representative at the 1975 All-Star Game and also his final appearance as a player. Ironically, it was to be Bonds' final midsummer classic as well, in his only season as a Yankee. And it was a good one for Bonds, too. Remember, the Bronx Bombers played at the home of the Mets', Shea Stadium, in '75, for the second of two seasons while The House That Ruth Built was being refurbished.

Word was that Bobby spent a lot of time with Willie Mays (who was a coach for the Mets at the time) while he played for the Yankees. Bonds ended up smashing 32 homers for the Yanks, which was quite an accomplishment in spacious Shea – no Mets player had ever hit more than 26 while calling Shea Stadium home. Funny thing was, Kingman hit 36 for the Mets at the same ballpark in '75. The best home run hitters of all time to that point in Shea Stadium came from the Giants. How's that for amazing?

Murcer had told me Steinbrenner had promised to bring him back to the Bronx at some point. I could see the desperate hope in Bobby's eyes when he spoke those words, but I had to think, with an outfield of Elliot Maddox, who was hitting about .330 at the time, Sweet Lou Pinella and Bobby Bonds, the electric ballplayer made for the grand stage of New York, the cover boy of at least four or five sports magazines that spring, I wasn't sure this would ever happen. I remember thinking at the time, *"Who's gonna trade Bobby Bonds again?"*

* * * * *

I dropped Murcer off at the hotel and stayed out just a bit longer. My elbow was bothering me all through dinner, but the crisp May evening air kept me from returning to my room. I passed a nightclub with young people in suits and gold chains lined up behind velvet ropes. The days of flower children and casual dress on Saturday Night had all but ceased to exist. I made my way back to the hotel literally thirty minutes later, but not before poking my curious head inside the club. It was the first time I had heard KC & the Sunshine Band.

We were beginning the second half of the 1970's now, my innocence whittling away, the Psychedelic Shack of my Baseball youth dismantled and boy, does my arm hurt.

Miracles

So you wanna know what it's like? Ok...

You're under the brilliant lights on a gorgeous Tuesday afternoon in Los Angeles. There's not a cloud in the sky, yet your personal overcast surrounds you. You're indoors and yet the Astrodome is 1500 miles away. There's no pregame jitters; just the most important day of your life as what's left of your baseball career depends on the immediate performance of those all around you.

The very small crowd hovers above your body and then it begins.

The main man on the chessboard is not Bobby Murcer in Center Field nor Chris Speier running down a sharp grounder over the middle off the bat of Bake McBride. It's Frank Jobe, the Dodgers' team physician, chief medicine man for your hated rival. It's late May, 1975. Jobe's not the father of modern baseball surgery at this point; he's just a doctor who operated on a crafty lefthander, the full recovery of whom has yet to be determined. The reality of the circumstances beans you with scary questions you're not ready nor in any condition to answer. Logic and proportion gets tossed to the side as the anesthesiologist prepares to send your mind to the showers.

The white knight has you talking backwards as he prepares to cut into your precious, gifted right arm. 100...99...98...in a few moments, you'll no longer be that young phenom, the wunderkind with the 100-MPH gas, the rookie badass who earned that missing gold cup on his baseball card that only you know belongs there.

Soon you'll be the oft-injured hurler...96...95...94...as you hazily speculate if you'll make it to one, your eyelids slowly close and you take an extended timeout from consciousness, into a wonderland that very possibly does not include a major league pitching mound......

* * * * *

Sometimes you ask yourself what's the greater thrill in Baseball – that moment you witness a long fly ball pass through the sky approaching the fence, or the actual touching ground on the other side? The anticipation versus the realization. Everybody digs the long ball. The fans in the stands, friends and lovers, parents and children, embracing as it leaves the field of play. You felt that way last year when you jacked one out against Larry Demery in front of the home crowd at Candlestick. You don't see many hugs after a 6-4-3 or a bloop single. There's nothing as poetic and true in the game as the 4-base hit, nothing as picturesque, either. An amazing site to behold.

Except when you're standing on the mound and you're watching your 96 MPH heater travel 400 feet into the waving arms of the St. Louis Cardinals fans in right field. You shake your head as the great Ron Fairly takes his professional trot around the bases.

This was the fourth time in your first six starts of the 1975 season you watched this episode. The year before, you were 11th in the league in Homers Per Nine – gave up only 13 dingers in 215 innings. Now it's already four in 21. To be honest, it wasn't a major red flag – you made a mistake and Fairly, one of the most underrated hitters you ever faced (guy knew the strike zone as well as any batter in the league) made the most of it. Your manager Wes Westrum paces slowly out to the mound. The score is now 6-3 in the 3rd inning– your day is done.

No one in the Giants organization this year expects the team to compete for the post-season. The Dodgers are coming off an unlikely besting of the Cincinnati Reds for the division title in '74. Odds are the two of them will fight it out between themselves once again. The ballclub's financial situation remains in disarray. The last great link to Giants powerhouse teams of the 60's was traded to the New York Yankees. The pitching staff is mostly a bunch of youngsters like yourself – the slightly older Mike Caldwell; new rookie phenom Count Montefusco and spring training surprise southpaw Pete Falcone. You and Falcone became fast friends in Phoenix over spring training. Italian food and guitar jamming are among your mutual interests. Soon "Petey" becomes your primary dinner buddy on road trips. Official media guides in February praised the fact that you won more games as a rookie Giants pitcher than anyone in 20 years and more strikeouts since "early in the century." Others said you were probably the best young righthander in the league, who *could be the Giant ace of the future.* In addition to being 11th in the league in HR/9, you tied for 7th in Hits/9 and 4th in K/9. In many ways, you're no longer seen as a luxury. You're one of the team leaders. They're depending on you. You're on the cover of the team yearbook.

And here you are in the first 10 days of May and you sit at 1-4 with a double-digit ERA.

Something's wrong – you love pitching in Busch Stadium, if there was any place you could solve your problems on the mound, it would be in St. Louis. Your manager, a former catcher, says he's pulling you from the starting rotation. He wants to see if he can identify the problem so he has you throw the eighth inning of a blowout *the very next day*. You give up a run on two hits, walking one. The opposing pitcher, John Curtis, bunts off you with an 8-0 lead in presumably their final frame, but whatever. Not a great relief outing, but nothing physically jumps out at you.

You're at a late dinner with Petey Falcone after the game when you feel it in your forearm as you dig into a plate of lasagna. You wince and your friend checks in on you.

"All right, man?" Petey asks. You shake it off and wash down the flash of pain with a sip of Budweiser.

You wake up the following morning at the Gateway Hotel, reaching for your watch on the night table and the pain by your elbow returns. It stays a little longer but a hot shower relieves it. You still need to tell someone.

Al "Hump" Wylder, your team's trainer, monitors the situation as Dr. Stan London, the Cardinals' team physician, examines you in the clubhouse before that day's game, pinching up and down your arm, coming to a quick conclusion.

"John has serious bone chips," Dr. London says. Minutes later in Westrum's office, your manager is on the phone with Jerry Donavan, your team's assistant GM, back in San Francisco.

"I shoulda known," Westrum sighs through a haggard cough, "We ain't gonna know for sure 'til we get some x-rays. You wanna send him to Rocky anyway-"

Rocky Bridges is the manager for the Phoenix Giants. That means you're goin' to the minors.

"What about Kerlan? We gonna have him clean Johnny out and have the kid good for September...no....so should I just send him home?"

That means you're having surgery. September means you're probably out for the year.

"Right-o, just let me know what ya wanna do. I still gotta get another starter in here." Westrum looks up at you with the face of a man without answers.

"I dunno, Johnny. I think you're gettin' surgery later in the week. For right now you're still with the ballclub. Just not pitchin'. Keep it between us 'til I know more."

Your best case scenario is that you're healthy and you're bad at your job, headed to AAA. You almost want the pain, and throughout the next five hours, the pain is happy to oblige.

After another loss to the Cardinals, the beat guys are looking for answers to the team's issues from Westrum, pitching coach McMahon, even Petey, who started the game. As you're packing your uniform and cleats, a San Francisco reporter that you're friendly with steps over.

"Johnny?" he asks, almost concerned, "What's goin' on with you? Wes says he's taking you out of the rotation. When's your next start?"

"Heh-heh," you laugh, a little caught off-guard with your friend in the media, "Just as soon as the pain in my arm goes away."

Sudden silence in the clubhouse. There's like five or six words that can halt the chatter in a professional locker room. Trade. Release. Firing. Retirement. Injury.

Pain.

"What did you just say?" The beat guys inch closer, almost salivating.

You let the cat-scan out of the bag. You revealed after the game that you will require surgery at the end of the week and will most likely be on the shelf for at least a month and a half. The reporters from St. Louis, San Fran, UPI and AP all express sincere sorrow for your misfortune as they nearly thank you for providing them *Around the League* notes fodder for the next few days.

On the charter flight to New York, Speier and Rader sit together scanning the prep sheet, analyzing the hitters, making remarks on how to play Kingman, as they know everything about their former teammate's hitting tendencies. Murcer stares out the window, wondering what awaits his first trip back to the only big league city he ever called home. Gary Matthews and newcomer Derrel Thomas hang out with some of the other guys in the back of the plane playing poker. Sweet Matt jumps up, slamming his cards on the fold out table, yelling, *"Take that, sucka!"* collecting everyone's chips and slappin' five to whomever wants a taste. He wins the pot by bluffing, and you barely bluffed the reporters about the severity of your injury. The pain is real now.

You reach The Sheraton East in midtown Manhattan around 1 AM. You're more tired of focusing on the near future of your career than body exhaustion. Petey sees this, tries to cheer you up, offering to take you and Dave Rader to see what's up at The Bottom Line, a popular rock club down in the Village. You want to join them but don't want to be a downer. As you shrug and decide to call it a night, three stewardesses in Eastern Airlines uniforms roll their baggage past you. One of them, a petite blond with brown eyes and hair in a bun, probably 24 or 25, also notices your slightly pained expression, and lets her colleagues slowly walk ahead as she turns to get your attention.

"Are you lost?" she asks in lieu of *"hello."* The confusion as to where the next weeks lead your life must be all over your face. You're honest with her, which appears to be something she's looking for as well.

"Kinda," you respond with a smile. Rader taps you on the shoulder, nodding his head in a joking *"case-closed"* sort of way.

"Ooo-kay," Rader mutters, as he and Petey walk through the revolving door of the hotel to grab a cab.

Her name is Janice, which you find out a few minutes later.

* * * * *

The phone in your hotel room rings about 9 AM the following morning. It's Westrum. Your manager tells you to meet him in the trainer's room at the ballpark early to have your arm examined and x-rayed. You hang up the receiver and reach for your wristwatch on the nightable but instead grab the Eastern Airlines lapel pin sitting there under the light. The smile lasts about 10 minutes until you're riding in the the cab toward Shea Stadium when you notice the big city slip away at an accelerated pace once you cross the 59th Street Bridge. You arrive not knowing whether you're still a player or just a fan.

The examination reveals bone chips that have sat in your arm for over four years, probably developed during your season at Decatur back in 1971. The doctor isn't certain that major surgery is necessary, at least not season-ending surgery.

"You're probably going to Phoenix," Westrum tells you in his office.

"Shouldn't I go on the disabled list?" you respond, fully aware that a trip to the minors is often times a one-way ticket.

"Son, it's not my decision," your manager says, his head down.

"Can I call Jerry," you ask Westrum, seeking permission to hear it directly from his boss. Your manager nods, grabbing the phone and placing it across his desk before you.

"We wanna get Halicki up here," Jerry tells you minutes later on the call, "There's a hole in the rotation now and Halicki's earned his shot."

"But can't you do that just by putting me on the disabled list," you plead.

"What's the difference? You'll be back once you're better. We're not gonna leave you there." *But what if I'm not better*, you're thinking to yourself, "*And what if they leave me there? What If I go and my arm gets worse and then I need to under the knife anyway? Then I'm an injured minor-league pitcher.*"

"Jerry, look, you know this will affect my service time and my pension if something really, really bad happens."

Silence on the phone.

"Please?"

A sigh from Jerry.

"Let me talk to Mr. Stoneham. We have to think of the team first, and we have to know that surgery is the only option. Let me think about it."

Once you're suited up, you walk onto the field during batting practice and try to get your mind off everything by grabbing your former teammate Mikey Phillips, who was purchased by the Mets off the Giants roster a week earlier. He's as clueless about New York City as you are, but the team is making him feel very welcome. Dave Kingman stops by to chat a bit. He heard about your troubles in the paper and asks if you're ok. You nod and shrug, appreciate his thoughts and make your way back to the dugout as fans dressed in assorted blue and orange pour into the seats surrounding the field.

"Hey Johnny?" Murcer calls out as he steps down into the dugout, "See that woman over there? She wants to meet you." Bobby points to the seats right behind the backstop at home plate.

"Today's not the day for autographs." Bobby shakes his head.

"She *wants* to meet you. Really clear about it, too. I would go over there and introduce yourself." You roll your eyes, mutter *"fine"* and make your way to the backstop. You turn to Bobby for a moment, asking "Which one?"

"You'll know," Bobby nods. As you approach the seats, a woman in her mid-thirties steps down toward the field. One look at her and you ask youself, *"What is someone like her doing at a baseball game?"* Right away it's clear she comes from money, lots of money, or at least acquired it somewhere down the line and learned the body language. Golden brown hair, large-collared, white blouse and blue Capri pants with a white belt hanging from the side. She looks like a slightly older version of that model Cheryl Tiegs.

"Hello," she smirks.

"Hi, I'm Johnny," you reply.

"I know," she shoots back coyly, "I'm Marlene. Are you pitching today?" In some way, that's a shot to the gut, but you know she's not privy to your current circumstances.

"No, my turn is next Saturday back in San Fran," you fib, only because she doesn't need to know the details. Not yet, anyway.

"That's too bad," she flirt-frowns, "I was hoping to see you in action tonight." This is generally a polite statement, but you know a pitch when you see one.

"We'll be here again in September. Maybe you can come back and see us play?" Marlene smiles and nods slowly.

"Maybe. What are your dinner plans after the game? Have you ever been to Le Cirque?"

"Sure," I said, "Couple of the guys here like it a lot." You've *never* heard of Le Cirque, but you're guessing it's not Jack in the Box. The refined cadence of Marlene's voice tells you she dines at places like Le Cirque all the time.

"Would you like to go for a late dinner?" she asks. A father wearing a faded Mets cap with his young two sons sits in their box seats beside Marlene, listening to this entire exchange. You look over and his eyes revert to his scorecard, with a knowing little grin on his face.

"Sure," you respond, slightly embarrassed, "Where is it?"

"I think it's on 65th street in the Mayfair Hotel. I'll drive us over." You agree, end the conversation pleasantly and as you leave, you throw a quick glance to the father, with a smile that lets him in on the strangeness of Marlene's offer.

"I guess I got dinner plans," you tell Bobby once you reach the dugout, who's standing by the bat rack awaiting the story.

"Oh, she's got plans, all right," Murcer laughs, as you look over toward Marlene one last time before the lineups are announced over the loudspeaker. She's looking back.

After the game, once you've changed out of your uniform, you stroll over to Murcer, who's holding court with the New York beat guys he's known for years.

"Bobby, which ballpark do you like better, Candlestick or Shea?" one of them asks.

"Yankee Stadium," Murcer responds dryly, and the group erupts into laughter, writing feverishly. "That's enough for tonight guys, we'll see ya in the morning." Another writer calls out to you, "Hey Johnny, is it true the Giants are sending you to AAA-"

"I said that's enough," Bobby repeats sternly, protecting you, throwing his arm around you, walking you out of the clubhouse toward the players' parking lot.

"Is it true?" he asks you softly, once we're outside.

"I dunno," you shrug, "Jerry said they'll get back to me." Moments later, the biggest car you've ever seen pulls up. Silver, Cadillac limousine. The power window slides down. Standing a few feet away, you turn to Bobby.

"Is she a pro?" Bobby laughs.

"No, she's not a pro," Murcer said with a hint of nostalgia in his voice, "It's just New York." You walk over to the car and Marlene leans to see your face.

"You ready?" she asks with as much detached eagerness as possible.

You're actually nervous, as you step into the car.

"Maybe," you chuckle, as the telephone in the side panel catches you by surprise, alongside the fine crystal and champagne laying in ice beside the other door.

"Where to?" the driver asks Marlene from the front seat.

"Le Cirque, Ron," Marlene responds as she stares into your eyes.

"I'm hungry," you say, at an absolute loss for words.

"It's 11:15," Ron replies, obviously aware of the restaurant's hours.

"Hmmmm," Marlene purrs, and you see a notion cross her face, and her eyes sparkle.

"Have you ever been to the Hamptons?" she asks. Ron knows what that means, raising the privacy partition as the big car slowly drives away.

* * * * *

Your eyes open about nine hours later staring at a bizarre work of art on the bedroom wall you find out later is a privately commissioned Andy Warhol piece. The décor of the sparse, spacious bedroom matches the modernist design of what you've seen from the rest of the house. You throw your clothes on and step outside onto the balcony overlooking the beach. The sun struggles to emerge from behind the clouds. Rays of shine fight through the morning mist. The waves insist you're a million miles from your problems. Marlene joins you out there, offering a mug of coffee.

"Good morning," she says softly. You put your arm around her and she nuzzles against you for a moment. No words for these next few minutes, just some much-needed peace and quiet.

"I assume you have to get back," Marlene sighs and you know the encounter is ending.

"We have another game today," you nod as you take your final sip.

"If it doesn't rain. There's a car for you downstairs." You kiss Marlene on the forehead and release her back to someone else's world and make your way through the balcony into the bedroom, down the cast iron spiral staircase to the kitchen, past the tulip table in the breakfast area, the black leather modular sofa and ball chairs in the great room, out the front door to the idling Town Car in the circular drive.

"I hope your arm is ok," Marlene says as you leave her. You step into the car, but not before getting one last glimpse of this graceful, mystery woman.

"Thanks," you say and you mean it. Marlene smiles widely and turns away, closing the front door, as well as the chapter on your involvement with this person. You hear the oncoming raindrops tapping against the car and the crackle of moving tires along the pebbled driveway. You are being transported from this fantasy back toward the continued shitstorm that awaits you in Flushing.

Marlene was right. Your game gets rained out. You stay in the clubhouse a little while longer waiting for the call from Jerry, a message from your manager about next steps in his awful process and you hear nothing, nothing but rumors about a flight to Phoenix. You have thoughts about catching an authentic Italian meal in Brooklyn with Petey, but you just head back to the hotel. Where the night before you were the best of Johnny in a 25-room mansion on the tony South Shore of Long Island; tonight it's a half-eaten cheeseburger and soda at 11 PM watching The Best of Groucho on the small TV, your throbbing elbow slumped in an ice bucket, your future the only thing on the rocks at the moment.

* * * * *

Two days later, Friday May 16th, back in California, you finally wake up in your own bed after the eight-day road trip that felt like forever.

Your arm does *not*.

Your right elbow is locked, like *locked* locked. No mobility. Maybe you slept on it wrong? After a few moments, you know it's not that. You wiggle your fingers, they're fine. Elbow still locked. After waving it slightly about, your right arm now sits in a complete, unmovable right angle.

You know you've got a problem.

You get to Candlestick Park, walk swiftly into the clubhouse. One of the beat reporters tries to get your attention.

"Johnny, I thought you were sent down," but you ignore him and grab Ozzie Virgil, the friendly coach, at his locker.

"Something's wrong, Oz," you tell him. He senses your deep concern.

"Hey Johnny?" he reassures you, rubbing your shoulder, "Let's go throw in the outfield. Let's go play catch together." Oz walks you out of the clubhouse, through the tunnel and onto the field from the dugout. You both jog toward the warning track. You grip the baseball but you're afraid to throw it. You take your time as Oz waits patiently. It's like you're stalling.

"Johnny, don't worry," he says quietly, "Maybe it's muscle tightening. Let's work it out. Just toss it over."

You're always the optimist; you're always the bright, smiling Johnny D. That's what has you wrapped with anxiety. It's not paranoia. You just know what awaits you.

Finally, you toss the baseball, a dribbler 15 feet awkwardly to Ozzie's left side. That was supposed to be a soft liner. From a big-league pitcher.

Your elbow locks. You cry out in pain and profanity. Oz walks over quickly.

"Can't lift it," you say a couple times, worried sick. "Just can't lift it."

"Ok ok ok, Johnny," Oz replies calmly, "Let's get you back inside."

Oz gently leads you to the dugout and as you step down toward the tunnel, you turn back one more time, stealing a glance at the pitching mound. You know why, but you're not ready to admit the reason to yourself. Sure, once inside the clubhouse, the ice that Hump Wylder, your team's trainer, applies to your arm in addition to some basic massage therapy alleviates the momentary pain, but the reason throbs in your head. Especially as Dr. Campbell, the ballclub's specialist who hurries over from his office, checks out your elbow, considers the initial symptoms, then turns to the trainer as if you're not even there and says the next-step phrase a pitcher never wants to hear.

"We need to take x-rays, Hump."

As you drive over to Dr. Campbell's office at Stanford University Medical Center, all the soothing sounds of country rock from the car radio can't keep your nerves in check. You just keep thinking, *"This is bad. This is bad. This is bad."* You hate it when your instincts know what they're talking about. X-rays. Tests. Tests. X-rays. Never a good thing when the doctor swallows before delivering the news in his office.

Multiple bone chips in the back of your elbow, as everyone expected.

The bone on the ulna (the "funny bone") cracked in half.

Your Ulnar Collateral Ligament – your UCL - snapped at the elbow. *Snapped*. Dr. Campbell immediately reaches for the phone.

"We have one of our guys here that needs your help," he states into his office speaker during an impromptu conference call with two other specialists.

"Send him down," replies one of the men on the other side.

"Thanks, Frank," Dr. Campbell says as he hangs up, turning to you like a father reluctantly sending his son off to war.

"That was Dr. Frank Jobe. He's in Los Angeles. He's the surgeon who's working on Tommy John."

"Oh, God, is it that bad," you gulp.

"Well, I spoke to Jerry earlier," Dr. Campbell replies, "You're going on the disabled list. They're not sending you down." You're way past that point now. That's just baseball politics, in your mind. You just want answers about your arm.

"How bad?" you ask again.

"We don't know," Dr. Campbell replies.

He knows.

So do you.

*****

One of the lonelier cab rides of your life. You're uncomfortable and distracted and you're not even driving. The pinky and ring finger on your right hand are tucked into your palm. The nerve has expanded almost 1/3 more than its normal size. You're closer than you realize to being crippled. Even your thoughts about your favorite bands go negative. You hear a new song from a legendary rock group on the cab radio, a sweet ballad, very trendy for the time period. You think it's sad that this amazing band, who authored so many hard-charging, fantastic tunes during your high school years, is now throwing this soft slop at the pop charts. You wonder what happened to their fastball.

You reach Dr. Jobe's office. By yourself. No one is around to help you through this. The team didn't send anyone with you. Your parents are still in San Diego. Why didn't you tell Mom? Because this shit is going so fast, you're 23 and not thinking straight. Mom should be here with you. Someone should be here with you.

Dr. Jobe takes additional x-rays, additional tests. Soon you're standing in another surgeon's office, with two men in lab coats who wish they could smile at you, but don't want to give the impression that there's an easy way out of this. Dr. Kerlan is the other physician in the room. You both recall he was the doctor who examined you at your draft induction five years earlier. His inviting smile tries and fails to reassure you that everything will be fine. Dr. Kerlan looks down at the x-rays, handing them to Dr. Jobe before speaking. He's buying time, as people do when seeking just the right manner to deliver devastating news. Enough with the damn pauses, you yell in your mind.

You say the words "How bad is it," yet again, just to get the man to open his mouth.

"Have a seat, John," Dr. Jobe says. Not Johnny. Not Johnny D.

John.

Shit.

"This is a new procedure," Dr. Kerlan says, "We don't know if it's gonna fix you."

You're numb.

"At this stage, we're not sure if you need *full* UCL repair surgery," Dr. Jobe says next, "But since the ligament appears to be intact, we might have to staple it to your elbow and you'll probably lose about five degrees range of motion."

"Do you have a job now?" Dr. Kerlan interjects, very concerned about your answer. *What an odd question to ask,* you think to yourself.

"Yeah," you reply earnestly, snapping back for a moment, fighting the inevitability of this conversation's direction as best you can, "Starting pitcher for the San Francisco Giants."

"No, John," Dr. Jobe interjects, "That's not what he means." Dr. Kerlan repeats himself.

"Do you have a job? There's only a 40% chance you'll ever throw a baseball again."

Dr. Jobe and Dr. Kerlan detail the nuances of the surgery. You don't hear a damn thing for five minutes.

"You may never play baseball again" is the only phrase playing in your mind right now on a somber loop.

All the joy within you dies, and you start to cry.

* * * * *

Two days later, you're driving over to Centinela Hospital in Inglewood, a suburb of Los Angeles. *"It all ends here,"* you think, *"All that work, the high school years in bed by nine, missing out on the surf parties and bonfires, the dedication, years of rooming houses in Great Falls, Montana, riding through parts of Illinois on surplus Greyhound buses, seemingly endless nights touring towns of the Pacific Coast League. Why would the Baseball gods give you such a rich taste of the dream saturated with life's great flavor, then grab the plate from your hands, as if to say, 'You've had enough?'"* The nurse at reception receives your papers with a blank expression. Last month, you were digging into a juicy ribeye at a five-star steakhouse in Los Angeles, laughing and telling stories with Murcer. Soon you're checked in, tucked in, fiddling with the adjustable mattress, watching Mike Douglas on the smallish TV in the corner of the room, eating jello. You begin compiling a list of promising pitchers recently felled by injury. Gary Gentry. Chuck Seelbach. Balor Moore. Gentry – the Mets chose to keep him over Nolan Ryan. Chuck Seelbach was drafted before you in the first round by the Tigers in 1970, had an amazing year out of the pen in '72. Guys who were supposed to be gamers at this stage of their career, barely hanging on at the fringes of the league, if not out of the game entirely. You remember Jim Maloney at the end of his injured line with the Giants organization in Phoenix few years back at age 31 and he had Hall of Fame stuff. Joining this rotation of "what could've been" goes through your mind as you spend the night in the hospital before the surgery.

The following morning, you slowly drift into the operating room on a gurney. The valium helps your anxiety, though now you're just sort of this passive observer to the death of your youth more than cool with what's happening. The starting lineup enters the arena. Three nurses.

The anesthesiologist. Dr. Kerlan. Finally, Dr. Jobe. In some way, you're impressed with the collection of top-shelf medical talent here to put you back together. It's like an All-Star Game for doctors and you're Baseball's version of Steve Austin, a man barely able to throw 10 feet. They have the technology, only you may never be better than you were before.

* * * * *

As you awaken, for an instant you're relieved that this was the ugliest, most vivid dream you've ever experienced. Your mind is still cloudy, but at least you'll be driving to the ball park shortly, rocking the Led Zeppelin as you buzz across the Golden Gate Bridge. Facing Andy Messersmith, Randy Jones, Jack Billingham, head-to-head against some other team's ace. Then you try to wipe sleep sand from your eyes and find that your arm is wrapped to your chest. Then you remember.

You're on the disabled list.

Your right hand is wrapped under your left armpit by a slew of ace bandages. Bags of ice sit on your chest to cool down your heartbeat due to the stress of the operation. Terrible body chills. Nurses swaddling you in blankets. Everything iced down. Soon Dr.

Jobe enters the room to check on you. He makes a joke about tying you up to keep you from beating his Dodgers, but you're not in the mood for levity, good-natured as it was.

"How'd it go?" you ask him wearily. Dr. Jobe gives you the play-by-play.

They had to re-tunnel the nerve from the funny bone, he says. Drilled a hole in the elbow, re-attached the nerve and the bone grafted shut so it would slide. The ligament was cleaned and re-attached to the ulna-elbow area, resulting in the five degree range of motion loss he mentioned in his office earlier. Dr. Jobe goes on and on, as your head turns to gaze out the window and his words melt into verbal white noise.

You spend close to a week in that cold, bland hospital room. Private. Isolated. Going through this alone. The nurses took good care of you. Fed you dinners, cut up your steak because you couldn't move your arm. Brought you wine. Mom and Dad still have no idea what you're going through. You need to tell them.

* * * * *

You return to see Dr. Campbell in San Francisco, who is extremely impressed with Dr. Jobe's work and signs off on your regiment. In your mind, you're thinking, *"How will you come back from this?"* You're instructed to remain with club and rehab your elbow at the ballpark. This isn't 1988. There will be no rehab starts at Phoenix. Everything will be done at the team level. You stay with the ballclub during homestands, you're in uniform, but you're distracting your mind, almost preparing for the future with that fancy offseason job you have with Bank of America making $45K a year handling airline accounts for the company's credit card division that will soon be renamed VISA. The team is actually a couple games over .500. The pitching staff is relatively stable. Count Montefusco is the new wunderkind, already considered a Cy Young candidate. Your friends on the ballclub aren't treating you like a guest, but you sure feel like one. You start believing the most depressing part about getting injured is not that you let your teammates down, but that they don't need you anymore. This is where the doubt starts kicking optimism's ass.

The ballclub goes on a 12-game road trip and leaves you behind. B of A asks you to go visit the Pacific Southwest Airlines Headquarters down in San Diego, but you really use this work trip as an excuse to do what you should have done right after surgery.

You go home.

Mom's waiting for you on the front porch as you drive up with your brother Fred. She doesn't ask questions, doesn't hug you because she knows your arm is a mess, simply smiles as she reaches up for your head and gives you a kiss on your cheek, her expression a mix of affection, reassurance and determination to make her son whole again. You appreciate her love, half-hug her hello then excuse yourself to go inside and lie down because it's late, you're tired and you're still not certain you're ever going to see another inning on a major league mound.

As you face the ceiling that night, lying in the bed of your childhood, you receive a visitor. The ghost of brilliance past stops by, spends awhile by your side, calls attention to the many trophies on your shelf, the important baseballs on your teenage desk in the corner of the room, reminds you of your ability, your gift, comforts you then leaves you with this message. *"Baseball isn't your pastime. Working for Bank of America – that's your pastime. Baseball is your life. 20 wins, 20 losses, 200 K's, 200 walks, Cy Young, Cy Never, none of that matters. You're not done yet, Johnny. Baseball is what you were meant to do. Your journey back to the game begins now. Take heed in Dr. Jobe's words. Have faith in his direction. Everything will be ok."*

You rise in the morning to Mom's hearty sausage and eggs, and as she catches you up on family gossip and the latest news about the neighbor's kids, you hear the words, *"You're not done yet."* Later that day, at a business lunch with executives from PSA as the VP of marketing breaks down the promotional needs of the airline, you're saying to yourself, *"You're not done yet."* Couple nights later, as you're out for a beer with Fred and his buddies reminiscing about the quirks of girlfriends from seven years earlier, you sip your Coors while whispering in your mind, *"You're not done yet."* In two weeks time, as you're ready to leave for the airport back to San Francisco, Mom kisses the same spot on your cheek, glowing with pride because she still has that maternal fastball that can make everything all right for her grown son and you step into the car confident with the knowledge that Stage One of your rehab is now complete.

* * * * *

You arrive to an empty ballpark. Your teammates are in Atlanta splitting a four-game series, living their lives. You step out onto the field to resume yours. You remember what Dr. Jobe said.

"One day, you will have to pop the adhesions in your elbow and that is going to make it feel like you hurt yourself again. In the meantime, I suggest you throw the ball against the wall. *Do not play catch with anyone."*

Even away three weeks, you missed the ballpark smell of residual hot dog smoke and stale beer. After taking in the vacant, silent view, you run. You run and you run and you run and you run. Up and down the first base line, across the infield, foul pole to foul pole. Back and forth that warning track. You run. You prepare your body for the fight of its life and your mind takes command of the mission. When your body feels it's done, your mind shakes the head. *"Nope. Keep going."* And you run some more. This is how you're told to start every day for the rest of the summer.

You take a racquetball everywhere you go. Squeeze the two fingers you use to pitch and squeeze that racquetball completely, almost folding it in half. You wince slightly the first time. Gonna hurt for awhile. Hand squeezers, too. It all starts in the hand, up the wrist, through the forearm toward its destination, the elbow. *Do not lift weights.* Pretty soon, by yourself, you start playing catch with the bullpen wall using a tennis ball.

* * * * *

Ten days later, the Dodgers come to town. Walking around the cage during batting practice, your eyes meet Tommy John's across the field. He nods, walks over and you both meet in the middle of the diamond. You swap Frank Jobe stories, recall the good doctor's corny jokes to keep you at ease, his pleasant demeanor.

"How's it going for you?" Tommy asks. He's surprised to learn you're already throwing. He took longer to heal than you. He had a big knot where his elbow was, a knot more than 1 ½ times raised above normal. They had to take the entire ligament out and replace it with a leg ligament and re-attach it to the elbow. You still had your ligament – big difference, but you both share the same journey.

Through every cool morning in empty Candlestick Park that June and July, you're tossing a tennis ball by yourself against the bullpen wall. Soft toss after soft toss. The tedium tries to beat the process, but you believe in Dr. Jobe, and you work through it. July becomes August and that furry, yellow Wilson becomes an official major league hardball. You know every bounce, every nook, every crevice in that wall like Carl Yastrzemski knows every carom off the Green Monster in Fenway. Soon the tosses become throws and your frowns become grins of confidence. You look down at your elbow and know it's time. You run to the clubhouse and call your medicine man.

"Feeling pretty good," you tell Dr. Jobe, "Think it's time to pop 'em."

"When you pop the adhesions, you're gonna see little pustules come up in your scar. And then that's gonna tell us that you popped your adhesions loose, the internal stichings on the collateral ligament where we wrapped the elbow."

Couple days later, all alone, right there in the bullpen, you pop the adhesions. Your screams of pain echo throughout the barren stands, and when it finally goes mute, you look up at the auburn, empty seats and you want to hear cheers. You step off 60 feet from the wall. You pick up the baseball and make the most important pitch of your career, the invisible crowd roars with encouragement in your mind like a child in the backyard pretending it's Game Seven as you whip that damn ball against the bullpen wall, grunting through your delivery. It makes a crackling sound that reverberates throughout the park. It's the most exhilarating pain you ever felt. You see the result of your work and run to the clubhouse.

"Hey Hump?" you call over to your trainer with a beckon, "Come check this out."

"You take care of business?" Hump asks, with some ice and an ace bandage at the ready.

"Just c'mon," you wave excitedly as you leave the clubhouse.

You jog over to the bullpen wall like a proud son presenting gold-star schoolwork to his father as Hump walks slowly behind. Hump approaches the wall and touches the crack in the concrete, the crack you made with your broken pitching arm, then offers you a sly grin.

You found The Heater right where it was all along.

* * * * *

A week later, September 15th, you're driving to the ballpark. Today might be the day. The song from that washed up band you love so much comes on the radio. You hear it differently now. You identify with them now. You both had to move heaven and earth to find your way back. The cool, detached DJ says the band is Jefferson Starship, *"but to me they'll always be The Airplane."* You know that life happens. Jefferson Airplane went through their own reconstructive surgery, having to replace musical tendons and arteries in their group. They're not rocking out psychedelic tunes but using mellifluous curveballs and sliders to be relevant again. They fought through their troubles and by revamping their sound they returned to the top ten of the music charts for the first time in eight years. Their fastball is long gone, but they're still winning fans over. The ballad is like the knuckleball of rock n roll.

They'll always be The Airplane to you, too, but now you know their voyage.

You're in the top of the fifth inning. There's less than 1000 fans in the park. The Braves lead 5-0 and looking to blow this one out.

Charlie Williams just intentionally walked Dave May to load the bases and the opposing pitcher Jamie Easterly steps to the plate. An error at second brings in another run. Dusty Baker smacks a double to left-center, plating Vic Correll and Dave May. Wes Westrum needs to stop the blood-gushing as the score is now 8-0. Your pitching coach Don McMahon sends the sign to Ozzie Virgil to get another right-hander up in the pen. Fast. You hear the loveliest request in the past four months.

"Hey Johnny?" Ozzie calls over to you with a laugh, "Wanna play catch?" You wanna burst with glee.

"Nope," you shake your head, stepping off the bullpen bench in right field, toeing the rubber as you let that fastball loose.

Two batters later, you see Westrum walk to the mound. He taps his right arm and calls for the first day of the rest of your career.

Your journey is complete as the PA announcer tells the fans you're back.

Your walk across the first base line is slow and deliberate. You want to savor the moment, as it took every fiber of your being to make it through this time in your life. Sure, there's only 900 people in the stands, but you would do this in front of one person and you did for four months.

The ghost of brilliance past only promised you the strength to work through the process of reliving the dream of doing the thing you were always meant to do.

Sometimes faith in yourself may be the difference between triumphantly walking back under the lights before a crowd of thousands, just like that September afternoon in 1975, or taking yourself out of the game and calling it a day.

If only you believe like I believe.

Mahogany

Confidence.

That's it. That's what gets a talented, major-league pitcher through nine innings. It's the fuel for the engine and the fuel for your mind to pitch successfully in the bigs. When you hit 100 on the gun, there's no time for doubts. I loved that feeling of airing it out, blowing it by Mike Schmidt or Jimmy Wynn, especially those players who possessed a keen eye to lay off the junk and work the count if they couldn't capitalize on a mistake. Feel the same way about driving. Nothing like goin' fast. Open-road, blazing past the other cars and trucks on the highway. No room for questioning anything or hearing the doubts of others.

The last thing I needed coming into the 1976 season was a lack of confidence. After the previous summer's surgery, I couldn't completely straighten my arm when pitching, which hindered my control. Had to learn a few adjustments, especially making my crooked arm throw 96 MPH. I'd start my release at the edge of the corner of the plate and the pitch would be six inches off the strike zone - *ball!* I had to learn how to start the release at the middle of the plate or the right to throw a strike - I could still bring some gas, but it was going all over the place. Part of the healing process includes the mindset that you still are the player you once were. Confidence.

Spring training was interrupted by another labor dispute between players (still represented by Marvin Miller) and owners. This time, the issue was free agency. The players wanted a new labor contract but the ballclubs were busy contesting Peter Seitz' ruling of the Messersmith-McNally arbitration case which gave players the right to put themselves up at auction to the highest bidder when their contracts ran out. The owners engaged in a *"lock out"* of the players that disrupted spring training in 1976. Count Montefusco and I basically worked out in San Fran while we waited for Marvin and the owners to come to terms. Count was pissed because, as Rookie of the Year for 1975, he was due a hefty raise. He didn't keep quiet about it, either, especially when the reporters came calling.

"If it wasn't for him (Messersmith), *we'd all be in spring training now, and baseball wouldn't be getting all this bad publicity,"* Count said to a UPI reporter, *"I'll tell you this. We need those camps open to get ready and play baseball."* Count would eventually receive a big raise from the Giants – the largest salary ever awarded to a second-year player. He wanted to get his money sooner rather than later. We sat around for a good month waiting for this issue to resolve itself.

It seemed to happen overnight. Where we were reading headlines on March 17th like, *"No Vote Jeopardizes Baseball Season,"* and *"Grave Doubts 1976 Baseball Season Opens on Schedule,"* I woke up the next morning to a phone call.

"They made a deal. Get down here. Now."

Baseball commissioner Bowie Kuhn put his foot down and demanded owners open spring training and get the season going.

Marvin Miller ultimately secured a player's right to test free agency when his contract expired, which would aid many financially strong ballclubs the following October and make many players much wealthier. For me, for Count and the rest of the Giants, it meant time to go back to work.

We were directed to report to Casa Grande for Spring Training. We had one day to get to Arizona. Now we could've easily flown from San Fran to Phoenix. That's how the players and coaches usually arrived for pitchers and catchers – there's a van that picks you up at the airport and onto the training facility. Count and I, however, felt something bold was in order.

We weren't just taking our cars. We decided to engage in a pitcher's duel – with our Porsches.

* * * * *

Count Montefusco had a 1975 Targa. Sleek, burgundy coupe, two-seater, half-convertible, 164 cubic rear engine, 2.7 liter, rear-wheel steering, Pirelli tires, 143 horsepower, could go from zero to sixty inside of five seconds. Kind of car you would expect the most recent MLB Rookie of the Year to own. Especially one with as much confidence as John. Count loved a challenge. He was the guy who would tell the hitter what he was gonna throw before his windup, then blow it right by him. John made his presence felt since his debut at Dodger Stadium late in '74. From that point, the Giants knew Montefusco would be at the front of the rotation.

I picked up my Porsche 911 Carrera after the 1973 season. An amazing machine, stick-shift, six-cylinder, twin-valve induction engine. No radiator. Didn't need one. Porsche has a protective reservoir, shielding the engine from frying, so when you burn oil it starts injecting new fluid, because they are air-cooled – not refrigerated by anti-freeze or water. My confidence car of choice.

There was also the issue about where the Giants would be calling home for the '76 season. Our owner Horace Stoneham was very close to selling the club to an investment group led by Labatt, the largest brewer in Canada, and moving the ballclub to Toronto. The money was in the bank – they verified funds and everything. There was talk that a Major League franchise would be in Toronto for 1977 regardless of how this played out. With all the chatter about moving the Giants to another city, the organization had sparsely prepared anything in terms of promotion. The media books were barely thrown together. There were also whispers about well-heeled investors in Florida. Where were we going?

Most of this was settled when local millionaire Bob Lurie bought the ballclub from Stoneham and promised to keep the franchise in San Francisco. Word soon circulated that former Giant manager Bill Rigney once again was going to be our skipper. National League President Chub Feeney was very close to Rigney (as was new owner Lurie) and with the Giants going through serious financial issues at the time, strongly suggested Bill to take over for the dismissed Wes Westrum. Wes had to be one of the nicest men in the league, but we were a pretty young ballclub and he was the ultimate old-school guy.

He couldn't control us. Had run-ins with most of the staff, especially Jim Barr. JB, a really talented and smart pitcher, liked to call his own game. Westrum, a former catcher, insisted that everything come from the dugout. The two of them blew up at each other a number of times, and Barr wasn't the only player, either. Baseball wasn't quite at the point where young managers like Joe Torre or Tony LaRussa had innovative thoughts about massaging a roster of competitive, twenty-something athletes. A move needed to be made.

Count and I lived near each other in Foster City, about 22 miles outside of San Francisco. When a few of the guys on the team heard we were driving to spring training, they asked to join. Randy Moffitt wanted to come – so did Halicki, another starting pitcher on the club who hung out with us. Just by checking out Ed's baseball cards, with his tall frame and long, blond hair, you would think he was one of the Southern California boys. Halicki was from Kearny, NJ. With Count born and raised on the Jersey shore, they became close quickly. Being something of a newlywed, the road trip would give "Hoho" a chance to spend some guy time with Count. They drove together.

I was very close to Randy. We also lived near one another, we knew each other's families – went to many barbecues at the Moffitt house. His sister is Billy Jean King – when she wasn't traveling the world as the ambassador to professional tennis, we'd see her sometimes at family gatherings. Our parents would sit together when we played at Dodgers Stadium. Our Dads were close.

I picked up Moffitt at his place. Randy's wife came out to see us off. I threw his bag in the trunk and handed him the keys for the long journey. Count and Ed had followed us to Moff's house as we mapped out the race. Moff and I shared a quick laugh watching the six-foot-seven Halicki trying to pack himself into Count's Porsche.

"How's that big son of a bitch gonna get himself in?" Moff laughed, scratching his head as he opened the driver's side door to my car. We had to report by 7 AM in Casa Grande or else we would be officially late. There was a sense of urgency, but also pushing the limits, the adrenaline rush of crossing the finish line our way. Only bragging rights were at stake, but when you're in your mid-twenties, sometimes that's all the currency in the world. We started our engines with 12 hours to get to Arizona and sakes alive, we had ourselves a convoy.

* * * * *

Our course took us from Foster City onto Interstate 101 to The 5. Figured going late we'd see less traffic and of course, less CHIPS. Most likely not running into Ponch and Jon at this hour. The idea was for Moff and me to split the driving so we could each catch some shut-eye, but we were both too pumped to sleep much. Moff was trying to recapture the glory of 1973, where he pitched to a 2.42 ERA. You rarely see more than a handful of 3 WAR relievers every year, it was a good season for him. He had two relatively mediocre seasons since then and with the depth of our pen as well as our minor-league system, you were always looking over your shoulder. Gary Lavelle gave us a nice rookie season, ERA under 3, but was great in the 9th inning and especially against left-handed hitters. Dave Heaverlo was another rookie with amazing stuff who showed he could be a tremendous 8th inning guy, with a 0.50 ERA in 19 games right before the 9th. You also couldn't count out Charlie Williams, who threw with excellent movement on his ball. None of this includes rookie Greg Minton breathing down everyone's neck, who had a solid season at AAA Phoenix as a swingman, or Bob Knepper, who was just about ready to take a spot in the starting rotation.

It was a fun ride. Lots of laughs, great tunes. We wore out my Bachman-Turner Overdrive and Doobie Brothers 8-tracks – this was well before Michael McDonald became an ironic punch line and snide remarks about Bachman-Turner-Overplayed. We would flick on the radio for a break and through the sounds of religious programming and random Top 40 hits, we'd come across a particular song I just didn't like. Not that it wasn't a beautiful melody, it's a classic, just that if you ever wanted a thought-provoking tune to ruin a good time vibe it was this one. A sweet, gentle tempo, leading into an inspiring, orchestral sound, though ultimately rather melancholy. Last thing I wanted to wanna hear. I shut it off immediately.

As we cruised down The Five, we eventually had to stop and grab a bite. Of course, 1976 wasn't the consumer smorgasbord that you find on road trips almost anywhere in America today. Obviously you had McDonalds and Burger King, Carl Jr's, Hardees, Bob's Big Boy in Southern California, but for me none of them compared to the best burger on the West Coast: The Jumbo Jack. Sure it was Jack in the Box's answer to the Big Mac, but ohhh, that mayo-onion sauce was so much sweeter than the "*Special Sauce*" found on McDonald's premiere sandwich.

We hit Jack in the Box, grabbed a few burgers, then stopped at a Union Oil 76. As I gassed up, I stared at the logo. I knew that 1976 would be a pivotal year in my life. Staring at the gas station sign was almost as bad as hearing that song on the radio. Didn't need any more reminders that the season may not work out. That's the thing with standing still in time; when you're not in motion, you start thinking. Just like pitching. Don't think. You've gotten to this level as much for your ability as for your instincts. Your ability gets you here. Your instincts keep you in the game.

I filled the tank, quickly replacing the gas cap and jumped in the driver's seat. I threw on an eight-track of BTO and we were back to the race.

*　*　*　*　*

We would gun it to well over 90 MPH for extended periods as we made our way down The Five. I was behind the wheel now making sure no one caught us, not Count, certainly not the highway cops, as well as insuring we didn't smack into the 18-wheelers we would occasionally come across. As Randy slept in the shotgun seat, I switched to the radio. The standards of the day came on – *"Sister Golden Hair"* a couple times, some Stevie Wonder, *"Kung Fu Fighting."* Of course, that song I didn't want to hear chased me across the dial over the next two hours. I couldn't escape it. I switched the station every time. It had to be the most overplayed tune that month, as if some cosmic force insisted I listen to its lyrics. I wasn't in the mood for that message. Had so many things on my mind. The new manager – new pitching coach, Buck Rodgers. Another song that haunted the ride was the latest Paul Simon hit.

Made me count in my head 50 ways I could leave the Giants. Trade? Waivers? Outright release? Purchase? I changed the station before I got to 10. I felt there were some in the organization who didn't want me there in 1976 and as any observer of corporate psychology could tell you, new management loves cleaning house. I felt I had a great rapport with the fans there, the media, too. I always believed my popularity (as well as my relationship with the recently replaced Mayor Alioto, a distant relative) is what kept me in San Fran. Granted, with my arm injury, I thought management wanted to give it one more year and see how things played out. I really needed these 12 hours to clear my head properly before suiting up in Casa Grande.

As I fought off the urge to really ponder my issues, Count and Ho-Ho beeped the horn beside me as we merged onto I-10 near San Bernardino, gave me the one-finger salute and flew right past us.

The four of us played cat and mouse for the next few hours, swapped driving, another Jack in the Box stop, jumping lanes, gunning it up off-ramps, trying to out-duel one another. It was reckless and exhilarating as we crossed into Arizona, neither of us letting up.

Still had a few hours to go. Moff woke up and we started talking about the team, what we would experience when we got to Casa Grande. We talked about how much we would miss Petey Falcone. If management hadn't traded him to St. Louis over the winter, he would've been on this trip with us somehow. Actually, skips my mind now but one of the sports mags, probably either The Sporting News or Baseball Digest had me, Count and Petey on the cover during the '75 season: "[Pitching Coach Don] *McMahon's Mafia*," it was titled, a very cool and sort of politically incorrect profile on the Giants' Italian fireballers. Besides all the joking, all the good-natured East Coast-West Coast Italian food rivalries, Petey and I became very, very good friends, always there to talk, hang out, a great guy to have a beer with. We got Kenny Reitz back in the trade, a player who's been sort of lost to baseball history, but, man could he glove. They called him *"The Zamboni Machine."* His greatness on the field doesn't really show up in modern statistical analysis, but in the '70's he was known as one of the best third basemen in the game. As a team, you loved having him behind you; another fun dude to hang out with, but I missed my buddy Petey terribly.

* * * * *

Finally, we got off Interstate 8, close to Casa Grande. Rancher country at this time, cowboy hats, long stretches of nothing but farms and horses. By about 6 AM we turned off at this gravelly, two-lane road. Not the most conducive to driving, but we were in the midst of a race against time, against each other. We weren't about to get fined and definitely not coming in second.

"Hit it, JD," Moff commanded.

I didn't pay attention that Count, who wanted to beat me as much as I wanted to come out on top, abruptly eased off the pedal, Moff and me kept going, until the barbed-wire fence 100 yards at the end of the road came at us. I got my foot through the floorboard, now we're bookin' at 130 MPH plus.

"Oh shit, there's a T in the road," Moff yelled, *"STOP!!!!!"* The foot brakes weren't helping, the Porsche spun out without my permission, the barbed-wire jumped in our faces like a tragic 3-D movie…

I reacted, pulling the emergency brake. Tires screeching, semi-circle spinout, avoided the barb-wire fence by inches and drove left down the road to the facility. Let out the most relieved sigh of my life.

"Wow," I turned to Moff, "That was cool."

"Yeah," Moff breathed slowly, rolling his eyes. As close a call to a major wreck as I've ever gotten. We buzzed down to training camp, a little slower than before, but at least in one piece.

* * * * *

Man, those cars were machines. We could've gone 24 hours at that rate and the Porsches would've taken it. We waited for Count and Ho-Ho to get there before we all went in together. They arrived about five minutes after us.

"We made it," I said, half-implying we won. Count took one look at the front of my car and laughed.

"Congratulations," he replied, nodding at the nicked-up bumper, and that was the best of it.

In the end, they had to replace my windshield as well as additional body work, thanks to all the pebbles and gravel popping onto my hood and side doors. Was it reckless? Maybe that drag race on barely-paved road wasn't our best idea. Still one of the highlights of my fun times with the guys, though.

We checked in a little before 7 AM, received our room keys to the motel. Giants' management and the coaches stayed at the swanky condo building, which was also on the grounds. The players weren't allowed there, either, nor could they eat at the steakhouse located on the premises. We were served buffet food for breakfast, lunch and dinner. None of that mattered to me at this point. Just relieved to get to my room for some sleep.

I opened the door and found Onti half-awake in the other twin bed. "Roomie," he said drowsily, "You made it."

"In one piece," I replied. "Crazy night." Onti rolled over and packed it back in.

"Tell me later," he muffled into his pillow and fell back asleep, "Good to see ya." I unpacked my clock radio, set it for sometime in the afternoon and passed out in my clothes.

* * * * *

The alarm went off around 3 PM. Onti was long gone. I recalled something about late golf, but all I could do was stare at the ceiling, wince from my aching body and here comes that damn song.

Too exhausted to reach for the snooze, I had to endure her words, her voice, Diana Ross' lovely, sultry, soothing voice of doubt. I was no longer a rookie phenom with the whole world ahead of him. Starting to let some dreams slip through my hands. So many questions in my head and I wasn't one hundred percent certain I wanted the answers. Would I get my fastball back? Will I ever throw it in triple digits with command? What's life gonna be like for a 23-year old, injured pitcher? Will I get along with Rigney and Buck Rodgers? Now that Labatt is most likely bringing expansion baseball to Toronto, will Bob Lurie keep the Giants in the Bay Area as promised, or would we end up in St. Petersburg, Tampa Bay, Seattle, or some other God-forsaken town? What if I am not selected for the starting rotation? Can I make it as swingman? There's absolutely no room in the bullpen for me, right? What if Bob Knepper is dynamite in Spring Training? Will I get traded at the end of March?

Will I get released?

Do I really have my confidence back?

Do you know?

Rumors

"*So how long have you been in the mob?*" Hank Sauer asked me on the field one morning at Candlestick Park in early September, 1976, "'*Cuz that's what everyone's sayin'.*"

When your teams' hitting coach approaches you by the backstop before a game against the Dodgers, you might expect him to ask you your impressions of the opposing club's starter that night, any tendencies you may have observed, any tells that can be exploited, who is tipping his pitches, that sort of thing. Whether or not you are an organized crime figure is generally not among the litany of queries.

"I beg your pardon," I replied, taken aback, annoyed, irritated.

"People are talkin' that you're in the mob."

"Just because I have an Italian name?" Hank threw me an eye-roll, a "*c'mon, man*" sort of look.

"Well that's what's goin' around."

"It's not true."

"What's goin' on over at the restaurant?"

The restaurant. Heh. Where do I start?

* * * * *

Spring Training wasn't my best. Still had control problems. Rigney kept having me throw only fastballs in the games to fight my wildness. In my last exhibition against Oakland, I walked five batters in five innings. Not a great kickoff to the season. Rigney still told the beat guys I would be the fourth starter in the rotation. I had no idea what that really meant. Or how close I came to truly going home.

I attended a labor meeting at a Phoenix hotel during spring training where Marvin Miller discussed what we accomplished from the lockout. During the cocktail party afterward, my old teammate Willie McCovey came up to me with a big grin on his face.

"I hear the boys are trying to get me back in town," Mac said.

"Seems like the ballclub's trying to bring in all the old favorites," I replied. Made sense with Rigney, the manager of the Giants from their first season on the west coast in 1958 at the helm, old Giants players like Davvy on the coaching staff. Anything to get their fans through the turnstiles.

"Who would we have to give up?" I asked, sipping my beer.

"You don't wanna know," Mac said through his classic heavy laugh.

"What?"

Yup, yours truly. The Padres were making a concerted effort to bring me home to San Diego. New Giants owner Bob Lurie passed on the deal. I stayed in San Fran. It wouldn't be their only attempt to bring McCovey to the Bay Area. Or the other thing.

* * * * *

Labor strife in April 1976 wasn't simply relegated to the baseball world, either. Around this time, San Francisco city workers went on strike about a week before the season began. Newly elected Mayor George Moscone made a promise that 100,000 fans would show up for the new owners of the club. The chants outside the ballpark weren't for Murcer or Count. At least 50 workers picketed Candlestick before our opener against the Dodgers. Didn't turn into a terrible scene, but the mess was pretty close to a fine analogy for our season. Count won the first game for us, but there were many signs that things just weren't right with our ballclub. A swarm of maybe five to 10 thousand bees attacked our dugout in Cincinnati on April 18th, the first Giants game televised before a national audience that year. Ten days into the season, I still hadn't started a ballgame. Finally, on April 27th, I saw my first start against the team I always seemed to dominate, the St. Louis Cardinals. I didn't last two innings, getting touched up for four runs before Rigney came and got me. Two years ago, Bob Gibson and Joe Torre were singing my praises to the St. Louis press corps. Now Lynn McGlothen was offering sympathy wishes. 0-1.

I knew something was wrong right then and there. This level of failure never happened to me before. I was hurt last year. Could I blame my awful start on needing another year of rehab? I was running out of personal scapegoats.

After the game, I went into Rigney's office.

"We got ya the coaches ya wanted," Rigney said, "You boys wanted Frank Funk here, he's here. You boys wanted Davenport here, he's here. What else ya want us to do?"

"I need to fix what's wrong," I pleaded, "Can you help me? Please?" Whenever I had a problem in my career, I always went to the manager, who was there for me. When you're 23 and have never experienced failure in your life, you don't always handle it properly.

"Ya wanna be fixed?" Then he cupped his hands to his mouth like a bullhorn. *"Stop throwin' the ball all over the goddamn ballpark. There, you're fixed. We done now?"*

Maybe I couldn't have been fixed in 1976, but Rigney and I were really done as soon as I left his office that day. Never before had I played for a manager who didn't take me under his wing. Harvey Keopf treated me like a student he cared for. Frank Funk was the heavily involved uncle. Jim Davenport, a much older brother. Charlie Fox, my baseball father. Even Wes Westrum possessed kind, paternal instincts at times. Not Rigney. Was it my fault for expecting some kind of personal relationship with my manager? Looking back, probably, but that's what I was used to my entire life in baseball. Needless to say, the worst pep talk in the history of sports surprisingly did not improve my work.

May 8th: Montreal touched me up for six runs on six hits and a Pepe Mangual dinger before I helped myself to a second inning shower. Expos cruised to a 7-5 victory that wasn't nearly as close as it looked in the box score. 0-2.

Rigney had a great relationship with the press, especially the older writers. They were his drinking buddies. He tended to take his frustrations with the ballclub to the media. Picked up the paper one morning and found some quotes attributed to "ol' Q-Tip" (Rigney's nickname) after a night of drinking with reporters in Los Angeles.

"I got this one pitcher I can't figure out at all. One game he got the side out in the first inning with four pitches, the second inning with eight

pitches and the third out with 12. Perfect ball for three innings. He's got it all together, right? Wrong! The next inning the other team blasted everything he threw. I mean he got murdered. He's got real problems and he's not even a lefthander. When I tell him he's gonna start, he worries himself into a frenzy and he's no good by the time he gets on the mound, and if I don't tell him, he bugs the hell outta me. Maybe I'll wait until five minutes before a game, then tell 'em. Maybe he'll throw a no-hitter!"

He never used my name, but everyone knew it was me, basically because the reporters asked me for comments one afternoon before a game against Montreal. Of course I told them that must've been another pitcher and as they all gave me knowing glances, the writers smartly changed the subject. I was standing in Rigney's office soon as the writers had moved on to Halicki.

"What the fuck is this?" I asked him, as I dropped the newspaper one of the reporters handed me on his desk.

"What?" Rigney grabbed and read the paper, sighing like a man that knew he had some explaining but pride kept him from coming completely clean.

"Why are you worrying about this stuff?" he defended.

"I'm not worrying about it, but when the fuckin' beat guys are throwing it in my face and asking for a response-"

"My team's 23-40, John-" I didn't care to hear his explanation. I knew an apology wasn't coming. My pitching coach Buck Rodgers was no help at all – most of us on the staff basically ignored him and listened to Frank Funk, the man who cared for us while we played for him in the minors. I was extremely uptight at this point, but many veteran managers back then rarely communicated with their pitchers. It would only get worse.

June 12th: I gave up one hit over six innings. Of course I walked nine, on the losing end of a 3-1 snoozer against the Mets. 0-3.

June 22nd: Even sleeping in my boyhood bed, eating a home-cooked Italian meal from Mom, even after a long chat with Dad and a beer with Fred, even against my hometown Padres, against my buddy Randy Jones, regardless of the fact he's pitched out of his mind the last year and a half and would go on to start the All-Star game, I had nothing. Six-plus innings, seven hits, three runs, three walks, no strikeouts. Randy tied Christy Mathewson's mark for 63 straight innings without walking a batter. At least the game ended in less than two and a half hours. Giants lose. 0-4.

July 3rd: Three and two-thirds of an inning. Three runs, four hits, six more walks against the punchless Atlanta Braves. 0-5. ERA of 6.75. Rigney removed me from the starting rotation.

Drove home that night alone beside myself. 0-5. No post-game drinks with Count. No dinner at Bertolucci's. No friends over the apartment. I just didn't know what to do or when it would all turn around. A 40-minute ride back to my place punctuated by Fleetwood Mac repeatedly asking me *"Will you ever win?"*

* * * * *

Next morning, I woke up and made Count and me a pot of coffee.

"You hear the news?" he said, staggering into the living room.

"What, that I'm 0-5?" I replied.

"Worse than that. They're closing the Playboy Club."

"You're kidding."

"'Connie says it's next week. It's gone. Where the hell we gonna go now?"

The Playboy Club had been open in San Francisco since 1965. Back in the early '70s, there were bunnies hopping all over that joint. By 1976, there couldn't have been more than 20 fatigued women working all shifts. Was really the only spot in town where the players could go and just chill out.

"We gotta find a new place," Count said through a coffee slurp.

My off-the-field activities were the last thing on my mind at this point.

That would soon change.

* * * * *

"You guys want me and Count to open a restaurant?" I asked *"Danny Cooney,"* a short Irishman in his late '40s, a few days later at a bar near Candlestick, "I'm a baseball player, what the hell do I know about entrees?"

"Johnny, we're not asking you guys to work the prep lines," Danny laughed. "We just wanna put your names on the sign." Danny had been part of the management group that ran the Playboy Club in town, and much like Count, had recognized that the young elite of San Francisco needed a high-end place to go that wasn't your everyday bar or restaurant.

"I'm having a terrible season, I know the restaurant business is usually a loser's game. I really don't need to be worried about sinking my baseball money in an establishment-"

"We're not asking for any money. In fact, we want to pay *you* to get involved."

That changed my stance a bit.

"You guys take anything you want. You wanna grab a few bottles to take back to your place, fine. You wanna come in every night for dinner, great – we'd actually love that. You wanna bring your other ballplayer buddies, you're more than welcome. "

"If we say yes, how much would we get paid?"

"$200,000. Between the two of you, of course."

"This sounds too good to be true. Let me talk to Count." The next day, I brought it up while we were chatting in the dugout before a game against the Phillies.

"A restaurant?" Count joked, "What???!? What do we know about the fuckin' food business?"

"My Dad's been involved with restaurants my whole life," I replied eagerly, "Free meals when we're in town. It'll be like our own personal liquor store. At least we'll have a place to go."

"All right, that's cool. What are they gonna pay us?"

"We get a piece of the joint, and if we wanna get out, they pay us off and take our name down."

I met up with Danny the following day in the bar at the Fairmont Hotel in town.

"As long as everything is above board, as long as there's no hanky-panky, you can use our names."

Danny was thrilled.

"You know something, this is gonna be cool, you guys are gonna love it, it'll be nice, really be a lot of fun-"

"No hanky-panky, no funny shit-"

"None at all-"

"Danny-"

"I swear on my mother's grave, everything on the up and up."

"You know, our names and reputations and everything-"

"Johnny, stop worrying. This is a good thing."

We shook hands. The deal was done. Then we began strategizing the marketing of the restaurant. First things first.

"How are we gonna get women to show up?" The grin wrapped around Danny's face, the sly nod of his head told me he already had this part of the plan all laid out.

* * * * *

The restaurant was located in a strip mall on the corner of Bay & Powell Street close to Fisherman's Wharf in San Francisco. Solid area for tourist foot traffic but the point of it all was really providing affluent locals an after-hours spot. They had been working on this for months before Count and me were involved. I had never seen construction of a restaurant come together so quickly. We'd walk in there and the workers moved with such swiftness aware they were on the clock to get the place up and running as soon as possible. Music blasted throughout the joint as they painted, installed the bar, sanded the floors, like a construction symphony as "*A Fifth of Beethoven*" blared from someone's portable radio. They completed construction of the bar and applying the brick face to the walls with incredible efficiency. Count and I were brought in to interview the waitresses. One by one, Danny brought each of the girls into the room that would ultimately serve as a corporate meeting/dining room. We sat behind a table on fold-out chairs as each lady walked in. Blondes, brunettes, redheads, long-flowing hair, ponytails, all tall, all gorgeous.

Nearly all the women were former Playboy Bunnies. Count and I turned to one another, amazed that a couple of twenty-something kids were getting paid to act like judges in a never-ending beauty pageant.

Finally, I had something to think about besides my 0-5 record, my terrible control problems, the fact that my manager wasn't in my corner, my overall awful season.

And guess what happened?

July 20th headline: *D'ACQUISTO REVIVED; Whips Cardinals 5-3*

Eight innings, four hits, struck out six. I did walk eight more, but was able to continually work out of jams. Also went 2-for-4 with a double off Bob Forsch.

And then this happened:

July 24th headline: *D'ACQUISTO HELPS S.F. SPLIT PAIR*:

Six innings of two-hit, four-walk ball against the Astros in the Astrodome. Fanned five. Still hadn't given up a dinger since April.

And then this happened:

July 29th headline: *D'ACQUISTO SHINES IN RARE SHUTOUT*:

Kept the World Champion Cincinnati Reds in check for six and a third, giving up only four hits, two walks – by far my best game of the season. Wanna know what else? Didn't strike out a batter, beat them with off-speed stuff, had them guessing fastball all night long. A lot of lazy fly balls. I stopped worrying about the beat guys, I stopped worrying about the walks, stopped worrying about

Rigney, stopped worrying about not living up to the nickname given to me by my teammates. I just pitched by instinct.

* * * * *

Count and I stopped by the restaurant once we returned home from the Cincinnati road trip. Danny was there placing the finishing touches on the establishment.

"We open next month," Danny bragged, "Whaddya think?"

Man, the place was gorgeous. Oak wood bar encircled by brass rails right off the floor. Dazzling chandelier. Tables that could seat 100 guests. It was almost time to get the action going.

"Only one thing," I said, beckoning to the dining area, "Let's change up the table cloths. I want white table cloths, not this checkered crap."

"Well, every Italian restaurant has red and white-checkered table cloths. It's a staple."

"Not this place. Maybe during the week or weekend afternoons. At night, it's all white."

Danny nodded. As we left the restaurant, Count and I were walking down the street.

"I can't believe this is happening so fast," Count said, as we reached his Porsche.

"I know, they're working their asses off," I replied as I reached the passenger's side door.

"Nahhh, I'm from Jersey. Nothin' gets built this fast. Permits, county supervisors, all that shit. This thing's gonna be done before the end of the season."

"I think these guys really want to have a place to get all the Playboy Club business before someone else does."

Count shrugged and dipped into the Porsche.

"Yeah, maybe you're right," Count nodded, still a bit skeptical, driving me to my re-match with the Reds.

* * * * *

I made the Big Red Machine look pretty silly with my off-speed stuff in the last game. I felt ready to win my fourth start in a row. I held them scoreless through six. They would get a walk here, a single there, but I finished them off when I had to. We took a 1-0 lead into the seventh, two quick outs and then Pete Rose stepped to the plate. Working the count on me, Pete slapped a single to right. Crazy thing was, it seemed like Pete always knew what was coming. Ken Griffey, next at-bat same thing. Griff smashed a triple down the line, scoring Pete, tying the game. The following inning was even uglier. George Foster, single; Dan Driessen, single. Bench, single. They started waiting on the off-speed stuff, stopped guessing fastball and just timed everything I threw.

Like they knew what was coming. I lost the game 4-1, which put my record at 3-6. The rest of the month was the same. Two more losses, couple of no-decisions, especially a six and two-thirds innings effort shutting out the Expos. I ended August with an atrocious start against Pittsburgh, not even getting out of the first inning. By the end of the month, my record was 3-8.

* * * * *

Darrel Chaney's the batter facing me in an early September game against the Atlanta Braves. Jerry Royster, the rookie leadoff hitter, stepped a few paces off of first base. I had just walked him.

Fuckin' walks. I look out to the dugout, seeing ol' Q-Tip's obnoxious demeanor, one of those expressions of people when you can't tell whether they're smiling or sneering. Before I left the clubhouse, I found out Rigney made some comments again. Apparently, Rigney had drinks with famed San Fran sportswriter Bucky Walter. Walter asked Rigney about certain players. Rigney proceeded to rip them in detail, one by one. Then it was my turn. *"John D'Acquisto ," Rigney said, "Ball one, Ball Two, Ball three, Ball Four. Ball Five. Ball Six – that's John D'Acquisto."*

I was so furious reading his comments in The San Francisco Examiner that day. Why would a manager say something like that in the press about his own young player? You want to bust a veteran's balls, that's one thing. Then, I saw Royster getting cute leaning off first behind my shoulder, well, fuck him –

Picked him right off. There, sit your ass down now. Didn't matter much. Ended up walking Chaney. Two strikeouts later, I was back in the dugout. I've never pitched with such anger. Problem was, it wasn't fuel anger, the punch outs of Willie Montanez and Dave May notwithstanding. It was self-destructive anger. How I got those two dudes out was nothing short of a miracle.

The next inning, I started off with a walk to Kenny Henderson. After a strikeout and force-out at second, I gave up a single to Pete Varney and then the opposing starter Bruce Dal Canton came to the plate. A pitcher who barely had seven plate appearances during the season. I walked him. I walked the pitcher to load the bases. It was almost as if I *wanted* to walk him to get Rigney to come out to the mound so I could let him have it in front of 4500 Candlestick fans. Jerry Royster came back to the plate and – yup, you guessed it – walked him to force in a run.

Rigney jogged out to the mound and reached out his hand for the ball.

"You're done, John," he said coldly.

"What's your problem with me?" I snapped, "Why are you always shitting on me? I'm giving you guys everything I got-"

"Well, you ain't got a whole lot these days-"

"Fuck you-"

"Go take a shower-" Rigney deadpanned as he waited for Dave Heaverlo to jog in from the bullpen.

"If you're old ass is here next season, I better not be-"

"We can arrange that."

I stormed off the mound. Turns out, the beat writers were very good at getting Rigney liquored up. He had a tendency to talk colorfully after a few whiskeys. I could have almost forgiven his public openness about my struggles if he just fessed up about it.

I wasn't the only Giant who had issues with ol' Q-Tip. Count was fined $500 two weeks earlier for calling Rigney *"a loser"* in the papers. Jim Barr admitted publicly that Rigney had severe communications issues with the young Giants. Some teams can overcome the generation gaps between players and manager, but not when your record is 61-78. Rigney and I would "patch up" our public disagreements, but I didn't pitch for another 17 days. Much like I had feared during spring training, Rigney gave my spot in the rotation to the rookie lefthander Bob Knepper, just off the shuttle from AAA Phoenix. September meant something different to him than me at this point.

The restaurant was due to open one week later.

* * * * *

The night played out as I imagined a Hollywood premiere. Seemed as though every boldface name in the Bay Area was there. My parents, Fred, my sister, my roommate Jim Colton, who was the PR guy of the local ABC affiliate in San Francisco. A few of my teammates and some opposing players, too. Count and I were extremely proud of what we helped create. The finest Italian dishes steaming from every table. Butterfly Steak Parmeasan, Four-Cheese Baked Ziti like you've never tasted, Minestone Soup rated the best in the Bay Area at the time, gelato to cleanse the pallid, and the main course, nine former Playboy bunnies strutting around the joint. The finest roster of September call-ups you ever laid your eyes on. There was *Sandy*, 22, 5-foot-9 from Van Nuys, Ca, flowing, dirty blond hair, the first time I'd ever seen the Farrah Fawcett feathered style, handled the tables in the back; *Debra*, 23, a 5-foot-6 inch redhead from Albuquerque with a trim figure, worked the center of the restaurant; *Marcia*, 24, 5-foot-10 inch, white-haired blond with a Dorothy Hamill-esque wedge cut from Missouri, serving drinks, and of course, *Corrine*, 24, a gorgeous, nearly six-foot brunette from Boulder, who received the guests at the door with a sultry, *"Welcome to Montefusco's & D'Acquistos."* During the day, the girls wore tuxedo shirts and smart black pants as the restaurant took on a more family-style sensibility, balloons, ice cream sundaes and chicken parm for the kids, but after midnight, the top buttons came loose and those foxes had their run of the place.

Danny had set up the back of the restaurant as a stage for performers the night of our opening. I wondered who would come in to play. As I stood with Count against the bar, I saw Danny lead our entertainment for the night through the door of the restaurant.

The Chairman of the Board.

Count and I looked at each other.

"How does Danny know fuckin' Sinatra?" Count asked me.

"Your guess is as good as mine." With his small entourage of a band already set-up, the legendary crooner made his way to the stage, the lights went down, the room went quiet as the former leader of the Rat Pack began singing *The Summer Wind.*" Danny walked by Count and me with a very self-satisfied grin.

"How did you guys get Sinatra," I asked him. Danny just smiled.

"We got Stevie Wonder next week," he replied. He never answered the question, but sure enough, exactly seven days later…

"Johnny, this is insane," Count said in my ear, trying to talk over the blaring trumpet in Stevie Wonder's small-set rendition of "*Superstition,*" "This is crazy!"

"I know," I replied, a yell only he could hear, "Isn't it great, though?"

"Well yeah, the girls are hot stuff, but Stevie Wonder?"

"Isn't this what you wanted?"

The restaurant was rocking and the girls were very appreciative of our nightly presence in the restaurant. For those final two weeks of the season, opposing players approached us, behind the backstop during batting practice, knocking on the clubhouse door before games, running across the field, pre-game, asking for rides, times, directions to the restaurant soon after the final out was recorded. Colorful players, "wholesome" players, rookies, All-Stars, everyone hung out at the restaurant after dark. *Everyone.*

"Johnny, pick me up at the Hilton," players would say, *"I wanna check out the restaurant."* I became the most popular player on the ballclub in those final days of '76. We'd walk into the place and the women would be waiting for us, for my fellow ballplayers. I didn't have a single lonely night that month.

As for Rigney, he had no control of any of us. He resigned on September 22nd with 10 days to go in the regular season, our record standing at 70-83, worse than the year before under Wes Westrum. Although he did finish the season in the dugout, Rigney was one of a good handful of old-school skippers in 1976 having trouble relating to what was then considered "the modern player." I understood Bob Lurie's process – he was very nice to me that year personally - he was close to Rigney, wanted a friend running the team at least for the first year while he tried to figure things out in the front office. That said, Rigney was the wrong fit for that clubhouse from day one.

* * * * *

All things considered, September wasn't all about hot girls and the restaurant. I was asked to attend this fan appreciation party, a get together between us and the Dodgers, held in the private dining club of Candlestick Park, hors d'oeuvres, open bar, socializing between sponsors, certain season-ticket holders and league VIPs. Suit and tie kind of gig. One of our car advertisers was pitching me a promotional idea. I nodded along and listened intently because that's what you did at these things when Susan caught my eye. A lovely young woman, petite, movie-star blue eyes. Always well-dressed, well-spoken. Ready for a business meeting or an upscale function at The Fairmont. Simply a classic San Francisco brunette. I walked over and we hit it off instantly. Easy talking between us, where I do hang out, where does she hang out, that sort of thing.

Soon enough we're heading down the elevator to take this to another bar and continue our conversation. As we're leaving the stadium, the doors open to Lurie, Rigney, my favorite manager and Chub Feeney. They were not thrilled to see us together.

After all, Susan was Chub Feeney's secretary. She knew about every trade that went down in the National League often before the players, agents, some of the managers, too.

Fraternizing between the players and League employees even in the most innocent of situations was frowned upon with extreme prejudice. Chub was a great boss, Susan said, a wonderful man who looked after her like his own daughter. Off the field, players were dogs in Chub's eyes, and rightly so, I suppose. This was a problem, a problem all parties decided not to deal with in this moment and we left the gathering.

Susan and I enjoyed a nice relationship over those next two months, nice dinners at places like The Velvet Turtle in Redwood City, romantic weekend drives on the 101 to Big Sur and Carmel. I kept stealing glances of the perfectly winged flip of her jet black hair that would make Jaclyn Smith fire her stylist in a jealous rage. One October evening, as I parked the car in front of the restaurant, I caught a sense of despair in her voice.

"Everything ok?" I asked her.

"I don't know how to tell you this," she said with a smile that wasn't sure of itself, "You're about to be traded to the St. Louis Cardinals. There's a lot of chatter about it in the league office."

The topic monopolized the rest of our night together. Later at a nearby bar, we talked deeply about what the chatter she heard meant for us as a couple. The gossip coming from the league office was almost always true. My days were numbered. At the same time, ownership was telling my agent I would receive a multi-year deal. So my head was spinning a bit. That night, Susan would be talking, I would be listening, but really looking beyond her, beginning my mourning process, realizing I wouldn't be have too many nights like this left in the Bay Area. Baseball was above us on the TV that night, in the corner of the bar, the Reds finishing off Philadelphia on their way to the '76 World Series. Baseball was always in the air with us, always hovering over our relationship. Ironic that it was baseball that brought us together and would inevitably break us up. I really liked her, but with the scuttlebutt about the trade, this wasn't a good idea. Working in Major League Baseball, she knew protocol.

When we got back to her place, we sat in the car for a few minutes. This trade news sort of ruined the night for us. She told me my Giants career is over, the only team I'd ever known and loved. *"Landslide"* played faintly through the crackle of an AM radio station. "I'm guessing something will be announced soon." Susan said softly, caressing my back, almost consoling, "I just thought you should know."

* * * * *

The restaurant was hoppin'. Packed every night. Soon, I would see more and more women coming in, drinking, but not drinking. Just sitting at the bar. We also had our local regulars. There was this kindly old man who would come in a few nights a week. We called him *"Uncle Jimmy."* Always a warm smile, some funny jokes. Thought nothing of it, just an older man who wanted to be around hot women but with an unusual amount of discretionary cash to eat out every other night. The bar was this large rectangle – and in the back corner there was a gold plate that read "Uncle Jimmy," where he sat night after night. The owners trusted us because we rarely took anything from the restaurant to bring back to our place, but there were some incidents that began to raise our suspicions.

One late night after the restaurant had closed, Count and I and drove up to the back door of the restaurant for loading/unloading into the kitchen– we went there to grab a case of wine to take home for a small gathering of friends at my apartment. Going through the back with our key.

"Leave a note for Danny what we're taking," I said to Count, which was our standard procedure. We bumped into Tommy, a busboy, walking out with a case of wine.

"Hey hold on a sec," I said to him.

"What," he replied nervously.

"Whatcha got there?"

"Some wine."

"You supposed to have that?"

"No."

"No," Count said, looking toward me as if I would follow the line of inquiry.

"You must be bringing that out for us."

"Yeah, sure." Tommy gently handed me the case.

"Thank you very much." Before he even got a chance to mutter *"You're welcome,"* I said, "Get your fuckin' ass in there." We led Tommy back into the storeroom of the restaurant.

"Don't let me catch you pulling this shit again. Next time, you're gone. Don't steal from us."

"I'm so, so sorry, Johnny."

"Yeah, yeah, go home, get the fuck outta here," Count said from behind me. Tommy left pretty quickly.

"The nerve of that kid," Count said to me.

"Little asshole." I handed Count the case of wine and we left the restaurant.

"C'mon, let's go."

* * * * *

About a week later, I came home from horseback riding in the Half Moon Bay area with my roommate Jim Colton. My apartment in San Mateo was pretty sparse; 15-inch TV, barely a kitchen. We were just chilling out for a few minutes when the doorbell rang. I found Giants executive Jerry Donavan standing there with a package. There was no phone in our apartment – the only way the club could deliver news to me in the off-season was either by mail or knocking on my door and hoping I was home.

"You've been traded." One hellvua hello, you might say. I had to act surprised because I didn't want to get Susan in trouble, as if I was tipped off to the whispers.

"We traded you, Mike Caldwell and Dave Rader," Jerry said, walking only a few steps inside my place, "You're all going to St. Louis." I was very friendly with Caldwell, Rader, too, but again, we didn't have a phone in the apartment, so there was no comparing notes on what we were told by the team. Donavan said, "Be honest, I wanted them to keep you, but management told me you wanted out."

"I only wanted to go if Rigney was still around, and we got rid of him," I defended.

"Too late now," he shrugged, patting me on the back as he left the apartment. That was my goodbye from the Giants organization.

Before heading home to San Diego for Thanksgiving, I saw Susan one more time. We talked about how to possibly to make this happen, but in the end, the National League offices were moving to New York City. With me in St. Louis, it simply wouldn't work. "I'll see you when I see you," meant something else, something I didn't want to say. I left her place and drove up the coast to collect my thoughts. I wanted to see Rocky Point one more time. I was really going to miss Northern California, especially San Francisco, but the trade winds dictated that it was time to leave my baseball home and loved ones behind.

A couple hours later, I entered my apartment and Jim's there with one of his close friends who lived down the block.

"What's up, Johnny," Keith Hernandez said, sitting on the couch with a smoke hanging from his fingers, "What are we doin' tonight?"

* * * * *

So we're at the restaurant two hours later. It's me, Keith, Count and Jim. This was just what the doctor ordered. I had hung out before with Keith; he grew up with my roommate in the Bay Area. Different circumstances now, though. This was my teammate.

"We should work out together," Keith said through cigarette smoke and gorgeous ladies in low-cut tuxedo shirts passing our table on all sides. I had no objections – I thought this would be a perfect way to prepare for the spring. I did have a ton of questions about St. Louis.

"Where should I get a place?" I asked him, "Where do we hang out to meet girls?"

"Pheasant Run is the place to be," Keith assured me in between beer sips, "Near U of M. A lot of stewardesses there. College girls, too." We might have been veterans, per se, but man, we started in the league at 21. We were still kids. Kind of. This information was important. It's not like anyone from the organization reached out to me. It was three weeks already and no one from the ballclub sent me anything outside of salary and insurance-related paperwork. The traveling secretary called my parents asking where to send the plane tickets for St. Petersburg. That was it. Not my manager. Not Bing Devine, the general manager. Not my pitching coach, Claude Osteen. No one. This isn't to say I wasn't grateful for the raise they agreed to give me. Yet, with my injury resume, you would think someone would check in and see how I was preparing during the off-season. Didn't happen.

* * * * *

Over the next two months, Keith and I would meet up a few times a week. We would soft toss, I would throw him live BP for 30 minutes. We had a catcher join us and simulate games. Keith would point out when I was tipping my pitches. We'd work on the pickoff move. Keith would go into the tells of every speedster in the league, from the established stars to the emerging players. "Omar Moreno, the kid from Pittsburgh, when he leans to the right, that means he's going. He's planting. When he does that, we're gonna nail him." Keith always had the answer. One of the smartest minds in the game, even at 25, great baseball instincts. Then it was on to the restaurant. Keith knew how to have a good time, too. We were all young, single, typical ballplayers doing well, going out, busting each other's balls.

* * * * *

The restaurant continued filling the place to capacity well into December. Continued seeing new faces, mostly new women. Uncle Jimmy wasn't the only colorful character who would frequent the bar area. Pretty soon, another older gentleman named Mickey started coming around. Mickey was friendly to everyone, a jovial Irishman who loved his J&B. *"Hey, how ya doin?" "How's things?" "How's the old arm holdin' up?"* That was Mickey. He started showing up at the bar a couple nights a week; sometimes alone, every so often with a woman. Mickey made himself at home with stories about The Korean War and San Francisco in the '50s. I really enjoyed his company. Mickey really got a kick out of Uncle Jimmy's tall tales and remarks, as if he were his biggest fan. On the nights where I would come in and the restaurant was relatively empty, I would find Uncle Jimmy at the bar, as well as Mickey a few stools away.

"Quiet here," I said to him as the bartender poured me a whiskey.

"Don't have to be," Uncle Jimmy said.

"Oh yeah?"

"I can get 10 of the finest women in town standin' right next to ya in 30 minutes."

"What are you talkin' about, old man?" I said with a grin.

"C'mon, kid," Uncle Jimmy laughed, "Ya know what I'm talkin' about." Mickey, of course, was sitting at the bar, laughing his ass off.

"I know what that's about," Mickey laughed, raising his glass to Uncle Jimmy.

"You lonely, too?" Uncle Jimmy asked Mickey.

"Not tonight, I got a headache."

I thought it was the musings of a couple of bawdy old men. I just laughed with him, said "Yeah, sure," and then walked into the back to talk to Danny.

The women didn't swing by that night, but it got to the point where you had no idea who would be there when you stopped by. About a week later, I entered the restaurant alone after a long workout with Keith. He was out at another bar with our friend Jim; Count had started seeing a nice stewardess and spending less time at the place. As I approached, I looked over at the table in the back and my eyes nearly shot out of my head.

"What's Uncle Jimmy doin' having dinner with the Mayor of San Francisco," I thought to myself, but there he was, Uncle Jimmy, Mayor Moscone and another guy I later learned was named Harvey Milk. The Mayor and Milk seemed to possess remarkable personal chemistry. One moment Moscone and Uncle Jimmy were laughing like old college buddies, then in an instant turn serious as if they were business colleagues. I gulped down my drink quickly and left, starting to wonder what was going on with *"my restaurant."*

This would not be the only time I found Mayor Moscone dining with Uncle Jimmy.

* * * * *

I spent the holidays mainly in San Diego with my parents, sister and brother, trying to wrap my head around what was going on at the restaurant. It was good to have that time with them before entering the unknown of the Cardinals organization. I started thinking less about the restaurant and more about 1977, as the whole pitching situation dawned on me. Where do I fit in here? How am I going to make this work – I only know four guys on the team (Rader, Caldwell, Falcone, Keith.) Will I start or sit in the bullpen? They brought over Larry Dierker from the Astros – he was practically an ace. There's John Denny, Bob Forsch, Caldwell – am I going to be the fifth starter? Falcone had a decent year, that's six starters. Haven't even mentioned Eric Rasmussen. Seven established starting pitchers in camp. Where will they fit me?

* * * * *

After the new year, Count received a five-year deal with the Giants. He wasn't going anywhere for awhile. As brash and outspoken as he could be, Count was still extremely popular in town. One night soon after, Count and I went on a double date, ending, of course with late-night cocktails at the restaurant.

"C'mon, let's go to my place," I said to everyone, "Don't know how much longer I'm gonna have it." We left the restaurant at closing time and walked around the block to my car beside the back alley that the restaurant used for pick-ups and sanitation. Before we knew what happened, two broad-shouldered men grabbed us and threw us into the alley.

"Hey, what the," Count yelled out. The girls were too scared to talk, just shivering beside us.

"Don't fucking move," one of the men said, slamming us against the wall.

"The fuck is going on??!?" I yelled, as the men patted us down, holding our arms behind our backs.

"Hey, watch the arm," I said, as he revealed himself from behind the wall.

"Holy shit," Count said as he saw the man.

"Mickey," I said to the man, "What the fuck's going on?"

"My name's not Mickey," Mickey said quietly.

"What are you, a cop?" Count said, "Please get this asshole off my arm. You know what I do."

Mickey directed the big guys to lay off, though they finished by pushing the both of us against the building.

"Guess again," Mickey replied chillingly.

"Mickey, I dunno what the-"

"I'm FBI. Your restaurant's been under surveillance for the past three months."

"Whaddya mean, under surveillance-"

"Who's Uncle Jimmy-"

"I dunno, you know him, he's some old guy that comes in a lot."

"Are you related to him?"

"I don't even know his last name. He's just a customer of the restaurant who likes the waitresses."

"He's Jimmy 'The Weasel' Fratianno, head of the West Coast mafia. *You* don't know that? He's dealing drugs from behind the bar and running prostitution in the place."

"Bullshit," I said. Count was really shaken up. At this point, Mickey realized we weren't involved with anything shady. After being in the FBI for a couple decades, you could tell the difference between someone scared and someone scared of getting caught.

"I haven't seen either of you do anything stupid, so I'm just gonna say this. You boys have four months to get outta this place.

If I come back here in June and you're still hangin around, I will drag your asses off to jail. Now get lost." Mickey walked away and I never saw him again. As soon as Mickey left with the other FBI agents, Count turned to me, shaking his fists in frustration.

"I *knew* this place was mobbed up," he said. "Johnny, you gotta get us out of this."

The next day, we saw Danny at the restaurant.

"We're out," I said.

"Out?" Danny replied, "What? Why? Everything's going so well-"

"We're out," Count said, "Take our name off the building."

"I can't say why, just we need to be taken out of here." Danny sighed, didn't say anything, but he knew.

"You really have to do this?"

"We really have to do this."

"We're out."

"It's gonna take a little while-"

"Just buy us out. We're done." Danny eventually paid us off. Count and I were done with the restaurant. Just like that. The place was called *"The Good Earth"* by the spring.

Just another reason to clean out my memories from San Francisco. Was gonna miss The Count. He'd become my best friend in the Bay Area. I moved all my stuff down to my parents' house in San Diego temporarily and moved on to my new life with the St. Louis Cardinals.

* * * * *

I told Keith I would pick him up at the airport in San Fran and then we would go to St. Petersburg together. I found him standing on the curb outside the Eastern Airlines terminal of San Francisco International on our way for the flight to Tampa-St. Pete.

The two of us waited at the airport bar with our carry-on bags. The flight wasn't for a couple hours. We filled the time with roster chatter and my questions about the ballclub.

"Just have fun," Keith said, his voice muffled from lighting a smoke, "Great spring training facility. One of the best organizations, they really take care of their players. If you pitch well, you're gonna be fine." Sounded good enough to me.

"What about Vern Rapp?" I asked, "I don't even know who this guy is." Vern Rapp was the new manager of the Cardinals, replacing Red Schoendienst, another legendary skipper in the game who at this point had the misfortune of being featured on more black and white footage than color.

Keith paused a moment, considered the question.

"Neither do I," Keith finally said, downing what was left of his drink, then chuckled to himself, "But we sure as hell gonna find out, aren't we?"

Keith was as uncertain of Rapp as I was, and Keith was certain about everything, always knew the score. He knew the organization backward and forward. For him to not be 100% on Rapp made me more than a little nervous.

Our flight to Tampa-St. Pete was announced overhead. Time to board.

Keith put out what was left of his cigarette in the ashtray, tapped me on the shoulder and beckoned to the gate with a confident grin. "You ready," he asked, checking in one last time. I grabbed my bag, the chorus to *"Go Your Own Way"* stuck in my head from the car ride over as Keith and I left the airport bar, toward the plane and onto the next adventure.

* * * * *

We touched down in Tampa and then drove across the Gandy Bridge heading into St. Petersburg. It would be a whole new spring training experience for me. Up to this point, I had always spent March in Arizona. All the West Coast teams except the Dodgers were based out there, as well as many American League clubs. The weather was more humid in Florida versus the dry western climate. Different cuisine, too. Arizona was all steak and potatoes; Florida was seafood. The Florida facilities blew the Arizona fields away. There was simply no comparison.

Keith was right again. Everything related to the St. Louis Cardinals organization was top-shelf all the way. Everything. The team put us up at the St. Petersburg Hilton, back when The Hilton was The Hilton. We wanted for absolutely nothing. Al Lang Field was a fantastic complex. Gussie Busch treated all of us as if we were his own children. Every player had their own hotel room on the road, where the Giants had the players bunk together. Double meal money for the stars and established veterans. Then we entered the clubhouse for the first workouts. Three uniforms in your locker – home whites and away grays. On other clubs, if something was ripped and you ran through your allotment, you got a bill. Not in St. Louis – everything was provided at no cost. The organization only asked the players to tip the clubhouse guys, which was my pleasure.

I threw on my St. Louis whites. You know there are some teams where people say it's special to wear their colors. St. Louis was like that. One of the classiest uniforms in the game. Everything was perfect. Saw a couple familiar faces. Gave Petey Falcone a big hug. Even chatted with Steve Dunning, the old San Diego high school and Stanford phenom, the number two pick in the draft back in 1970. Arm trouble had curtailed Steve's career and here he was trying to hang on with the Cards. Then Vern Rapp entered the clubhouse. He treated us like his children as well. Only he was the teacher. Kindergarten teacher.

"Everybody get in here," Rapp said, waving the few early reporters out of the room. Closed, clubhouse meeting – day one. "This ballclub lost 90 games last year. There are gonna be some changes. Lots of changes. I want to be clear that certain things will not be tolerated." I looked at Keith, who shrugged with his eyes – we both had a hunch we were in store for something like this. Keith rubbed his moustache almost the moment Rapp went into the next of his demands.

"The beards, the facial hair, that's gotta go." Rapp looked right over Al Hrabosky's way. The Mad Hungarian was instantly pissed. The beard was one of the props in his act on the mound, as much as a part of his repertoire on the field as his blazing fastball and one of the best forkballs in the game. The Mad Hungo simply shook his head. "Nope." Rapp stopped and turned to Al. "Beg your pardon?"

"Ain't doin' it. That's me. Just ain't doin' it." Rapp was taking none of this.

"There's nothin' else to say. I want it gone." Al started walking toward Rapp. They got into a face-to-face, had to be broken up. We knew right then and there, this guy had no real future running the ballclub. Rapp, a little unnerved by Hrabosky, continued his laundry list. "Now that we're down here, we're down here to work, not bounce around town chasing women. The hotel bar at The Hilton is off-limits." This was too much.

"Hold on a second, that's just crazy," I chimed in. Vern Rapp, meet John D'Acquisto. "We need an outlet after a day's work."

"Well, not in my house," Rapp snapped.

"I didn't know your name was Hilton," I said, "Is your last name Hilton?"

Rapp cocked his head, basically saying *"Don't be an asshole,"* but I was rolling.

"It's our house, too. Besides, Skip, c'mon, the guys are gonna go do what they're gonna do. Wouldn't it make more sense for us to be in a spot where you could watch us?" Rapp, to his credit, thought for a moment, then barked at me. "Fine, you guys can be in the hotel bar, but I got my eye on everyone. No messing around. 1977 is not gonna be 1976. Not on my watch. Now let's get on the field." Rapp gave me an extra glance, just to let me know I'm on his radar. Not in a good way. Some of the players nodded their approval of my bravery. Ted Simmons leaned into me before walking out to the field.

"You're fuckin' nuts," Simba laughed quietly, "I like that." I turned to Keith with a chuckle as we walked out. He made a face that said *"You just made Rapp's shitlist."* Of course, Keith was right again. The following afternoon, we finished a full morning of bunting drills, long-tossing and other exercises. Around 1 PM, I see Rapp walking with Clay Carroll, another veteran reliever the ballclub picked up in the off-season. Rapp carried a bat and a bucket as he stopped at the dugout.

"John," Rapp called over. I'm thinking this is some kind of fungo exercise. As I got closer, I see Carroll's expression. He's pissed. I also see the bucket. Not filled with baseballs. Iced Bud Tall Boys.

"I think you guys need a little endurance work," Rapp said, helping himself to the dugout bench. "Foul line to foul line. Let's go." There was a hint of a smile in Rapp's expression. Carroll and I looked at each other, "I guess we're doing sprints." We start running as Rapp pulled the lid off his first Bud. The implication was when the bucket was empty, we were done running. Rapp made sure to take really long sips. "This is horseshit," Carroll said as we sprinted back and forth on the field. Carroll was an excellent reliever (had the major league single-season saves record for exactly one year) and now at 36, was definitely in the twilight of his career. I had no idea what he did to Rapp that got him this gracious gift. It was a horseshit move. Two hours. We sprinted for two hours while Rapp finished his bucket of the King of Beers. This is why Skip had no need to frequent the hotel bar. He was out there downing tall cool ones while players were killing themselves. I didn't make it out that night, either. Not even sure I ate supper after that. Went straight to the Hilton and right into bed. Maybe that was Vern's idea all along.

This happened at least ten times that spring to Carroll and me. Just to put us in our place. A costly price to pay for nighttime cocktails.

* * * * *

Truth be told, there wasn't a whole lot of carousing and chasin' happening in St. Petersburg. It was a relatively quiet retirement community. We shared the facility with the New York Mets during spring training. There were a few places to go out and get in some trouble, but the truth was, we really just stayed at the hotel bar. The Hilton was fine. Not too many fans bothered us there, we had our own space to hang out. The writers knew when they could and couldn't approach us. Still couldn't get away from the gossip. Even at night late in spring training, when I was at some open-air restaurant with Keith, Rasmussen and Falcone, the talk was always about who was getting cut on the other ball clubs, who looked great in our exhibition games, which veterans seemed like they were on their last legs.

The roster was taking shape. I had a good spring, but the math wasn't really working in my favor. The starting rotation at this point was probably Bob Forsch, John Denny, Petey Falcone and Eric Rasmussen, who also became a close friend. Larry Dierker from Houston had gotten hurt and wouldn't be on the opening day roster. Mike Caldwell was also in the mix. The bullpen was looking like The Hungarian, this rookie John Urrea, a great kid, Clay Carroll the veteran and maybe another rookie, Johnny Sutton. Where was my spot on this team? I still didn't know. Forget about the writers in the bars, in the clubhouse or the guys at dinner, the self-generated, self-consumed gossip in my head had me going to one of many different organizations, via trade, waivers or purchase. I started reading the paper every morning, checking out the transactions to see who else was getting cut, mentally pasting together rosters of other ball clubs that needed my fastball. I never felt I would be cut; being traded was a different story. I got to the ballpark that morning and the picture became slightly clearer. Caldwell was shipped off to Cincinnati for Pat Darcy, the kid who gave up Fisk's Game Six dinger in the '75 series, and he was sent down. As this news made its way around the clubhouse, in walked

Joel Youngblood, who we got from the Reds in a separate trade the day before. "*Blood*" (as we called him) was my age. He and his wife owned the coolest van in the league – of all the vans you've seen in '70's films or recall that sweet ride buzzing by you down the street when you were younger – 'Blood had *that* van. Captain's chairs, tremendous sound system, all the fixins. Me and 'Blood would end up living close to one another, commuting to the ballpark together on days his wife couldn't take us. Some late nights after a rough game, she would drive us home in the van while me and 'Blood got wrecked downing tall boys. It became one of the better friendships I made in the game.

'Blood was frustrated, too. Buried in the Reds' organization for six years, waiting behind Ed Armbrister on the depth chart, who himself was behind Griffey, Pete Rose for a spell and Cesar Geronimo. He spent three years starting at AAA Indianapolis. Finally got his chance but was literally the 25th man on the roster for a World Series team. Sort of a bittersweet situation. 'Blood was excited to leave the logjam at Riverfront Stadium behind, but when he got to the Cards on March 29th, the team was basically set. Kinda like walking into a party when all the guys and girls had already matched up. 'Blood and I were in the same boat; talented enough to make the roster, but there was really no role for either of us. 'Blood was the utility player; I, the spot starter who would come into some games in a mop-up situation.

We flew into St. Louis. Longtime broadcaster Jack Buck was on our plane, walking up and down the aisles, checking in with everyone. Not just Lou Brock, the elder statesman of the ballclub, but also the rookies, a Red-labeled Bud Longneck in his hand, offering encouragement or telling great stories. Jack Buck was an extremely nice man. I remember talking with 'Blood on the plane about St. Louis. I couldn't wait to wear that uni in a regular season game and couldn't wait to pitch at Busch Stadium in front of some of the best fans in Baseball.

It would be a longer wait than I expected.

* * * * *

Opening Day in Pittsburgh. Freezing. 29 degrees out, snow on the ground. The game was called, but I still wanted to get some air with the guys. Rasmussen and I went out to run a few sprints. As we were racing through the outfield, a spiky sensation shot through from my left calf. I crashed to the ground. Rasmussen ran to my side.

"Johnny, you ok, man?" he asked, kneeling down beside me. Unbearable pain. Few minutes later, I limped into the trainer's room and onto the table. The trainer, Gene Geiselman, massaged the leg, searching for any possible source of the pain, looking for an injury.

"How's it feeling," he asked. "Not great," I replied, "But I think it might only be a cramp." The trainer placed my leg down slowly back onto the table. "Get some ice on it," he said, "I'll be right back."

Thirty minutes later, I found out the Cardinals placed me on the 21-day Disabled List. Buddy Schultz would be taking my spot on the roster. I was pretty upset about this. The protocol at the time was that the player rep had to be posted on any listing of guys on the injured list before the actual announcement. That didn't happen. Lou Brock, the team's player rep, came into the clubhouse pretty quickly. I was sitting in an armchair.

"Did that S.O.B. put you on the DL?" Brock asked me. I nodded, still very surprised.

"It's only a cramp," I replied. Brock shook his head, helping me up.

"That's not cool." We walked into Rapp's office.

"What's goin' on with Johnny?" Brock demanded.

"Just a precaution," Rapp said. That was it. That was the explanation. I was fine the next day, but the following game, they had me walk in the dugout on crutches just so everyone could see I had a "real" injury," so no one would look foolish. I was in uniform for the next 30 days, suited for every game, riding the pine, idle.

"We have an excess of pitching at the moment," Claude Osteen, our pitching coach told me, "Just in case the organization wants to make a move. It's for the best."

* * * * *

Hrabosky's beard was gone. Same with Keith's moustache. They were annoyed and I was frustrated. The ballclub was taking their time with me on the disabled list. 'Blood was upset, too – he started only three games in the first month. The gossip would get to both of us. The uncertainty that we would wake up one morning and be in the paper, on our way to another ballclub, ate away at our insecurities. I remember 'Blood going on about this guy that might get traded, that this other guy's leaving, too, the team isn't happy with another player's off-the-field activities, what does this mean for us? It was May and I still hadn't pitched for St. Louis; 'Blood only played 10 games. The following afternoon would make things clearer in my mind. I was starting my first game in a Cardinals uniform against the Houston Astros.

I experienced some butterflies the day of my debut in front of the home fans, but they were great. Everything they say about Cardinals fans is accurate; joyous, dedicated loyal folks. Before the game, as I warmed up in the bullpen, I heard the supportive yelling, the encouragement and good wishes. Once I finished throwing, I turned to the stands. All the magical elements of the big league baseball audience experience hit me. These people spending their dollars just to watch me play. The glee that would race across their faces when they realized I was smiling directly at them. Eye contact is something the fans never forget; it cost the player nothing and the fans remember the moment for the rest of their lives. With these people behind me, I was ready to conquer the earth.

Top of the first, Enos Cabell smacked a double to right field. I pitched around Cedeno – the old *"unintentional intentional walk"* - to get to Willie Crawford, the guy the Cardinals traded for me. Willie wanted to show these fans they made a mistake and did so immediately, smacking a double to left - Cabell scored, Cedeno, one of the fastest guys in the game, actually stopped at third. That was kind of a break. I got Bob Watson to groundout and caught Jose Cruz looking. Minimal damage, only one run.

I got through the second inning with only a walk, but then came the third. Cabell had my number that day, smacking a single deep in the hole at short. I walked Cedeno again and here comes Willie Crawford. It was important for me to get Willie out this time. I owed it to these fans to give them a thrill. Willie hit .304 for them last year. I'm sure there were a few St. Louis fans sad to see him go. Since the Cards basically sent Caldwell packing, the only thing in their minds they got for Willie was Dave Rader, Ted Simmons' backup and me. I *had* to get him out. Willie was patient, had a great at-bat, ran the count to 3-2. Cabell and Cedeno took healthy leads.

I'm thinking double steal. Not getting any tells from Keith or Rader. Rader was just concerned about keeping me focused. Willie is the only thing that matters. Let's get Willie. The pitch....*The runners going!!!*

Willie smacked the hardest line drive I had ever seen right at Mike Tyson (*one*) who chucked a bean to Kessinger at short, doubling up Cabell who was halfway to third (*two*) and fired a rocket to Keith at first to catch Cedeno off the bag (*three*).

Triple play. Inning over.

I ran over and slapped Tyson five, patted Kessinger on the fanny and nodded Keith my appreciation. Keith winked back and jogged to the dugout. All business on the field.

We scored two in the bottom of the inning, still psyched from the triple play. The fourth was easy for me. So at the bottom of the inning, I reached for my helmet. I heard Vern Rapp call out, *"Youngblood, grab a bat, you're hitting for John."* I looked over, Keith looked over. We looked at each other. There was no doubt now.

I was being showcased for other ball clubs.

'Blood, one of my best friends on the team, knew what this meant, too. Embarrassed frown on his face as he stepped into the on-deck circle. Four innings, one run, four hits, walked three, struck out four. Not a great line, but not worthy of this treatment.

This is how the gossip starts. A teammate in the dugout witnesses this, they talk amongst themselves, with a guy on another ballclub having drinks after the game, or trying to impress some groupie in a bar offering a flavor of the life in exchange for heading back to his room together. A beat reporter trying to fill his *"Around The League"* column and a player offers gossip to the reporter with the old, *"but you didn't get it from me,"* caveat. A simple managerial move becomes chatter that I am being shopped and showcased. And the chatter is almost always true.

I started again at home on three days' rest at Busch Stadium, a Thursday afternoon matinee against the Reds. I tried to keep the gossip out of my head. I'm walking across the field during batting practice when I saw a familiar face in the stands close to the dugout.

"Hey Bob?" I smiled, "Imagine seeing you here."

Bob Fontaine was the General Manager of the Padres, whom I knew through San Diego social circles. Bob was a gentleman, but also a smart guy. He got it.

"Johnny, nice to see you. You're starting today, right?" I grinned and nodded.

"The main attraction, apparently." We had some small talk, it was all good between us, but we both knew the deal. I walked back toward the bullpen thinking to myself, *"Bob wants a show? Okay....."*

Cincy rested Johnny Bench for this game, but the lineup still contained Rose, Morgan, Griffey, Foster. Had a rocky first inning, 1-2-3 in the second, three walks in the third, but this was also me pitching this lineup carefully. The fourth inning Cesar Geronimo and Dave Concepcion went down 1-2. I was getting stronger as the game wore on. By the way, I had a no-hitter going. Four Ks in three and 2/3s. Out comes Vern Rapp. Simmons was behind the plate and jogged quickly to the mound. Keith did the same coming from first. Kessinger in from short.

"You're done for the day, John," Rapp said, "Gimme the ball." He hadn't yet called for a reliever. Had he done that, there would've been no discussion. Something else was at play here. I was….I'm still flabbergasted. "Do you see the scoreboard," I said to Rapp.

"I know we're down 1-0, gimme the ball." Even the umpire walked over from behind the plate, "We all right here," the ump asked.

"He wants to take me out of the game," I said.

"Really? You have a no-hitter going?"

"Stay outta this," Rapp snapped at the ump. "Gimme the ball, John."

This was the only time, *the only time*, in my *professional* life, where I didn't do what I was told.

"Fuck you, get off my mound." Rapp nodded his head, a smart baseball man wasn't about to make a scene in front of 20,000 fans. Rapp walked back to the dugout and I faced Bill Plummer. I was so mad and made easy work of Plummer, striking him out. Of course, when I got to the dugout, Bake McBride pinch hit for me. That was my last start in a regular game for the St. Louis Cardinals. Buddy Schultz again replaced me, got the win but gave up a lone Ken Griffey double in the eighth. The Hungarian got the save. A one-hitter. Oh and by the way, we won 10-1. All the reporters afterward asked about the mound meeting. I did the right thing.

"Vern's the manager. It's his call how he wants things handled."

Manager's prerogative? Yeah maybe, but the manager's job is to make decisions to win the game. This move had nothing to do with victory. The Cardinals were showcasing me, like a movie trailer to entice the audience of general managers from around the league.

The 1977 Cardinals were better than the previous season, no question, but Vern was beginning to lose the clubhouse, let alone burning through the bullpen. This was before the Tony LaRussa days – not every manager was Sparky Anderson, who knew how to work his relievers. A few managers tried to emulate this. Rapp was one of those guys, especially being the Reds' AAA manager the previous year. Down in Atlanta, three days later on Sunday, I joined Lou Brock in the outfield to shag fly balls before the game.

"It's blowing in the breeze, Johnny D," Lou said, sort of sing-songy. As our player rep, Brock at this point was privy to all the chatter before it hit the rest of us.

"What kind of things?" I asked, knowing where this was going.

"I dunno," Lou replied, catching a fly through the early afternoon sun, "But I think you might be happy. I just hope it doesn't happen." I took a few more flies then jogged toward the dugout. My friend from the Padres was there in the stands, following me around the league like my biggest fan. I nodded to Bob with a knowing smile. Had a rough outing that night, we got knocked around in the eighth inning for six runs in a game where the Braves put up a football score on us, the wrong side of a 15-12 slugfest. Part of this game, at this level, is working through the chatter and the gossip, not allowing it to mess with your rhythm on the mound. Most of the time you can ignore it. It was not one of those days. For many players, the mental element of the game is what separates a starting player from a AAAA superstar.

The following day, we played our Triple-A affiliate, the New Orleans Pelicans on the way to a two-game series in Houston. I started on the back of my relief appearance the previous afternoon. I pitched four innings, threw fairly well. It wasn't until the fourth inning when I realized Bob Fontaine was at this game, too. A general manager from another ballclub watching our minor league exhibition, my God. Bob's appearance at this game was a walking *Sporting News* headline; *"Padres and Cardinals talking trade."* Was only a matter of time now.

* * * * *

There was a knock on my hotel room door the next night in Houston. Woke up with a bit of a headache. I got out of bed and looked through the peephole. It was Cardinals' pitching coach Claude Osteen holding a bottle of red wine and two glasses, making an unsuccessful effort to stand up straight.

"Two in the morning," I said, a bit aggravated, as I opened the door. A buddy like Eric or Keith could convince me at this time to throw on my clothes and go get in trouble.

This was not a buddy.

"Can I come in?" Claude asked through slurred speech.

"You're hammered."

"This stuff is never easy. Can I come in?"

Then I knew. These conversations are difficult for everyone involved. I threw up my hand with a shrug, inviting him inside.

Claude took two steps into the room.

"Oh, excuse me," he said softly with a polite drunkenness to the woman sitting up against the headboard of my bed, under the covers, wearing one of my T-shirts.

"I'm sorry," Darlene replied in her sweet Texas drawl, turning to me. "Should ah go?"

"Stick around," I said, "You're about to see how baseball players get traded in the majors."

"Aww, come on, Johnny," Claude said, looking away guiltily.

We sat down at the table in the room as I turned on the light. Claude slowly poured a glass of Red. One of us was celebrating.

"So who'd they get for me?" I asked.

"Bucc...Butch Metzger. They saw Pat Scanlon yesterday at the exhibition game and asked for him, too. You're goin' home, Johnny."

I was happy. And sad. And shocked. And really annoyed.

"Why didn't you protect me?" Claude sipped his glass sloppily, glanced at Darlene, then barely placed his hand on my shoulder.

"What's the difference now? You're goin' home."

"You never spoke up-"

"There's gonna be more trades. You're not the only one. There's too many pitchers. Too many outfielders." We finished our drinks and then he raised himself slowly and awkwardly from the chair.

"Put your clothes on. They're waiting upstairs." Half-asleep, in shock, I threw on my suit because that's what you did back then. I walked toward the door. Claude was already out of the room.

"Should ah go?" Darlene asked again. She was a really pretty blond, but I had a feeling I was checking out very soon.

"Probably a good idea. Sorry." Apologized again, but Darlene got dressed and grabbed her purse. I offered her cab fare, but she refused it, just stood at the door for a moment, scrunching her nose.

"Sounds serious. Ah hope everything's ok."

"I hope you'll be ok getting' home." Then Darlene had this *"Who me?"* grin on her face as she kissed me gently on the cheek.

"I'll be fine. Call me when ya'll back in town."

* * * * *

We entered the suite a few minutes later and there's Bing Devine, the Cardinals GM, sitting on the couch, Vern Rapp, standing and Tom Sullivan, the traveling secretary. Everyone still in suits.

"You need to meet the Padres tomorrow in Montreal. Flight's at 7:30," Sullivan said to me. The whole scene had a Godfather feel to it, handing me my plane ticket like I was Carlo headed to Vegas. Was waiting for Clemenza to walk me to the elevator. Trades never feel good. Anyway you want to look at it, I just got whacked.

* * * * *

My Cardinal career was over. Youngblood would be traded to the Mets a month later for my old Giants teammate Mike Phillips, where he would finally get a chance to prove to the league how talented he was. The same day, the ballclub traded Bake McBride to the Phillies, a move I thought was hasty and wrongheaded on so many levels. The 1977 Carindals won 11 games more than the previous season, but only four games above .500. They were 10 games above at the end of May. Rapp just lost the team over the course of the year. He actually considered benching Keith to play his favorite son Roger Freed, the guy he brought with him from his previous stint managing AAA Denver, full-time at first. To be fair, Roger was pinch-hitting out of his mind, but possessed an absolute iron glove. He most certainly would've cost the Cards as many runs as he could produce at the plate, probably more when exposed to everyday play.

Suffice to say, Vern Rapp would be fired 17 games into the 1978 season.

In the end, I never had a chance to say goodbye to my friends. Just me catching a ride to the airport alone. Goodbye, Eric. So long, 'Blood. Be good, Petey.

Take it easy, Keith. We had a great, short run.

As I stepped into the cab outside the hotel, the emerging Houston sunrise told me it was time to start thinking about tomorrow.

* * * * *

A day later, I entered the Padres clubhouse in Montreal. Lots of new faces. A few old ones, though. No greetings from anyone. Definitely wasn't the St. Louis clubhouse, not by a long shot. The clubhouse guy gave me my gear except they had no spikes for me. I ended up having to borrow shoes from Doug Rader.

My locker was placed in between Rollie Fingers and Randy Jones, The guys were getting dressed for the game. I knew Rollie from charity functions when we both pitched in the Bay Area and of course I worked out with Randy during the off-seasons when I came home for Christmas. It was oddly quiet. Neither of them said a single word. I was slightly taken aback. Wasn't expecting a marching band or anything, but these guys were supposed to be friends. Randy stood up from his stool to leave, without uttering a sound, then swiftly spun around and grabbed me with a buddy embrace and hearty laugh.

"You're here, Bud," Randy cackled, "You're with us now." Rollie joined in.

"Welcome home, Johnny D." Randy looked me right in the eye with his crazy, curly head of blond hair.

"You know how hard we've been riding these guys to get you in here? I've been up Fontaine's ass to figure out a way to get you on the team. Heard you were dyin' over there."

"This is gonna be good," Rollie added, "This is gonna work out."

"Thanks, guys," I said, genuinely touched at their enthusiasm. Finally, in a spot where I felt good, where I felt wanted, where I felt....home. The friendly harassment was interrupted as a new teammate walked over to introduce himself. Extended his hand, asked if I needed anything, glad I was on the ballclub.

"Yeah, actually, where's Skip?" I asked, standing up. John McNamara was in San Francisco with the Giants as a coach a few years earlier when I was a rookie, a well-respected baseball guy. The player laughed a little and pointed me in the direction. "Sure, he's down the hall over there," the player said, "But I wouldn't get too attached. The word we're hearing is that Johnny Mac's out and Al Dark's coming in to manage. Any day now."

"What?" I asked, turning to Randy and Rollie, who both said nothing but half-ass nodded in agreement. I thought I left this all behind.

More of the chatter. It never ends. Gossip is as much a part of the Baseball experience as groupies, balks and strikeouts. It's stitched into the fabric of the game. I tapped the player on the shoulder, muttered *"thanks,"* nodded to Randy and Rollie, then walked out of the clubhouse, through the shadows of the tunnel leading me to the Olympic Stadium dugout, knowing that the chain of hearsay, scuttlebutt, whatever you want to call it, would follow me as long as I took up a spot on some team's 25-man roster.

Just listen to the wind blow.

Hotel Oahu

*"*A*ll good teams gotta start somewhere. We can only go up from here. Now, I know Rollie and Geno, but I'll be lookin' forward to gettin' to know y'all a whole lot better…*

The rumors were true, of course. John McNamara was fired as Padres manager in what seemed like ten minutes after I arrived in the clubhouse. I liked Johnny Mac, everybody liked him, but the club was struggling to stay out of the cellar. Alvin Dark was a World Series winning skipper, although he really inherited most of the club from Dick Williams, but back then your record was your record. Judging from the look on Rollie's face after our first clubhouse meeting, he had heard all this before.

"Yeah, Dark never spoke to us except on the mound during games," Rollie laughed as the players dispersed throughout the clubhouse. Randy didn't take it so well, either.

"Johnny Mac didn't deserve this," Randy said, shaking his head, "He always made us play better than the talent on the field." The problem was that the 1977 Padres *had* some talent on the field now. Owner Ray Kroc spent big bucks in the free agent market bringing in Rollie, Gene ("*Geno*") Tenace from Charlie Finley and Oakland; he traded for George Hendrick, who had potential superstar written all over him. The Padres were getting their money's worth out of Rollie – they pitched him five days in a row between Johnny Mac's firing and Alvin Dark coming on board. There was just no starting pitching behind Randy, and even he was trying to come back from elbow surgery. The rotation was so weak that Randy pretty much blew his arm out throwing every fourth day for two seasons. The beauty of Randy Jones, one of the reasons I liked him so much, was that he never let it get him down. Rollie and Randy became my dinner buddies on the road. The best part of all this was that I was home again. Dinner a couple times a week at Mom and Dad's. I saw my brother Fred and my sister Jeannette a whole lot more. We had one of the most respected pitching coaches in all of baseball with Roger Craig. In a home ballpark even more spacious than The 'Stick. Everything was in place for me to succeed and live up to my potential.

That's the other problem. Everything was in place for me to succeed and live up to my potential.

No more excuses. A manager that didn't love me? Tough.

"Hey, JD?" Randy said as we sat on the bench during Dark's first game, at home in San Diego Stadium against the Houston Astros, "I spoke to Marvin last night. He wants you to help me out with union matters on the team."

"You mean like player rep?"

"Yeah, you would be co-player rep with me, making sure the players don't get taken advantage of, grievances, that sort of stuff. You good with that?"

"Sure. I'd love to help out."

"Good," Randy laughed, "'Cuz, no one else wants the fuckin' job, hahaha. Congrats, Bud." Marvin Miller had taken me under his wing during the Union strife last season. I was very happy to lend a hand. I was not very happy with my performance that first month. 0-1 in four starts, gave up 13 runs in less than 11 innings. 17 walks, including my first start in Candlestick as a Padre, where I was touched up for five hits and four walks in two-plus innings. Where in St. Louis I had a walks problem, once I arrived in San Diego, I had an everything problem. I lost my spot in the rotation by the middle of July, with a total of 12 days elapsing between the starts of July 10th and July 23rd, when I didn't last two innings against the Mets. I only gave up one dinger to this point in the season, but I just wasn't getting it done. There were no distractions. Wasn't running around much. The occasional beer with Randy and Rollie at dinner. I just wasn't getting it done.

Four days after the Mets start, we were at San Diego Stadium before a game when some of the position players were going through batting practice. Dave Kingman had just come over from New York about a month earlier at the trade deadline and wow, could he put on a show at BP. Seemed like every toss from Roger Craig, who was throwing us batting practice, ended up 450 feet away in the seats. After Kingman finished, I grabbed a bat. Took one swing, hit the pitch a good 430 feet over the left field fence. Would've really impressed myself had I not suddenly fell to the ground writhing in pain. The trainer ran out to the backstop.

"Johnny, you ok?" he asked, rolling me over. I was holding my right side, my pitching side.

"Think it's my rib," I wheezed back at him. The trainer picked me up and hopped me back to the clubhouse.

"Does that hurt?" he asked, once I was on the table in the trainer's room.

"Ah-ah, yeah a little," I replied. The trainer applied a heating pad and some other stuff as Randy entered the room. All smiles, of course.

"Hey, Slugger?" Randy joked, "The fuck happened?"

"Think I pulled something in batting practice-"

"Serves you right trying to swing with Kingman. Need me to get Roger?"

"I think I'll be ok, thanks. Just gonna lay here for a little while." I stayed in the trainer's room for most of the game before driving home shortly after the ninth inning. I woke up the next morning to a phone call from my general manager Buzzie Bavasi.

"Johnny?" Buzzie said, "The organization is sending you down."

I was blown away by this.

"Excuse me? Sending me down?"

"Yeah, you're going to AAA for a little while. Fix up your rib cage. Kind of a rehabilitation assignment."

"Shouldn't I be going on the disabled list or something? Sending me down?"

"It's the best thing for you and the ballclub. We're activating Randy and we need a spot on the roster. We'll see ya soon, son."

I couldn't believe what I was hearing. It wasn't like today where players go on rehab with the minor league clubs *after* they're placed on the DL. I called Marvin immediately.

"They can't do that to you," Marvin said, "That's a violation of the agreement. We can sue the ballclub." I considered it for a moment. I really didn't want to make trouble with the team, but I didn't want to go to AAA, either.

"Let me think about it. I'll call you back." Few minutes later, I spoke to the Padres player rep, the man who was replacing me on the roster.

"What's up, Bud?" Randy answered.

"The Padres are sending me down."

"Assholes."

"I know. Marvin thinks we should sue the team."

"You really wanna do that?"

After a pause. "No." Silence on the other end.

"Aw hell, JD, it's only a month. You know they're gonna call ya back in September."

"How do you know?"

"Because our pitching staff sucks. Shit, I'm fuckin' 4-7. Nobody in the organization throws as fast as you do. Think of it like a working vacation. You'll be back here in 30 days and if you're not, well then ya got yourself one hellvua grievance."

What Randy said made sense. This was my third organization in less than a year. Of any place in the majors, I wanted to be here. Buzzie was thinking more about Randy, the team's star pitcher, than me, which I sort of understood. I was just mad. I wasn't about to make a problem for Bob Fontaine and the front office.

"I'll talk to Marvin," Randy assured me, "Nobody's suing anybody. I gotta get myself straightened out, too. You'll be fine. Go to AAA, Johnny." Then Randy cackled, as if what he was about to say was the funniest thing in the world.

"Go get laidddd."

Our AAA affiliate was the Hawaii Islanders.

* * * * *

Palm trees? Check. Grass skirts in the airport? Check. White, sandy beaches? Eh, more light brown and a bit clumpy, but check. As I hopped into the cab outside Honolulu International, I expected to hear ukulele-fueled music, but all they played on the radio was *Hotel California*. Actually, Hawaii (at least the mainland) resembled the 5-0 long-running TV crime drama much more than the tour books – saw them filming the cop show a couple times by the Princess Hotel. Kinda reminded me of downtown Phoenix a little. Congested with peddlers, walkers and shady characters on street corners. A few skyscrapers that grew out of the coconut trees and adobe construction. The song resonated a great deal with me that month. Hawaii was all sunshine, beauty and heat, but something wasn't quite right about this place, something ominous. The cool breezes, the shapely women, the 90-degree evenings and every-single guy in that clubhouse would kill to be freezing their nuts off during a September night game in Toronto.

My first start I was firing on all cylinders; ended up with the win leaving in the eighth inning with a blister on my throwing hand. Got the victory in my second start, too – don't remember much about that one as I was cooked on a ton of Darvon the team doctors prescribed for me to deal with the agonizing pain stemming from the broken cartilage in my split rib cage. Mike Dupree saved the first game for me – here's an interesting story. 1977 was Dupree's fifth year in organized ball – had a cup of coffee with the

Pods the season before but was cut once again in spring training. Pitched in 36 games for Hawaii in 1977 – *played* in 70. Batted .352 in 108 at-bats. ERA of 4.75 in 97 innings. The franchise had no idea what to do with him. The story of many players on the Hawaii ballclub. Jim Fairey was hitting over .300 himself – he was 32 and a major league veteran of five seasons, an original Montreal Expo back in '69. John Balaz was our home run hitter – he spent a half season with the Angels before finding himself back at AAA. Eddie Watt was our closer. He was 36, an outstanding, underrated big-league reliever spanning close to a decade, 11 strikeouts in over 10 post-season innings. This was Eddie's third season trying to get back to the majors. Amidst the sadness there were pockets of glee in the clubhouse. The ballclub was a contender – how could they not be with all the major-league, replacement-level talent on the roster. Tons of AAAA guys. I made friends with Kala Kaaihue, the team's third-string catcher and native Hawaiian. Kala took us to all the local hangouts and nightclubs, where we'd drink and and cavort with 20-something, effervescent dancing queens until dawn. In many ways, Randy was spot-on. This *was* a vacation. Kala introduced me to his cousin Henry, who was part of a popular local music group, Cecilio & Kapono. We would play background bongos as the popular twosome sported an assortment of instruments, original songs and a select number of Top 40 tunes. Heard many different cover versions of Hotel California. Some nights I would leave early, stopping by Chuck's Steak House, which was close to my suite at the Outrigger Hotel in Waikiki. They were a major sponsor of the ballclub; the players enjoyed steak and lobster on the house every night in town. Amazing balcony overlooking the Pacific filled with a lineup of ladies across the bar. Was all a pretty neat scene for being stuck in the minors. And then I saw my teenage role model on a stool, leaning against the bar.

Alone. Head staring straight, eyes reading the mirror wall behind the bartender. Almost catatonic. Cigarette in one hand. Bourbon and water – hold the water – in the other. He wasn't there looking for anything, other than if you believe Buffett's classic song, his lost shaker of salt. He didn't recognize me at first, but the moment I saw Clay Kirby, former ace of the San Diego Padres pitching staff seven years earlier, by himself in a bar filled with friendly women and colorful locals, I got a sick pit in my stomach.

"Clay," I said, extending my hand to greet him. He cocked his head toward me, as if he was supposed to recognize my face, but it juuust wasn't coming to him.

"D'Acquisto," I continued, hands out as if I just delievered the punchline to a joke that confused the audience.

"Ohhh," Clay replied with slightest slur, "Johnny D. Heard a rumor about you comin' down to these parts. How ya feelin'?"

"Split my side in BP," I replied, as he ordered me a beer and himself a backup, "Buzzie decided to give me some all-expense paid R&R in AAA. Sure hope it's a round-trip ticket." Clay finished a drag and raised his eyebrows all too knowingly.

"Buzzie," Clay laughed, "How's the old bastard doin'?"

"Heh-heh, you know Buzzie." I couldn't and didn't want to get into it.

"God, what's it been? Two years?" Clay took a drag and thought for a moment.

"The Giants? '74, right? I think I struck out 11, maybe 12." Clay's eyes flashed a hint of youth when he said that. Pitchers remember their great games. Every single one of 'em. Sometimes when opposing players run into one another off the field, they talk baseball, especially their own accomplishments. Sometimes you're in the mood to bust each other's balls. Oftentimes, it's the only thing you have in common to keep the conversation going. Sometimes you just look at the women in the bar. This was Clay's moment. Seemed like he needed it.

"You were dynamite that night," I said. "None of us had a chance."

"Yeah." Then he glanced down and studied his drink with a faint smile. "Wonder where that guy is today." What I appreciated about Clay was his quick East Coast wit, which got sharper as more drinks were placed in front of him.

"How's life down here?" I asked, just trying to change the subject, looking around Chuck's Steak House and out toward the ocean.

"It's gorgeous," he half-laughed, "People are friendly. Our manager's not a shithead, but...you know...," as if Clay's expressive left hand and trailing off response said *we're still in the minor leagues*, regardless of the locale.

Clay Kirby was the bright, shining hope for the first five years of the Padres organization. Struck out 231 batters in '71. Won 15 games for a team that lost 100. As electric stuff as you'll ever see. Ended up with the Cincinnati Reds for a couple years, got a World Series ring even though he never pitched in the postseason. Right now, he was just a man trying to figure it all out in the minors. There were a lot of *"formers"* and *"one-timers"* littering the Islanders' roster if you read the Hawaii Tribune-Herald. Former Orioles ace reliever Eddie Watt. One-time original Montreal Expo Jim Fairey. Former stud major-leaguer Clay Kirby.

Wouldn't be the last time I heard about Clay's 11 strikeouts over a pack of Marlboro reds and Johnny Walker black that month.

* * * * *

Obviously, the primary difference between playing AAA in Honolulu versus, say Syracuse was the travel issue. The other ball clubs of the Pacific Coast League were located in Phoenix, Tucson, San Jose, Albuquerque, but also Salt Lake City, Spokane and Tacoma all the way up in Washington. It was probably the most expensive minor league in all of baseball. The teams would play two weeks in their home parks and two weeks on the road, due to all the travel, it was pretty set in stone. The thing to me was that I wasn't on a Pacific Southwest Airliner up and down the coast; I was on this time machine, stopping for the night through the corridors of my Baseball past. The phenoms that were rushed to the majors while I chilled in Phoenix back in '73 were still down here; Eddie Bane, who pitched in the big leagues straight from college by the Twins, was now languishing at Tacoma. David Clyde, the most sensationalized rookie pitcher before Mark Fidrych came along, sat at AAA Tucson trying to find his way. Close friends were all sprinkled around the league, guys I ate and drank with for years, guys I shared deep heart-to- heart talks. My high school buddy Kyle Hypes, still with Giants, but still with Phoenix. My best friend in Fresno, Skip James, was still there, too. This would be his *fifth* year at AAA for San Francisco. I lost a game in Spokane, a pitchers' duel against Willie Prall, a close teammate of mine in Decatur back in '71. That team's home run hitter was Gorman Thomas, a drinking buddy of mine from that same season. AAA can be the loneliest place in baseball. When you're in single A, everything's new, you probably have your first taste of freedom, first real exposure to girls, and yet you're not exposed to men who had earned and lost a taste of the bigs. Double-A's fun too, as you just received a promotion, the college recruits and draft picks come into town with their campus stories and slightly more mature (or perhaps enlightened) outlooks on life. The only former major leaguers you see at AA are players the organization is grooming for managerial or coaching roles. AAA is different. The kids are anxious to meet major league women and enjoy major league perks – and know they're prized possessions of the organization. The formers and one-timers are just looking for another glass of champagne on ice at the big league level. I finished up with a 4-3 record going into a playoff game against Phoenix. These feelings swelled up in me every time I watched Clay pitch. Game after game, I would see him step off the mound in despair, unable to do what he had done all through high school and through much of his time at the major league level: pitch competitive baseball. Clay would finish the season with a 1-7 record, an ERA close to eight. He would sit in the dugout, broken and disheartened. I had no clue what to say to him, how to comfort him. All you could do was walk by and slap a half-hearted tap on his knee. Many nights I would be going out with Kala to the clubs around town. I would stop by his apartment and invite him out. Clay would just be sitting there on his balcony, a light coastal breeze coming off the ocean, drinking whisky, smoking, talking about San Diego, our game in Cincinnati. Anything but the current situation. I would stay and keep him company for awhile. Sometimes he'd join us, sometimes he preferred to be alone. Clay lost his will to compete, his balls-to-the-wall spirit of 1969 as a fresh-faced rookie for the expansion Padres.

Last thing I remember about Hawaii was a call from Buzzie.

"Johnny, get up here for the team photo," he barked through the phone.

"But we're in the middle of the playoffs," I replied, "Don't you think I should be here and help them-"

"Nah, don't worry about that. We need you in the team picture. Your plane ticket is waiting for you." Click.

I wanted to remain in Honolulu to finish out the series against the Phoenix Giants, but I always did what I was told. Wanted to help these guys win. Came to really care for all of them, but I heard the mission bell. Time to come home. Taught me a real lesson about the lack of importance of minor league victories in the scope of the parent club. I knocked on Clay's door to say goodbye. He was sitting on his couch smoking a cigarette watching a game show, in the dark with the drapes closed. He saw me with luggage in my hands.

"You goin'?" he asked.

"Got the call," I sighed. Clay nodded with a slight smile. He didn't say anything.

"I'll see ya soon," I said, but we both knew that was bullshit.

"Yeah," he continued to nod. "I'll walk you out."

Clay grabbed one of my bags and dropped it in my trunk. I waved goodbye and drove away from the hotel wishing I knew him better back in his day; a very witty guy, even with a few in him, *especially* with a few in him. In the end, Clay checked out long before I arrived. Never left, either, at least not as a major leaguer. 1977 was his final season in professional baseball.

I wasn't gonna end up like that.

* * * *

"Fastball Johnny's back," cackled Randy, giving me a big hug as I made it onto the field at San Diego Stadium in time for the Padres' team photo, "How was Hawaii, Bud? Lots of bikinis, right?"

Randy made me chuckle a bit as the photographer had us ready for the picture, even if I was still feeling very guilty for leaving the Islanders during the championship series. "There's bikinis here."

"Ahhhh, c'mon, Hawaii's not San Diego, man."

"Eyes up, guys," the photographer yelled and snapped the photo.

"No, it's not," I said to Randy through a forced smile, "Not at all."

* * * * *

I didn't pitch for a good 10 days, and once I did, I still couldn't kill the beast. Knocked out in the second inning of a game against the Astros; gave up two runs on six hits. A relief appearance the next day saw me surrender another two runs in an inning's work. Five days later, against the Giants, I was touched up for four runs, five hits, three walks. After Derrel Thomas sliced a liner down the right-field line for a run-scoring double, the manager came and got me.

"That's enough, John," Alvin muttered, barely looking at me, taking the ball from my hand. It's the loneliest walk in the world coming out of a game during an inning. What makes it worse is you have to sit there and watch the next pitcher toss kerosene on your brush fire of an outing or show you how it's done by getting your team out of the jam. It's being fired in front of 100,000 people. You want to throw things and extinguish your self-hatred somehow, but the TV cameras cut to you as the color man explains how you failed, and again when the inning ends to watch you grab your jacket and mope into the clubhouse. I looked over and found Roger Craig, my only friend on the coaching staff, staring at me, trying to figure me out. You don't know if he's thinking, *"How the hell am I gonna fix this kid,"* or *"How the hell am I gonna tell the hometown boy there's no spot for him on the team next season."* The worst part of all is when no one in the dugout wants to say a damn word to you. The only contact comes from the funniest, most animated dude on the roster, Randy Jones, walking by solemnly.

He offers a supportive tap on your knee, adding a lifeless, "Get 'em next time, JD."

Humiliated, helpless, possibly out of answers. Had yet to find the passage back to the place I was before. One fear crept into my mind and haunted the remainder of my season, especially since the Eagles' monster single continued to enjoy what seemed like non-stop radio play, the spiritual soundtrack to my month in "paradise."

There might still be plenty of room at the Hotel Oahu for *Former Phenom John D'Acquisto.*

The Alternate

Imagine you're behind the wheel of a 1977 desert beige Porsche Turbo Carrera, ignoring the speed limit with extreme prejudice down Interstate 805, open sunroof, fiddling with the radio, searching for some Led Zeppelin as you approach the glistening sightline of San Diego Stadium. But dammit, all you're finding across the dial is Disco. You shrug, sigh and settle on Donna Summer's "*I Feel Love,*" which oddly starts to rev you up. The riveting, pulsating bass line behind the pop superstar's voice settles in your mind for awhile. It's now your personal soundtrack, as the most exhilarating night of your life is about to begin.

Here we go.

Imagine it's about five hours and seven local media interviews later. You're chilling in the National League dugout beside the legends of the game. Seaver. Morgan. Stargell. Niekro. You're sitting on the bench next to Pete Rose bullshitting about last night's gala thrown by Major League Baseball for the dignitaries of the host city.

Now imagine the public address announcer calling out your teammates' names, who trot onto the field in uniform to the enthusiastic applause of the crowd. Rollie Fingers. Dave Winfield.

You imagine your name will be called at any moment. Obviously, you're one of the hottest relievers in both leagues right now. Your ERA is 1.94 in 45+ innings. You've given up one home run all season. Mike Schmidt, "The Cobra," Dave Parker, up and coming Keith Hernandez are all counted among your many strikeouts. You're with esteemed colleagues on this day and you know what, you have their complete respect.

Now imagine this happening in your teams' home ballpark, in front of fans that absolutely adore you, who can't wait to see their guy standing shoulder-to-shoulder with the greatest ballplayers on the planet.

Now imagine this happening in your hometown, the town where you were born, where you were raised, in the same stadium where you tried out for the majors eight years earlier. Your Mom, your Dad, brother and sister sit right behind home plate alongside the league VIPs, beaming with pride, leaning over to catch a glimpse of your face in a dugout surrounded by future Hall of Famers. You receive a nod from your hometown buddy Graig Nettles across the field, with whom you also downed a few beers at one of the three functions you attended last night.

Yeah, you feel love all right. You feel recognition, you feel affection, you feel things in this game you've never felt before, like you're in the right place at the right time and your badass, 100 MPH-throwing right arm brought you here.

Imagine it's July 11th, 1978 and you're at the Major League All Star Game in San Diego, California.

Imagine 51,549 fans, mostly locals, a time when a family of four from La Mesa could afford and access All-Star tickets, fans that know your name, that want to see you on the field in the worst way, in front of Commissioner Bowie Kuhn and former President Gerald Ford, who's about to toss out the first ball.

Now imagine if you could change just one critical element to this picture…

* * * * *

1977 ended with some pretty rough performances on my part. George Foster and Johnny Bench teed off on me in my final start, with Foster wielding that famous black bat of his and connecting on a perfect dinger to straight away center for his 52nd Home Run of the year. As for Bench, well, he jacked a moon shot grand slam into the left field seats, on the way to a brutal 8-0 loss at Riverfront Stadium. My stuff was simply flat, a lackluster curveball to go along with lifeless heat that everyone knew was coming. I was also messing around with a slurve that Steve Carlton had taught me in Spring Training when the Cardinals faced the Phillies in Clearwater, but I hadn't quite mastered it. The day after the season ended, I had a beer with Roger Craig. We had just gotten out of a meeting with Bob Fontaine, the Padres' General Manager, a really great guy who did his very best to look out for me.

"You gotta do something about this, Johnny," Roger said, in a fatherly manner, "You gotta be better than what ya shown us, unless ya wanna end up back in AAA next season. Or worse." I didn't want to consider "*or worse*," but there was nothing to say. He was right. I suffered an oblique tear, pulled hamstring, I was traded, whatever, I had a very bad year. At age 26 now, no one wanted to hear excuses.

"I need ya to pitch in Tijuana over the winter," Roger said as we finished up. "You can work on a few things, ya can still live at home in San Diego and drive over the border and sleep in your own bed after home games. This ain't about off-years anymore, Johnny. We're talking about saving your career before ya get lost in the mix of young prospects." It bothered me that the conversation sounded more like a friendly reminder about last chances.

"We want ya to make the team next season," Roger continued, walking me to my car outside the restaurant.

"Really?" I replied, not 100% sure about Alvin Dark's feelings on the matter.

"*I want ya* to make the team. Bob wants ya to make the team. You're a San Diego kid, of course the organization wants ya to succeed here. The only way you're gonna do that is if ya get out of the gate quickly in Spring Training. The way for ya to get out of the gate quickly is to go to Winter Ball. We think it's a good idea that you play for them and it's good relations between the Padres and the Tijuana Potros (Ponies)." So I did it. The fact wasn't so much that Bob liked me or Roger liked me, but that I still had a lively arm and I was a local San Diego kid. If I could somehow get it together, I could become one of the team's top ambassadors to the city.

"One more thing," Roger asked before driving away, "You're not throwing to the glove. All year I watched ya throwing to the batter, to the plate, everywhere but the glove. When you're in Mexico, throw to the glove."

"Is that your big fix, Doctor?" I laughed, "Just like that?"

"It's a fuckin' start," Roger shot back, shutting me up. "Call me if ya need anything." He drove away and I started plotting routes to my new ballpark.

In another country.

* * * * *

There are worse things in life than Winter Ball in Mexico. Of course, Roger's advice was spot on. I started just throwing to the glove, not concerned about any external factors. Just the glove.

I went 9-0 for Tijuana, spoke enough Spanish to conduct interviews with the local press and they called me "El Gigante" (*"The Giant"*). I averaged 16 strikeouts a start. I felt healthy, I felt strong, most important, I felt ready for 1978.

Arriving at Spring Training in Yuma one month later, there were a stockpile of former Number One draft picks in camp. Me, Mike Ivie, Billy Almon, Dave Roberts, Dave Winfield, of course. While all the other pitchers I competed against were just beginning to get into shape, I'm in mid-season form. I already threw about 110 innings or so down in Mexico.

There wasn't too much room left on the staff. Randy Jones, Bob Shirley and of course Rollie Fingers were set. Holdovers from the Johnny McNamara years Dan Spillner and Dave Freisleben were making the team. The ballclub brought Gaylord Perry into town a couple months earlier, so you knew he had a spot. Mickey Lolich was invited to camp to see if he had something left and would most likely make the club. The front office really wanted Brent Strom to overcome his injuries. Bobby Owchinko, Dave Wehrmeister, Mark Lee – tons of rookies vying for the last three spots. This wasn't an open and shut case for me at all. Especially with Alvin Dark in the managers' seat. He didn't like me one bit.You would be shocked how much that matters even in the majors. Doug Rader was the funniest guy in the clubhouse when I first arrived in '77, wonderful teammate, a true life-of-the-party type, the one you always wanted hanging out with you on the road. Ten days later, Rader was sold and shipped to the Toronto Blue Jays. Not traded. *Sold.* He was batting .271 with a .392 OBP. 'Nuff said.

I knew the deck was really stacked against me. Two months earlier, my brother Fred, who was working for Pacific Southwest Airlines at the San Diego airport during this time, recognized Dark's name on a charter flight list and introduced himself. Remarkably, after some polite chit chat, Dark admitted to my brother that he's gonna send me down to AA. Not AAA, not Hawaii. Alexandria, Virginia. Could Dark have been sending me a message to get my ass in gear? I suppose, but I was lights-out in Winter Ball and I'm sure Dark was receiving the reports. There was no reason to motivate me. I had been told Dark was not happy with my living arrangements at the time.

I had two female roommates – both stewardesses I met on flights the previous season - at a condo in Tierrasanta, right outside San Diego. The TV show *"Three's Company"* was closer to the truth of the times than you could ever imagine. My brother called me immediately to warn of the situation. I was extremely aware I had to prove myself, but now I knew there was a chance it wouldn't matter. I couldn't let that affect me. My career was at stake. It was a pretty groovy arrangement with the ladies, until the phone rang one morning a couple weeks before spring training began.

"Is *Jackie* there?" this gruff guy asked me, a little curiousity in his voice that a man answered the phone. He sounded familiar. *Really* familiar.

"Who's this?" I answered.

"Who's *this?*" he answered back, annoyed.

"Who is calling?" I said.

"*All-Star Player***," he replied.

"Hey, this is John D'Acquisto. What are you doin' calling here, man?"

A guy I'd met 10-15 times easy, teammates with a buddy of mine on another ball club, didn't even respond in kind. Didn't care.

"I wanna talk to Jackie. Can ya just put her on the phone?"

"She's not here. Don't call back." Click. Total asshole. I faced him a few more times over the years. The phone call never came up, but I knew right then and there, beyond Dark's issues with my roommates, I should probably get my own place.

*****

After settling in at camp, I met with Roger Craig and Chuck Estrada, my AAA pitching coach in Hawaii. Roger knew what Dark's plans were and said he would go to bat for me, at the very least, get me in AAA Hawaii rather than on the other side of the country. Estrada walked me out of Craig's office and toward the ball fields.

"Johnny, you did great in Mexico, but Tijuana's not the majors," Chuck said. "Let's see how you throw here and we'll figure everything out."

Over the next two weeks, Chuck and I worked side by side, with Roger checking in on the progress. It was like a sports movie montage.

"No, no, no," Chuck would wave his hands at me, examining my mechanics on the practice fields, "You're going too fast. Keep the motion fluid, but slow it down."

He analyzed the manner my arms would swing. He grasped my shoulders, bringing my palms into my face instead of over my head, the way Roger Clemens and Andy Petitte used to wind up, how they peek over their glove, their arms don't go over their head. "You need to simplify your motion. Needs to be more compact."

Roger tried to teach me the split-fingered fastball, but with all the surgery I'd been through, the force of the pitch placed too much pressure on my elbow, so that was scrapped. Still trying to master the slurve. I was getting there, but something just wasn't quite right.

Outside of the failed split-finger experiment, I was throwing strikes consistently, with heat, with command, with location. From the backfields, I was soon chucking unhittable gas in spring games. The more I threw strikes, the more confidence I had.

Meanwhile, Dark was having a terrible go of it communicating with the players. Same story as my previous year's spring training with Vern Rapp and the Cardinals. The old generation of manager, the more contentious, lights out at nine, no facial hair-types, were falling by the wayside all across the Major League landscape, while younger men with evolved philosophies in handling the clubhouse, guys like Joe Torre with the Mets, were popping up everywhere. Dark had an absolutely awful relationship with the players. He tried to get Mike Ivie back behind the plate, but Ivie still had issues with tossing the ball to the pitcher. A week later, Bob Fontaine ended up trading Ivie to San Francisco for Derrel Thomas. Players started complaining about Dark to Fontaine, his approach, his Christian preaching in the clubhouse, among a much larger laundry list. Something had to be done.

The other issue was Billy Almon, our starting shortstop. He had a so-so year with the bat in '77, but a fourth-round draft pick, a non-roster player named Ozzie Smith, with only a single year of minor-league seasoning came out of nowhere in camp and covered everything on the field. He pushed Billy off of shortstop, which wasn't that hard to do because Billy made 41 errors with minimal range the previous season. Gaylord would say to Rollie, "*Man, if the kid plays like this in the regular season, I might win 20 games this year.*" Young Ozzie Smith was like a Kirby Vacuum Cleaner out there. He covered the third base hole, behind the bag at second and was smooth as silk. He was also one of the sweetest kids you'd ever want to meet. Everyone liked Almon, too. Smart guy, graduated from Brown and never threw it in anyone's face, but he was no Ozzie. From Day One, we all wanted Ozzie behind us. I don't know if even Ozzie himself was aware of this, but Roger had Chuck speak with the veteran pitchers to get their opinions on whether to keep the light-hitting Ozzie on the opening day roster. "*You're crazy if you send that kid down,*" I said to him. Now none of us had any idea that he would become a Hall-of-Fame caliber player. We just knew he would save us a whole bunch of runs. Ozzie and I had an excellent rapport, especially in the field, exceptional timing. We picked off maybe three or four guys in spring training from second base. I would be on the mound, look over, Ozzie would wink at me, get behind the runner. I would set, lift my leg, turn and throw. It was like picking cherries from a tree. Problem now became where Billy would play in the field. Almon ultimately ended up at third, but wasn't much of an improvement. While he didn't make 41 errors, he wasn't a third baseman. Really could've used Doug Rader's glove at the hot corner in '78.

* * * * *

The team bus was a very status-filled place in spring training. The manager sat up front with his coaches either beside him or a couple rows behind. Then rookies and veterans in the back. Late in spring training, there was a roster sheet of who was going on the road trips during the end of March, and if you weren't on that list, you were staying behind and your ticket was most likely headed to minor-league camp. Chuck found me outside the clubhouse before I found the roster sheet.

"I need to tell you something," Chuck said. "You're going on the road trip." I was a veteran by this point and knew not to take anything for granted.

"Gotcha," I shrugged.

"You know the rule of thumb, Johnny. I dunno anything for sure, but I think you might've made it."

"That's nice to hear," I said, "But I won't believe it until I see the final roster in the Sunday paper."

Chuck tapped me on the shoulder to get my attention.

"Hey, just hang tight, don't get in any trouble, don't piss off Dark, don't make any waves. I think something's up. Just hang in there. Now c'mon, let's get on the bus."

I had no idea what moves could possibly be made. Blockbuster trade? One of the veterans got hurt? I never considered what he could have meant that.

As we stepped onto the bus, I knew exactly what Chuck meant.

Roger was sitting in Alvin Dark's seat in the first row.

I was stunned, then amused. Craig greeted me with this sly-dog wink, a cocky nod hello. I laughed and he smiled, then threw me a playful *"Get your ass in the back of the bus"* beckon.

Alvin Dark was fired. It was only the second time in baseball history that a manager was fired in spring training.

The headline was that Dark was gone. The story was that I made the team.

*****

I felt great being in San Diego and making the roster. Besides having a spot on the pitching staff, I was amongst very close baseball friends. Randy Jones, Rollie Fingers and me continued to hang out all the time on the road. Soon enough, Roger would ask me to add another fellow to our gang.

"You did good this spring," Roger nodded later as we packed up on the last day of camp, "We're trying to figure out where your place is on the staff, but we know we need your arm. We're thinking you could really help us coming out of the bullpen, pitching an inning or two before Rollie gets the ball in the 7th or 8th. Maybe a spot start here or there."

"Roger, thanks for believing in me," I replied, "I feel good this year."

"Ya look good, Johnny. Keep it up. Let's go home." Roger slapped me on the back as I left his office.

"Oh, one more thing," he said, slowly spinning around, "Looks like Mickey's coming back with us, too. He's gonna need a place to stay in San Diego. You have room?" I had just found a new townhouse in La Jolla. I welcomed Mickey into my home until his wife Mary Ann was able to move out west and join him.

Mickey Lolich had taken off the 1977 season after being very unhappy with the New York Mets. Bob gave him a shot in camp to see what he had left. Turns out Mickey could still get batters out, though his fastball wasn't nearly the same. I made some room in the townhouse to let Mickey stay with me. One of the best moves I made all year.

Mickey loved motorcycles almost as much as I loved cars. Most mornings when I made breakfast, we'd be talking Porsches, Harleys or pitching. It was the best situation for me. I had Roger Craig, one of the greatest pitching coaches in history as my manager; Chuck Estrada, my friend and new pitching coach and World Series hero Mickey Lolich, my roommate. I always had knowledgeable, friendly people around me to talk through any issues I might have had on the mound. Hell, I even ran across Lefty Carlton during batting practice when the Padres played against the Phillies at Veterans Stadium in late April.

"What am I doing wrong?" I asked Carlton, "The Slurve's not workin' for me."

"How are you grippin' it?" replied Professor Carlton. Lefty examined my hand on the ball.

"I see the problem," Lefty nodded, "You're not placing enough pressure on the seams." I took that knowledge to the bullpen and worked on it later during the game. It was like a whole new pitch.

Now you could say I was getting too much advice that could be completely confusing and with some guys, you'd be right. To me, it wasn't a matter of too many cooks spoiling the broth; it was a group of brilliant celebrity chefs and I was the innovative dish being prepared in the San Diego test kitchen. We would soon find out if the meal was a success.

* * * * *

"I could really get used to this," I said to Donna, half-asleep at the Hyatt in Atlanta, a week into the season. Donna rolled over to face me with a curious smirk, her eye-liner slightly smudged from the night before, surrounding long lashes.

"Get used to what?"

"This," I continued, half-ass wave right above us, "Waking up with a girlfriend. Not just a girlfriend, but a girl who's my friend, ya catch my drift?"

Donna had light blond hair and quite a figure, but more than that, she was educated with a sense of humor that was flirty-sarcastic. She had the wit of a Hollywood writer and the body of a Showcase Showdown model. We met a few years back during a stop against Phil Niekro and the Braves.

"Are you asking me out?" she giggled, sliding her fingers down my arm. That was the great thing about Donna: she was always in on the joke.

"I dunno. It'd just be nice to have someone you like to do crossword puzzles with."

"I've never seen you read a newspaper-"

"No, crossword puzzles are a drag, that's not what I'm saying. I'm saying I like you. More than just…I don't think of you as a road-trip gal." Donna gave me this *"hmmm"* face, slowly rolling back, exploring the ceiling fan as if it held the answer to our problem.

"How would this work with me in Atlanta and you all over the country?"

"You're from California. You don't think there's social work jobs in San Diego?"

"Well, what about your two room-mates?" Donna hit me a smug grin when she said *roommates*. I returned the volley.

"I traded them for a 38-year old guy."

"You did that for me?"

"Oh yeah." Donna threw me the *"bullshit!"* leer and laugh-snort as she kissed me.

"Will you think about it?" I asked her. She nodded and got up to get ready to leave.

I walked Donna to her car outside the hotel.

"I'm serious," I said. Donna studied my face, her expression a duel between skepticism and hope.

"Okay," she said, still not certain what to make of the offer. I kissed her goodbye as she hopped in and turned the ignition.

"Think about it," I said one more time, ducking through her window.

"'Bye, Johnny," she said, driving away. Sure, I was running around with my head in the clouds all across the National League, but when I came home after away games to each town's Hilton, Sheration, Marriott, whatever, I kicked off my shoes, closed my eyes, and thought of Donna.

I hoped she thought back.

* * * * *

As April came to a close, it was clear Ozzie Smith was something special. No one could field the position like him. First and third situations with nobody out in 1977 became two gone with none on in '78. Roger placed Mickey in the bullpen and Lolich was firing on all cylinders. Just one problem. Mickey pitched five times in the first 12 games. Seemed a little much for someone who hadn't thrown at all the previous year. By the middle of the month, Mickey blew out his knee and was gone for three months. So my workload increased shortly thereafter.

The outfield was a whole other story. Dave Winfield continued to blossom, securing right field, not at all intimidated by San Diego Stadium's cavernous dimensions. Left and center were sort of a revolving door. Oscar Gamble was a free agent we brought over from the White Sox after he hit 31 dingers in the Windy City.

San Diego Stadium was not Comiskey Park, though. He didn't hit one out at home until May 24th. Gene Richards was our leadoff hitter and left fielder, but played more than 50 games in center and first base when Tenace was behind the plate. Then there was George Hendrick, who had been our center fielder in '77 but got off to a rough start with the bat, only had like two homers during the first month of the season. George was a real quiet guy. Some people labeled him moody, sullen, all those words you would read beside his name in the newspapers. He was a great teammate, he just kept to himself. I will say I didn't notice him smile much, but we didn't chat all that much, either. When I would see him in the players' parking lot, I would catch his eye staring at my Porsche, but he never said a word. I walked by him again a few days later, still staring, said nothing. As I was entered the clubhouse the following day, I walked by George's locker.

"I like your car," George mumbled.

I stopped and looked over.

"What's that?" I asked casually.

"Your car. I like your car. It's a nice car."

"Thanks, man."

"Very cool." I laughed a little, then reached into my pocket.

"Wanna drive it?" George's head inched up slowly until his eyes met mine. We stared at one another for what seemed like an hour.

George smiled. I threw him the keys.

We got out to the car, George stepped in, turned the engine over and listened to the purr of 400 horsepower. It's one of my favorite sounds in the world. He looked over to me and I saw the first George Hendrick smile in my career.

"Shittt," George laughed and nodded, grooving to the motor's melody as we pealed out of the parking lot.

We flew down Interstate 8, Hendrick was shifting through gears, squeezing the pedal, the odometer on the verge of 100, "*Disco Inferno*" screaming through the cutting-edge Quadraphonic Blapunkt stereo, swerving in and out of lanes like an All-Pro running back stepping between holes in the offensive line, commanding everyone's attention on the road. We're not talking, but he's got a grin from ear to ear. It's moments like this between teammates, where you share a piece of your life away from the game, that really stays with you.

Cruising off the freeway, we stopped at a red light.

"I want one," George stated, serious as a heart attack. I glanced at my watch.

"We still have a couple hours before first pitch-"

"Let's go now," George interrupted as the light turned green.

"Hit it," I nodded, and George just floored that puppy, getting us back on the highway.

As cool a teammate bonding experience as I ever had. We actually ended up going back to the stadium, but George bought a Porsche for himself shortly thereafter. The best part of all this was seeing the other guys tell George how cool his car was, Hendrick's proud papa smile, the joy in his voice as he described his new wheels. Became the conversation piece that broke the ice with the other players.

* * * * *

Although I was pitching very well, the team wasn't playing that great. By the end of May, we were 13-10 at home, but ran a 9-16 record on the road. I felt great personally, though. I had a 1.12 ERA and hadn't given up a home run to this point. All the work and advice Roger, Chuck and Mickey offered was paying off beautifully. When The Dodgers came to town around this time, I was chatting with my Dad on the field during batting practice when Tommy Lasorda came walking over. He knew my Pop for a few years and complemented me in front of him.

"You know, Johnny's doing real well this year," Tommy said, "If he keeps this up, I might pick him to be on my All-Star staff."

"Is that so?" Dad replied, turning to me with a proud smile.

"Sure, I'd love a good Italian boy to represent the Padres, why not? He just has to keep this pace."

"If you do that, I'll kiss ya. You'll have free meals at Anthony's for the rest of your life."

"Now that's something I'd have to think about," Tommy laughed. I honestly thought this was a game-changer with Tommy, as the next thing he said was one of the great complements I'd ever heard in my career.

"Oh, by the way, Fred, I'm trying to get your kid on the Dodgers."

"Why the hell would you do that?" Dad laughed, "Make me drive 90 minutes to see the boy pitch? Leave him here in San Diego." That's when I knew things might happen, that I might end up in that All-Star dugout come July.

* * * * *

Outside my personal success, some changes had to be made on the roster. I got into the clubhouse the next day only to be told that we just traded Hendrick to the Cardinals. I was kinda disappointed. I had just gotten to know George a little bit and felt he would eventually get it together. That was the bad news. The good news was that my buddy Eric Rasmussen was coming to town. Rassie had been a much better pitcher for the Cardinals in '77 than his 11-17 record would indicate. The club figured in spacious San Diego Stadium, Rassie could perform.

By the end of June, my ERA increased a bit to 1.35, but the front office let me know I was on the short list to be named to the All-Star Team. The general manager came by my locker before a game against the Giants.

"Don't make any plans for the break," Bob said, "Even if you don't make the team, if someone drops off the roster, you're going to be named. In case someone gets hurt, they want an arm from here to take his place. That's gonna be you, so be ready." I'd never been so thrilled in my life. To even be considered an All-Star was something I always dreamed of. Like the understudy in a Broadway play, I was backstage in the wings, an All-Star in waiting.

After the game, a few of my teammates made plans to head into Mission Valley. That was where all the after-hours action happened in San Diego back then. So many ways for a guy to get himself in trouble down there – especially young men with money.

"Yo, Johnny?" one of our position players asked me, "Hang out with us tonight. You're Mr. San Diego. Show us where all the shit gets funky." There were a few of my teammates who liked to stay out until dawn and get in the thick of it. While I spent most of my nights on the road at dinner with Rollie and Randy, once the team returned to San Diego, Rollie did his own thing and Randy ran straight home to be with Marie, his wife. You usually didn't have to twist my arm to have a reasonably good time, but as I replied to the fellas, I felt a tap on my shoulder.

"Hey JD?" Gaylord said, "Wanna go get some grub?" I turned to my other teammates. Didn't want to be rude, but I knew a night with them wouldn't end until the sun came up. Plus, Gaylord wouldn't have asked me if he didn't really want some company.

"Guys, I gotta go put the old man to bed," I laughed, handling the declined invitation as delicately as possible, "Maybe I'll catch up later." My teammates left and I took Gaylord to The Old Ox, one of the finer steakhouses in Misson Valley at the time.

"You know Roger wants me to keep an eye on ya," Gaylord said through his thick, North Carolina drawl, as we plowed through a couple of 14 oz ribeyes, "Doesn't want anything happenin' to his prize pupil." I appreciated the affection and concern, but I was slightly offended. This was my town. I knew where to go, who to avoid, where the spots were that people found *"activities."*

"I can handle myself, Gay," I replied, "I don't do any of that stuff anyway."

"'Cuz, ya know, you're makin' Roger look real good. You make a man look smart, he'll always watch out for ya."

"I'm makin' Roger look good? When's the last time you had a year like this?" Gaylord reached for his drink, considered my thought, then raised his glass to me and laughed.

"Good point, pardner." The fact was, Roger was doing a trememdous job getting the most from Perry as well as myself. If you look closely at his stats, you'll see that Gaylord was 8-3 with a 2.80 ERA around the beginning of July, clearly having his best season in close to four years. All-Star numbers in any league. Thing was, Gaylord wanted no part of the festivities. As great as he was pitching, he was also 39, living alone in San Diego while his wife Blanche was back at the peanut farm in North Carolina with the kids. He needed the break badly, and made it clear to all parties involved; he was going home for those three days. We also needed Gaylord to be in a healthy frame of mind and body, so he was never considered. Really had me wishing I had a meaningful person in my life waiting for me somewhere. Donna had yet to reach out.

Now on the surface, I could never legitimately complain about my life during this time. Driving to the ballpark in a Porsche each morning during a home stand, in a workplace where I enjoyed the company of all my teammates, had zero enemies either in management or among the employees, at a job I always adored, playing in games like that one against the Dodgers, relieving Gaylord with the bases loaded, the crowd of 27,100 behind me as I faced Rick Monday and Billy North, freezing them both with my 100-MPH heater, trotting off the field to the cheers of thousands, locking down the last three innings, some good-natured back-and-forth ribbing with the Union-Tribune beat guys in the locker room, but then I'd look around and everyone had already gone. I would leave the clubhouse and just head down the freeway toward La Jolla, *"Baker Street"* blasting at full volume on the Blaupunkt, arrive to an empty house, there's nothing in the fridge but sliced lemons and olives, turn on the TV just in time for the late news, watching myself on the sports report. *By myself.* I managed to avoid the trouble that can find you when extreme loneliness sets in and sure, I enjoyed some pre-dawn visitors, but there were getting to be too many nights I fell asleep alone. I couldn't handle much more solitude and I was tired of making that phone call. You know the one:

"Hey Julie....yeah, it's me, how ya been....I know, really sorry....yeah, just me...that'd be dynamite....see ya soon...and Julie....can you bring some Jack in the Box?"

I made that call, because of course I did, but it was time for a serious change in my home life.

I was there for the emotional taking.

* * * * *

A few weeks later, I spent my day off at the San Diego Convention Center as Co-MC of the 1978 Miss San Diego Beauty Pageant. This was the preliminary to the Miss California spectacle, leading up to Miss USA, America's original Final Four competition. As my pitching improved, the front office leveraged my status as the local boy made good and increased my personal appearances around town. The pageant featured the most beautiful and intelligent single women in the area. Of course, there's an element of ambition to any person, man or woman, who enters themselves into such a parade. The appearance was not much more than the MC, Brian Main, announcing to the crowd of 250 people that I was there as a judge, didn't speak much. Wasn't televised or anything, just me conferring with other local celebrities over which young woman would represent the county in the state competition. I was about to discover competition didn't merely exist on the ball field or even the pageant stage.

The after-party was held at the Intercontinental Plaza hotel in the banquet room. I chatted with Brian afterward by the open bar when I caught the eye of this gorgeous, 5-foot 9-inch blue-eyed blonde standing by the sternos in the corner of the room. I curved through the cattle of local sponsors and their friends in suits and dresses and made a beeline toward the warmed over Chicken Marsala and asparagus.

"I'm Missy," she said, "I work for a PR firm down on Broadway." Missy was this bright, charismatic woman from Iowa. Very Midwest America. Reminded me a little of Katie back in my Decatur days in the minor leagues. We chatted for awhile enjoying one another's company, comparing notes on her Iowa upbringing versus my Illinois experience.

"Hi, I'm Missy's friend," Liz greeted me, interrupting us. Liz had short, sandy-blond hair, brownish eyes, well-manicured, very intelligent with a trim figure. Both women were very attractive.

"Nice to meet you, Liz," I replied, as I glanced quickly to Missy.

"Liz won one of the local pageants last year," Missy remarked, nodding to her friend.

"Oh, that's interesting." I remained focused on Missy. As the night moved forward, the three of us continued conversing.

"Missy, can you come with me for a sec?" Liz said about 30 minutes later.

"Sure," Missy replied with a quizzical look, and the two of them headed toward the ladies' room. Not five minutes later only one of them returned.

"Missy apologizes," Liz said politely, "She has to finish her work for the night."

"Oh really?" I said, "She didn't mention to me that she worked for the pageant."

"Oh no, she doesn't. She's my assistant." The picture came together rather quickly. I should've made a stronger gesture toward tracking down Missy, but if I'm honest with myself, Liz was pretty much the whole package. The daughter of an influential businessman in town, very presentable, not at all a groupie. All things considered, Missy for Liz was an even-up swap.

Still would've traded both of them and a handful of prospects for Donna.

As Liz and I left the after-party about 90 minutes later through the hotel lobby, we passed Missy in conversation with the other judges. She gave us a gracious send-off, but as I departed toward the car, I looked back and my eyes caught Missy's. Regretfully, I wanted to get to know Missy better. Even more regretfully, I allowed someone into my life that I probably shouldn't have.

Wouldn't be the last time.

* * * * *

Today, people wonder if an All-Star Game is truly necessary, but I believe that having the Midsummer Classic in San Diego in 1978 gave the franchise the jumpstart it needed with the fan base. Remember, only four years earlier, the team was all set to be sold and moved to Washington, D.C. Now the Padres were becoming a scene, and we were among the best teams in baseball when we played in San Diego Stadium.

About two weeks before the All-Star break, I was hanging out with Rollie in the clubhouse. Fingers was told he was probably going to represent us at the game, along with Winfield.

"I may sit this one out," he told me, in reference to the All-Star Game, "My arm hurts." Being so close to Rollie, this put me in sort of a tough spot. I wanted to go in the worst way, and if Rollie bowed out, I would've been an All-Star – that's something that no one can ever take away from you. Nowadays, cute writers like to take dopey potshots at average players who made one random All-Star Game in otherwise nondescript careers, but when all is said and done, you were still an All-Star, and none of the snark or sarcastic remarks can ever change that. No matter where my career would take me, I would always be *"All Star John D'Acquisto."* It's a tough situation when you want something your friend possesses. I felt guilty wanting it so badly.

* * * * *

A few days later, I was driving toward the stadium when I heard on the radio that it was official, Winny and Rollie were named as reserves to the All-Star squad. I didn't feel snubbed in any way, but yet of course I was disappointed. Really wanted to be out there and receive that validation. As I got out of my car, Randy Jones drove into the players' lot. He honked his horn to get my attention.

"Hey Bud, look what I just got?" You guessed it; a Black Porsche Carrera.

* * * * *

Sad as I was not to be on the official roster, the league took care of me. In exchange for staying ready in case a pitcher went down, they awarded me four tickets behind home plate for my family to come see me in case I made it. Bob reminded me that I was still "*on-call*," which meant in addition to possibly playing, I was required to attend every league function surrounding the game, as if I was an actual All-Star.

"Johnny, you need to head to the Marriott," Bob said the night before the game, "Go to the ballroom for the MLB gala. The league's having the big party there, all the players will be there, we want you there, too."

The city was buzzing. Everyone from the league offices was there, retired players flown in as guests of Major League Baseball showed up. You couldn't get a hotel room in town if you tried. They didn't have Fanfest or anything back then, but they had parties, media parties. Multiple cocktail hours and sit-down dinners over those two nights. Late-night after-party drinks with major advertisers, getting caught in the corner by some rep from a candy company, nodding my head and listening for 30 minutes. I was all over the place. I'd go out in the hallway from the party and chat with the Union Tribune guys or the sports reporter for local CBS Channel 8 news. Everywhere I went during those three days, there was someone with a microphone in my face. I did get some face time with Goose and Nettles. Rollie was there, too. Even Gene Tenace popped his head in at one of the parties. Geno was beloved in San Diego and still very tight with Rollie from their A's days. I remember that night, Rollie leaning into me, softly saying, "I think I'm gonna play. Should be a lot of fun."

"Your arm, ok?" I replied, sipping a beer. Rollie chuckled, curling his handlebar moustache even further, nodding his head.

"Nope. Still hurts."

I didn't blame him, not at all. Seeing how the whole city embraced this event, of course you'd want to be a part of it, too.

* * * * *

When I arrived at the ballpark on the day of the All-Star Game, I mingled in the press box conducting still more interviews with local media. Bob Fontaine stepped over to me after I was finished.

"I need you to go down on the field," he said. "Stay in the clubhouse with the players. Tommy told me they still might need you to suit up." The dream remained alive. I walked quickly through the press area, down the elevator and into the clubhouse, where I found the best of the best. Garvey. Bowa. Foster. Vida Blue stepping through on his way to the pen to warm up. Tommy John. Reggie Smith. The top players in the league getting ready for the game. I looked over and found my uniform hanging in my locker. My teammates' gear was cleared out to make way for the All-Stars. Mine was still there in the event I had to come out in relief and make an appearance. I waited and waited, as Luzinski, Rick Monday and Ted Simmons began walking down the runway toward the dugout. Tommy saw me and trotted over.

"Hiya, Pal," Lasorda greeted, slapping me on the back. "Are you ready?"

I wasn't quite sure what he meant by that, but I hoped. Boy, did I hope it meant what I wanted it to mean.

"As soon as you tell me," I cracked.

"Well, it looks like we're gonna be okay, but stay put. We still may need ya."

"Thanks, Skip," I said, knowing my uniform would remain untouched.

I was the last one to leave the room, walking toward the dugout. I chatted with a few more of the guys on the bench before the lineups were announced. Once I saw the microphone being placed at home plate for the singing of the National Anthem, I knew I would be a fan for the rest of the night.

I stood by the dugout door, and watched the players' names get called one by one to the delight of the crowd. I knew my family would not get to see me run on that field, have my name announced by the great John DeMott, the Padres' beloved public address announcer. Obviously, it wasn't the worst thing in the world. It just would've been nice.

As Paul Pryor, the Home Plate umpire for the game cried "*Play Ball*," I enthusiastically clapped, nodded, smiled and turned away, disappearing through the dark tunnel and into the clubhouse.

* * * * *

My relationship with Liz escalated quickly. I mean *quickly*. I was so impressed with her wonderful family and Liz herself, actually. We made a good pair at social gatherings, and with my continued success on the field, I felt I needed a life partner. Liz eagerly accepted my marriage proposal and began plans for a 1979 wedding. Two weeks after the announcement, Liz told me she had business meetings all morning and afternoon. I was home on an off-day when the doorbell rang. I got out of bed curious, as by this point, Liz had a key to the townhouse.

"Hi, Johnny."

Donna.

"I took the job at the hospital here in town. Isn't that great?" I hadn't heard from Donna in months. So I thought, that's that, right? Donna was my first choice out of all of them. We just clicked on an emotional level rather than me being impressed for all the semi-wrong reasons.

"Can I come in?" she laughed.

"Yeah," I replied with a soft uncertainty in my voice, "Absolutely." I sat there having coffee with Donna explaining the situation.

"You never....you never called me."

"I know, Johnny, I'm so sorry. It was between this job and another in the San Francisco – I'm still waiting to hear back from the medical center in the Bay area, that's a super job. For right now, I got a month-to-month place here in town. I should've dropped you a line."

"No, it's okay, I just-"

A knock at the door. Probably don't have to tell you who was there.

"Hi, Liz," I greeted her.

"Who's car is that in the drivew-" Liz poked her head inside to find Donna on the couch sipping coffee. My life was turning back into that bad "Three's Company" episode by the second.

"Who's that and why is she drinking out of my mug-"

"Liz, an old friend just stopped by-"

"You don't have any old friends-"

"She just stopped by, nothing happened-"

"You're a bastard." Liz removed the ring, chucked it at me and through tears, ran back to her car.

"Liz, hold up, why you buggin' out-" Liz got in her Honda Accord and slammed the door.

"Don't call me. Weddings off." Liz drove away, leaving me standing there on my small lawn, holding the ring between my fingers. I turned back to find Donna leaning against the front door with a knowing grin.

"Congratulations on the engagement, Johnny." I didn't know what to do. I just laughed.

"Wanna get a bite to eat? Talk about it?" Donna suggested. I tell ya, she was one of the coolest women I ever knew.

Wasn't before long that Donna and I were dating again.

* * * * *

An enjoyable month had passed. The team was 10 games out - we weren't playing for the division crown, but rather our first winning season and league respectability. Also wouldn't hurt to try and knock the Dodgers off their perch. In August my ERA fell from 2.54 to 2.06 until the last game of the month. Didn't give up a single run in five appearances until the Phillies tagged me for four runs in an inning and two-thirds, easily one of my worst outings of the season. I also had one of the most difficult adult conversations of my life the night before.

"I heard back from the hospital in San Fran," Donna told me over a late dinner at my house, "It's a super job and they want an answer pretty quick." I knew where this was going.

"So I'm guessing *you* want an answer pretty quick," I replied.

"I like it in San Diego. I love being with you. But I need to know if we're just a lotta fun, or if we're serious-"

"We are serious, and it's been loads of fun, but you see what I've just been through with Liz-"

"I need a commitment." Right then I knew. She knew my answer. There was silence across the table. Maybe I should've ignored it, but those three months I didn't hear from Donna gave me pause from making any kind of long-term obligation.

"You know what?" she said with a resigned smile, "Let's have fun tonight. Tomorrow's tomorrow." I agreed, and we had enjoyed each other's company well into the evening, knowing fully well I wouldn't see Donna after the sun rose.

Or ever again.

* * * * *

1978 would prove to be The Padres' finest year in franchise history, as they finished 84-78. Trying to jump over the Dodgers, Reds and even the Giants proved to be too much for us, but there were many, many individual achievements on the roster. Winfield set the tone with an outstanding second half. Ozzie finished second in the Rookie of the Year voting behind a straight-to-the-majors talent named Bob Horner. Gaylord's prediction of winning 20 games came to fruition - 22, actually - en route to his second Cy Young Award. Rollie tied the NL record for saves with 37.

* * * * *

I packed and hauled my things out of the clubhouse at the season's end, throwing them in the back of the Porsche, leaving San Diego Stadium with a genuine sense that as long as Roger and Chuck were in my corner, one day I would eventually replace Rollie as the team's closer.

Driving back home up Interstate 805, still couldn't find a song I liked on the radio. With the death of Disco less than nine months away, Donna Summer still led the league in appearances over the airwaves. I finished 1978 among the top 15 relievers in baseball – 2.13 ERA, 104 strikeouts in 93 innings - only J.R. Richard sported a K/9 above 10 like me for hurlers who threw at least 90 innings. It was an off-season of preparing for the rest of my career in the town that I loved. The rest of my life, too.

About a month or so later, I was arriving home from a personal appearance and found her car idling in my driveway. Still sitting behind the wheel. Radio on. I pulled up beside her in my Porsche, this expression on her face asking me if we could give it one last try without saying a word.

Liz.

Maybe she just wanted to be Mrs. John D'Acquisto and much like free agent signings in the off-season, on paper, Liz made the perfect spouse for my needs at the time. Don't ask me why, but right then and there, I knew she would be my wife sooner rather than later. At that moment, I carefully measured every element to this partnership, except the most important consideration piping through the speakers of Liz's Honda Accord.

It's gonna take a lotta love or we won't get too far.

Wild Pitch

"All right, Johnny, can ya give us one more?" the sound engineer shouted over to me from behind the glass.

I nodded, corrected my back and gave the thumbs up that I was ready to go.

"Dow Sound City radio ad, take three – action!"

"Hey there, this is John D'Acquisto for Dow Sound City, the one-stop shop for all your electronics gifts and accessories. Check out our selection of TVs, radios and cutting-edge, high-fidelity stereo equipment. You'll always hit a home run and never strikeout with us! So c'mon down to Dow Sound City - over 10 San Diego area locations, open seven days a week, and tell 'em Johnny D sent ya!"

"How was that?" I said into the mic as I removed the headphones.

"Great – exactly what we needed," he replied, "Thanks, Johnny."

Wasn't quite Gillette Foamy or a Lite Beer from Miller commercial. I wanted one of those in the worst way, but it seemed that only retired ballplayers were chosen for beer ads. Still, it was a start to receiving endorsements off the success of my 1978 season. I began getting calls from other ballplayers asking for support with their charities. Willie Stargell got me involved with Sickle Cell Anemia. It felt much more rewarding than the next request the ad agency for Dow Sound City made a couple weeks later when I visited their offices.

"Okay, Johnny, picture this. You're gonna blaze your famous fastball through a sheet of plexi-glass at home plate as the announcer brags about Dow Sound City's low, low prices-"

"That's kinda silly-"

(Ad man cupping his hands like a cheesy announcer) "'Dow Sound City smashes prices, just ask Johnny D', and then we cut to you blasting away-"

"And I don't say anything?"

"Well, I think 100 MPH of pure pitching firepower speaks for yourself, don't you?"

"I think this is ridiculous," I sighed, but agreed to film the commercial, because I always did what I was asked.

Few days later, I showed up at San Diego Stadium where the ad was filmed. I walked out onto the mound in my uniform. The clapper shouted to begin filming.

"Dow Sound City Fastball Johnny D Take One."

"And action!"

I wound up and gave them the best heater I had....and missed the camera lens at the plate. By a lot. Aggravating. The director was gentle and reassuring.

"That was great, Johnny. Why don't we give it another whirl-"

"What are you talking about, I totally missed it-"

"Amazing form, let's go again, get him the ball, please — "

"Dow Sound City Fastball Johnny D, Take Two-"

"Action!"

I wound up, thought nothing of it, delivered the pitch, and missed the glass again. I was starting to get annoyed.

"That's all right, you came closer, we're gonna get it. Let's go again."

"Dow Sound City Fastball Johnny D, Take Three-"

Low and away. Far from the glass.

"Dow Sound City, Fastball Johnny D, Take Four-"

High and outside, above the glass-

"-Fastball Johnny D, Take Five-"

Against the backstop-

"Take Six-"

In the dirt-

"Take Seven-"

Bounced in front of the plate-"

"Take Eight-"

It took eleven pitches before I hit the lens. Of course, I shattered the damn thing in a million pieces once the ball reached its intended target. You know, someone once said, *"Johnny D could throw a coin through a car wash and it would come out dry on the other end. Hitting the car wash was always the problem."*

Welcome to my 1979.

* * * * *

Expectations were pretty high within the organization to build off the success of 1978. We figured Ozzie would continue to improve at the plate and that Winny was on the verge of a superstar season. None of us thought Gaylord could possibly top his Cy Young Winning '78. We picked up Mike Hargrove and a couple of other guys from the Texas Rangers for Oscar Gamble. Oscar was a great teammate, but he really belonged in the American League. The organization thought Hargrove would be an excellent table setter for Winny and Gene Tenace. The other issue for Oscar was the ballpark – it was just too big. The Padres couldn't sit still with the big changes happening in the NL West.

The Dodgers lost their number two starter in Tommy John, who fled via free agency to the Yankees. The Reds fired their manager, Sparky Anderson and Pete Rose took millions from the Philadelphia Phillies to leave his beloved Cincinnati, who seemed to lose a peg of the Big Red Machine every year. The sense was if Winny could put it all together, if Geno could keep getting on base, if Hargrove could hit .300, if Gaylord could be even half of what he gave the previous year, if Rollie and I did our jobs in the pen, this might just work out for us.

It was a rather non-descript spring training in Yuma, Arizona. Being engaged to Liz, I spent much of my free time on road trips with Rasmussen, grabbing a quick dinner then heading back to our rooms for a jam session. I had been playing guitar off and on since the age of 12 and Eric improved dramatically in a year, to the point where his playing was close to performance-quality.

Eric and I got a call toward the end of spring training to perform at Callernos de Yuma, a venue in town. We would be playing among a number of other groups. The band was me, Rasmussen and a handful of local musicians. We jammed for a good 80 minutes, mixing rock classics with a few country standards. I had never experienced the exhilaration like this – not even on the mound. By the time we gave our final bow, we had the audience on their feet. I turned to Eric, who had this proud grin. It was an amazing moment for both of us. Later that night, over beers at an open-air bar, we clinked our bottles in appreciation for the others' work.

"You ever get a standing ovation like that?" I asked Eric.

" I threw a four-hitter against the Reds back in St. Louis once," Eric replied after a moment of thought, "The fans got on their feet and clapped pretty loudly."

"I've had that, too, but this was different."

"Yep, it sure was."

"I think we're on to something."

Eric joked. "I'd like another standing ovation like that."

I would experience a standing ovation a few days later, the type of cheering that would set the tone for the rest of the season.

* * * * *

We were in San Francisco for our fifth game of the year. Gaylord gave us eight innings of two-run, six-hit ball. Roger pinch hit for him with runners on first and third in the top of ninth with the score tied at two, hoping we could get a lead against Vida Blue, who wasn't in his top form, but we still had trouble catching up to his fastball. After Vida fanned Kurt Bevacqua to end the inning, Roger brought me into the game. I made quick work of Mike Ivie with a strikeout and as I was pitching to the Giants' catcher Marc Hill, I noticed Willie McCovey in the on-deck circle whispering to San Francisco's third-string catcher John Tamargo. Mac had returned to the Giants in 1977 – had a great season, too. He was now 41, his status intact as a Hall of Fame-level ballplayer, a legend in the Bay Area, and still something of a drawing card. With the former A's dynasty now disbanded and floundering, there were only a few reasons for Bay Area fans to come to baseball games. There was emerging star Jack Clark, alongside Vida Blue and McCovey, who still possessed an instinct for the game. Even though I felt pretty confident out there, I could feel Mac studying my every move. I looked over to the Giants' dugout, and there was Mac chatting with Tamargo, eye-balling me. I actually had decent success against Mac in the past three years, but he saw something that day.

When Mac came out to pinch-hit for shortstop Roger Metzger, the crowd came to their feet. It was a pretty thrilling moment. Mac was one of those sluggers – and there were a couple on the Giants at that time – that knew how to lay off bad pitches and work the count. I felt I was throwing well. I was just gonna try and blow it by him. Mac dug in, I set, pitched and Mac drove a soft single to right-center. Three years earlier, that pitch would've been in the parking lot. Mac would be quickly replaced by a rookie pinch-runner named Max Venable, leaving the game to a standing ovation.

Giants' manager Joe Antobelli went all-in to win it at that point, having Tamargo bat for Vida. I couldn't worry about the speedy rookie on first; just fan the backup catcher and we could go into extras, where we would have the top of the order coming to bat.

"*C'mon, Johnny,*" I said to myself, "*Just blow it by him. He's not gonna touch it.*"

I checked the runner, kept him close, from the stretch, set and threw a 96-MPH heater right down the plate.

John Tamargo hit that fuckin' ball at least 450 feet into the stands.

Game-winning Home Run.

Standing Ovation.

Not for me.

* * * * *

The first half of the season played out about as well as opening day. I had blown four saves and had an ERA over six. It was as if 1978 never happened. Hargrove wasn't nearly the savior to the batting order we were expecting. Just like Oscar Gamble had trouble adjusting to the National League, Hargrove suffered the same fate. The NL was a league where the pitchers offered mainly fastballs and sliders. Mike Hargrove was an off-speed and curveball hitter-type guy. He had a hole where the slider would fall – he'd swing right over the top of it. Either smack it into the ground or strike out. An outstanding contact hitter back in Texas, Hargrove was batting .151 for us when Ray Kroc decided enough was enough and sent him packing to Cleveland in the middle of June. Wouldn't you know it – once Mike returned to the AL, he batted over .320 for the Indians, and it wasn't as if he was excited to be playing for a contending ballclub, either. The Indians were close to a last-place team just like the Padres. He just couldn't hit in the National League. Happened to a lot of guys.

By the end of June, Roger had a hunch that I needed to change things up. My won-lost record stood at 4-5 and he noticed that my two best performances during the season were pitching long relief. Won two games when I pitched more than five innings. Roger placed me back in the starting rotation. Still no one could figure out what the problem was.

No one except the smartest baseball man in the game at that time.

We were in Philly at Veterans Stadium around early July. I was walking through the tunnels toward the clubhouse when I passed by an old admirer and opponent.

"Hey Johnny?" Pete Rose said, grabbing at my shoulder, "Gotta tell ya somethin'." Pete took a liking to me from my days in San Francisco. We would grab dinner a couple times a year after ballgames throughout my career.

"Hey, what's up, Pete?" I replied.

Rose led me to the entrance of the Phillies clubhouse.

"I know why ya stink this year."

Any other person in the world, I would've been furious, but with Pete I kept my cool and listened.

"Okkkk...."

"Everyone knows what you're throwin'. Ya know that finger hole in your glove? Whenever you're about to throw a curveball, ya wiggle that finger. The guys know to lay off the pitch and wait for the heat and then they're teeing off on your ass. There's other stuff, too. Go check out the film. You're tippin' your pitches quite a bit."

"Why are you telling me this?"

"I dunno, I wanna beat ya at your best. See ya out there." Then he slapped me on the shoulder and walked into the Phillies clubhouse. I pitched seven innings that night, walked three, struck out seven, beating the Phillies 7-3.

I went 3-3 in the month of July – started seven games, got my strikeouts up and my walks down, but pitched rather streaky – three wins in a row, three losses in a row. All my wins came on the road – while I was playing music with Eric in our hotel rooms. Our guitar licks improved greatly and we seriously considered forming a band – no longer three-beers-in dreaming during impromptu road trip jams. I mentioned the notion of a band to my cousin Jimmy D'Aquisto, who was a world-famous guitar maker. Jimmy introduced me to Tony DeCaprio, guitarist for Diana Ross and Paul Simon. My friend Steve Laury re-acquinted me with a former high school classmate, Mark Augustine, who advised Eric on his initial music equipment purchases. Mark also brought in our drummer, Tommy Boyd. Through all their contacts, Eric and I would meet other musicians and jam alongside them on off-days. Still had to address my inconsistency on the mound, though. I would be taking a short break from jamming and guitar-pickin' for the upcoming series against my former Giants teammates. As our charter touched ground, I still had that opening day loss in San Francisco gnawing at my insides. I needed to redeem myself.

* * * * *

"Johnny?" said Count, who came to get me at SFO. He picked me up in his Porsche and drove us to his house in Foster City. I usually stayed with Count when I was in town, who by now settled down and married this lovely woman, Dory. Neither of us were crazy chasers any longer. The night would be basically a home-cooked meal and a few bottles of wine. Count was a close friend but tended to give me the business about how the Giants were so much better than my Padres. He was even more outrageous on this night. This would be a very special series.

"You saw the pitching match-up, right?" he laughed as we headed west over the Bay Bridge.

"I did," I replied. For the first time in our careers, the pitching matchups in the newspaper read like this:

J. Montefusco (3-4) vs. J. D'Acquisto (7-9).

Neither of us were having a good season at all. We both needed something to get us going. Dory's meal was delicious and we sat outside, enjoying cigars, more than a few glasses of merlot and busting each other's balls.

"You're gonna get your ass kicked tomorrow, ya know that, right?" Count bragged, "I mean, you're still a fastball pitcher, but you're not a starter anymore."

"I'm gonna be ok," I replied.

"You're gonna walk the ballpark. You don't have a chance."

"I don't have a chance? You're not exactly Bob Gibson out there these days-"

"Hey, I've been hurt all year, and now I'm back and you're gonna get smacked around."

I nodded, thought for a moment then sipped my drink.

"Wanna make it interesting?"

"What, you wanna bet?"

"A friendly wager."

"What are the stakes?"

I glanced over at the table beside his ashtray, toward the keys to Count's Porsche.

The next day, the former prodigious fireballers would face off in the Driver's Seat Game.

* * * * *

Count and I breezed through the first inning. We each issued a walk in the second; he to Gene Tenace; I gave Darrell Evans a free pass. Geno and Evans had two of the best eyes in the game, both regularly among the league leaders in walks. They would become the early poster boys for a baseball theory called The Three True Outcomes; expect a walk, a home run or a strikeout every at-bat. Man, if Evans and Tenace played in the age of sabermetrics, they would be like Greek gods to the stat crowd, and definitely a lot more Hall of Fame talk surrounding their careers. Neither guy hit much for average, but they smacked the ball a country mile, or got on base easily against guys without pinpoint control. Guys like me.

It was the bottom of the third. Still no score. I drilled Giants second baseman Joe Strain with a pitch to the shoulder. Then Jack Clark got around on my fastball and smacked a double into left-center. Then it was time for McCovey. He flew out to center last time up. Again, a couple years earlier, that ball would've been in the seats. I wanted to beat him with high heat. That's what I did – nothing but high fastballs – gave him my best, but gave him a chance to compete. Mac went down swinging for the first out. Was so excited to fan Mac that I walked Mike Ivie to load the bases. Now it was time for Darrell Evans. Geno jogged out to the mound. The crowd is starting to get worked up.

"How ya doin'?" Geno asked me.

"Doin' all right. How you doin'?"

"Evans thinks you're gonna walk him again."

"Why you say that?"

"'Cuz I *think* you're gonna walk him again, or throw another high fastball that he's gonna hit all the way to fuckin' Sausalito."

"Just get your ass back there. We're gonna be fine."

I really love Geno. There was no animosity at all – this was just heat of the battle talk, especially with the crowd noise drowning out our words. Geno handed me the ball, but not before looking me in the eye.

"Outside corner. Don't challenge him. Outside corner."

"I know-"

"Outside corner."

-"Heard ya the first time-"

I was beating these guys with my best. And I was gonna win this game, I didn't care if I walked the ballpark. No one was scoring off me. Geno was right, though. I would throw to the outside corner. I set, I wound up and as I delivered the pitch, *holy shit, Darrell stepped into it – he's totally expecting the outside corner!!!* – he just swung a little too late and popped the ball up to Paul Dade at third. I quickly struck out Giants' shortstop Johnny LeMaster to get out of it. Shows the importance of having a smart catcher. Regardless of whether Darrell Evans guessed right, Geno knew. In that situation, our only shot was the outside corner, and even then, Evans nearly made me pay. He would've crushed my high fastball.

On the other side, Count was throwing serious heat. Seven strikeouts through five innings; two walks, and only a single. We were both inspired to turn back the clock, not for money, not for the glory of the postseason. Just mano-e-mano, just for the competitive desire to shove it in your buddy's face. It was the best we looked in a few years. Funny thing about this game, both Geno and Evans walked twice. In the seventh, after that second Evans free pass, I noticed Count wincing slightly in pain, then saw Terry Whitfield grab a bat. He hit for Count, who was coming out of the game. I managed to get Whitfield to swing at another outside corner pitch and turned it into a third-to second-to first double play.

We managed to win the game with four runs in the ninth off a Johnny LeMaster error, couple Greg Minton walks and a single, but that wasn't the point. I still gave Count crap for winning as we walked out of Candlestick.

"Naw, that's bullshit," he protested, "If I hadn't had the blister-" I made a mocking movement with my fingers.

"Yeah, yeah, hand me the keys." Count tossed them over, muttering "Asshole." I got a good laugh out of that. I started the Porsche, revved the engine and turned to my former roommate.

"Pitched one hellvua game, Count." I said. He chuckled.

"Yeah. Been awhile since I've seen Fastball Johnny."

Sure the outcome was determined by a ninth inning Johnny LeMaster miscue at short, but all everyone talked about was how Count and D'Acquisto managed to show a glimpse of not just what could've been, but what *should've been* and what still might be.

* * * * *

Pete Rose's heads-up about my tells notwithstanding, I still had issues with my control, finishing the season with a 9-13 record and an ERA close to five. While the team didn't perform quite as badly in '79 as the fictional Padres in the Gary Coleman TV movie, we were still in our own little dogfight for last place with the Atlanta Braves. Team batting average and OBP fell 10 points and suddenly all those one-run victories we collected the previous season were going to the other guys. We went 14-13 in July after our rough first half, thought we were turning a corner, but an 8-19 August pretty much finished us off. The Padres ended 1979 with a 68-93 win-loss record, barely out of last place were it not for the lowly Bravos. Ray Kroc was not happy at all with the results. Talk around the clubhouse was that Kroc wanted to replace our manager Roger Craig with one of the coaches. Don Williams and Jack Krol were stand-up guys, fiercely loyal to Roger and both turned down the position. To be fair, Kroc was as meddling with baseball decisions as he was generous to the players when things went well. As the season mercifully came to an end, we began speculating about who Kroc might hire. With some ball clubs like the Yankees and Royals underperforming, the thought was there might be some A-list field generals to choose from. The Phillies' three-time division-winning manager Danny Ozark was on the Dodgers' bench after being dismissed in mid-season.

So I was working out at the Stadium the day after the last game of the season. Randy came out onto the field. "Guess what, Bud?" he said, chucking a ball at me, without leaving me a moment to reply, "Ray asked Jerry to be the manager."

"Jerry who?" I answered. Randy raised his glove and bare palms at me, "*Jerry. Jerry Coleman.*"

Took me a little by surprise. Never occurred to me that a broadcaster without any coaching experience would be asked to move down into the dugout. Obviously, Jerry knew the ballclub and the organization up and down, but in my eyes, he was coming from a completely different perspective. Maybe Kroc could've waited a few months. Billy Martin would become available. Whitey Herzog would be out there. There were still other managers to choose from, I thought. We all loved Jerry, but it didn't matter to Ray Kroc that other quality skippers were on the beach, waiting for another shot in the spotlight.

In his mind, Jerry Coleman was the only kid in the picture.

Randy was really excited about this. Jerry and Randy were like father and son. Coleman was so proud of Jonesy, another local California boy who battled through a tough 1974 season where he lost 20 games, turning it around to a 22-12 record in 1975 before his even greater Cy Young campaign in '76.

Jerry was the type of person who would sit down with us in the clubhouse, go into stories about the glorious Yankee ball clubs of the 1950s. He was something of a Baseball historian, a plethora of information and color. He flew well over 100 missions in World War 2 and Korea – just shrugged it off humbly when asked about it. A true war hero and most unassuming guy you'd ever meet. Very warm, very sincere – you just wanted to reach out and hug him.

A few specific moments between us stand out in my mind. Jerry, the American original that he was, loved his hot dogs. I used to eat franks as a ritual before every game. Jerry would stroll into the clubhouse, pass by my locker and slyly inquire, "Are they good today?"

"Oh, they're excellent," I would nod, barely audible, cheeks stuffed, sauerkraut hanging off the side of my mouth.

"Should I have one?"

"I think you should get two," I would smile. We'd enjoy a quick laugh, he'd grab a dog and then we'd get down to some thoughts on the game, providing background for his broadcast. We were hot dog buddies in 1979; got pretty close that year, not dinner mates or anything like that – Randy Jones would go out to dinner often with Jerry when the team was on the road – but we talked quite a bit that summer. Kroc adored Jerry, as we all did. Beyond sentiment, though, the move made sense. Kroc wanted to keep the attention of the fan base on their beloved Jerry Coleman, while trying to figure out how to handle the feared exodus of its superstar player.

Dave Winfield led the league in RBIs in '79 with 118, hit 34 homers and batted over .300, all outstanding accomplishments considering no one else on the ballclub had more than 67 ribbies. Very similar to Nate Colbert in 1972. Winny carried the ballclub, received his first all-star selection by the fans and really took his place as the star of the San Diego Padres. Winny had also become well-known for his charitable efforts – he bought so many seats for underprivileged kids every game. The organization adored Winny, but this was the time where every major player was either handed a handsome contract to stay in place like Mike Schmidt or looked to their agent and wondered what else was out there. Keith Hernandez was the coolest customer in the league and Willie Stargell was everything you could ask for in a team leader, but by any metric you care to utilize, Winfield was the best player in the National League that year. An absolute superstar. He knew it. His agent knew it. The team knew it, and he only had a year left on his contract. It was no secret. Winny probably wouldn't be a Padre for much longer.

"Oh, he's gone," Randy would say to me over beers when we talked about the team, "He's got Madison Avenue in his eyes. He's done with Friars Road."

By this point, I had become very close to Bob Fontaine and Ray Kroc. Unlike San Francisco where I rarely spoke to Horace

Stoneham and never chatted with Gussie Busch in the few months I was in St. Louis, I would see Ray Kroc every two weeks or so. Part of it of course was the organization keeping ties with the hometown boy, but Mr. Kroc appreciated my candor and he knew how much I loved the franchise. One night in late September after a game, I found myself in Mr. Kroc's office, talking over cocktails.

"Johnny?" Kroc asked me, "What are we gonna do about Winfield?" I didn't want to get in the middle of this. Kroc gave me a lot of respect, mainly because I treated him like a regular guy. He respected that and trusted my opinion on matters from the personnel moves to the 1980 uniforms.

"Boss, I just want your McDonald's location in Villa de la Valle. Please don't get me involved."

"Johnny, I'm askin' your opinion..."

"Well, if my boss is asking my opinion, two million dollars a year is a lot of money."

"It is a lot of money. But David's a great player. We did come in fifth place this year, though. How worse can it get without him?"

I knew where Dave's head was looking. Every so often, as co-union rep, I would talk to Winny about labor matters and eventually his impending free agency would come up.

"So is it true?" I asked Winny hanging out one night after a game.

"Is what true?" David replied. I gave him one of those "*You know exactly what I'm talkin' about*" looks. David flashed that soon to be million-dollar smile.

"Oh, I'm testing the free agent market." Superstar talent like that, well-heeled owners like George Steinbrenner, Gene Autry and

Ted Turner getting bolder and bolder with their contract offers. You knew George would make a big play for Winfield. There was no way around it. A five-tool guy with his numbers. They'll pay him anything he wants, and what he wanted was $20 million dollars. An insane amount of money by 1979 standards.

I had my concerns about what one guy making that kind of dough would do to the fabric of the ballclub. I know a lot of other ballplayers felt the same way. My mistake was conveying my thoughts to the wrong person. After the season ended, I ran into a writer from UPI at a Padres' charity benefit. He asked me about Winfield in what seemed like an off-the-record conversation.

"Any guy making as much as say, $ 1million a year, is set for life," I told him, *"Why would he want any more? If Winny gets that kind of money, it's going to hurt all the other guys on our team and that's bound to cause dissension."* Of course, I didn't stop there.

"I know when my contract runs out next year, I hope to sign for a little more, but I'm never gonna ask for the moon."

I actually said that. Marvin never called me out on it. Neither did my agent, Jerry Kapstein, the most powerful agent in baseball at the time. Not even sure Winny saw it. If he had, I'm sure I would've heard something. The players' union made great strides and a number of ballplayers enormously wealthy. I don't know why I said it. I wasn't envious – I made pretty good money and felt confident that with a good year, I would receive a generous contract – but $2 million a season? I really couldn't get my head around the idea. While I was generally quite savvy with the media and rarely ever said the wrong thing, this was probably the biggest press slip-up of my career. None of it mattered, though. 1980 would be a year of experimentation, of transition…and transactions.

* * * * *

In the midst of the chatter about our new manager and Winny's aspirations, Eric and I made good on our plan to start a band. Steve Laury, Tommy Boyd and Mark Augustine were solid professional musicians. Steve later became a member of Fattburger, a popular jazz group in California that turned some heads before disbanding. We rehearsed every day and after awhile we sounded pretty good. Mark and Steve were very close. Steve was the consummate jazz musician. The group still needed a name, though. One night after a gig in November, Eric turned to me at the bar and was like, "We need a name." I sipped my beer, nodded and said, "Wild Pitch."

"What?"

"Wild Pitch. How great is that?" Eric just laughed.

"That's really funny."

This cool establishment, the London Opera House in San Diego, auditioned us and ended up booking Wild Pitch from December through the beginning of February. We were the contract group for the whole off-season. We packed the place – 50 to 100 people every night. Got so successful, we ended up having to join the musician's union. We played throughout the new year and into February. The band performed every free moment we had during spring training. Young Padres infielder Tim Flannery joined our group. He was an amazing guitar player to go along with his glove work in the infield. We played mostly country rock, America, Pure Prairie League, a few originals. Even Bobby Owchinko, our Padres teammate, jammed with us one night on the sax.

The off-season also brought my wedding. Finally married Liz at a 1200-plus person affair at All Hallows Church on the hill in La Jolla. Two priests and the monsignor from USD where Liz went to school. Fred was my best man; Eric and Jim Colton from San Francisco were my groomsmen. Half the ball club was there, Randy, Winny, Bob Fontaine, Ballard Smith, our owner Ray Kroc and his lovely wife, Joan. Mrs. Kroc gave us beautiful Waterford crystal. I remember so many friends and teammates asking me about honeymoon plans. *"Well, obviously Eric and I have to finish out our engagements with Wild Pitch,"* I explained. *"We still have five or six more dates to play, then it's spring training, so......"* People would nod their head, sip their cocktail and move on to talk about home furnishings. As much as I was beginning a new life with Liz, my family was still Eric, Randy, Bob Fontaine, the Krocs and Major League Baseball.

* * * * *

As for baseball at the start of the 1980 season, Jerry Coleman ran a very easy-going clubhouse. Bob Fontaine had treated me great, but the ballclub has gotten lackadaisical. Sure Kroc had brought in Willie Montanez to play first and Dave Cash to play second, Jerry Mumphrey to man center, but Ozzie Smith and Gene Richards were still there, Randy was still the ace of the staff, and Rollie and me headed up the bullpen. Jerry decided my best spot was not starting, but rather setting up for Rollie. Jerry just let us play and it all seemed to be working. As of May 22nd, our teams' record was 22-19, all alone in 3rd place. Randy's record stood at 4-2 with an ERA under 1.90 – pitched three shutouts in a row, including one against the World Champion Pittsburgh Pirates. I had an ERA under 2.50. I was pitching well. And then I got a call from Bob Fontaine.

"Johnny, let's talk about your contract." My agent, Jerry Kapstein and I met with Fontaine.

"We want to extend Johnny's deal four more years at his current salary – and we'll guarantee it." Now I was making about $185,000. Jerry said, "$225K to $250,000 a year and you got 'em, along with a little signing bonus of $300,000." Fontaine ran it up the flagpole to Team President Ballard Smith who said, "We'll get back to you." Ray Kroc pulled me aside a day later in his office.

"If you promise me you'll pitch like the way you did in '78, I'll give ya the money."

"Ray, I can't promise you that," I replied.

"Then I can't give ya the money."

"I don't mean it like that, I mean I'll pitch well for you, but someone has to make sure I'm out on the mound every other game. I pitched three times in April, for God's sake."

Ray said, "I can guarantee that." The problem wasn't Ray Kroc. It was Ballard Smith. Not a week later, Ballard fired Bob Fontaine as Padres General Manager and replaced him with Jack McKeon. Ballard didn't care that the team was performing somewhat to expectations. Ballard wanted everyone gone, and wanted Mckeon (who would later earn the nickname "*Trader Jack*") to do his dirty work. Rollie. Randy. Winny. Montanez. Dave Cash. Jerry Mumphrey.

Me.

He and McKeon wanted to remake the Padres in their image. Don't get me wrong, Jack McKeon was a stand-up guy, a smart baseball man and a loyal employee. Problem for me was his loyalty was to Ballard.

Business is business.

At the beginning of August, I was sitting with Randy Jones on a bus headed to the airport and we were talking about the potential of trades coming and coming soon.

"Ya know they're gonna trade ya," Randy said to me with a friendly chuckle, "You're probably gone." I nodded somewhat in agreement knowing the rumors, as I started singing the Canadian National Anthem a little too loud. Trader Jack was traveling with the club on this trip and when he turned to the back of the bus, McKeon was staring right at me, not so much angry, but rather an eye-rolling, "*Stop-busting-balls*" demeanor.

"Cool it," Jack said.

It was my fault that I allowed the negotiations to mar what was looking like a decent season out of the pen. Randy tore his biceps tendon and his performance fell off a cliff. He went 1-11 from May 24 until August 22 when he was shut down for the remainder of the season, after a loss to the Montreal Expos at Olympic Stadium in Canada. I didn't pitch in that game, but I was there.

Just no longer as a Padre.

* * * * *

A phone call woke me up on August 11th, 1980. One of *those* phone calls.

"Johnny D?"

"Yeah?" I replied, half asleep, just 45 minutes into a slumber coming off a 17-day road trip, flying in only two hours earlier.

"It's McKeon, you awake?"

"No," I grumbled. Jack laughed.

"C'mon down to the ballpark. Soon as you can." Which of course meant *now*. Which of course, meant one thing to this kid who loved his San Diego Padres and the spacious ballpark he called home.

Go grab your passport.

Game 161

"I *have some good news and bad news*," is what you hear before you find out you've been traded over the winter. "*Can I see you in my office*," during the season if you're already at the stadium and it's a few hours before game time. "*I need to see you in my room right away*," if you're on the road after the game at the hotel, as I learned in St. Louis. On an off-day like this morning, it was "*C'mon down to the ballpark.*"

Sure enough the call came and I was crawling out of bed, heading down to the stadium to presumably collect my plane ticket and a handshake.

* * * * *

"I just did you the biggest favor in the world," Jack McKeon bragged in his office a half hour later, "I sent you to a first place team." I asked where.

"You're goin' to Montreal. You have a chance to play in the World Series." The Expos were tied with the Pittsburgh Pirates at the time for the division lead. The ballclub was loaded with young talent – Andre Dawson coming into his own, Warren Cromartie holding down the fort at first, Gary Carter finally emerging from the shadow of future Hall of Fame catcher Johnny Bench. An exciting staff anchored by Steve Rogers, a core of outstanding young arms in Scott Sanderson and David Palmer as well as rookies like Bill Gullickson and Charlie Lea. The Expos' main man in the bullpen, 40-year old Woodie Fryman, was ailing with a sore arm and I was brought in to help out. The Expos' relief corps was filled with cagey vets like Woodie, Stan Bahnsen, Fred Norman. There were a good number of ex-teammates and old friends on Montreal. I played with Gordy Carter, Gary's brother, in A Ball at Fresno in 1972 where "Kid" used to come up and visit. Elias Sosa was with me in San Fran back in '73-'74, as was shortstop Chris Speier. Speier is one of the good ones in the game – throughout the pennant race in 1980, you could find him at the ballpark early working with the other infielders, teaching them the right way to glove grounders and short-hops off the turf. Now while it was a true hop, you needed to be concerned about the seams in the turf – Spei learned this while playing on the tricky Candlestick Park surface all those years.

In the end, Jack did me a favor by swapping me to a contender, an opportunity to play in September games that meant something. Montreal, to this point, was the most successful ballclub I'd ever played for. So, in that sense, Jack McKeon was happy, trading an impending free agent for another player and cash; my agent was happy, as going to a contender could possibly increase my value *plus* I'd be getting more money because of the currency difference playing in Canada; I was happy to get a chance to possibly compete in the playoffs. Then there's the side of this story you rarely find in the back of the newspaper.

"What do you mean you got traded?" Liz said to me as I entered the house with a plane ticket in my hand, "Where are you going? What does this mean for us?"

"I'm going to Canada, and I have to leave now." It was a very, very tough conversation, especially when you're packing two suitcases through it all. She's in shock because forty minutes ago we were all set to spend the day at the beach together as a couple and now she's going to her mother's house wondering what the next two months of her marriage will be like as I'm heading out on a flight to Montreal. With both of us being born and raised in San Diego, my wife and I had friends and family all around us. It's the part of this game, most sports really, that few fans ever consider. When you call up a sports radio station and discuss a trade, you rarely consider or say "*I think Hanley Ramirez should go to L.A. because he just spent the last four months interviewing pre-schools with his wife and there's a number of quality Goddard locations,*" or "*A certain outfielder can't be traded to the Rockies because his son has asthma and can't really handle the Colorado atmosphere.*" These are the stories you never read about in the "*Transactions*" section of the sports page. Sure, you get compensated beyond your wildest dreams, even back then, but sometimes when you play the salary negotiation game, this is the risk, that the personal side of our business results in a pretty lousy outcome at times. Most of the time, actually.

This is why the clubhouse can be so important, why clubs go out of their way to ensure the players' comfort. Not simply because they want to pamper you, but to distract you from the loneliness of missing your family. This is why the Expos put me up in a five-star hotel, everything top-shelf across the board – who's getting an apartment or a house with 50 days left in the season? I arrived in Canada, dropped my stuff off at the suite, still in a bit of a daze from the whirlwind, hopped on the train that takes you straight to Olympic Stadium. Who do I see as I step off the platform? Fred

Biletnikoff, the former Oakland Raiders great and an old friend from my Bay Area days with the Giants. Fred was finishing up his football career with the Montreal Alouettes in the CFL.

"Johnny D, they got you, too," Fred laughed, "Everyone's up here now. Speier's up here, your old buddy [Elias] Sosa's up here. Saw Charlie Fox with [Expos' General Manager at the time John] McHale out at dinner the other night."

And then I knew why I was in Montreal.

Charlie. My beloved manager with the Giants back in the '70s was now an assistant to GM Jim Fanning.

It's so funny how you can be a journeyman player, but that scout that discovers you, that first coach, that first manager who witnessed you achieve amazing things, even years and sometimes decades later, fondly recalls when you hit triple digits on the gun, who you were and sometimes in their mind, who you still could be. With Woodie Fryman hurting, Charlie recommended me, that I could fortify the pen. Charlie was a great baseball man and a wonderful person in general. He definitely felt like a father to me and sometimes that's the silver lining of life with trades; if you have that special relationship, that bond with a coach, manager or owner somewhere around the league, they'll always have an eye on you as long as the bottom doesn't fall out of your ability, and even then, they'll still give you one last shot if the emotional connection remains in place.

* * * * *

Olympic Stadium, the Expos' home ballpark, was this concrete slab of a building with a tiny hole in the top. I really didn't mind pitching there. Upon walking out onto the field for the first time as a member of the ballclub, I was introduced to the owner of the

Expos, Charles Brofman, who was shagging fly balls with the outfielders. I always thought that was pretty cool. Mr. Brofman welcomed me with open arms. Kid Carter came over and eagerly said hello. We chatted for a few minutes; I asked how Gordy was doing. Many players approached me warmly. Speier, Sosa, Charlie, of course (even my starting first baseman from San Diego in 1980, *"The Hot Dog,"* Willie Montanez, would follow me to Montreal at the end of August in another pennant race swap between the two teams.) This didn't at all replace the sense of loss of not spending time with Liz much over the next 50 days, but the breakfasts with Speier, the dinners with Charlie. They made me feel like I belonged to the group and I'm sure this helped me turn my personal season around a little bit. Landing on a contending team didn't hurt, either.

* * * * *

Expos' manager Dick Williams put me to work pretty quickly once I got there, pitching in seven games over my first 16 days in Montreal. I blew a potential save against the Dodgers, giving up run-scoring hits to Jay Johnstone and Rick Monday that allowed L.A. to grab the lead. Coming back into the clubhouse, I heard Williams say loud enough, but not directly, for me to hear, *"Knew I should've brought in Bahnsen."* After two years of Roger Craig and four months of the relatively docile Jerry Coleman, I certainly wasn't used to open hostility from the manager.

"Don't worry about him," Carter assured me later, "He has his own problems. Don't take it personally." I let it go, pitched again two days later – three innings, three hits, two walks, no runs, kept a 5-2 deficit from getting out of hand. Again, Williams laid into the relievers after the game. This time it was Elias Sosa. My turn would come six days later.

* * * * *

We were in San Francisco. Bottom of the sixth of a 3-3 tie. I struck out two in the previous inning to keep us in the game when Dawson slammed a homer off Vida Blue to even it up. I started the next inning against Darrell Evans, who walked of course. I also walked Jim Wohlford and Williams brought in the southpaw Fred Norman to pitch to Milt May, who bunted the runners over. Dick left Norman in there to face a rookie, Guy Sularz. A routine ground ball went right through the legs of Larry Parrish our third baseman, allowing the go-ahead run to score, which hooked me on the losing end. Dick was furious for the rest of the game. The Giants tacked on another run to close it out 6-3. Our manager didn't yell or scream. He saved that for the charter flight home.

I was sitting in the middle of the plane next to Carter, who had become my closest friend on the team. We heard Dick mumbling and grumbling a few seats in front of us. Gary was flipping through a magazine. I was cooling my heels with a Canadian Club whiskey. I only walked two batters, but still felt extremely guilty. These games meant something. I had never been this close to it this late in the season. Thankfully, the Phillies lost as well, so we maintained our one-game lead. Dick decided after his fifth bourbon to get up, come toward us in the back of the plane and offer his post-game observations of the night.

"I'm sorry that our shitty, fuckin' relievers blew the game for us," Dick slurred, "Especially this one," pointing right at me. I tended not to get into many – don't believe any, actually – bar fights during my career, but I've seen a few go down. Dick looked like he wanted to mix it up with someone.

"We'll get him tomorrow, Skip," I said calmly, trying to defuse the situation. Williams was having none of it. He stepped toward my seat and leaned right in my face.

"I think you're a weak mother fucker."

"I beg your pardon?" This was getting very ugly, very quickly.

"I said you're a mother fucker. You need to grow some balls." Players and coaches crowded around us, because they knew what the next move was. I stood up in a flash and took a swing-

Only my arm didn't go anywhere. I turned and Kid Carter had a hold of my arm.

"Lemme go," I said to Gary.

Gary nodded to Galen Cisco and the other coaches.

"Get him outta here," Gary directed, as Cisco dragged Williams to his seat, who was still slurring obscenities.

"You wanna get thrown out of the league?" Gary scolded me, "Black-balled, released?"

"No one's releasing me," I shot back, "Why should I take that?"

"You touch him, you're done. I don't wanna see that happen."

"Who is he to talk to me like that?"

Then Gary let me go.

"You wanna go hit 'em, go. But you hit him, your career's over." I banged the arm rest with my left hand in anger. I was so embarrassed that I couldn't wipe the floor with Dick Williams, and how I just had to take that. Gary was right, of course. I remembered my old Giants teammate Bruce Miller punched out the traveling secretary in 1976 and was out of organized ball one month later. I didn't exactly keep my calm but I thank Gary for being there when someone had to think for me.

* * * * *

Couple weeks later, the plane rides were much less chaotic. I'm lounging back, seat reclined, eyes closed, my light slumber brought to you by Led Zeppelin on this new music device called the Sony Walkman which was sweeping the planet at the time. It was September at this point and my Expos had just taken two out of three from the Philadelphia Phillies.

The Phillies of Mike Schimdt, one of the greatest third basemen to ever play the game; of Steve Carlton, one of the top left-handed starting pitchers in baseball, hell, one of the best pitchers in baseball history, period; Tug McGraw, that quirky reliever, the classic oddball southpaw who seemed to have discovered the fountain of youth, placing the final touches on what was arguably the greatest season of his career; my old Giants teammate Garry Maddox, who by now was among the three best defensive center fielders in the game. By the way, Pete Rose also played every day at first base for them. The Phillies had barely any weakness and we were ahead in the standings by a half game with six to play.

We weren't confident we would bring Montreal to the playoffs for the first time in its 11-year existence. It was a sure thing. We felt that. Management felt that. Our fans felt that. As our charter flight came to a complete stop, I peered through the small window and found one of the most beautiful images my eyes had ever seen to that point. Hundreds upon hundreds of Expos fans were waiting for us, under the moonlight, signs, banners, kids and grownups jumping up and down with joy, with affection, anticipating that moment when we stepped off the plane. We hadn't won anything yet. They didn't care. They were just happy to see us. A whole lotta love indeed.

We still had six games to go. Imagine what this city will do when we actually make the playoffs. What will they do when we win the World Series?

There was no *"if"*. Just *"when"*.

The Cardinals were coming to town for their final three-game set with us. We basically split the season series. I think we won maybe one or two games more. Didn't matter – we were pretty loose. I walked into the clubhouse at Olympic Stadium before the first game and there's Gary Carter, hanging out with Steve Rogers, our ace, on the couches, taking in some daytime TV. Bad daytime TV.

"What the hell are you guys watching?" I asked with half a chuckle. Gary beckoned to the end of the couch for me to sit down. "C'mon, Johnny, this is the good part."

"I got better things to do than watch soap operas. Isn't there anything else on?" Carter shook his head with a laugh – remember, this is 1980, cable is in its infancy, ESPN isn't everywhere yet.

"Ah, it's just something to pass the time. How's your arm feelin'?" My arm was fine; I just hadn't pitched much during September. I made 49 appearances in 1980 between both the San Diego Padres and the Montreal Expos.

The next time I toed the rubber my 50-game bonus would kick in. I had a hot August for Montreal, pitching my best in almost two years, but Dick had his guys, wanted to leave the dance with those that brought him to this point. I knew I was going to pitch in at least one of the final six games, but there were a ton of mouths to feed in that pen. I understood the deal. One of the best relief corps I've ever seen. Between the ageless master Fryman, crafty southpaw Fred Norman, Sosa, Stan Bahnsen, the group was so solid, the team ended up releasing Dale Murray, a one-time lights-out reliever who came up with the club in 1974 and was on his second tour with Montreal. Once Fryman was healthier, manager Dick Williams had a tough time finding innings for all his guys in the pen. Staff ace Steve Rogers seemed to throw 250 innings every year, was one of the most talented hurlers in the league. Scott Sanderson, Bill Gullickson – Gully struck out 18 guys in a September game and this was his rookie season. This isn't even mentioning Bill "Spaceman" Lee was also one of our starters. Quirky element of the 1980 season; we were only behind the Cardinals by one for Most Team Complete Games in the National League. Wasn't easy for Dick getting work for his relievers with the starters going so deep into ballgames.

We made pretty easy work of the Cardinals – a tough win that ended with my new teammate Johnny Tamargo – remember him? - slamming a pinch-hit 3-run blast to win 5-2; a 7-2 victory for Gully and a David Palmer 8-0 shutout. Woodie appeared in the first two games and Palmer went the distance in the third. We were just giddy – in first place, breezing through a Cardinals squad that would get a Whitey Herzog facelift during the 1980 off-season – four of their nine top position players and basically the entire starting staff outside of Bob Forsch were sent packing that winter as Whitey made the ballclub his own.

I was sitting at my locker, listening to some Clapton on the Walkman, starting to get into my groove, my back to the rest of clubhouse. Not being anti-social, it was early; no one was really there, just doing my own thing. I felt a tap on my shoulder. It's Dick. Half street clothes, half uniform; his untucked Expos jersey hanging over tan slacks. We hadn't spoken since the plane incident.

"Hey, Skip?" I nodded. Dick cleared his throat. It wasn't so much a speech as it was a declaration.

"We're, uhh, we're adding you to the postseason roster. You're coming with us to the World Series and playoffs." I got choked up. This was it – my first time going to the NLCS and possibly the World Series. Through also-ran clubs in San Fran, St. Louis and San Diego, now I was finally headed to the playoffs. I was really excited about the opportunity to shine on a national stage. The exposure to other clubs didn't hurt, either. I would most likely be a free agent after the season ended. So much at stake in my life, but with the pen they had here, Dick didn't need to add me. No joke, I very nearly started to cry.

"What'sa matter?" Dick asked.

"I'm honored, you just made my day. You made my fuckin' career. I appreciate it, Skip." We didn't see eye to eye all the time, but I was very touched at Dick's efforts at apologizing. Not too-many old-school guys knew how to say *"I'm sorry."* This was my manager's method of expressing his remorse for the airplane episode. All was forgiven, as far as I was concerned.

* * * * *

We were unstoppable. Winning five in a row and still only up by a half game over Philadelphia? Sure it was annoying, but it didn't matter. We all thought we were going to the playoffs. I remember our bullpen coach Ozzie Virgil, yet another guy I worked with in San Fran, said to me, *"I'm gonna get my airplane now."* He was a fully licensed pilot. *"That's what my playoff check is going towards."* Guys were talking about winning the whole thing. Fine line between confidence and taking the Phillies lightly? Maybe. It's not that the team was overlooking the regular season; it was simply a fact in our minds that we *were* going to the playoffs. The Phillies can't stop us. Second place was never an option.

Everyone in the organization was drinking the Kool-Aid. The team had us measured for World Series rings, playoff tickets were printed. We had a team meeting to talk about post-season bonus shares. Kid insisted I join the conversation. They gave me a full share, which floored me to even be thought of as a full-season Expo when I was only there a month and a half.

I know Gary had an awful lot to do with this. No one was better than us – not the Astros, the Dodgers, the Yankees, KC, no one could beat us. We just took two of three from the Phillies at The Vet last weekend. Doing the same at home would be no problem.

And then the Phillies beat the Cubs the night before playing us at home in the final series of the regular season, tying us for first. Didn't matter. We were still the best team in the National League. The buzz in the stands – the seats were packed. 57,000+ came out to Olympic Stadium that Friday night to witness the Montreal Expos get closer to their first playoff berth. You wanna talk about adrenaline - it was like someone placed a battery pack on my shoulders and the electricity just flowed throughout my body. I pitched exceptionally well against Philadelphia over the course of the year. I wanted in this series more than any other in my career.

Game 160 would have no need for me. Top of the first – Sanderson vs. Dick Ruthven, a good pitcher in his own right. Rose singled. Bake McBride doubled. Sac Fly from Schmidt. 1-0 right off the bat. Game was 1-1 until the sixth, when Schmidt smoked a Sanderson fastball into the seats. Philly came out on top 2-1. We just couldn't hit Ruthven. Philly took over first place.

Saturday afternoon was the most important game of my career. I was still on 49 appearances. That day was so cold, windy, rainy, which delayed the start time. I was rested, prepared to get my teammates into the postseason. This was my moment. The Montreal faithful waited, all 50,000 of them, through the multiple delays to see the Expos just get to Sunday. No one was printing tickets on Saturday. There were no ring fingers measured on the day of Game 161. No one asked about playoff shares. Let's just get to Sunday.

Philly's bats threatened every inning, but our ace Steve Rogers kept us in the game. Striking out "The Bull" Greg Luzinski with McBride on third in the first inning; Dawson nailing McBride at third for the final out in the third inning. At our turn up in the bottom half, lead-off hitter Jerry White blasted a two-run dinger to get us on the board. By the sixth, we were up 2-1. I was sitting in the bullpen – I hung out there usually from the very first pitch, best seat in the house for my money. Come the seventh inning, Steve gave up seven hits.

"They're gonna need me," I'm thinking.

Greg Gross grounded out to Chris Speier at short. Pete Rose strolled to the plate. Being an important moment in the game, Pete singled, of course. Bake McBride, who seemed to be on base the entire series, also singled to center. First and second. Schmidt to the plate. The park was deafening. You couldn't hear yourself think, it was so loud. We were right there, me, the city of Montreal, I wasn't about to let Philly take this from me, from them. Without being asked, I started stretching. I wanted Dick to think I was there for him if he needed me. Touched my toes, stared at the cracks in the asphalt of the bullpen concrete under the bench. Didn't matter, as Sosa and Fryman started warming in the pen. Turned away from the field for a moment before I heard the letdown sound of the crowd as Schmidt danced that two-step batters make as they round first base after a single – Bake was nearly caught in a run-down between second and third. Bags were loaded and Greg Luzinski came to the plate. I had good numbers against The Bull and Rogers was on fumes at this point, going 3-0 on Luzinski. I wanted that ball, but if this was anyone's game to be won or lost, it was Steve's. He had been there since the Parc Jarry days, battled through a 15-22 season in '74 that he didn't deserve, with Kid Carter coming a year later – this was their club. They deserved to battle it out together. Steve delivered the pitch. Given the green light, Luzinski smashed a ground ball single to center. Pete scored! Bake scored! Phillies took the lead, but again bad baserunning cost them. Schmidt was caught assuming the throw from center was going to the plate, but Dawson threw a perfect strike to Larry Parrish at third, who found Schmidt between the bags. Not only was Schmidt tagged out by our first baseman who jumped into the run down, but Cromartie also nailed Luzinski rounding the bag too much at first. Carter ran over from home plate to cover first and tagged out The Bull when he tried to retreat!! Just your everyday 8-5-2-4-5-3-2 double play. Phils took the lead, but the inning was over and so was Steve's night. Now it was up to us in the pen to keep our club in the game. I was ready. I started throwing. *I know I'm pitching tonight,*I thought, *I know I will save it for Montreal.*

Oh, it was a sloppy game. Philly gave us so many chances just to take it. McBride making the final out of the inning at third. Manny Trillo's unlikely error at second in the bottom of the seventh. Dick took Speier out of the game and had Ron LeFlore run for him. That was like just handing us second base. Ron was fast, but he was out of his mind in 1980, stealing 97 bases, to that point only Maury Wills, Lou Brock and a sensational youngster out of Oakland named Rickey Henderson stole more in a single season. Obviously, Ron stole second. Phils reliever Ron Reed inexplicably tried to pick LeFlore off and chucked the ball into center field. Dick pinch-hit Steve with lefty-swinging Willie Montanez. I start throwing in the pen. *I know I'm getting in this game.* Dallas Green countered with Sparky Lyle, who needs no introduction for most of you. Dick called Willie back and sent righty-swinging Johnny Tamargo up in Willie's place, hoping to catch the game-winning lightning in a bottle from the other night. Sparky pitched Johnny carefully. Too carefully and walked him. Thinking back now, it's incredible all the important names and folks who stepped between the lines during this game. A young, smiling rookie named Tim Raines ran for Tamargo. Guess what happened? Yup, he stole second. Raines on second, Ron LeFlore on third. No one was considering this during the inning, but it was pretty clear that Raines, who played second base in AAA that season, was going to replace Ronny in left field. We all knew that LeFlore was a one and done in Montreal. Amazes me to think what the Expos could've done with an in-his-prime Ron LeFlore and a rookie Tim Raines at the top of the order. It's a shame we never found out. Jerry White faced Sparky with two men on and flew out to Unser in center. LeFlore scored – tie game. Rodney Scott stepped to the plate. Another speedster. Raines. Rodney. LeFlore. Even Rodney Scott, our starting second baseman, stole 63 bases. Scottie doubled to left field, Raines scored and now we were up by one. I know I'm getting in this game. Woodie, the 40-year old man, pitched the day before. Bahnsen threw almost two innings yesterday as well. *I know I'm getting in this game. I know I'll save it for Montreal.*

Dick called for Elias Sosa to start the eighth inning. I sat back down. Del Unser, who started in place of a day-to-day Garry Maddox, singled to right field. Sosa got Keith Moreland to ground to short, forcing Unser at second. Trillo popped up and then Bowa singled deep in the hole at short. Dick called on Woodie, a southpaw, to pitch to Greg Gross, a lefty. *"Strictly a situational move,"* I explained to myself, because I know I'm getting into this game. Dallas Green took his chances and countered with an ailing Garry Maddox. Dick kept Woodie on the mound to face the right-handed hitter.

Woodie fans Maddox. 4-3 Expos going into bottom of the eighth.

Conflicted feelings all over the place. Happy, we're winning. Unhappy, I'm not in the game, contributing to this wonderful group of guys that considered me one of the 25 that began together in April. I wanted to show my appreciation by closing this one out for them. I also wanted to pitch in my 50th game.

Ninth inning. I'm not that upset I wasn't brought in here because, remember, this is 1980 and the notion of the one-inning closer hasn't been conceived yet. Woodie walked Pete. Bake grounded to second, where Pete got forced out. Schmidt hit a slow roller to third, where Parrish could only get the play at first. Bob Boone stepped to the plate. I began warming in the bullpen again. *I know I'm getting in this game.* Especially here, against the right-handed hitting Boone. I'm not sure I've ever felt that much sadness in my heart when Boone smacked that single to center off Woodie to tie the game in the ninth. I was hoping Woodie could close it out – it was pretty clear that Dick was gonna lose this game with Woodie on the mound or go to extra innings – I just sat down on the bench. Dick had Woodie intentionally walk the next batter and put the go-ahead run on first. Ramon Aviles, a utility infielder, hit for the pitcher. Woodie used all the guile left in his tired arm and Aviles went down on strikes. What kept me going was the thought that if we go to extra innings, *I know I'm getting in this game.*

Tug McGraw started the bottom of the ninth for Philadelphia. It was as if the gods of Baseball gave this funny man, this walking anecdote from 1970s counter-culture baseball, one more outstanding season in the sun. There may not have been a better reliever in either league than Tug in 1980, and here we were trying to win our season against him. Tug's famous screwball didn't let him down, striking out both Larry Parrish and Jerry Manuel (subbing for Speier) rather quickly. Obviously, with the pitcher due up, Dick hit rookie Tim Wallach for Woodie. I start warming up yet again. *I know I'm getting in this game.*

Stan Bahnsen threw one and two-thirds innings yesterday. He began warming up, too. It's now 28 degrees out. As we were throwing, it was obvious I would be starting the 10th.

"Johnny, " Stan says, rubbing his pitching arm,"It's killing me. It's too damn cold. I can't feel a thing."

Dick was pitching Bahnsen quite a bit over the final two weeks of the season. He was burning him out. But I knew what my numbers were. Schmidt was hitting .181 at the time against me. Small sample size, you say? Maybe, but in 1980, those stats were the only tools a manager, a scout or pitching coach had at his disposal to make an informed decision. The bullpen phone rang. Bill Lee answered the call.

"They want Bahnsen," Spaceman said.

I was beside myself. At this point, this could go to the 20th inning, didn't matter. Now I knew I wasn't getting in. Facing Trillo, Bowa and Maddox, Stan shut them down rather easily. In the bottom of the inning, we threatened, with the man who seemed to be our MVP of that final week, Jerry White, promptly singled to left and made it to third with two out, only for Tug to get it together through the crowd noise of 50,000 strong, striking out Dawson to take the game into the 11th.

Dick stayed with Stan. I was resigned to not pitching in the game. Rose led off. It's the most important game of the season so Pete does what Pete does, he got on base. McBride popped out. Schmidt stepped to the plate. This was supposed to be my moment because I felt I was the best pitcher in this moment for the ballclub. I should've been in there. This was the thought that ran through my head as soon as Schmidt dug in, the thought when he smacked the pitch over the left field fence, the thought to this day, 36 years later.

I should've been in this game. The Phillies poured out onto the field from the dugout as they do in 2012 when a hitter jacks a walk-off dinger, celebrating Schmidt's 2-run blast even before the game was over. Might as well have been. Bahnsen stayed in after the home run, but Dallas Green pretty much said to us it's closing time by having Tug bat for himself in the 11th. We had our 5-6-7 coming up to bat, Kid, Cromartie and Larry Parrish. Great hitters all of them, but we knew it was over. After Parrish struck out, McGraw jumped straight in the air, the Phils celebrated on our mound and I sat there, stunned. Then angry, angry because I would never know, in the annals of playoff-level baseball, who I was. *Am I Mike Torrez? Am I Bucky Dent? Am I Calvin Schraldi? Am I Mariano Rivera? Who am I?* No one wants to honestly admit we define our players in the post-season by these small sample sizes, but we do. We sure do. Am I the hero or the goat? Baseball history will never know. I will never know. With all sincerity in my heart, I would rather be Donnie Moore, giving up a classic TV-worthy, game-winning, career-altering home run and at the very least experience the chance to revise baseball history, than sit on a paint-chipping, wooden, bullpen bench in Canada and watch it happen to someone else.

After the game, still in my uniform, I walked by the manager's office. Dick owned two rings from leading the Oakland A's. He brought the 1967 upstart, *"Impossible Dream"* Boston Red Sox to a seventh game. He experienced great victory and heart-breaking defeat. This was nothing new. Still hurt, I'm sure. The difference was this was his fourth or fifth trip to the rodeo, to the sensation of playoff or near-playoff baseball. This was my first – wasn't sure if I would ever get another one. I just stood in the hallway, in front of his door, staring at him. He looked over. I couldn't speak – just raised my arms, opened my palms, with body language that basically yelled WTF.

"What?" Dick said, sipping a beer, hunched over his desk.

"Why didn't you pitch me? You know Schmidt's batting .181 with 10 strikeouts against me. Bull (Luzinski's) just as bad."

"Why didn't you tell me that?" Dick fired back. "I didn't know this."

"Is it my job to be your pitcher *and* your scout? My job is to go out and pitch."

"I didn't know…ok….I didn't know. I'm sorry."

Although Dick did apologize, I wasn't in the mood to accept it, and I walked away. A beat reporter stepped quickly behind me, catching up to ask the same question I was trying to figure out myself. I was having none of that. "You have to ask Skipper," I replied, nodding to Dick's office, walking toward the exit, "He makes the moves, not me."

Carter caught up with me as I was leaving the clubhouse.

"Johnny?" Gary said, grabbing my arm, "You OK?"

"No," I laughed, "I'm not OK. I shoulda been in that game." Kid patted me on the shoulder.

"Look, we have a tremendous pen out there, but if the game's on the line and I hear you're throwing 97-98, I'm taking my chances with you. I really don't know why they didn't put you in. I'm sorry." I thanked Gary for his kind words, and on some level I understood Dick's motivation. I wasn't here from Day One. Even if the team voted me a full share of playoff money, I wasn't in the pen with Woodie, Stan and Sosa from Opening Day.

I left the ballpark that night, rode the subway back to my hotel apartment and tried to go to sleep. When that didn't work, I got up and walked down the block, grabbing a pie at this place called Pines Pizza. Ran into a couple of the fellas, enjoyed some sad laughs and proceeded to close a bar or two. I tried to wash down the end of our playoff hopes with a few beers. Succeeded, too.

The next day was Game 162. Didn't mean shit to anyone but a select few. Pete Rose, of course played because that's what Pete did. Schmidt sat, Maddox sat, Tim McCarver played his final game at first base, replacing Rose in the fifth inning. Tim Raines started his first game ever in left field. He would play alongside Andre Dawson for the next seven seasons or so. Really though, it was a throw away game.

Not to me. I was still at 49 appearances.

I found our pitching coach Galen Cisco, in the dugout alone before the game.

"Galen, I need one more appearance to get my bonus. You think I could pitch today?" Galen Cisco is a class act, and offered a very concerned response.

"Why didn't you tell me earlier?"

"Pitching in games shouldn't have anything to do with a bonus, but since this is a throwaway, I'd like to get my bonus." Galen asked me to sit on the bench.

"I know you're pissed off you didn't get in the game. We found out you didn't give up shit against Philadelphia. We're not happy about that, either, the scouts should've told us. That's why you were brought here. To go head-to-head with Philly. I dunno why didn't Dick use you."

Galen was called away, but left with a light slap on my knee, mouthing *"Don't worry,"* as he left me sitting there. I know he had to get the permission from Dick to play me in the final game.

In the fifth inning, with the Phils ahead 5-2, I got the call from the bullpen. My 50th appearance. Pitched two innings, kept us in the game, gave up a hit and struck out one. Got 'ol McCarver to line out to short in the next-to-last at bat of his career. I was glad to get my 50th appearance – it was a not an insignificant amount of money for 1980, to be honest. But, damn, did I want Game 161. Sometimes I think maybe if I got into that game, maybe we win, maybe we don't. Maybe my career changes, maybe it doesn't. I'll just never know. I really believe this state of being is much, much worse than losing.

I really enjoyed my time in Montreal. The city is absolutely gorgeous, the fans were special. The front office treated me well. Day after the season ended, I packed up my hotel apartment at La Cite' and jumped into a cab toward the airport. When I arrived at Dorval for my flight back home, there were no banners. No fathers and sons waiting for hero ballplayers. No signs with my name on it. Just other people in transition.

As I reclined in my chair on the plane, I placed the headphones from the Walkman over my ears, gazing out the window overlooking Montreal, reflecting on Baseball in Canada, wondering what the cap on my 1981 baseball card would look like. A part of me hoped it would be the Expos. The other knew what team I truly played for.

The Jerry Kapsteins.

Call Me

"I don't wanna go to New York," Liz said, a half-empty glass of Cabernet accentuating her words, "I don't care how much the Yankees will pay us."

It's October 1980. We enjoyed some wine while standing on a wraparound porch in Providence, Rhode Island, a gorgeous 100-year old Victorian house, walking distance to the ocean. Six, seven bedrooms. High ceilings. Lovely neighborhood; expansive front lawns, personal tennis courts. The choppy wind and constant drizzle would be the perfect analogy for the conversation my wife and I had at the time, trying to figure out where my career would be taking us.

This was my agent's house. Four years past the death of the reserve clause, those who figured out the system were doin' all right. If you thought Scott Boras was the ultimate super-agent, then you never met Jerry Kapstein.

After the Peter Seitz decision allowed Andy Messersmith to seek any team he chose, it ultimately allowed a number of ballplayers to seek free agency following the 1976 season. Smart, young men seized upon the moment to represent these players in their negotiations with owners around the league. Jerry Kapstein was one of these clever young men. Brilliant, Harvard-trained, remains one of the smartest guys I know. It was a whole new ballgame for athlete compensation, and Jerry got on the field in the very first inning.

For some of you who were old enough to collect baseball cards at the time, but still too young to read newspapers, you opened packs of TOPPS 1977 and found new ball clubs you never knew existed like the Toronto Blue Jays *and* the Seattle Mariners. Maybe you also found a bunch of players with painted caps from different teams that didn't seem quite correct. Bobby Grich on the *Angels*? You thought he was an Oriole, right? That was Jerry's work. Joe Rudi and Don Baylor, Angels, too? That was Jerry. Rollie Fingers and Gene Tenace were on A's, no? No, Padres, thanks to Jerry. Kapstein had represented close to 60 players in 1976, many of them tested the free agent waters and received more money than they could ever imagine. What this situation gave Jerry wasn't simply a steady stream of income. It gave him negotiating leverage with the owners, which got the players larger contracts and in the end, even more money and more players for him to represent.

Smartest guy I know.

After the 1980 season ended, Liz and I flew out to Rhode Island to spend the week with Jerry at his house and discuss my options as a free agent. It was my first time at the re-entry draft rodeo, but I knew someone was going to pay me. There were a slew of teams with bullpen issues to address and my solid two months in Montreal enhanced my prospects for a nice contract. Jerry and I had some great conversations about each of the cities we felt would end up drafting me. We had a hope that at least four teams would get in the mix: the Expos, the Yankees, the Phillies and the California Angels. Through all the dinners that week, both in Jerry's house and at the Italian restaurants around Providence, it was the same discussion: my wife didn't want to leave California. I knew Liz had Jerry's ear. She made sure he knew her wishes.

"I want to stay on the West Coast, my family's on the West Coast." The last thing I wanted to do in the world was disappoint her.

Marriage is a great institution, but for baseball it's awful. Forget groupies and all the basic jealousy issues. If your wife doesn't want you playing in a certain city, you have to make some serious decisions not just about your career, but your family as well. Teammates were rooming together less and less on the road by 1980 and life could get very, very lonely. You're not out every night with the guys after a game in the majors; sometimes it's just you, room service and bad TV in the hotel. You find yourself wanting a relationship, meet somebody you like along the way, the pedal hits the metal and next thing you know, you're married. The choices and decisions you would make were no longer, "*Ok, I'm being traded to the Cardinals, I guess I'm goin' to St. Louis,*" or "*The Phillies want me, the area seems nice, think I'll live and play there for three seasons.*" It's a transient lifestyle. It's not for everyone. Now you have someone else in these conversations – sometimes within earshot of the agent – and it completely changes the dynamic. And yeah, this becomes information the agent factors into the final decision.

My wife adored Southern California, it was her home, and mine as well. Both of our families lived pretty much right around the corner. I had been playing at home parks with blood relatives in attendance virtually my entire career. From 1973 to 1976, I played in San Fran, where I had a host of cousins all around town. Outside of short, bookended stays in St. Louis in early '77 & the last two months of the 1980 season in Canada, I played nearly four years in

San Diego, my hometown. Sure, it was great to see a familiar face from my high school days or family at just about every home game, but I wanted something, I don't know, something....different.

The East Coast was very attractive to me. It was either that or return to Montreal. I liked it there. I had Gary Carter, my buddy and team leader to spend time with. I had a lot of friends on the ball club and got along well with just about everyone. My mentor and father figure, Charlie Fox, worked in the front office. It made a fair amount of sense for me to stay in Canada. These were the issues Liz and I discussed with my agent that week we stayed at his house. Jerry was an absolutely gracious host and clearly defined every single option available to us. It was very obvious, though, when we hopped on the plane to go home at Providence Airport, nothing was resolved. My wife was dead set against leaving California.

There was no good guy in this. There was no bad guy. There was only me and her and we just disagreed.

* * * * *

I got a call from Charlie Fox about returning to the Expos. I know Stan Bahnsen, the Expos' other right-handed reliever, was a free agent as well. Charlie asked me, "So, ya wanna come back?"

"I love the guys," I replied, "Of course I wanna come back."

"Ok, so that's settled, whaddya want?"

"Try to get me four years if you can, at least $300k per. If it's for three years, I want $400k. If it's four years, I'll take $300k. And I want a bonus of $600k."

Charlie's like, "Ok, Johnny, lemme see what I can do." So Charlie comes back the next day.

"So, I spoke with the guys here – they're interested, but they're not interested."

"What does that mean?"

"I dunno," Charlie said, "I'm not getting a good read from them on this." In hindsight, I was most likely their backup plan in case they couldn't sign Bahnsen, someone who could set-up, close and pitch a lot, just like me.

"They said they would like you back, but they are trying to sign someone else and if they can sign the other guy, well, you know, you're expendable." Tough to hear this, but right then and there, I knew I pitched my last game in a Montreal uniform.

"Look, if they can't sign 'em, they're gonna get you." Charlie was very influential with me, so I kept that door open. That was a sad feeling, even at this level of negotiation, that they wanted someone more than me. We're not robots.

The following month, the re-entry draft came and went. Jerry was right – there would be a strong market for my services, even more then he realized. I was chosen by seven teams: The Angels, Phillies, Pirates, Indians, Cubs, Royals and the Yankees. Some teams chose me simply to have a dialogue, but weren't terribly serious.

The Phillies asked Jerry about me. I thought a lot about living in Philadelphia. Pete Rose had called me asking if I was interested. Pete said his teammates loved the area; some lived across the bridge in parts of South Jersey, like Cherry Hill - others in the suburbs of the city – a beautiful section called *"The Main Line,"* where there's gorgeous towns like Villanova (where the college is located), Wayne, Radnor, Gladwyne. Would've been fun to play with Pete. Keep in mind, Philadelphia had just won the World Series, and postseason bullpen star Tug McGraw was also a free agent. There was an opening, if only a small one. Ron Reed, Dickie Noles and Warren Brusstar all had tough seasons in 1980, but as long as they signed Tug (which they did), going to the City of Brotherly Love was a long-shot, at best. They made an offer of three years at $400,000 per with a fourth year at $425,000, non-guaranteed. A very nice offer, no question. Something else, though, was brewing up the turnpike.

The Yankees made an offer, too – three years, $350,000 per, with a fourth year at $425,000 – less than the Phillies' offer, *but* included a $675,000 signing bonus – again the fourth year was not guaranteed. Here's the thing; Goose Gossage was there. Bucky Dent, another friend, was there. Graig Nettles too, – me, Nettles and Goose all shared the same agent. So you had a sense that while you played for one team, you were also part of another - the guys with whom you shared a common agent. Goose, Nettles, stars like Steve Garvey. All Kapstein clients.

Smartest guy I know.

I was hearing it from all sides about New York. You're good-looking, you're Italian, look what's going on with Rick Cerone – came into New York City from the Blue Jays, stepped right in and replaced Thurman Munson. Was it the best year of Cerone's career? Maybe, but it was the best season by a Yankee catcher in three years and no one knew in December 1980 that their 26-year old catcher (who finished seventh in the AL MVP voting) would never be this good again. Cerone took Madison Avenue by storm. He became *"The Italian Stallion."* They played the Tarantella every time he came to bat at the Stadium. There was a place for me in the Bronx if I wanted, and I really did want it.

"This all makes sense," Jerry said, "They want you there, there's endorsement opportunities you haven't even dreamed of, the money's right, I think we should do it. I know how Liz feels, but she married your career, this is your decision, we need to make this move." I wanted to see myself in the uniform. I wanted a baseball card that said *Yankees* above my picture. Jerry fed into all those dreams. "Look, you're gonna make more money off the field than *on* the field. You're gonna be Madison Avenue and if you pitch well, you're gonna be big time Madison Avenue. Most important, you're gonna be a Yankee."

During this time in my life, every discussion with Liz became about staying in California. Every night was a stressful debate about my future. To her credit, the fights were never about the money – we all knew someone was going to pay me, Jerry made sure of that. It was about consistency of a home life surrounded by extended family, multiple friends and acquaintances who had known me since grade school. A home life in California. What I experienced in Montreal at the end of 1980, made me think, maybe I needed a break from that for a few years. Too many people constantly coming by the house. No privacy whatsoever. Weekly phone calls about tickets. I left seats for my folks and siblings.

Occasionally, aunts, uncles, cousins would call, and even that was no big deal – they were family and I loved them. It wasn't them. People I knew in town who never reached out before suddenly found my number when I got to the Padres. People who I didn't get along with in high school suddenly called me to make amends. It was a situation I really had no problem leaving behind and I couldn't think of a better place than New York, a team as far away as possible and a ballclub who possessed one of the best chances to win a pennant. I knew this was the final contract I would ever sign

– I was constantly in pain, constantly hurt, nothing that would show up in a physical, but my body told me every day I wasn't 21 anymore. I could still hit 95 on the gun with consistency, but the pain was there.

So while I'm thinking *"Yankees vs. a team in California that may or may not want me," "Do I return to Montreal on a lesser contract," "How will I resolve this mess with my wife,"* Cleveland comes out of the clear blue sky and offers me $360,000 per for three years with a fourth year for $420,000, an option that was not guaranteed. Now the Yankees fourth year was not guaranteed, either. Why did the Indians jump into the mix? They had to part with their excellent closer in Victor Cruz to get Bert Blyleven, a great starting pitcher. They really had no closer now. They ended up moving a 16-game winner in Dan Spillner into the bullpen. Cleveland would've been nice – some of the suburbs outside the city are just beautiful. I was starting to have all these teams throwing money at me, the one club that mattered the most to my wife, the California Angels, didn't care at all. Jerry was sent a note from Buzzie Bavasi, the Angels general manager and my old GM in San Diego, basically saying they didn't want to negotiate with us. The West Coast was out.

So we were focusing on the Yankees. That was our best opportunity, the best money and I knew I would be comfortable with the other guys. So a few days pass and Jerry calls me.

"Go buy a new suit, we're going to New York."

"Did you commit to Steinbrenner?"

"Yes I did. He wants to talk to you."

So I received a call at home later that day from George Steinbrenner.

"Johnny, I'm gonna give you what you want, but I'm not gonna guarantee the last year."

"That's fair, George."

"If you do well on the three, we can talk on the fourth."

"I'm committing to you, George." Now, I stuck my neck out to say to George Steinbrenner, *"I'm committing to you."* That's like a handshake. Like signing in blood. Jerry said to Steinbrenner, "Okay George, you can go ahead and let it loose." *"Let it loose"* means he can tell the media we have a deal. I was really happy about this. Liz, not so much.

"I don't wanna go to New York, I don't wanna be on the East Coast," she said, and another grating discussion ensued.

"We're goin' to the Yankees," I nodded, "You better start looking for schools." We went to bed, didn't really resolve much, but I fell asleep peacefully dreaming of Monument Park, dreaming of playing in the center of the media universe.

This was the night of December 9th, 1980.

The phone woke me up at 2:30 in the morning, December 10th, 1980.

It wasn't Marv Albert looking to set up my first interview on Live at Five, the popular WNBC news program in New York at the time.

"It's Jerry," my agent mumbled into the phone, "Don't say anything, get your clothes on, get in your car and come to the house immediately. I got you four years guaranteed, $600,000 bonus with the California Angels."

"Huh?" I replied in a sleep daze, "What are you doin', we're goin' to New York later today."

"No, we're going to see Gene Autry later today."

"Whaddya talkin' about, I just made an agreement with the Yankees and Steinbrenner, it's been all over the news. New York Post, Daily News, this is dangerous, we just agreed to terms, what are you doing?"

"Your wife wants you on the West Coast, I worked my butt off to get you here-"

"But am I gonna pitch there?"

"Just get in the car and come down here before he changes his mind."

"But it's not good for my career-"

"Just come down here. We'll talk when you get here." I entered Jerry's place in La Jolla wearing a pair of sweats and T-shirt. He handed me a contract.

"No, no, no, I'm not signing that. This benefits you, not me." Of course, the money benefitted me, but I knew in my heart there would be long-term ramifications of blowing off the Yankees. No one does that to George Steinbrenner. God forbid you cross him, and this was a betrayal of the highest order. Embarrassing him in the newspapers.

"Just sign the contract, John-"

"This is gonna bite me in the ass-"

"Sign the contract-"

"This isn't good for my-"

"You're right, John. You're absolutely right. New York and the fans and all that Italian Stallion marketing would be much, much better for you and your career than Anaheim."

"Thank you, Jerry."

"Now sign the fuckin' contract."

I always did what I was told.

I never felt so lousy placing my name on a legal document. After receiving my signature, Jerry eased me into the thought of pitching with California.

"Don't worry, you'll be the closer. They don't have anyone else."

I wanted New York over all other places if I was only pitching the seventh and eighth innings. Goose Gossage was a superstar, all-star reliever, and a great guy. Would've been a blast hanging out with him in the bullpen watching six innings of baseball for six months. But being the closer, that's...

"So I'm the closer for the California Angels?" I repeated this.

"You're the closer for the California Angels."

"I have to talk to George-" Jerry waved his finger at me.

"I will talk to George." I laughed at that statement. It didn't matter. George would accept this coming from Jerry. Jerry had power. Jerry had leverage. Jerry represented his All-Star closer, among other important players. George would be mad at me, and hold it against me, but never the agent. Never an agent as powerful as Jerry.

Do you know what really happened? Earlier that night, the Angels acquired Butch Hobson and Rick Burleson, the Red Sox All-

Star Shortstop in a trade for Carney Lansford, Rick Miller and Mark Clear, the Angels, right-handed reliever. The trade was essentially a vehicle for the Red Sox to get rid of Burleson, who was having contentious contract talks with the ballclub. Through the mechanics of this trade, Burleson became the highest-paid shortstop in the game. Do you really have to guess who Rick Burleson's agent was at the time?

Yup, smartest guy I know.

There were so many moving parts to this situation, some I was aware of, but the largest piece, unbeknownst to me, was about to fall into place.

I understand the nature of leverage and its importance. If my agent was a relative or some obscure lawyer from Santa Monica, the terms of my deal would be different. The money would definitely be different and less of it. Did being with a prominent agent make things easy for me? Did I receive better contract terms than if I had a lesser agent? You bet. Don't forget, the baseball players' strike was the elephant in the room at this time. It was very important for me to at least be signed and secure.

* * * * *

Going to the California Angels and breaking the handshake deal with the Yankees was the worst decision I ever made. I regret it every time I see myself on a baseball card in an Angels uniform. All for an extra $300,000. Jerry Kapstein made me very wealthy. Just know, as a player, that when you make a choice to go to a ballclub, be conscious of every element to that decision before you sign. Most important, which people there have your future in their hands – that means the manager, the general manager, the owner and possibly veteran players with some persuasive power in the clubhouse and front office. This is vital to the free-agent decision-making process. I'm not talking about the superstar that should be set for life with a year's salary if he's smart with his money. What I'm talking about are those long relievers and fifth outfielders in today's game. They need to take this seriously.

* * * * *

I never had the chance to pitch in Yankee Stadium. Never had the chance to hear Bob Sheppard announce me into a 5-4 game in the seventh inning. Never had a chance to bust balls with Goose in the Yankees bullpen or jump on that pile when they clinched the American League championship in 1981.

From the moment I left Jerry's driveway, I knew this would be the greatest regret of my baseball career. George Steinbrenner would never forget, either.

Buzzing down the 101 at 4:30 in the morning, top down on the Mercedes, in my bed clothes, I could barely look at myself in the rearview mirror. Debbie Harry's beguiling voice boomed through the Blaupunkt, best encapsulating how I was felt about myself at that moment.

I know who you are.

Sacrifice The Pitcher

"*You know, Grandy Rice said that it makes no difference whether you win or lose, it's the way you play the game,*" announced Angels owner Gene Autry, "*The Cowboy,*" at the press conference welcoming Fred Lynn, Rick Burleson, Butch Hobson and me to the team, flash bulbs popping off everywhere, "*Well, Grandy Rice can go to hell as far as I'm concerned. I've spent 10 million dollars lately on this outfit and I wanna win.*" The Angels had us lined up at a table in front of the reporters, proudly boasting the pieces he put in place to claim the pennant. Thanks in part to super agent Jerry Kapstein, of course.

Autry had been the most active owner in the free agent game since the players received the right to auction themselves off to the highest bidder in 1976. Don Baylor, Bobby Grich, Joe Rudi, Lyman Bostock, Bruce Kison, Geoff Zahn, Billy Travers, me. Most of us were Jerry Kapstein clients. Jerry's close relationship with both Gene Autry and current Angels General Manager Buzzie Bavasi made a lot of these deals happen. There was also a new type of transaction perfected during the past four years: the "*trade and sign.*" When Minnesota Twins owner Calvin Griffith was unwilling to pay his star players ever-increasing market wages, Gene was all too willing to open his wallet and acquire the all-stars with the assumption being that they would be arriving with a brand-new contract, at a much higher salary. Think Rod Carew and Dan Ford in 1979; the deal Jerry negotiated with Buzzie for Rick Burleson just one month earlier, and now Freddie Lynn, also from the Sox. Boston's GM Haywood Sullivan had made the mistake of sending the 1981 contracts to Lynn and Red Sox catcher Carlton Fisk two days *after* the deadline. Jerry exploited the error, whereby releasing Fisk and Lynn from any further obligations to the Boston franchise. Red Sox ownership disputed this, claiming that under the 1976 collective bargaining agreement the team was entitled to an option year before their two stars would be able to file for free agency.

The Dodgers tried to coax Lynn from Fenway, offering Rookie of the Year reliever Steve Howe along with young pitcher Joe Beckwith and second-year outfielder Mickey Hatcher, which the Sox accepted at first. The problem was Jerry insisted Freddie wouldn't sign an extension. The Dodgers balked and Boston would wait for the arbitration hearing in New York to determine whether or not Lynn and Fisk could claim free agency. After placing Burleson, Hobson and me in California, Jerry remained in Buzzie's ear.

The Red Sox, fearing they would lose the case, jumped at the chance to get something for Fred Lynn, which turned out to be Frank Tanana and Joe Rudi. I would've liked the chance to play with Frankie, as we both went through painful operations on our arm and knew the other's injury experience. You know, to say that sitting on that lighted stage beside guys like Lynn and Burleson approached the surreal was a bit of an understatement, but at first Fregosi made me feel as if I would be the man in the bullpen. "*A lot of pitchers develop later in their career,*" Fregosi said to reporters about me, "*The type of arm Johnny has gets a great deal of velocity and he fits very well into our plan.*" After the presser, Fregosi told me, in no uncertain terms, I would be the closer for the Angels when we broke camp. "You're my guy," he said. That was the deal I was sold, that's the reason I signed with California, that's why I went there. With a starting lineup that fielded an All-Star or near Hall of Famer at just about every position, I could really get my chance to at last reach the playoffs. Heading down to Angels' spring training in Palm Springs, February 1981, I was ready for the universal dream of every ballplayer:to be part of a superstar team.

* * * * *

The Cowboy was a lot like Gussie Busch. Everything at the facility was first-rate, from the spring training complex, the clubhouse food on the road, extra spikes, uniforms – you wanted for nothing as an employee. Wasn't just because Autry was made of money or a great guy – and Gene Autry was a *super*, super guy – but the ballclub absolutely crushed it at the turnstiles. The California Angels lost 95 games in 1980 and still drew close to 2.3 million fans – second in the American League. This wasn't TV cable money fueling this team – the guys told me it seemed like every game was close to a sellout.

Entering the clubhouse at Palm Spring Stadium sort of felt like the first day of high school, lots of new kids but a few familiar faces. I shared an agent with Bobby Grich and Donny Baylor. Billy Travers I knew from the minor leagues. Andy Hassler, too. Of course, Dan Ford, the one hitter who really had my number back in the AAA and low minors days. We joked a bit about the moonshot dingers he smacked against me in the Midwest and Pacific Coast League games.

Upon entering the clubhouse, I offered my services to Baylor to help out with the players' union affairs. A big, bulky guy, even by ballplayer standards. Imposing figure, booming voice, Baylor was on the players' executive director board as well as player representative of the Angels for the Major League Baseball Players Association. To say the strike loomed large over baseball in 1981 would be an understatement. The main issue was the owners basically trying to get something in exchange for their fellow owners' desperation. Autry was the best example. From January 1980 to May 1981, Autry acquired six free agent pitchers, all in a vain attempt to replace his mistake of letting Nolan Ryan cruise outta town. He made us all multi-millionaires. His fellow major league owners wanted the ability to pick from a collection of other players – a *"compensation pool"* – to offset the loss of free agents like us. Marvin Miller vehemently opposed this. Anything that could possibly deter the escalation of salaries, Marvin challenged. That's what brought about the Baseball Strike of 1981.

"Marvin told me you'd be willing to help out with the union stuff," Baylor asked me as we stretched in the outfield at Palm Spring Stadium, "Would you be the team's co-rep?"

"I seemed to get asked that a lot," I laughed. Baylor smiled.

"Yeah, most guys want no part of it."

"I'm happy to help." Baylor updated me on the status of the meetings with the owners, which is to say, there was none. He was hopeful that the strike would be averted. Optimistic? Not so much.

After our workout, a few of us went to this open-air bar in Palm Springs. I was having a beer with Baylor talking labor stuff as Jimmie Reese joined our conversation. Resse was an 80-year old baseball lifer who was invited to Angels' spring training every year to teach bunting and supervise infield drills, but really just came down because Autry loved him and wanted him around. We all adored Jimmie – a baseball icon - he was Babe Ruth's roommate. Loved telling stories about the grand old game in the 1930s and '40s. Also loved his whiskey and cigars. As Donny stepped away to find the bathroom, Jimmie leaned into me, as if sharing a secret.

"Be careful with that shit," he spoke in this raspy whisper of a voice.

"What shit is that?" I replied, as I lit our cigars.

"We're just players. We ain't money men, we ain't the bosses."

"It's a different world now, Jimmie-"

"Bullshit. 60 years in baseball, know how many enemies I got?" Jimmie curled his wrinkled fist into a zero. "Don't get dirty with this shit."

* * * * *

There was another controversy brewing in camp. The Angels hired Gene Mauch, former Phillies, Expos and Twins manager as a "consultant" within the organization. Biggest open secret in the clubhouse was that Fregosi didn't inspire much confidence with Autry and Buzzie. They were simply waiting for the right opportunity to let him go. You'll see this often when a former respected manager joins a franchise where the current skipper is not terribly regarded. In this situation, Mauch spent the spring getting to know the hitters, the pitchers and the farm system. The plan was for Mauch to be completely prepared and aware of the teams' needs in the event Fregosi would be fired. This was not a good development for me at all.

Back in 1974 when Mauch was managing the Montreal Expos and I was a rookie with the Giants, he and his players were yelling things at Jim Barr and me through the pre-game warm-ups, the stuff you don't see on TV, trying to rattle my cage. After taking enough of their abuse, I stepped off the rubber and chucked a heater right past the old man's head. Not too fast, but enough to make a point. Then, I ran over to the Expos dugout, pointed at Mauch and said, *"You! I want you out here right now."* I wanted a piece of Mauch pretty bad. Both dugouts emptied. Jim Barr had my back, mixing it up with the Expos players as well. Mauch never accepted my challenge, but I certainly showed him up. Now, seven years later, he's my manager-in waiting. Jim Barr was also still with the Angels, though stuck on the 60-Day DL and no real timetable to return. If Mauch became manager, my California goose would be all but cooked. Suffice to say, Mauch never approached me during camp.

I began spring training pitching well in relief, started a game or two. Happy to be there, but something changed soon after Mauch arrived. Fregosi began dropping hints that Don Aase *"wanted to close."* Was kind of a chickenshit way to go about the process. I didn't help matters much, to be honest. I allowed my apprehensions get the best of my performance on the mound. We played a scrimmage against Fullerton State College toward the end of camp. I gave up five runs in seven innings. We won the game, but it was a prep team. I should've thrown much better. The next day, Fregosi called me into his office. The hints he'd been dropping all week soon became bombs.

"Aase's gonna be our closer," Fregosi told me, "You'll be in long relief. Some set-up work. Maybe, we'll see." If this happened today, I would've approached the Players' Association and complained about the chain of events. The General Manager told me and my agent one thing and then the manager and pitching coach told me something entirely different.

"What are you talkin' about?" I replied, "This wasn't what you said to me in January."

"Yeah, well, things are changed. You're not where you're supposed to be at this stage."

"It's spring training, I'm working my way into shape-"

"We were promised 98-99 MPH fastballs, you're only throwing 95-96-"

"Only 95-96??!? What the-"

"I just thought you should know-"

"Yeah, thanks." I walked out. I held it against Fregosi at the time, but the more I thought about it, the more I realized things had changed – Jim Fregosi wouldn't my manager for very long.

I was basically a mop-up guy when the season began. My first game was in a 5-0 laugher against the Seattle Mariners of all teams. I gave up five more runs in the final two innings. I wouldn't pitch for another 18 days. My next appearance would introduce me to someone whom I would eventually grow very close.

* * * * *

We faced Oakland at the end of April. Back in January, after Buzzie made all the free agent moves and trades, A's manager Billy Martin made a snide remark at him in the press. *"I have to laugh at Buzzie Bavasi. He's picked up all the old arms he could find. He ought go to the junkyard."* So in the sixth inning, Rickey Henderson stepped to the plate. Ed Ott was catching and gave me the thumb sign, which meant *"Flip him."* I nodded, wound up and took Rickey off his legs with a 96 MPH fastball right under his chin. Billy screamed at me from the dugout.

"That's a horseshit pitch, Dago! You do that again, I'll come out there and kick your ass." I looked over at Billy in the A's dugout, extended my arms as if to say, *"I'm right here, Skip."* Ott tossed me the ball back and called for an inside heater. We hit the black this time. Strike one. Ott called for the same pitch. Hit the black again. Strike two. This time, Ott called for the slider. I look over at Billy and smile, just to let him think I might get cute with some more chin music. "You do that again, Dago and it's your ass." I wound up.

Slider on the outside corner.

Called strike three.

Inning over.

Ott shook the ball right in front of Rickey's nose.

"Is this what you're lookin' for, asshole?" Ott laughed at Rickey. Hendu and Ott start mouthing face-to-face. Nothing came of it, but the scent of conflict was in the air. In the eighth inning, Dan Ford smacked a blast off Mike Norris. A's catcher Mike Heath had the umpire check the bat. Danny went nuts on Heath – benches cleared. A few punches were thrown, everyone settled down....until the end of the game. Both teams walked through the tunnels under the stands to reach their respective clubhouses. Our pitching coach, Tom Morgan, picked a fight with one of the A's players. Wrong move, as Billy was itching for a shot at someone. He pinned ol' Morgan against the tunnel wall and was about to beat the living shit out of him until cops and players pulled him away. Martin was laughing about it with the beat guys after the game. Billy just loved to fight. Loved it.

Dissension wasn't simply relegated to our opponents, either. With all the whispers about Fregosi's job in the air, the Angels' clubhouse was an absolute disaster. Mauch and Fregosi stopped communicating completely. Got so bad when they ran into each other in bars after the games, they hung out in opposite ends of the place. It was like Baseball's version of West Side Story. Brian Downing was pissed because most of the pitchers wanted Eddie Ott calling their games. One beat guy in particular, Jim Schulte from the San Bernardino County Sun, would stir shit up on a near weekly basis - which pitcher was unhappy with Fregosi, which reliever thought Fregosi would be gone within weeks. Fregosi was fed up at this point - commenting on the record to Schulte during nights drinking in the big sports bar behind Anaheim Stadium, saying things like *"If that white-haired son-of-a-bitch wants my job so bad, he can have it. I'm tired of the bullshit."* The main reason Autry, being a stand-up guy, stuck with Fregosi so long was because Jimmy was the Angels' first real star back in the 60's.

My season was a mess. I pitched four times in the first 27 games. I would sit in the bullpen with Jesse Jefferson, another promising hurler from 1973 the organization believed could be revitalized. Neither of us would pitch and just shake our heads.

"Johnny, man, we ain't never gettin' into a game," Jesse would laugh. He was closer to the truth than he realized.

My fourth outing of the season was one of the worst experiences of my career. May 6th, at home against the Yankees. Bucky Dent was enjoying one hellvua night. A two-run double to left and a dinger couple innings later off rookie Mike Witt that made the score

5-0 Yankees. I'm on the mound in the sixth, Bucky comes up and my 94-MPH fastball cracks him right on the wrist. Knocked him out of the game. All the papers were saying I threw at him on purpose. Yankees first baseman Bob Watson said the Bombers should come after us the next time around. It was not at all intentional. Bucky was (and remains to this day) a good friend of mine, one of my buddies from back in A ball. I reached out to him the next morning – he was cool about it, but it just gave Fregosi more ammo to freeze me out. I didn't enter a game for a week and a half after that. Few days later, I confronted my manager in his office.

"Hey Jim, can you tell me when I might get on the mound again?" Fregosi wouldn't even look at me. "Dunno, can't tell ya."

"Well, think about it," I said, "Because I'm not doing anyone any good just sitting on my ass in the bullpen." As I stormed out of his office, Fregosi called out, "Johnny!" I turned around and he motioned for me to close the door, lighting a cigarette.

"You see what I'm fuckin' dealin' with here. I don't like what's goin' on, Mauch's running his mouth-"

"-I'm in the clubhouse, too, I know all that, but I'm wasting away out there-"

"They're paying you a shitload of money, my hands are tied, just, just fuckin' deal with it. *Please*?"

I sighed, nodded and left his office. He had all but checked out at that stage. By the end of the month, Fregosi would be gone. Gene Mauch would be the next Angels manager. I always thought that Mauch through Buzzie had something to do with my inactivity. Turns out, it was even more sinister than that.

Rumors were floating around that Buzzie was also messing with Donny Baylor's head, too. The Texas Rangers caught wind and asked what it would take to get Baylor in a trade. Buzzie had a problem with Baylor and apparently a problem with me. The only thing that the teams' designated hitter and mop-up reliever had in common was that we were both heavily involved with the players' negotiation ahead of the scheduled strike.

* * * * *

We just got home from a road trip across the Midwest. I was finally sleeping in my own bed when the phone rang at 2:30 AM.

"Hey, Johnny, it's Donny Baylor. You have to come up to Anaheim tomorrow. We're sitting down with the owners. I need you here with me."

The players' strike was reality. This wouldn't be the week's extended golf outing like '72. This wouldn't be the abbreviated strikes of '73 nor the '76 lockout. This was real. Don had been up half the night for many weeks with the executive board, fighting for the benefits of every baseball player in 1981. The nights and worries about the upcoming work stoppage affected many of us, both off and on the field. Baylor himself was hitting .154 on May 22nd, a week before the strike, the lowest batting average of his career to that point in the season. Don had the responsibility for many players and their families in his hands. It's obvious that emotional pressure, in addition to long, stressful nights at the negotiating table, *and* the trade rumors, weighed down on his performance.

I sat up in bed after Baylor's phone call in May 1981. We were to meet with the owners. It was a ballsy posture the union was taking here, but it had to be done. This was going to test the resolve of the players' union. There was a lot of money possibly lost by everyone if it didn't work out. What kept us going was our faith in Marvin Miller. Even we knew the money had gotten a little crazy. Marvin had already made some of us wealthier than we ever dreamed, made near millionaires of Reggie, Rudi, Campy, Goose, Pete, among many others. Multi-millionaires of Winfield and Nolan Ryan. He made other players extremely comfortable. Let me put it in this perspective. From the first free-agent class after the 1976 season to the summer of 1981, just five years later – *I* was making more in salary than Don Baylor and Bobby Grich (this would be rectified a great deal in each of their next contracts, but just to illustrate the point). Marvin told us to have faith in him and this is why we did it.

And why I did what no other player was willing to do.

* * * * *

We were in an executive board member meeting for the player's association. Me, Donny Baylor, Steve Renko, Bob Boone, Marvin Miller, a few other players.

"The guys are starting to ask me questions," Baylor said, "*'Is the strike happening?' 'What are we gonna do?'* Some of them are asking me about money, a lot of the of the players are living paycheck to paycheck, *'I have enough to make it through a couple months, but that's it.'*"

Marvin was adamant. "Their resolve needs to be stronger. We can win this thing-"

"It's not a game, Marvin-"

"I know it's not a game, but the owners will crush you guys if we don't fight back in kind-"

"Well, what's your plan?"

"I have information that there's some serious cross-ownership issues happening all throughout the league."

Everyone's mouths hit the table.

"What?"

"Are you serious?"

Marvin showed us the documents that outlined the different owners who possessed stakes in opposing ball clubs, bank records, transaction documents, everything.

"Where the hell'd you get this?" Baylor asked Marvin, who shot back a *"don't ask questions"* look.

"Now which one of you is going to confront them?" You never heard laughter so loud.

"You out of your fuckin' mind?" one of the players said. *"Not a chance,"* *"No fuckin' way,"* *"Not me,"* was the response from every single player rep at the table. Then Marvin looked my way.

"Johnny?" Marvin asked me gently, "Can I count on you?"

I paused for a moment. A couple of players simply shook their heads at me, basically saying, *"Don't do it."*

"Lemme see the file." I was flabbergasted by the amount of evidence Marvin collected.

"It's all there, Johnny. You got balls enough?"

I folded the document and handed it back to Marvin.

"Bigger balls than you do." Marvin's famous moustache curved in a gleeful grin.

"That's why I like you."

I always did what I was told. Marvin Miller went to his head hunter in the bullpen to close it out.

* * * * *

Marvin and I entered the meeting with the owners. Gussie Busch, 82 years old, down-home, charismatic billionaire, was the leader of the owners' group. I glanced over to Marvin, who nodded his approval to move forward, and then I looked my former employer in the eye.

"Mr. Busch, it's been brought to my attention that you have interest in six major-league ball clubs, heavy interest to say the least. How is that possible? I know you're Budweiser and everything, your beer's in every park, and rightfully so, but this document says you have financial interest in six major league teams. Kansas City, St. Louis, San Francisco, New York Mets, teams that are financially distraught. New franchises. How is that possible?"

Busch's smile was gone.

"Where'd you get that information?" he barked at me.

I slid the document across the table. Busch placed his reading glasses across his eyes and perused the documents. He sighed slightly, then smiled again, the grin of one of the most powerful businessman in the world, like a general who just lost a battle. "It's true. It's all true."

"Thank you for being honest. How were you able to pull this off?"

"The owners allowed it." All the other owners grumbled, up to that point, the most serious moment of my life.

Leaving that meeting was very bittersweet. I was a strident union supporter, did whatever Marvin Miller asked of me, but on a personal level, Gussie Busch treated me well during my time in St. Louis. All of the owners treated me like gold, to be honest. Marvin assured me that the union would prevail, that the owners didn't want this information getting leaked to the press and they would cave.

A week later, I arrived at The Big A for another meeting with the owners, Buzzie pulled me aside.

"Let's go to my office," he mumbled.

"The organization's making a change," he said, as he closed the door, without giving me a chance to take a seat, "You're being sent down to Salt Lake City. You're not getting enough work up here. We need you to stay fresh, get your starts."

"What?" I replied, shocked at first, but not surprised the more he spoke, "I have a guaranteed-"

"You'll get your money. Plane ticket's waiting for you at the airport. Goodbye-"

"You can't do that, I'm a veteran-"

"I just did-" and Buzzie handed me my paperwork.

"Look me in the eye and tell me this isn't about the teams' cross-ownership-"

"This is about your 10 ERA-"

"I've pitched six games in two months-"

"We're gonna get you some work down there, we're converting you back to a starter, you'll get plenty of time in Salt Lake to work it all out-"

-"Because the teams' doing so well right now-"

"Goodbye, Johnny." Buzzie walked out of the office and into the negotiation room, where my presence was no longer allowed...being a minor league player.

I returned to the conference room, grabbed my jacket and walked out.

"Johnny, where ya goin?" Baylor asked me, following me down the hall, "Talk to me-"

"Buzzie sent me to the Mormons-"

"What the hell are you-" I showed him the slip.

"What...he can't," Baylor was furious, "Stay right there." I grabbed his arm.

"Don't get involved," I warned him, "There's nothing you can do."

"Call Marvin, he'll fix it." I rolled my eyes and slapped him lightly on the shoulder.

"Sure," and walked away. Baylor called after me.

"Johnny, man, I'm sorry." I waved back to acknowledge him and left the ballpark.

I was numb. The next conversation was with Marvin when I got home. "John, I feel terrible," he said.

"We need to fix this," I replied, "This is my job."

"I know, but I...I can't help you at this moment. You're gonna have to just go there for a little while." There were more apologies, more words of polite concern from Marvin, but the question that weighed on my mind was even worse.

What was I gonna tell my wife? She was out shopping when I got home.

"Honey, the Angels have sent me down to AAA Salt Lake City. I'm gonna be gone for a couple months. I'm angry, I'm embarrassed, these guys fucked me over pretty badly. I don't know what I'm gonna do."

"Oh, sweety, it's ok. Here's what you're gonna do. You're gonna show those young kids what Fastball Johnny D is all about. You're gonna be great. We're gonna be great. I have the baby here, my folks are just a few miles away. You'll be in my arms in no time. C'mere, gimme a kiss."

Except that's not at all how it happened.

She first asked me how the demotion would affect our income, and it went downhill from there.

* * * * *

As I loaded my bags into the trunk of the cab outside the house, I realized my only hope for survival in this chosen career was to put aside the alienation brewing inside me.

"Where ya going?" the driver asked me, trying to make small talk on the way to the airport.

I had no answer.

It would be quite awhile before Johnny D would be living in the limelight of a major league baseball game.

The Midnight Special

"The fuck are you doin' here?" the Salt Lake City Gulls manager Moose Stubing asked me when I entered his office at Derks Stadium the following morning.

"Nice to see you too, Skip," I smiled, extending my hand, "John D'Acquisto-"

"I know who you are. What the hell ya doing here?"

"What do you mean? Didn't Buzzie tell you?"

Moose dropped his pen in exasperation like some DMV worker who suddenly found two extra hours of paperwork on her desk.

"Buzzie didn't tell me shit. There's no plan or regiment for you here, just go find a spot in the locker room like the rest of 'em, drop your crap and go sit in the bullpen-"

"I beg your pardon? That's not how this works. I have a major league contract. Buzzie sent me down here to get work. That's a start every fourth day. Now if you got a problem with that, I'm sure the players' union would be thrilled to have a word with you."

Stubing was a baseball company man through and through. He had a cup of coffee with California in the bigs back in 1967. Minor league coach and manager in the Angels organization for over a decade. Definitely did as *he* was told. And sometimes, as in this case, not at all told. And not at all thrilled about having another Angels castoff dropped in his lap.

"Take your shit," Moose said deliberately, "And get in the clubhouse." Great, I thought to myself, another manager delighted to make my acquaintance. I picked up my gear and Moose picked up the phone instantly as I walked out.

* * * * *

The Salt Lake City Gulls' clubhouse felt like The Land of Misfit Big Leaguers. Pepe Mangual. My old Padres teammates Fernando Gonzalez and Bob Davis. Chris Knapp. Mickey Mahler. The older guys had their own corner reserved, as if the ballclub didn't want our seasoned influence put upon their up and coming stars, and there were a few. 21-year old catcher named Brian Harper was leading the Pacific Coast League in hitting, though his path was blocked at the major level by Brian Downing and Ed Ott. Tom Brunansky, a 20-year old slugging outfielder was also tearing up AAA pitchers, but Baylor, Freddie Lynn and Danny Ford sat in his way as well. 22-year old Daryl Sconiers was also hitting in the mid .300s, but where was he going with future Hall of Famer Rod Carew manning first base at the Big A? Steve Lubratich was the sure-gloved, 26-year old second baseman, but Bobby Grich's MVP-caliber performance kept him stuck at AAA. Seemed as though everyone in that room had reasons to be disgruntled. Barely had a few moments to get reacquainted with Gonzalez as he was released a couple days after I arrived in town.

Moose reluctantly stuck me in the starting rotation. I wasn't in the right frame of mind from the moment I got there. Lost three of my first four starts and it wasn't pretty. Toward the end of the month, I arrived at the ballpark one morning to find a familiar face waiting by my locker. I recognized a much younger version of the tall, 60-ish man not from previous interactions, conversations or any particular moment in my life, but rather TV, baseball cards and sports history books.

"Hi Johnny," Hall of fame pitcher Warren Spahn greeted me, "Buzzie sent me here to work with you."

Sure, it was always a thrill to meet legendary ballplayers, hear their stories and insights, but this felt like a perfunctory, ass-covering exercise, as if to say, *"We even had one of the greatest pitchers to ever play the game look him over and he couldn't fix Johnny."* Still, I shook Spahn's hand and soon we were on the field, going through my motion. He asked to see all my pitches. Never asked for any adjustments. Simply watched me throw for about 30 minutes.

So, I asked, "What's your diagnosis, Dr.?" Spahn, chin in hand for a few moments, threw his arms up.

"Johnny, I dunno what to tell ya," he finally said, "Ya look fine to me. Sharp slider, movement on the fastball, curve's doin' what it's supposed to be doin'. Everything ok upstairs?"

"Well, since you asked..." I went into the situation with Buzzie and the players' association. Spahn just shook his head.

"Ah, fuck. Don't think I can help ya with all that, son. I can teach ya how to throw a nasty curveball, but looks like ya got that already." I just laughed.

"So what's the scouting report back to Buzzie gonna look like?"

"Eh, just gonna tell him they didn't give ya enough work at the big club. Probably the problem here anyway."

Spahn didn't have a golden solution to my pitching woes. No one did. I was just miserable.

* * * * *

The players' strike finally hit Major League Baseball on June 12, 1981. This was the toughest negotiation in the union's short history. Marvin would be in meetings until three, four o'clock in the morning, with the owner's representative, Ray Grebey. Marvin and Grebey absolutely hated each other. The finest complement I could get from Marvin about Grebey was a simple, yet curt, *"That guy's an ass."* It was in-the-trenches war. We had the best negotiator in the world on our side. Hit the owners full-steam. This had the makings of a long work stoppage. When I called Liz and let her know about the strike, there were few questions about my loneliness and frame of mind stuck in AAA and more about the ramifications with the paychecks.

This was a very prevalent conversation in the living rooms of major league ballplayers at this time. I checked every so often with Marvin, who was besieged with calls and messages from guys regarding their personal problems during the strike. *"So-and-so can't pay his mortgage,"* that sort of stuff. For me, since Buzzie sent me down to AAA, I still received my major-league salary while everyone else was on strike. Felt awful about that, too.

I roomed with a young backup outfielder, Wayne Pechek, when the Gulls traveled. The Angels organization kept everything first-class for the guys on the major league roster, but cut corners where they could with the minor leaguers. Pechek played in college at the University of Oklahoma with my old Padres teammate Bob Shirley, so we had that in common. We'd have dinner on the road together, but I wasn't the greatest company during my time in Salt Lake.

Remember, Utah's not the easiest place to just go out and grab a spur-of-the-moment beer. We'd enter a random watering hole and it was a whole process just to order a drink. Food has to be on the table first before alcohol, things like that.

The hitters of the Pacific Coast League were smacking my pitches around with relative ease. So tired of losing, nothing to do away from the ballpark and all the time to do it. Unable to help the players' union negotiate a reasonable settlement with the owners. Sitting on the balcony of my hotel room in Salt Lake City, alone, staring out at the capitol building, left me with too much time on my hands and as my ERA drew closer and closer to 10, my career was ticking away. Fast.

* * * * *

By the middle of July, I won a few games, lost a few more, just resigned to my fate. The players' strike was over a month old, so even if I wanted to be back on the green field and rolling hills of the Big A in Anaheim, there was really nothing waiting for me there. We were in Spokane for a series against the Mariners AAA club, the Indians. I returned from the pool at the Sheraton in town where we were staying. Roadie types rushing back and forth around me in the lobby carrying musical equipment and luggage. As I entered the hotel bar to grab a sandwich, someone called out, "*Johnny?*" I turned around and found an old acquaintance having lunch with a friend.

"Charley?" I asked, looking closer at the forty-ish black man who caught my attention, "Is that you?" Charley Pride's face lit up. Charley was a very popular country singer at the time.

"Johnny D," he smiled in a sing-song-ish voice, "How ya been, man?" Charley got up and gave me a generous hug.

"I'm doin' all right," I replied, "Good to see you. Just out for a little swim. What brings you to town?"

"Ahh, I got a little gig tonight." Then he introduced me to the other person at the table. "Johnny, this is...."

Let's call her "*PTBNL,*" as in the "*Popstar To Be Named Later.*"

"Pleasure," she said to me. I wanted to tell her that I had all her records, but really only one or two of the huge LPs from the early '70s. Kept it as cool as I could. I met movie stars and singers before at parties in L.A. or the Hollywood Hills, but this was different. Right off the bat, I got a much more "*friends hanging out*" vibe.

"Have a seat," Charley offered, nodding to the spot beside her, which I obliged.

"I worked out with Johnny's team in Phoenix a few years ago," Charley said to her, "You know, he can throw a fastball a 100 miles an hour."

"Oh really?" she said, slightly intrigued.

"On the good days," I nodded humbly, "On the bad days, the ball flies off their bat twice as fast."

Charley Pride played in the Negro leagues in the early '50s. He was friends with many of the older legends, Willie Mays, Jackie Robinson – a lot of guys in baseball knew Charley and he felt very comfortable in the presence of athletes. We talked a little baseball, some music. I mentioned that my band opened for Chuck Berry at the San Diego Arena. She snickered slightly, like it was kind of a joke.

"Get outta here," she laughed.

"Oh yeah, we played mostly country rock, some originals, a little of the Laurel Canyon stuff."

"I'm a…I'm a little familiar with that," she smirked slyly, humoring me a bit, and at the same time holding the stare that extra second. As the waitress brought our food, I checked my watch and realized I was late. I paid the server, got up, shaking Charley's hand.

"Sorry, I gotta run to the ballpark," I said to him, "Double header today."

"Maybe if you're around later, we'll get a drink, catch up some more."

"Yeah, that'd be great." Then I nodded to her. "Nice meeting you." Her eyes stayed on me for a moment.

"Same," she chirped quietly. I turned back to Charley as I walked away, "Break a leg, tonight."

I went to the park that afternoon with this renewed sense of energy. Was nice to see Charley again. Was interesting to meet *her*, not so much for the star-quality, but when you're in the company of certain people who have achieved an element of fame, sometimes you recognize the magnetism that brought them such celebrity. It was a fun interaction. Barely paid attention to the double-header. Did I pitch? Don't remember. Did we win the first game? No idea. Did we sweep? Get swept? Haven't a clue. What happened after the game was a night I'll never forget.

* * * * *

I got back to the hotel around 11, 11:30 or so. The euphoria from lunch wore off a bit. Just wanted to get to bed and forget about my circumstances, my status as a minor-league pitcher, my guilt about the strike-

"Hey." I looked over.

PTBNL. She was walking the other way through the hotel lobby, like someone who just finished a hard day's work and wanted to shut it off for a couple hours and hang out.

"Hey yourself. How was your show?"

She smiled and shrugged. "Eh, you know. How was your game?"

"Does it matter?" I laughed.

"That good, huh?" I nodded with a chuckle.

"Need a drink?" she asked.

Her hair wasn't Harlow gold, her eyes more swimming pool blue than Bette Davis brown, but I didn't have to think twice.

"Sure." We entered the hotel bar and sat down at a table in the back of the lounge. A couple of patrons would get her attention, to which she politely acknowledged and smiled, but for the most part we were left alone.

"So what brings the 100 MPH man to Spokane, Washington?" she remarked with a sly grin, her throaty voice seeming to annunciate "SPO-CAN" in italics.

"Heh-heh, said the wrong thing to the wrong guys," I shrugged after a sip, "You?"

"Payin' bills. I have a place in Idaho. It's an easy gig."

"Always wanted to go there. Played in Montana one summer."

"It's nice this time of year, you should check it out." Sounded more like an invitation than travel advice.

We chatted for a couple hours, a few drinks, fair amount of laughs. She had this amazing personality, this sharp wit, easily one of the most intelligent women I had ever met to that point in my life. She didn't hit you over the head with it, either. We just talked about life on the road, people we knew in common throughout the L.A. area, the difficulty of relationships with such a transient lifestyle. She got it. Had been awhile since I had such an interesting adult conversation. She fiddled with her long, light brown hair, not quite curly, not quite straight, as the waitress approached our table for last call.

"One more?" I asked her. She smiled. Gorgeous dimples.

Toward the end of the night, I explained where I was in my life. She seemed to have so much figured out.

"You can't let all the bullshit interfere with what you need to do," she said, twirling the ice in her glass. As she spoke, I noticed a stray eyelash hanging off her cheek.

"Hold on a sec," I interrupted, reached over and gently wiped it from her face with my finger. She leaned into my palm, closed her eyes for what seemed like a minute, then beamed, mouthing *"Thank you."* We held the moment. That look you get when you know you've touched another's soul, however ephemeral that touch may last. It's like a striking out a .300 hitter. The rush stays with you for just a few seconds, but it happened, and you're glad it did.

"What was I talking about?" she smirked.

"Damned if I know," I replied softly.

That was the last night I ever saw her.

There was no denying that something was wrong with my life, and her words meant so much more to me when I would hear her voice on the radio from that night forward, and left me with the notion that maybe I could still harness the essence of the gifts God gave me.

Through the injuries, the control problems, the final, awful starts in Salt Lake City, I was just telling myself that I had been to the promised land, the majors, a place I left behind and I wouldn't rest until I got back again.

Final Cuts

The Major League Players Baseball strike ended on July 31, 1981. The resolution wasn't one-sided and Marvin fought for us but the owners received concessions as well. They got their free agent compensation pool (this was the vehicle that caused the New York Mets to lose Tom Seaver after the 1983 season). Marvin made sure we received the less-publicized concessions. *"Meal money"* (the stipend the players were given each day while on the road), got bumped up to $125 a day from $25. Rookies were thrilled with the increase because they could pay their rent with the meal money. Benefits and insurance now covered our families 100%. The animosity remained, though. Marvin and Grebey hated each other so much they refused to take the celebratory *"Play Ball"* end of negotiation photo together. Baseball was back and all was forgotten. Marvin fought the battle and won for all of us.

Well, almost all of us. And all was *not* forgotten. I remained in Salt Lake City until the September call-ups. I returned to California on September 2nd. Upon re-entering the clubhouse, I didn't get three minutes to greet my teammates when one of the attendants approached me.

"Buzzie wants to see you." At this point, I had no idea what he could possibly do to me that he hadn't already done.

"Here's our offer," Buzzie said to me, "You can go home, we'll pay you every two weeks, no one says a word to anybody, 21-Day disabled list, we'll figure out the particulars, or you can go downstairs and rot in the bullpen. 'Cause I know Mauch'll never pitch you unless I tell him to. And I'm not telling him anything. Your choice."

"I guess I'll see you on the field." Buzzie nodded and went about his business. The Angels were paying me. I felt it was my personal obligation to respect Autry's money and suit up. Didn't matter though. I didn't appear in a single game that September for the California Angels. Mauch didn't so much as look my way the entire month. My lone highlight from those last 30 days of the 1981 season occurred in the clubhouse the following morning. I got to the ballpark early – I knew I wasn't pitching but still kept a deep respect toward my contract. No one else was around. As I changed into my uniform, I heard spikes walking toward me.

"Hey Johnny?" someone called out. It was Baylor.

"What's up, Donny?" I replied, pulling my stirrups.

"You, umm, you gave up a lot for the guys," Donny said, "Just wanted to say thanks, and I'm sorry about all this."

"We're big boys," I replied, "I'll be ok." Two of the unsung heroes of the 1981 Baseball labor movement walked out of the clubhouse together and toward the field.

I hold no ill will toward Gene Autry. It was Buzzie pulling the strings all along behind the scenes. The way I saw it, I was probably overpaid by at least half the value of my contract anyway. Jerry Kapstein made that happen. That was Buzzie's issue the whole time, resentment that Jerry leveraged his stable of superstars to force me down the Angels' throat. They wanted Burleson, the steady, All-Star shortstop they lacked since Fregosi was traded to the Mets ten years earlier, and through the goodwill of signing me to a long-term deal, they got Jerry to blow off the Dodgers and steer superstar Freddie Lynn toward Anaheim.

* * * * *

1982 spring training in Palm Springs was pretty much a waste of my time. The Angels couldn't unload me at the Winter Meetings because of my contract as well as the fact that I barely pitched in the majors the previous season. My trade value was close to nil. Sure, I appeared in a few pre-season games, but that was more about showcasing me in the vain hope another ballclub would reach out with a trade proposal. I was released close to the end of camp – a spiteful move on Buzzie's part since all the other organizations had their rosters set. I reached out to someone I had played for in the past. We didn't always get along, but I know he respected my work.

"Dick?" I said into the phone, "John D'Acquisto."

"Oh, hey, Johnny, how ya doin'?" Like we just spoke yesterday. Dick Williams had his intolerable moments after he downed a few highballs, but he was a solid baseball man – and reasonable. You could engage in a knock-down, drag-out with him at night, and the following morning, everything would be fine.

"I was just checking in to see how things were down there." Dick was the new manager for the San Diego Padres.

"It's comin' along. Everything ok with you?"

"Not really, but I'm calling for a friend. Count's looking to land somewhere, he knows I know you, I think there's a fit." Count wasn't re-signed by the Atlanta Braves and asked me to reach out to some of the managers I played for. I thought San Diego would be a good spot for him.

"Montefusco? He wasn't that great last year."

"C'mon, you know that's the Launching Pad. Fuckin' band box. Count'll be much better at Jack Murphy. He'll give you a lot of innings."

"Hmmm. Can always use some more pitching. You vouch for him?"

"I vouch for him."

"Well, lemme talk to Ballard. What about you? What's your story?"

"I'm probably gonna get cut. It's not working out with Mauch."

"Eh, he's a real SOB."

"San Diego 's my home, you know."

"I know. I could probably use you, too, but they're still pretty sore over here that you turned down their offer. Tell ya what, gimme Count's number. I'll talk to Ballard. If somethin' can be worked out, I'll call ya back. If not, well, you know..."

"I know. Thanks, Dick."

The Padres signed Count three days later. Didn't work out for me in San Diego. Didn't think it would, but doesn't hurt to ask, right? My 1982 season would begin, just not at all as I imagined.

*****

I had thrown about 85 pitches. 14 strikeouts. Completely dominated the competition. Top of the ninth. We're up 8-0. The batter digs in. I toed the rubber. I set. I pitched. He had no chance against my heater. "*Strike three,*" the umpire growled. My catcher jogged over to congratulate me. Scattered applause from the crowd. I looked over to the stands...where a local little league team sat waiting patiently in their shorts and T-shirts to get on the field to practice.

"All yours, kids," I said to them collectively as I grabbed my gear from behind the fence.

"Hey Johnny?" my first-baseman yelled over, "We're heading to Danny's, you comin'?"

It wasn't the majors. Hell, it wasn't even Double A, but there's a lot of competitive lawyers, doctors and accountants in the San Diego area that can rake and glove it cleanly around first base. Semi-pro ball kept me in good shape during the month of April. Also was good to play baseball with my friends. Dad came to see me every time I pitched. I nodded at him, walking over quickly toward his proud smile.

"Nice game," Dad greeted, following me across the park grass toward my car.

"Yeah, if I'm not striking out at least 10 of them, I probably shouldn't be out there at all," I replied. Dad raised his eyebrows in agreement, as he reached into his wallet.

"Here," Dad said, handing me a business card, "I ran into him last night at the restaurant." I almost laughed.

"Didn't know they were in town," I replied, not that I was paying much attention to the box scores anyway.

"I said you were still working out. He told me they could use one more starter. After I said you were having games like this, he said *'It can't hurt to see what ya got.'"* To give you an idea of where my head was at this point, my other priorities kicked in.

"I'll have to tell the bank I need a couple days off," I said.

"I think they'll understand," Dad smiled, "Mom's got a pot of sausage on the stove. C'mon by the house." As I got in my car, part of me wanted to stick the business card in my glove compartment and never touch it again. The little boy in me who just struck out 14 of his friends went to sleep that night dreaming about his major league tryout the following morning.

* * * * *

It was no longer San Diego Stadium, but now Jack Murphy Stadium, named after a San Diego sportswriter who started the grass-roots effort to build a ballpark that could field both baseball and football. I still knew the grounds crew, ushers, parking attendants, ticket agents. Everyone who worked there always had a smile when they saw me and I made sure to return the gesture to each and every one of them. I was brought into the visiting clubhouse and made my way toward the manager's office. He sat at the desk studying scouting reports. I knocked on the door without saying a word, just a simple salute. He looked up and it felt like 1974.

"Johnny, glad you could make it," Joe Torre said, standing up and walking over to shake my hand.

"How ya doin', Joe?" I replied, "Great to see you."

"Great to see you, too. Nice to see your Dad the other night. They make a great swordfish over at Anthony's."

"Oh, yeah, I like the food there." Then we got down to business.

"Heard you had a tough break in California," Joe said, as we walked through the empty clubhouse, "New managers like to clean house sometimes. Bring in their own guys."

"Yeah, I know how it goes." Then Joe flashed a smart grin, bringing attention to himself.

"New managers." Joe Torre was less than one month into his first season as skipper for the Atlanta Braves. "Your old man says you still have your fastball. Is that true?"

"I can still throw 95, sometimes over that. With control."

"If that's true, I could probably use that." Then, from out of nowhere-

"You still got that nasty-ass slider you threw at me?" I spun around and there he was, leaning against the wall of the clubhouse exit to the field, holding a cup of coffee, with a mile-wide smirk.

Gibby.

"Well, suit up, Johnny," Gibby said, "Show us what'cha got."

* * * * *

"Damn," Gibby said 30 minutes later, as the catcher's glove popped again and again.

"Now show me the slider," Gibby continued. Hit the corners each time. "Inch 'em out now." I put the ball exactly where he asked me. We spent an hour in the bullpen, laughing about our games together.

"You never backed down to me, Johnny," Gibby said, "Always liked that."

"I'm sorry if you thought I was disrespectful," I replied, "You're one of the greatest pitchers ever. I couldn't back down to you."

Gibby laughed. "Back down? Shit, that's baseball." Then Gibby walked off the mound, toward the exit of the bullpen, sort of beckoned. "Let's go find Joe. I dunno who you pissed off, but you can still pitch."

Few minutes later, Gibby, Torre and I were back in his office.

"We're gonna sign you," Torre said, "I always liked the way you played. Maybe it works and maybe it doesn't, you know, no promises, but-"

"Can't ever have enough pitching," Gibby interjected.

"Never have enough pitching," Torre agreed, "Go home, grab your stuff and come on back. I'll call Hank (Aaron, who was now vice-president for the Atlanta Braves) and we'll have the paperwork waiting for you." No agents, no general managers, just a good-old fashioned pick-up game at the highest level. I was still being paid by the Angels, so there was no negotiation about salary or bonuses. I was just happy to be wanted. I turned around at the door.

"Thanks, Skip," I said to Torre. "Thanks, Bob," I said to Gibby. Torre smiled and nodded goodbye. "Anytime. See ya later."

Ran home, packed my stuff, kissed my daughter and told my wife the news before I had a moment to think it over. Nothing was stopping me from going to play baseball with my friends.

* * * * *

I traveled with the Atlanta Braves for the next 30 days. Didn't get into any games – just worked with Gibby in the bullpen. Every week I pitched a simulated game with the injured guys, utility players. I was never activated – not that they needed me or anything. The club held first place in April, off to a hot 18-8 start.

Again, I was basically an insurance policy in case one of their pitchers went down. No need to mess with a good thing, which I understood. When we got to Richmond, Va., their AAA affiliate, the Braves wanted me to get regular work, starting games, so they dropped me off there after an exhibition game.

"We're gonna leave ya here to get some games in and then we're gonna bring you up," Joe told me. Won my first three starts down there. Waited patiently for my opportunity to return to the big leagues and jump into the Braves' rotation. One evening in July, Eddie Mathews, who was a scout for the Oakland A's at the time, got to talking with my brother Fred, who was now the ticket manager for Pacific Southwest Airlines in San Diego. Fred knew almost everyone in the National League because he handled the flight arrangements for ball clubs arriving to face the Padres. I wasn't terribly happy as Atlanta had chosen to bring Pascual Perez to the majors instead of me a few weeks earlier. Right move, wrong move, I didn't care, I was a little upset. My brother had mentioned this to Eddie, who told him,

"Billy should hear about this. Can I use your phone?" Two hours later, I get a call in my motel room. It was Eddie.

"We sure could use your arm here in Oakland." Billy Martin had been the manager of the A's for close to three years at this point. He also had the authority to make player personnel decisions like this.

"Eddie, I would love to play for the A's," I replied, so happy with this, "I have to speak with Hank and get my release." The common practice was if a veteran of my standing was sitting in AAA and received an offer to play in the majors from another club, the team generally wouldn't stand in their way. Also, Hank Aaron played for years with Eddie Mathews on the Braves back in the 60's. I was sure they would be able to work this out.

Hank Aaron pretty much relayed as much to me on the phone.

"Johnny?" Hank said minutes later, "If there's a spot for you on Oakland's staff, then we'll give you your release. Just remember, we're not letting you go to play in Tacoma. We're gonna use ya next year."

"Thanks, Hank," I said, "I appreciate you understanding."

"Very well, you're done here then. I'll take care of the paperwork. Just pack your stuff and get on your way. Good luck, John."

I flew to San Diego, saw my family and then hopped on another plane to Oakland. Spent the short flight kind of concerned about how I would get along with Billy Martin. I appreciated that Billy wanted me, but I just remembered the last time our paths crossed on the field wasn't the most congenial.

So I wasn't completely certain what I was walking into as I stepped through the jet way of Oakland International Airport. The A's GM sent someone to get me. There was no sign from a limo driver or anything. Turns out the A's GM sent himself. Standing at the gate, leisure suit, slick cowboy boots, pencil-thin moustache, dyed black hair, classic late '70's/early 80's fogged out sunglasses. Puffing a smoke as he leaned against the wall. Nodding hello to random strangers that recognized him. That world-famous grin when his eyes met mine.

Yes, Billy Martin picked me up at the airport.

"How's it goin', Dags?" Billy greeted me with a friendly handshake. "*Dags*" is short for "Dago," an Italian reference, slightly friendlier than last season. I felt an instant comfort with Billy.

As we walked through the parking lot toward his car, Billy handed me a thick envelope.

"That's a little something for you. I know you're coming from Triple-A. Buy yourself some clothes, get what you need, then come back to the ballpark. Art wants to see you throw." Art Fowler was the A's pitching coach. Billy and Art's close friendship is well-treaded ground in Baseball. Few fellas in the game were known to be tighter than these two. Billy drove us to the Coliseum, handed me the keys to his car, shook my hand and said "See you in a little bit." After playing in San Fran all those years, I knew my way around the area pretty well. I went shopping at the mall, dropped my stuff off at the Hilton in Oakland and went to the stadium. All dressed in my new uniform, I walked out of the dugout. A photographer approached me.

"Hi, I'm with Fleer, the baseball card company," he said, "Can I grab a shot?" I shrugged, "Sure." Keep in mind, now, I haven't even signed yet. I walked over to see Art in the middle of the field – my adrenaline's pumping. I got on the pitching mound, there were hitters in each batter's box. Art stood behind me, speaking softly with that South Carolina drawl.

"Now, Johnny, this is what I call my focus drill. If ya can throw pitches in between these two bastards, you're gonna throw strikes in the game. Lemme show ya." Art got up there, set and hurled five straight pitches right down the pike. Art had great control when he was a pitcher, especially toward the end of his career. I got on the mound, digging back in. I lit it up, popping the ball on the black, in the zone. Throwing strikes. Art was impressed. "Good, now throw me a slider, a curveball, throw me a change-up." I said, "Don't have a change-up."

"What'cha got then?"

"I got a little type of sinker that I use for a change-up."

"Lemme see it." I threw for about 10 minutes more, as other pitchers started walking toward the mound. Steve McCatty, Mike Norris, Dave Beard, few of the other guys. When we were done, Art put his arm around my shoulder. "Go in and see Billy, he got your contract. He's gonna sign you up, son."

"Really?"

Art nodded. "Yep, you're an Oakland A. Now go on, get outta here." I jogged back to the dugout and quickly walked toward Billy's office, who was waiting for me with his feet up on the desk.

"Welcome aboard, Johnny! I always wanted to have my own Italian hit man."

"So you're gonna use me to start fights?" Billy smiled and shrugged as he puffed his cigarette.

"Well, I'm getting' pretty good at that, Skip," I replied.

"Man, I like you already," Billy laughed. "Yeah, I have a special sign when I want you to drill somebody."

"I can deal with that." Don't get me wrong, the last thing I ever wanted to do was knock guys down for the hell of it. Just when the manager told you to dust someone, he got dusted. Simple as that. Different world back then.

"Now, we're not gonna play you right away," Billy continued, "The plan is for you to get back in shape, hang out on the bench for about a week. A lot of guys here have spoken highly of you, so just hang out and get back into the swing of things. We have an exhibition against Tacoma in two weeks, you'll start that game. We're gonna leave you up there to get some work in, then we'll be ready to throw you out in the pen for September. Is that ok?"

"Yeah, Skip, that's fine." You see, what Billy was doing here was helping me get out of AAA limbo and back in the big league mentality. You talk about a Baseball man that cared for his players. If you gave him what he expected of you, you were one of his guys. Fowler, Cliff Johnson, he adored Chicken Stanley. His guys. Truth be told, Billy wanted me to be one of his guys, for whatever reason. Whether it was because I was Italian, my willingness to pitch inside, maybe, maybe not, but I was *his* guy. Leaving me in Tacoma wasn't a violation of the deal I had with Hank Aaron and Atlanta, either. It was more like an unofficial DL rehab assignment. Those three weeks in Tacoma were fine. Dave Heaverlo, my old teammate from the Giants was up there, transitioning from ballplayer to broadcaster. He's one of the nicest guys in the game. Was so happy to spend those few days hanging out with him. He made my time in Tacoma extremely warm and comfortable.

* * * * *

I got back to Oakland in early September. So many familiar faces in the bullpen. Dennis Kinney I played with in San Diego. Bobby Owchinko, too. Spent a lot of time with Brian Kingman, especially. We had such great talks sitting out there, chatting about everything in the world except baseball. The economy, politics. Brian Kingman is one of the brightest guys I ever met in the game. I had a blast in Oakland that September. I actually stayed at Billy's house in Danville, while he lived with his new wife in Berkeley. Gave me a chance to re-connect with old friends in the Bay Area from my years with the Giants. Spent most of the off-days playing golf in Half Moon Bay and late night drinks at the Lion's Den in San Fran. As for the team during the game, you couldn't ask a better defensive outfield behind you than Rickey, Dwayne Murphy and Tony Armas. Davey Lopes was there giving Rickey the final tutoring he would need to become the greatest base stealer of all time. It was just the pitching staff was toast from two years of Billy overworking them. Even as the team settled in 5th place, Billy remained in tune with every game.

We were in Detroit one night, I tried to handcuff John Wockenfuss with a high hard one, but he got around on it and the ball sailed over the left field fence. Billy's right in there, screaming at the umpire, "Check the bat! Check the bat! There's gotta be cork in that bat." Billy was constantly trying to find any edge, any advantage possible to win. He knew every trick in the book.

Flights were a great time, too. I'd be sitting in the back of the plane with Steve McCatty, chatting and drinking. Here comes Billy stumbling down the aisle, a brown paper bag in his right hand. "Dags, get up, move over, gimme the end seat." Billy pulled out a block of provolone cheese and a top-shelf bottle of Sebastiani Private Reserve Red, asking the flight attendant to remove the cork and slice our food. Then the stories of *"the old days"* would pour out of him. Billy loved to reminisce about his time with the Yankees, with Mickey and Whitey. Nights of all hell breaking loose in Manhattan. Days of hungover, pinch hit Home Runs and dugout vomit in the Bronx. History tells us Billy loved being a Yankee, but Billy really loved the Yankees of his youth. It's almost like time had moved on but to Billy, the world was a long-playing broken record, constantly skipping back to 1956.

* * * * *

In the real world, nothing was clicking for our pitchers. The season was clearly a bust at this point. The pressure to get the staff to be at least somewhat competitive for 1983 started to eat away at Billy.

One night against the Rangers, we're getting crushed 10-3. It was the ninth inning and as I was stepping from the dugout, Billy grabbed my left arm. Dave Hostetler is the first batter up.

"I want you to hit that son of bitch right in the ribs," Billy said softly with anger in his voice.

"What?" I replied. Billy looked at me like I asked the stupidest question. I nodded calmly and stepped onto the field.

As I am rubbing the baseball on the mound, I see Billy standing against the dugout steps. He sends the sign to me and Jeff Newman the catcher. Billy takes his thumb and gently pokes himself in the ribs. Newman approaches the mound.

"Did you see the sign?" Newman said, lifting his mask.

"Yeah, I saw it," I replied.

"And?"

"Get back behind the plate. You know what I'm gonna do."

Newman crouched down and called for the pitch. Billy started yelling the most unmentionable words at Hostetler, who then turned to me, I wound up, threw, the ball whizzed right over his head, hit the centerpiece of the backstop and ricocheted off Hostetler's ankle. Billy's screamed at Hostetler now, *"See that, you S.O.B.! He can even hit you on the rebound!"* I swear, I went to confession a few times over this one, but I dusted him again, barely missing his ribs this time. After the game, I was sitting at my locker enjoying a frosty tall boy when Billy walked over.

"Hey Dags, come in my office." He locked the door, broke out some more of his provolone cheese and a big bottle of Dago Red and handed me a glass.

"This one's for you." We sat there; Billy slapped me on the shoulder.

"Man, I was laughing so hard, you fired that thing, hit the pole, came back and smashed into that kid's ankle and knocked him on his ass. There was a fuckin' dent in the backstop pole. I know, I checked after the game." Billy was hysterical re-telling this. Other than his Mantle stories, I never saw the man happier. Sadly, for him, there wouldn't be too many laughs left in the season.

* * * * *

Three days later, we're in the clubhouse and we heard "*bang-bang, boom-boom*" coming from the hallway leading to the players' lounge. "What the hell's goin' on over there," one of the guys asked. We knew only one person who would make noise like this.

"I'll go check it out," I said, getting up from my stool. McCatty was all, "I wouldn't mess with Billy right now."

"I can handle him," I said, walking toward the office. When I finally reached his doorway, the noise ended, but it was like nothing I ever saw in the game.

The office was an absolute disaster. Papers and objects thrown all over the floor, pictures of Mickey busted amid broken glass, the desk turned on its side, blood on his chair, on the walls, everywhere. Billy's fingers were all cut up. He put his hand through the TV screen. Billy was curled in his seat, glasses off his face, calm but slightly shaking. His eyes seemed to be on the verge of a second round of furious weeping.

"You ok, Skip?" I asked quietly. Billy calmly replied and nodded, "Yeah...yeah I'm ok." I couldn't believe the mess I witnessed. Billy didn't look at me once.

"They won't extend my contract. I think this is it for me here." It wasn't as if Billy relied or assumed he was going back to the Yankees for the 1983 season. In his mind, Billy had no back-up plan. He truly thought in that moment this was it. He'd be out of baseball if he had to leave Oakland.

"Everything's going to be fine," I said, a total lie, "Just keep your cool." I bent down to turn the desk upright. Billy wouldn't have that.

"Leave it," Billy said calmly, almost zombie-like, still staring at nothing, "Just leave it."

The following morning, I walked toward the clubhouse wondering what the area would look like. Entering the players' lounge, the first room you passed was Billy's office. Sparkling clean. Like nothing ever happened. All the pictures were re-framed and hung back in their place. There was a new TV. The walls were repainted. Billy's desk was in order.

That night, after the game, I found Art alone in the trainers' room.

"Johnny?" Art said, "It looks like our little run here is over." He knew Billy told me, so I didn't have to act like I didn't know. Still, I just nodded the nod you might give a friend at a funeral trying to say something nice without words. "And remember this, son," Art continued, "Anyone who's considered a Billy guy'll probably be gone, too. So don't hold your breath too long here."

"Okay, Art, I gotcha."

"Ya best get your agent to get lookin' for another place for next year or else ya gonna get screwed."

Billy respected the fact that I kept it quiet about his not coming back for 1983 and I was honored that he brought me into his confidence as well. Art knew, but again, Art was Billy's best friend.

My last game that year in Kansas ended with a Hal McRae bases-clearing triple. Billy was let go after the World Series. Steve Boros was brought in a few weeks later with Ron Schueler as the new pitching coach. Regardless of my status as Billy's guy, the organization not only kept me on the roster, they asked me to join the offseason community outreach caravan, billing me as the club's closer. I felt peace of mind from this and perhaps Art was wrong. Maybe this wasn't a suicide mission after all.

* * * * *

Boros was definitely no Billy Martin. After he was hired, Boros' press conference and subsequent interviews around town let the writers know as much, saying things like, "*I have my own standards and I have to be guided by them. Baiting umpires and yelling at opposing players is not among them. I believe there is a different way to handle both situations.*" His way was early sabermetrics. Boros wanted to be a professor, graduated from the University of Michigan with a degree in literature. However, no knowledge of F. Scott Fitzgerald or deep analysis of "*Moby Dick*" can give you the insight to handle guys like Mike Norris or try to communicate with Rickey. Obviously, when you fire a manger, you look for the exact opposite qualities in the new skipper you bring on board. I started to see the club make changes that winter, cleaning out some of the more Billy-friendly players. They released ex-Yankee Mickey Klutts. They traded Cliff Johnson to Toronto for Al Woods, who would never see Oakland Coliseum from the A's dugout.

They let Chicken Stanley go. They sold Brian Kingman, my buddy, to Boston. They signed the veteran lefty Tom Burgmeier, a great southpaw reliever that doesn't get the historical credit he deserves. It also probably meant Bobby Owchinko's time in Oakland was over, though. In the end, while I felt confident and was given every indication I was an important part of the ballclub, I knew the days of drinking on the plane and eating cheese with my manager were lonnng gone.

* * * * *

It was the spring of 1983, on my way to A's camp in Phoenix from my home in San Diego. I was driving in my Mercedes through the dry heat across the state line into Arizona on an empty, desolate Interstate 8, just me, the cracked moon roof, that tangerine glow of the sun setting behind me and some of the best driving music from the '70s. Could've used a couple more albums from Boston. Sure *"More Than a Feeling"* can still bring chills in the right moment, *"'Long Time"* is an incredible number when you're buzzing down the highway hitting 100+ on Johnny Law's radar gun, but there's so many other songs on those two albums that are just outstanding – the songs you don't hear all the time - *"It's Easy," "Feelin' Satisfied," "Something About You,"* – man, did I wear out those cassette tapes. The A's had told me I would be the closer coming into spring training. It had been a long eight months to get back to this point where I felt settled in, concerned more about who I was facing in the Major Leagues that night rather than whether I would be wearing another uniform tomorrow. Or any at all.

When I finally arrived at A's camp, I didn't have much interaction with Boros. He spent most of his time analyzing the numbers and allowing the computer to dictate his managerial decisions. Guys like Davey Johnson would enjoy amazing success with this strategy, although having stars like Keith, Darryl Strawberry and Doc Gooden didn't hurt, either. The thing with Davey was that he was an intellectual *and* a players' manager. All the guys on the Mets knew they could walk into Davey's office at any time and talk with him about anything. Steve Boros was *not* that guy.

Oakland pitched me like crazy that March. I appeared in 17 games, sporting a 2.76 spring ERA. Sure, you can say pre-season numbers are meaningless and in many ways, you would be right. What matters for hitters is bat speed, not striking out and possibly home runs. For pitchers, it's just like real estate – location, location, location, and for one of the only springs in my career, I had it in spades this time. Something was wrong, though. No "*AttaBoys*" from the coaches. No ass-slaps from Boros after solid outings. No confirmations about places on the roster. But I was getting guys out, the impressive way in spring, with dazzling off-speed stuff and 95 MPH fastballs. Maybe affirmations just weren't Boros' way and I was just being paranoid. The camaraderie was different than other places, too. Sure I was older now, but there was no palling around with guys like Keith Hernandez, Randy Jones or Eric Rasmussen. It was all business. Just watching the days go by and making sure I never got tapped on the shoulder by the wrong person on the coaching staff.

When I heard Bobby Owchinko was finally released toward the end of March, I felt my spot was secure. We were in Yuma, Arizona after a game against the Padres. Ron Schueler approached me.

"How do you feel about starting in Palm Springs against the Angels tomorrow?"

"Sure thing," I replied. I got a chance to face my old club and show them they made a mistake cutting me. Most of all spend some time with my family. San Diego's barely a 2 1/2-hour drive to Palm Springs. I spoke with my wife that night and she made arrangements for everyone to see me pitch.

The next morning, I had breakfast with the family before the game. Got to see Liz, my parents and even Liz's parents. It was to be a very special day.

About ninety minutes before game time, I was in the clubhouse getting a rubdown, mentally preparing for the start. There was a knock on the door. Schueler entered and tapped me on the shoulder.

"Boros wants to see you."

Shit.

After being in the major leagues for close to ten years, you realize certain phrases mean something else. When the manager approaches you on the mound and asks *"How you feelin,"* he's really looking for a reason to take you out of the game. When the manager asks you to grab a drink with him, he's really saying he wants to take you into his confidence or perhaps convey a message to the rest of the ballclub. When you hear that the manager wants to see you, in spring training, it's not sweet music. It's the Executioner's Song.

If you've ever seen Palm Spring Stadium, the dugouts are recessed. You really can't look inside from the stands. I walked through the tunnel and found Boros on the bench.

"What's up, Skip?" I asked, but I knew what was up.

"You're not coming with us," he said, stone-faced, staring out to the field, "We're letting you go."

The worst thing about this is not that the club was outright releasing me; it's the timing of the thing. If I get released on March 10th or March 15th or even March 20th, I still have time to hookup with another club. When you're the last guy cut, that's it. All the other teams pretty much have their rosters set. Even if you get signed by another organization, you most likely won't see a major league pitching mound before June, if at all.

"You're letting me go now, when every other team's packing up their equipment trucks?"

Before Boros could answer, guess who walked out from the clubhouse?

It was Bill Rigney, my old manager in San Francisco. Remember, Rigney and I weren't the best of friends. Actually, I'm not sure I liked anyone less in baseball than this man. It started making sense now.

"Bill, did you have anything to do this?" I asked him, face-to-face.

"Well, I am the special consultant to Mr. Eisenhardt (the A's owner)," Rigney replied. There was a vague hint of a smile on his face.

"Is that my answer?"

"That's your answer." And that was it. I said thank you to Boros for the opportunity and walked back into the clubhouse. I removed my A's uniform for the last time, threw my stuff in a bag and headed out. Kept my jersey, though. I wanted something to remind me of the month I enjoyed with Billy, Art, Kingman, McCatty and the rest of the guys from that club.

I stepped back out of the dugout, saw my wife in the stands and got her attention.

"Meet me outside," I said calmly. She didn't understand, but then realized I wasn't wearing my uniform.

"What's going on?" Liz said, her voice cracking a bit.

"Meet me outside the stadium and bring everyone. We're going home."

As I left the clubhouse to meet up with my family in the parking lot, I just wanted to get in my car and drive away. From everything. From everyone. I stood there, prepared for the tears, the questions, the whys, the what ifs. All I wanted was my car, an open road to nowhere and my Boston cassette tapes.

There would be no Peace of Mind. Outside the stadium in Palm Springs, I took a look ahead and in the distance, I didn't see a ballpark on my horizon. Didn't see teammates. Didn't see three beat reporters surrounding my locker after nailing down a crucial save in a September division matchup.

I saw nothing but desert.

*****

The post-script to this story is not much brighter. Days after Oakland handed me my release, I called Billy, who was once again managing the Yankees. He said he could find a spot for me in the bullpen.

"Let me check with George and I'll call ya right back."

He returned the call in 15 minutes. There was a bit of a laugh in his voice, but not funny ha-ha.

"Jesus, Johnny," Billy snorted, "What the hell'd you do to George?" "Whaddya mean?" Of course I knew exactly what he meant. "I dunno, after I mentioned bringing you on board, he said 'No Fucking Way,' and slammed the phone down."

I didn't blame George, either. I was paid $300,000 in 1981 dollars to hear that response. Doesn't make it any less painful. I thanked Billy, ended the call and did what anyone who just lost their best job lead would...I walked into the den to watch a movie.

I've always been a big James Bond fan, owned all the films on Betamax and decided to throw in *The Spy Who Loved Me*. I plopped down into my deep-pocketed couch and enjoyed the opening scene where Roger Moore skied off the mountain, pulling the cord on his parachute and escaping the bad guys.

Billy was my parachute, and I felt there would be others, but for the moment, as Carly Simon exclaimed praise and affirmation during the credit sequence through the projection tv, my eyes wouldn't waver from the cordless phone on the coffee table.

The Boys Of Autumn

"Now batting for the pitcher, Craig Lefferts, Tim......Flannery."

John Demott's booming voice announced my former band
mate into the game. I was there for Timmy's first major league
game, for his first spring training with the big club, his first
performance in Wild Pitch with Eric and me. I'd witnessed his
growth in the game and in life. Not that there were too many ex-
teammates on the club anymore. It had been four years since I wore
a Padres uniform and only three players remained from my 1980
Padres ballclub; Timmy was one of them. Extremely popular with
the fans. Now here he was, the tying runner on first, seventh inning
of Game Five for the 1984 National League Championship Series.
Rick Sutcliffe was on the mound – he dominated the NL after
coming over in a midseason swap with the Cleveland Indians. This
was an amazing NLCS, one of the most exciting in the relatively
short history of the match. Thought it was great that so many
players in their 30's, known for earlier post-season highlights, were
involved in the series. Goose and Nettles were now Padres; Steve
Garvey, too. The Cubs had *"The Penguin,"* Ron Cey and Davey
Lopes, who both shared the Dodgers' infield with Garvey. Gary
Matthews, my old teammate we called *"Sweet Matt"* when I first
came up in San Francisco, now answered to *"Sarge"*; Rick *"Big*

Daddy" Reuschel, who came back for a second tour with the Cubbies; Larry Bowa, the former Phillies all-star shortstop. Sutcliffe had practically carried the Cubs on his back in the second half of the season, pitching out of his mind, winning 16 of his 20 starts, losing just one. *"The Red Baron,"* as they called Sutcliffe, looked spent. Watching him struggle just to get to the seventh inning made me think to myself, *"What if I was in the Cubs' bullpen right now? Maybe I could've helped him."* Really not a question coming out of left field, either.

* * * * *

The Middle of the Road and baseball was trying to find me.

Walking down Rodeo Drive in Beverly Hills with my dreams behind me in January of 1984. A desk job, business lunches with women wearing big diamond rings alongside Hollywood agents in silk suits with a smile for everyone they meet. I just finished a working meal with legendary TV actor Lorne Greene at the Polo Lounge in the Beverly Hills Hotel, assisting him with his investments. The phone rang as I entered my office in Century City about 90 minutes later.

"Johnny D, whatcha doin' in L.A.?" Spider Jorgensen, an elderly baseball lifer working as an advanced scout for the Chicago Cubs, asked me on the other side of the receiver. I had recently separated from Liz and relocated to the Los Angeles area. Turned out that the problems we had were much deeper than me being away from the family in New York or Salt Lake City.

Spider had been a friend of mine from the San Francisco days. I had a second surgery on my elbow just a month earlier. Hadn't picked up a ball in almost half a year.

"Been awhile since I've stepped on a mound," I replied, "Doctor cut me up few weeks ago. Really don't know what you're gonna get."

"Ahh, why don't ya come down to Commerce Field anyway," Spider said, "All it's gonna cost ya is some gas money. Maybe there's somethin' left in that arm of yours."

Say what you will about Major League Baseball being a cold, heartless organization, but if you have a reputation of being a good teammate, a decent clubhouse guy and of course, an alleged blazing fastball, teams will give you every shot in the world to make it back. In the end, if you have nothing, it's 90 minutes of their time and usually an extra half-hour reminiscing about the old days. It's not just the fans that get nostalgic about great moments in baseball. And if the scout somehow catches lightning in a bottle, he's a genius.

"Ehhh, come on down anyway," Spider laughed, "Haven't seen ya in awhile."

I hung up the phone and sighed. I guess I was taking the day off.

* * * * *

It was a simulated game against players the Cubs were considering inviting to spring training. Chicago was 71-91 in 1983, worst ERA in the league. They had some solid veterans on the staff like Dick Ruthven and Steve Trout, a few free agents and Fergie Jenkins, their legendary ace whom they weren't certain had anything left. To the Cubs credit, they searched everywhere for pitching help. Obviously. I basically told them I wasn't interested. They didn't care.

It had been months since I toed the rubber. The first batter I faced stepped into the box. I set and threw – swing and a miss. I managed to strike him out on five pitches. The next batter couldn't get around on my fastball, hitting a foul pop off the end of the bat to the first baseman. The third batter slapped a weak grounder to shortstop. Out of the inning on nine pitches. I walked slowly to the dugout and Spider yelled over to me, "Whaddya mean ya can't pitch anymore?"

"Can I have some ice, please?" I replied quietly. God, I was in so much pain. I applied the cold press to my elbow, then went out and pitched another hitless inning. After that, I walked over to Spider.

"How was that?" I asked him.

"You should come down to Mesa," he said to me as I grabbed my gear. I reached out and shook his hand.

"Always good to see you," I replied quietly, "Thanks for inviting me."

"I'll call ya tomorrow," Spider said, as I waved politely behind my back, walking out of the dugout.

Of course, the next day, Spider lobbed in a call to my office. "How's the arm?"

"Hurts like hell," I said, rubbing my elbow through the suit I was wearing.

"Aww, you're just a little rusty. Ya looked great yesterday. The ballclub wants ya to come down to Mesa."

"Yeah, then what?" I said.

"Well, ya know, show us what ya can do, and then maybe spend the first month in Iowa, you know at AAA, then the ballclub will come get ya when you've gotten some work in."

At this point in my life, I was considering starting a financial advisory firm. My office was in Beverly Hills, I was taking meetings with sports agents and film producers about managing investments. Had one more year of Gene Autry's money coming to me from my Angels contract – I didn't need the cash. As sincere as I believed Spider was, I'd heard the "no promises" story before. I was having lunch that afternoon at Spago in West Hollywood – there was no way I going to Iowa.

"I think…I think I'm done, Spider," I stuttered slightly into the phone.

"Well, we still got a couple weeks before spring training," Spider sighed, "I'll call ya back in case ya change your mind."

"Thanks, man," I said as I hung up the phone. The feeling stayed in the air for a few moments. I actually picked up the phone to dial Spider back, but then stopped. You know why I stopped?

I didn't feel like dragging a bunch of bags down to Mesa, meet a whole new group of guys, go through the hassle of getting a place for 30 days, relive old times with the one or two dudes I played with, run sprints, get on that mound and blow out my arm on the first day, see those looks of disappointment from the manager and coaches, the "*I told you so*" from the one coach who said this was a bad idea – because one of them is always there – and then answer questions from the beat guys who have to fill out their columns. The process would be exhausting with not a whole lot accomplished.

So why did I go to Commerce Park when Spider asked me knowing in my heart I was done?

Because I'm a ballplayer. It's what I am, and when a guy in the game asks you to play ball with him, you play ball with him, but a larger part of me wasn't the fun-loving, rookie phenom anymore. Had a kid, was 33, all that jazz.

MLB came calling once again. I just kept walking down the middle of the road.

* * * * *

So there I stood alone, nine months later, watching in a trance as my buddy Tim Flannery hit a routine grounder that eased through the legs of Leon Durham to tie it up at 3-3 in Game Five of the '84 NLCS. The crowd roared, egging on my hometown Padres and their aging veterans. Third-year speedster Alan Wiggins came up and singled. Then young Tony Gwynn, the Padres' emerging star and batting champ who complemented the older players' wisdom and savvy, laced a double to center field scoring Flannery and Wiggins. Sutcliffe, the warrior on the mound, fought tirelessly to keep this game from getting out of hand, but he had nothing left. He gave the fans of Wrigley four months of cheers, of achievements, of smiles, but there were no more tricks left in his bag. His first pitch to Garvey was a clutch single up the middle, scoring Gwynn. And then it was time for my other friend to take the mound for San Diego holding a 6-3 lead. Nothing left to chance; Gossage was finishing this game. Seeing The Goose get himself in and out of an eighth inning jam, even if he lost a foot or so off his blazing fastball, got my own juices flowing. Standing in the dugout tunnel reserved for VVIPs, I watched from field level as Goose delivered a final message to Cubs catcher Jody Davis who grounded weakly to Nettles at third for the final force out. Goose jumped into his catcher's arms. Nettles, Garvey, Padres shortstop Garry Templeton, another former '70s star, the rest of the ballclub, drifting, falling into the triumphant baseball pile, players floating almost weightless atop the collection of victorious players which formed on my hometown field, fans streaming from the stands to join in. It was the coolest thing I'd ever witnessed on a baseball diamond. All the players joyously charging past me through the dugout tunnel heading to the champagne gala that awaited them in the clubhouse. The San Diego Padres were now in orbit, champions across the National League stratosphere. A couple of the guys invited me to join them in the party, but obviously it wasn't at all my place to be there. My friends were going to the World Series.

I walked through the tunnel by myself and headed to my car in the parking lot.

I was going home, because that's what *fans* do.

* * * * *

I was divorced soon after this, looking around to find what retirement would bring me. I was hired by INTERBANK Financial Services, a large institution based in New York City, as director of securities. I handled investments for high-net worth individuals, basically a high-net worth stockbroker. The firm was impressed with my background at Bank of America and Sun Savings & Loan in California. I passed all the exams for the securities licenses and started my life in New York. The go-go Manhattan lifestyle didn't bother me much; kind of enjoyed it at first. I lived in Hell's Kitchen off Ninth Avenue and 48th street. Could've probably gotten a much nicer co-op somewhere uptown, but luxury was never really important to me, as long as the basic needs were covered. Count was married and living in New Jersey, but we would get together every so often and have a nice meal in midtown. Baseball was a million miles away in my life, but always still in my veins. I was happy with my job, and still providing for my daughter.

As amazing as many claim New York to be, this California surfer still found some drawbacks. No car, the beach felt a million miles away, or at least, an absolute hassle to reach. Sure, I never ate better outside of my Mom's home cooking, but I had more than my share of meals alone. The people are much nicer than every cliché you've read or hear about The Big Apple. They're just hurried and crowded; even in 1986, there was just too much human congestion. Folks who lived in New Jersey and Long Island were forced to work in the city because that's where the lucrative jobs were, creating an awful commute. It was impossible to drive over the bridges and not get stuck in traffic. Obviously, there's nightmare jams on California highways as well. You're just face to face on the streets in New York City much, much more than somewhere like L.A. after they've drudged through a 80-minute drive or train ride. Every movie theater, every Broadway play, every comedy club – always booked solid. It was a life of endless lines and waiting at the bar. The women were beautiful, funny and sophisticated, but waking up felt so lonely, regardless if there was someone else in my bed. My naïve melody of those few years living in Manhattan was convincing myself that I could live a great life in the greatest city in the world, but even watching the sun rise above that impressive skyline, as much as I tried to convince myself this must be the place, home is where I wanted to be.

Home, home.

* * * * *

"You played with Willie Mays," this overly-exuberant colleague from the bank in his thick, Staten Island accent asked me one late night over drinks at The Palms, a legendary restaurant in midtown, "Get outta here." I nodded as I sipped my scotch. It was mid-summer, 1986, and I still hadn't felt comfortable in New York.

"What about Stretch McCovey? You know Stretch, too? What about Marichal? I had all their baseball cards."

"Yeah, I was a San Francisco Giant."

"Get outta here. Wow." This was the drill for me at least twice a week for two years. Stuff like this.

"What about the other one – Cepeda – you play with Cepeda?"

"I didn't play with Cepeda."

"Ah, that's ok." As I called the bartender over to handle the check, my colleague was stunned. He tapped me on the shoulder and nodded across the bar.

"Hey, hey do you know *that* guy?" I turned around and saw a couple men dining at a table. I handed the bartender my AMEX, then leaned into my colleague with a grin. "Watch this." I walked over to the table in the middle of the restaurant where the men were finishing their meal.

"Hi, stranger."

It was Keith. He looked over and smiled like a long-lost college buddy.

"Johnny D?" Keith exclaimed as he got up to hug me, "How's it goin'? Good to see ya." Keith introduced me to his party.

"Doin' allright, how you been?"

"Pretty good, enjoying New York. It's fun. Never thought I'd like it here, but you know what? It's home now. You living here?"

"Keep trying to love it, and it's great and all, but, eh...." Keith nodded. He got what I was going through.

"I know. It'll grow on ya. You wanna join us?"

"I'm actually with some people from work, I don't wanna be rude, let's grab dinner-"

"Ya got a pen?" We exchanged numbers. "I get back in town in a couple weeks. Let's do that – or come by the ballpark whenever."

I hung out with Keith a bit during the rest of my time in New York City. Went to a few games at Shea, followed by drinks afterward at the clubs around town. He left tickets for me down the first base line for the 1986 World Series. Yeah, I watched the ball trickle through his legs. I wonder how many people in this world can say they witnessed both the Leon Durham and Buckner errors live at the park. Even so, by December I decided in my mind to give New York one more year. Right then and there I should've realized it was time to leave. Work was fine but unfulfilling. Had a female friend who would stay with me every so often but nothing serious. I missed California terribly. All throughout 1987, my colleagues would drag me out to the nightclubs, the Limelight, the Palladium, but this, this pulsating UK alternative dance music that captured the nightclub culture in the mid-80's; this was not my true faith. I was more mojitos in Santa Barbara, maybe some CSNY faintly in the background, maybe some Buffett, not living life as some one-note character in a Jay McInerney novel. Even while mindlessly dancing with pretty, big-haired, shoulder pad-clad advertising executives and book editors at these "hotspots" all around New York, I used to dream of buzzing down The 5 in my long-sold off

Porsche, T-tops down, rocking out to a band that might've been at Monterey or Woodstock. I also realized something else.

I wanted to see delight in the shade of the morning sun. I wanted the childhood I lost. I wanted a glove back on my hand, a ball pressing against my fingertips, trying to break a wooden bat in two pieces with my bare velocity. I wanted clumps of clay stuck to the bottom of my cleats. And my arm felt *fantastic*. Didn't care if it was for the Padres, the Albuquerque Dukes, or Chico's Bail Bonds.

I wanted to play baseball again.

I used to think that the day would never come.

I was wrong.

* * * * *

I remember when we were driving, weekend driving in my Mercedes coupe, down the Pacific Coast Highway at irresponsible speeds, her arms wrangling me in laughs, glee and contentment, those stolen glances you make to the woman beside you while focusing on the road, this was my wish while drudging through the New York snow. Well, at least half of it came true at first.

I moved back to Southern California in 1988. I enjoyed working for INTERBANK but I had enough of Manhattan. I ended up in commercial lending out of La Jolla. Nice, easy living. Sometimes traffic, often times not. Met Michelle, a smart, attractive woman and settled down in a nice community outside San Diego. We had been dating for three months when we were out at Bully's West restaurant in Del Mar – Don Johnson and Barbra Streisand were dining at the table beside ours.

"I'm not getting younger," Michelle told me over dinner as she peeked at the movie stars, "You seem to have a good heart, I like your parents."

"And I like yours. Very much."

"I'd like to have a baby. How do you feel about that?"

I almost choked on my scotch.

"Honey, we haven't even had our entrees yet-"

"I know, I know it's a lot to ask, but I want a son-"

"That's a really tall order, I already have a beautiful daughter-"

"I know, and that's great. She'll have a sibling. No strings attached"

"C'mon, we'd be attached forever-"

"Maybe that's not such a bad thing?"

"Maybe."

"Can you help me with this? Please, I really want a boy."

"I'd like to have a son, too."

I was 37 at this point. The more I thought about the notion of a boy as I sat there, the longer I waited to decline her offer, the wider Michelle's smile extended. It wasn't a matter of me always doing as I was told. The truth is, I really wanted a boy in this world. *My boy.* Michelle was pretty and intelligent. This was a gamble worth taking.

"Let's try it," I said, as our server arrived with the steaks. Michelle had this look on her face like her whole world changed – right there, at that table. Beyond spending a lot of time with a lovely woman, kinda made me feel good to provide such a moment of joy to another human being.

Soon after that night, Michelle and I would be living together.

* * * * *

Right around this time, the other half of my wish began to reveal itself. Got back involved with semi-pro baseball. The La Jolla Profiles. Lots of ex-major leaguers were there. Even my old roommate from the early days, Steve Ontiveros, was there too. Pitched once every 10 days, then we'd all grab beers at the local bars after the games. No post-victory steaks like when Onti and me played in Phoenix, but it was always a good time. Was I dominant? Kinda, we went 25-0. It almost wasn't fair with the club we had, but that didn't matter. I stayed in shape and all the local aspiring ballplayers wanted their shot to get a hit off the guy who struck out Hall of Famers. It was a pretty good deal for everyone involved. Competitive, but the stakes were never too high. Still, my juices were flowing like crazy and my arm felt great. This was my life for the better part of 15 months and it was delightful. It would get even better one September Sunday afternoon when Michelle asked me to go walk the dog.

I saw one of my neighbors rolling his garbage can to the side of the road. I nodded hello as I normally would when his face lit up.

"John D'Acquisto," Graig Nettles greeted me, "You're just the man I'm lookin' for."

"Oh yeah?" I laughed, holding my palms up, "I didn't do it."

"Ha, not this time," Nettles, ever the wise guy, cracked back, "Can you hang out for a little bit? I'm inside watching the Chargers game."

"Lemme bring the dog home and I'll see ya in 10 minutes."

* * * * *

"It's called the Senior Professional Baseball Association," Graig explained to me while we watched football in his family room over cold beers, "There will be about seven or eight teams spread all over Florida, Orlando, Winter Haven, Fort Myers-"

"Using all the spring training facilities," I replied, glancing at the business plan.

"Yeah, about 70-75 games a year, you know, *little less than half a regular season*. The players must be pros, must be over 35, the catchers could be a little younger, but I'm calling everyone I know to play. There's a lot of ex-major leaguers that are gonna be involved."

"What about money? I know it's not gonna be millions of dollars, but at least enough to live on?"

"You wanna play ball or sit behind a desk the rest of your life?"

"Of course I wanna pitch again, but I'm gettin' married soon, you know, expenses-"

"There'll be some money there for certain guys. But, you know, I just wanna make sure you're interested in being eligible for the draft. Not everyone who wants to play will be picked, and even the guys that get picked may not make the rosters."

"We're all big boys, we know how these things go-"

"That's what I'm counting on. Big boys that wanna play one more time."

The more I studied the business plan, the more I knew this was exactly what I wanted.

"The St. Lucie Legends. You're managing the team?"

"Yep," Graig nodded.

"Onti would be great for this," I said. Nettles assured me all the San Diego area ex-players would be or had already been called. For now, he just wanted my verbal ok.

"Are you in, Johnny?"

* * * * *

My old teammate from A ball, Larry Milbourne. Walt "No-Neck" Williams. Oscar Gamble. Chicken Stanley. Graig's brother, Jim. George Foster. With a little input from Nettles, the St. Lucie Legends, led by former Yankees employee Ray Negron, drafted a number of old Bronx Bombers, a few of Nettles' pals and former superstars. Vida Blue, Ross Grimsley, Jerry Johnson. It was like a high school reunion. I flew to Miami with Onti, then drove up to Port St. Lucie. Michelle understood my need for this. She would join me out there eventually. As much as I wanted this to work, the ballclub was sort of Nettles' baby. I knew Graig was pumped less about playing, as he had only retired one year earlier after serving as a pinch-hitter deluxe for the Montreal Expos in 1988. He was excited for his chance to show the major league teams he could manage a ballclub. Upon arriving at the training complex, we dropped off our gear in the clubhouse and walked out onto the field. As soon as the man standing behind the backstop in a black sweat suit turned around to greet us, the toothy but ebullient grin on his face and a cigarette dangling from his right hand told me I was back with the in-crowd.

"Hiya, Rook."

Bobby.

"Mr. Bonds," I exclaimed, "Been awhile."

Bobby let out a joyous laugh, offering a handshake that led into a hug, "How are ya, Johnny? Been a long time. Took a little work for us to get ya out here."

"Thanks for the invite," I replied, taking in the smell of the grass and the fresh air.

"You ready to have some fun?"

"Sure am. How's my little buddy doin'?" Bobby knew exactly who I was talking about.

"Barry's good," he said about his son, who now was on the verge of becoming a superstar outfielder for the Pittsburgh Pirates, "He likes Pennsylvania. Likes California a whole lot more."

"He'll be home one day," I said.

"Probably," Bobby replied as he stamped out his smoke. "You ready to play some ball?"

I was ready to be back with my baseball family.

* * * * *

There were eight teams in the Senior Baseball league; West Palm Beach, Fort Myers, Gold Coast, St. Petersburg, Bradenton, Orlando, Winter Haven and us, the St. Lucie Legends. Sure guys like Bert Campaneris couldn't run as fast at age 47 as his big league prime, but he could still read pitchers and catchers then steal a base on ya. George Foster could hardly get that black bat of his around Major League gas at this stage of his life, but he could still take an 85-MPH fastball for a ride. There was an expectation that with the popularity of spring training, the New York snowbirds who were die-hard baseball fans and the relative prosperity of the Major

Leagues, that this concept was something of a no-brainer. Few things they didn't count on. The television deals, which are ultimately the greatest method for creating awareness of any media product, weren't in place. Fans didn't always know where to find the games, or that the games even existed. With the exception of only a couple of owners (such as John Henry, who backed the Bradenton Explorers), most teams only possessed the funds to pay their players and open the gates, but not properly promote the league, which itself wasn't properly financed. The other issue was essentially philosophical. While many of the players took the game seriously, and even others who actually depended on the league as a primary source of income, a good number of guys just came out to have fun and assumed there was a good chance the league wouldn't be around for more than a year or two. This created many conflicts on many clubs. Old rivalries were rekindled. Some teams drafted players that didn't necessarily get along well. Billy Martin and Bobby Bonds had problems in New York back in 1975. Nettles was the ultimate Billy guy, so naturally, Graig and Bobby didn't really see eye-to-eye. Vida Blue was the ace of our staff, but had a number of issues with Graig's leadership right off the bat. Soon Blue enlisted Bobby's help in getting ownership to make a managerial change. The team started off poorly, losing 10 of our first 16 games.

There wasn't a slew of media following the teams outside of the Associated Press, and after awhile that ended. The great baseball author Peter Golenbock, who co-wrote *"The Bronx Zoo"* with Sparky Lyle and Graig's autobiography *"Balls,"* was following Bobby Tolan and the St. Petersburg Pelicans in the hopes of writing a book about the league's first season. We spoke a couple times before games – his was a book about the business of the league's formation and the actual game results. He assured me that none of the off-the-field shenanigans would be chronicled, and there *was* some fun being had by the guys after hours. Being close to Nettles, I took Peter at his word, especially since there were many players concerned about his presence.

Michelle had recently given birth to our beautiful baby boy, John Paul, and had joined me in Port St. Lucie for a couple weeks. I missed them both very much. They came to the ballpark a number of times to cheer me on. As we finished a late afternoon game against Fort Myers, I was getting ready to take my family out to dinner when I clicked on the TV in our hotel room. Flipping the channels I came across ESPN and there at the bottom of the screen I saw it:

The St. Lucie Legends of the Senior Baseball League traded manager first baseman Graig Nettles and Pitcher John D'Acquisto to the Bradenton Explorers for first baseman Willie Aikens.

The phone immediately rang in my room.

"Did you hear the news?" Graig asked me.

"Yeah, thanks for telling me," I snapped at him.

"Sorry, Johnny. This thing has been a clusterfuck since day one. They sent me too."

"Yeah, we'll probably be better off." Look, it was annoying – I had to pack up my fiancée, the baby, send them home and *then* move my things to another hotel, but really, it was pretty low-stakes stuff. It wasn't the majors.

"We'll be ok," Nettles assured me, "I hear the owner is the classiest guy outta the whole bunch."

"Who's manager again?"

"Clete Boyer. He's a good guy. I know him from the Yankees. We're in good hands."

After dropping my family off at the airport, I drove to Bradenton and met with the owner of the Explorers, John Henry. It was no coincidence that the best-run organization in the fledgling league was also in first place.

"So what do you think is fair?" the owner asked me as we sat down to talk salary.

"My expectations are low, you know, compared to the big leagues, but I'd like $10,000 a month, plus $500 for every save and $1000 for every win." John Henry was extremely open-minded, extremely generous and extremely curious about the process of running a sports franchise. Just like Graig wanted to manage a big-league team, it was clear to me that Henry had his sights set on owning a Major League franchise someday. The Explorers were his financial tackling dummy of sorts. Everyone had their ambitions in baseball; it was only a matter of degrees.

"I think we could do that," Henry nodded. We shook hands, the checks arrived every two weeks and I pitched my butt off for him over the rest of the short season. My final record was 5-4 with four saves. Enough incentive money to pay for diapers and children's books. We ended up losing in the playoffs to Bobby Tolan's Pelicans. Would've been nicer to win but a number of guys achieved something even better than their SPBA Champions Trophy.

Danny Boone, a former Padre lefthander who last pitched in the majors in 1982, signed a minor-league deal with the Baltimore Orioles after the SPBA season ended. He spent most of 1990 in AAA but appeared in four September games for Baltimore. Pitched well, too.

Ozzie Virgil, Jr. and Paul Mirabella also signed contracts after our season ended, but they had played in the majors at some point in 1989. Same with Joaquin Andujar, the flashy right-hander for the Cardinals back in the 80's. He signed a minor-league deal with the Montreal Expos, but was cut at the end of spring training.

There was one more pitcher who was scouted a bit during the playoff series.

As I walked off the mound in my final game, a vaguely familiar face caught my eye behind the backstop. Not a boisterous fan, certainly not a groupie, not an ex-player. He had a notebook in his hand and spent a fair amount of time talking to the team official handling the radar gun.

Really? Is it possible? Am I being scouted? *At Age 38? Five years out of league?*

I wondered if it was a dream.

* * * * *

I had just gotten home from the SPBA playoffs. Spent a relaxing weekend with Michelle and John Paul mostly finalizing wedding plans for that summer and the life we would live together. I had just come back from a very rewarding baseball season with my friends, a rival or two, but I had an absolute renaissance in Florida. I went back to my 9-to-5 job at the bank after having one more dip in the baseball pool. My life was now settled.

And then the phone rang.

"*Johnny, mah boy.*" When you play a sport or work in some hands-on level of show business, you meet thousands of people.

You don't remember everyone's voice by heart. This one I knew and from the moment he spoke, I remembered who was in the stands that night in Bradenton.

"Roger," I replied, "How're ya doin'?"

I hadn't heard from Roger Craig in at least five years. You know how you have people in your life that you care for and maybe they don't call, maybe they don't write, reach out in any way, but you still possess affection for them? That was Roger.

"Doin' pretty good. Would like the Giants to be playin' better, but what can ya do, right?"

"Sure. That was a tough series last year for you guys." The Giants had just been swept by the Oakland A's in the 1989 World Series, a post-season interrupted by the tragic San Francisco earthquake.

"Eh, the teams played their hearts out, but those A's, tough sons of bitches. Beat ya with pitching *and* hitting."

As much as I loved hearing Roger's voice – and I love the man to pieces – I knew there was more to the call than catching up.

"So what's a busy man like you doing on the phone with an old fart like me?"

Roger chuckled.

"Well if you're old, what the hell's that make me?" We both laughed.

"I know, so what's up?"

"We're in town against the Padres this week. I want ya to come to the park. I need to ask ya somethin'."

"Ya got me on the phone now."

"Just get in the car and have a beer with me, will ya? I wanna see your face."

"I'll, umm, I'll come down tomorrow."

"Right-o. Talk to ya then, Johnny." As I hung up the phone, it hit me. The face in the crowd at the ballgame? Dave Nahabedian, the farm director for the San Francisco Giants. The scouting director? Bob Fontaine, my general manager in San Diego, the best executive I ever played for.

This was not a friendly visit with an ex-manager.

This was business.

* * * * *

"You still wanna pitch?" Roger asked me pretty much point-blank the moment I stepped into his office, "Because we need another arm in the pen. Our guys were sayin' you had that up to 95-96 in the old man league three months ago. You think you can still miss bats in the majors?"

"I know I can," I replied, because as I have been trained all my life, when the skipper asks you if you can get guys out, your answer always always *always* is yes.

"The team's lookin' to sign Mark Thurmond for the final pen spot. If we can't get him, we wanna bring ya back."

I laughed my ass off.

"Roger, you gotta be kidding me. I'm gonna be 39 years old this year."

"Well, the plan is this, we don't sign Thurmond, we're signing you. We do sign Thurmond, we're signin' you anyway and sendin' you to Phoenix-"

"C'mon Roger, AAA?"

"Not just that, you'll be a pitching coach, too. The organization thinks you'll get along real good with the younger guys. Me, Fontaine, we know ya. We're comfortable having you babysit our kids. Ya do a good job, there's always teams looking for a pitching coach that kids listen to."

I read through the contract. I wanted to sign it so badly. Roger had great people instincts. He knew I was dying to put pen to paper.

"Roger, I'm making a lot of money now."

"I know, son. That's why life's about the decisions ya choose." I must've sat in his office for five minutes silently. Roger dropped a pen on the contract.

"Do this. Sign the contract. Take it home. Talk to your family. If ya come back here tomorrow and shake my hand, there's a jersey waitin' for ya. If not......you retire as a Giant. The way you were supposed to."

Roger's words touched me in a way I hadn't been reached in years. Baseball kept inviting me back into the family, again and again and again. It was the hardest drive home in a long time.

As I walked in the side door of my house, Michelle was holding John Paul, sweetly singing to him. Wedding magazines all over the kitchen counter, surrounded by Williams Sonoma catalogs. Plans were in place. Michelle greeted me with a sweet kiss on my lips.

"Hey Honey, you have a nice visit with your friends?"

By now, you know how this moment ended. The only logical conclusion.

I always did what I was told.

The next day, I walked into Roger's office. He glanced over, saw the liquid forming in corners of my eyes.

He knew my answer.

He just sighed, then stood up and gave me a hearty hug.

"Men gotta do what men gotta do." I raised the contract in my hands.

"Can I keep this?" I asked. Roger nodded.

I shook his hand one more time and walked out of his office. As I left the stadium, I wanted to run back in the worst way and tell Roger, *"I'm here, Skip. Anything you need, ready to leave, wherever, whenever."* Of course, all I did was leave Jack Murphy Stadium through the general admission's entrance.

Because that's what fans do.

* * * * *

Driving home, I nearly turned the car around at least five times, but that little voice inside my head said don't look back. Not a single day goes by that I don't regret not running off to join my friends in the major league circus. My whole life would be different. Strike fights, one or two asshole managers, labor bullshit, trades, outright releases – so what. Someone, somewhere, at one time or another in that entire sport, that entire organization, always looked out for me. Baseball was my family and I turned away from them and toward the real world. You can always see your opponents' faces on a baseball diamond. You can look the opposition in the eye across the field. Whether you can catch up to the fastball or not, maybe you can out run that screaming line drive or maybe you can't, you always see it coming.

The real world is often the exact opposite.

The little voice inside my head said those days are gone forever and I should just let 'em go.

That stupid little voice had no idea what the coming decade had in store for me.

Stop Motion

The book was entitled *"The Forever Boys."* Peter Golenbock had finished his year-long project to chronicle the start-up senior baseball league where I played. It was a great read and he remained true to his pledge to keep the narrative focused on baseball matters. I flipped through the pages as I sat on a jet headed for Asia in the summer of 1991. It had been less than two years since I pitched for the Bradenton Explorers but it felt like a lifetime ago. After baseball, my boss John Smith at First Commercial Bank in Kearny Mesa, a small San Diego suburb, welcomed me back with open arms, but he knew my true love was to be involved in sports. One of my clients at the bank was a company called Ariel Life Systems. My contact there was Chuck Erickson, the sales and marketing director who also happened to be my catcher at Great Falls back in 1970. His bosses were Dr. Don Brucker, the inventor of the gas permeable contact lens along with Dr. Gideon Ariel, the father of the Ariel Performance Analysis system with 3-D motion capture. We held a meeting in my office to discuss their financial situation. The company numbers were all in place. As I walked them to the parking lot, the conversation took an interesting turn.

"Chuck had an idea," Dr. Brucker said as we reached his car, "Why don't you come down and meet Gideon. There might be a spot for you with us."

"Really?" I replied, "I'm extremely flattered, but the guys here at the bank, they take good care of me."

"I don't doubt that, but we need someone with your background, and to be frank, your rolodex. We believe sports analytics will become a growth industry, but we could use someone with your reputation to preach our gospel."

I thought for a moment before extending my hand.

"Well, I guess it couldn't hurt to swing by Friday and talk," I said as we waved goodbye.

As much as I liked and respected everyone at the bank, this was an exciting opportunity. Later that week, Chuck and Dr. Brucker introduced me to Gideon Ariel. The location wasn't far from my house. The money was comparable to my salary at the bank, so I would have no issues at home with jumping to what was sort of a start-up company. I told my boss I would be leaving, stayed around for a couple weeks to assist with the transition and then began work for Ariel Life Systems as director of sports marketing and technical advisor related to baseball.

* * * * *

It didn't take me long to fall in love with the operations. Analyzing elite athletes, performance enhancement, injury prevention – these endeavors were right up my alley. It was almost the same as coaching and I could sleep in my own bed every night. Gideon believed that motion analysis could revolutionize the sports industry and it began with me calling everyone I knew from my office at Ariel.

"Galen," I said, "It's Johnny D! Been a long time since Montreal......"

"Leo, John D'Acquisto. Right, how ya been? I know, great to hear your voice, too. You have some amazing young guys down there in Atlanta...."

"Billy Connors, please? John D'Acquisto calling....."

My first meeting was with the Toronto Blue Jays at their spring training facility in Dunedin, Fla., 1991. Galen Cisco was my pitching coach with the Expos for that month back in 1980. I made the presentation of Ariel's work to the Blue Jays' young pitchers. Analyzed the motion of David Wells and Al Leiter. My old catcher in San Diego, Gene Tenace, was also on the coaching staff – there were a fair amount of familiar faces. Cito Gaston was the Blue Jays' manager at the time, open-minded enough to allow us to analyze his guys. Toronto ended up buying our analytics program. Our next stop was Atlanta. Leo Mazzone had pitched with me in the Giants' organization. He brought us in to look at some of their prospects. Leo introduced me to Tom Glavine and John Smoltz. There wasn't a huge need to fix them at all, as they were developing nicely within the system. For those two, it was a matter of merely checking for red flags or the tendencies that lead to arm injuries. In the end, Leo liked our work and had the Braves purchase the program.

Word about Ariel Life Systems' motion analysis began to spread not just throughout baseball but all over the sports world. Our work provided valuable information to major league clubs and college teams alike, with other sports checking in on us. The city of San Diego was especially proud of our product – one local television network, Channel 10, named Ariel Life Systems the most innovative company in San Diego for 1991.

It wasn't long before the baseball leagues of the Pacific Rim heard about our breakthroughs in sports technology and next thing I knew, Gideon had me on a flight to Tokyo. We were big in Japan. Nagoya, the Lotte Orions, Yokohama, Yakult swallows, Saitama Seibu Lions, Chiba Lotte Marines, Tohoku Rakuten Golden Eagles, Hanshin Tigers, Chunichi Dragons, Hiroshima Toyo Carp – I met with all the ball clubs of the Japanese Baseball Association. Demonstrations at the stadiums, office meetings, dinners at the finest restaurants in Tokyo - we pitched this to everyone - ended up selling over a million dollars worth of systems. Dr. Ariel was extremely appreciative of the job we did.

I learned so much working alongside Dr. Ariel, to the point where he sponsored me for the academic work necessary to achieve my degree as well as the beginnings of a PhD program in bio-mechanics. Was it easy working for Dr. Ariel? Sure he was very demanding, played it close to the vest with his creations, as many inventors in the technology world have been known to act. Couldn't blame him as another company in the same field, *Motion Analysis*, was founded from a former Ariel employee who had a falling out with Gideon – we lost a fair amount of first-mover advantage to those individuals.

After our success with baseball organizations around the world, we began to look at other sports. I hosted a clinic sponsored by the PGA for the golf pros in San Diego – great turnout, some of the guys saw a computer breakdown of their swings that they had never seen before, issues they were never aware of. We had access to all the golfers through what was then-called the Andy Williams San

Diego Open. We sponsored a tent - took a number of analytical photos and video analysis of golf greats like Jack Nicklaus, Lee Trevino, John Daly, Daly especially was one of my first golf subjects.

We branched out to work in Tennis – Ariel sent me to the Nick Belliterri Tennis Academy in Sarasota, Florida. Andre Agassi, Jim Courier, Pete Sampras, everybody used our programs. Through Dick Dent, my old trainer with the Padres, I was introduced to Bill Koch's America 2 sailing team, training the crew to improve speed for hoisting the sails in competition.

As our success grew, of course the number of companies in the space increased as well. Motion Analysis as well as Sony jumped into the market, developing copycat programs based on Dr. Ariel's principles.

Around the third year with Ariel Life Systems, business continued expanding, but like most geniuses, Dr. Ariel became bored once he achieved his goal. In his mind, he accomplished everything. Money wasn't at all a motivation – acceptance and achievement triumphed the almighty dollar. His first love was medicine. The systems were falling off the shelves as fast as Gideon could program them. He had his validation; it was time for something else. Gideon wanted to explore the medical field - gait analysis, specifically - where he began his career.

"Do you think we'll match the volume selling to the track and field world?" I asked at our third anniversary team meeting in 1993, "It's seems like there's thousands of college teams around the country that are dying for our product."

"I think we've done all we can do here," Dr. Ariel replied, "There's another mountain to conquer."

"There's so much support revenue we're leaving on the table with baseball," I shot back, with the tacit approval of my colleagues in the room, "We're the best at what we do."

"Right," Dr. Ariel nodded, "And now it's time for us to be the best at something else. Something I'm very passionate about."

It's hard – no, it's nearly impossible – to tell a brilliant man who's hearing from everyone how enlightened and ahead-of-the-curve he is, that his next idea is the wrong move. Although I was making good money working for him, I certainly didn't want to be knocking on the doors of doctor's offices selling what was basically elite-level medical equipment. I was offered the opportunity to work for Ariel's competitors, but in my heart, that would've been wrong. It's not like professional sports, where you play for another ball club when you become a free agent – we pretty much invented the sports motion analytics industry – I couldn't bring myself to pitch product for a copycat company. I respectfully thanked Dr. Gideon for his education and support and moved on. He accepted my resignation and genuinely appreciated the doors I opened for him in the sports world.

I was still well-off at this point, money wasn't a major issue, but I needed to be working in some capacity.

I also realized, with the success I enjoyed at Ariel, I felt it was time to work for myself.

* * * * *

It's a well-documented fact that many professional athletes face serious financial difficulties when their playing careers end, even sometimes before. You need to only check out the bottom of baseball cards to recognize certain guys hanging on at the end of their careers. Makes you scratch your end as to why Hall-of-Fame caliber players would subject themselves to a bench role. Some couldn't get enough of the locker room camaraderie, or simply didn't know anything else in life. The next time you're in the rabbit hole of a sports reference website and you come across a star-player who spent their final seasons bouncing through the league, chances are money played more than a cameo role in their decision to stick around, especially players who came up before the free agency era. Athletes don't pay much attention to their legacies when they need to make child support payments or even sustain a lifestyle for their family based upon their previous lucrative contract.

My mom gave me a lifelong education in living below your means. Sure, I always treated myself to a nice car, but that was my lone extravagance. Always had a nice house, but never a McMansion or anything. Even by mid-1993, when I was long out of baseball and the generous contract I signed with the Angels had long expired, I remained quite comfortable. Money was necessary to live, obviously, but it was never the endgame for me.

After Ariel, I had explored working in Major League Baseball again. There were no positions open with the Padres in town. I received a call from Jimmy Leyland, then manager of the Pittsburgh Pirates, inquiring about my interest in a pitching coach role with the organization. Jimmy said Rollie Fingers recommended me based upon my work with pitching computer analytics back at Ariel as well as my general ease and communication skills with young players. Another situation where Major League Baseball reached out their hand to keep me in the family, to keep me warm and safe within the secure bubble of sunshine and stadium lighting. Another situation where Michelle suggested months away from home would hamper our marriage, which of course, was correct. I genuinely thanked Jimmy for the offer and regretfully declined. I began what was my next career step.

Ultimately, the only two things I knew were sports and banking. Turns out I knew one better than I realized. The other, I knew barely more than I was supposed to.

In any event, I leveraged my existing contacts and of course, my license as a registered investment advisor, and opened the D'Acquisto Financial Group. I hired an attorney, Thomas F. Goodman, to establish and design a trust for the company, along with all the necessary protections. Our investment process was similar to a fund of funds structure, whereby venture capital seekers would come to us for investment. The hedge fund world wasn't in its infancy in 1993, but it had yet to become the group of rock stars that gets paraded across CNBC and FOX Business News every day. Finding funding wasn't the easiest task in the world back then, and someone with my rolodex was able to procure investments easily. We were welcomed into the Southern California financial community, many of whom I knew growing up, played against or hung out with in high school, successful to the point where I received a phone call related to melding the expertise I gained over ten years in baseball with one of the more complicated investment opportunities.

The San Diego Padres.

Stakes

The primary investment strategy for the D'Acquisto Financial Group was international interest rate swaps. While I possessed a banking background, my partner knew a lot more about this than I did. These type of transactions were frowned upon in the United States, but overseas was a different story. It was legal to invest in swaps in Europe, as long as they didn't involve American depositors. My partner Tom designed the Doubleday Trust and composed all the protections for investors. Using my banking contacts and Tom's relationships, we were able to raise $7.5 million dollars. We established trading relationships with many Wall Street firms and money center banks – Merrill Lynch, Prudential Bache, Shearson Lehman Brothers, Wells Fargo as well as my former employer Bank of America. We also engaged in venture capital investing, and dabbled in stocks and bonds. I enjoyed trading commodities. We executed our commodity trades through the Sheraton Management Group, based out of Chicago. I had a good relationship with their head of commodities trading, Jeff Kollar. Jeff fancied himself a quantitative expert, always had designs on creating an electronic analysis tool to measure the moves of coffee prices, oil, wheat, cattle futures, everything in the space, basically an early-stage algorithim. From 1993 to mid 1994, we accumulated nearly $22 million in assets based upon the interest-rate swaps and commodities trading, a monthly return of 16% off of Jeff's commodity trades alone.

We sunk nearly every dime back into the business. As successful as we were, it didn't change my lifestyle much. I did treat myself to a new Porsche, but that was an expenditure which came from my personal savings – at that stage of my life, I wasn't the kind of guy who used his company to write everything off. Still lived in the same ranch home I shared with Michelle and John Paul. We hired a couple of employees – one of my family members, a former IRS veteran, to ensure our books were compliant with all the proper and ever-changing tax laws. With the success of DFG, we started looking toward interesting ventures.

And some came looking for us.

* * * * *

"We think it would be a great situation," Tom said to me, "You're a former player, a former *Padres* player, local kid, you're the perfect candidate." The notion of owning a baseball club wasn't completely foreign to me. I had been asked to join the ownership group of the Palm Springs franchise for the Senior League Baseball organization at the time the league disbanded. Tom and I had also explored bidding on a club in the Mexican League right across the border and made a $50,000 good-faith deposit, but at the time we were unsuccessful in raising the $5 million and for the most part received our deposit back. A Major League team, though, one located in my hometown, would be a much different story. It wasn't as if I had a lust for money, I just wanted to be involved in Baseball and still be home for my family. I turned down the Pirates' coaching position, but this situation would keep me in the San

Diego area. One of my clients, Mercury Investment, told us that Farmers Insurance Group had an interest in financing the acquisition. Tom ironed out the details.

"Are you sure we have the money?" I asked him in our Del Mar-based offices.

"Everything's covered," Tom replied. At this time, my old friend, Hank Bauer, was a sportscaster for Channel 8 News in San Diego. During our off-the-record conversations, I showed him the line of credit (or, the "*LOC*") we received from Farmers. Of course, it would eventually get leaked that we were prepared to make an offer. I wanted to make sure everything was in place before going public with our intentions. Finally, I sent a letter to Dick Freeman, who represented Padres' ownership.

"We are prepared to submit a bid for the San Diego Padres." Around this time, John Moores, a wealthy tech investor, called me on the phone.

"Johnny, congrats on getting to this point in the process," John said, "Must be an exciting time for you."

"Yeah," I replied, "Maybe we can make this work."

"I have an idea. What would you say if I came in with you on the ownership group? I think the two of us together to put this over the top."

I listened to John's proposal. Basically, he would come in as 49% partner versus my 51% backed by the Farmers' Group financing. It was a fair request, but I felt that circumstances like this rarely work out. I also believed with the support from the Farmers Group, I didn't need to bring anyone into this.

"I appreciate the offer, John," I told him, "But, to be honest, I would rather work alone on this one."

"I understand. Thanks for hearing us out."

My group submitted a bid for $350 million to purchase the ball club. Padres' ownership rejected our offer. John Morres would team up with Tom Werner, producer of TV's "*Roseanne*" as well as "*The Cosby Show*," and ultimately became the new owners of the San Diego ball club. While I was slightly disappointed, it wasn't the end of the world for me.

That would come soon enough.

* * * * *

With our success trading with the Sheraton Management Group, we began receiving calls from bigger players seeking investment in our ventures as well as wealthy individuals seeking capital. Soon, the guys at Sheraton presented us with an electronic trading project.

"It's bascally an algorithim," Jeff Kollar said to Tom and me on a conference call in September 1993, "I believe this program can predict the swings in wheat prices, cattle futures, you name it, and yield one hellvua return. I just need to raise additional capital and we're off and running."

Tom and I had been making impressive returns with Jeff's commodities trading. Jeff suggested we could take it to the next level with more money. I liked being part of a sophisticated, successful business. We decided to help raise funds for the commodities algorithim. Through Tom's friends and contacts, as well as my decades-old banking relationships, we were able to pitch Jeff's algorithim and investment strategy. We approached a number of banks, both domestic and international, to build out the trading program. In the midst of all this, I was introduced to Davide Siniscalchi, a wealthy, Chicago-based executive with a desire to invest in intricate trading strategies. Jeff flew out to San Diego and met with Siniscalchi, myself and Tom. Jeff and Davide got along very well, almost too well. They had mutual acquaintances and many people in common. Ultimately, Davide invested in my fund and we prospered for the first six months. Soon after this, I created an investment trust that would invest in overseas interest-rate swaps. Davide introduced us to his European banking relationships. The nature of the arrangement called for Davide and my group to split any profits from the venture 50-50. Since the D'Acquisto Financial Group (or "DFG") was leveraging Davide's contacts for Jeff's swaps trading, the agreement called for us to split the profits down the middle with him, which was fine by me. Upon receiving the document outlining the agreement, Tom came across some language in the contract.

"Johnny, check this out," Tom said to me in our office, handing me the document, "Says here that as co-trustee, if you are charged with any civil or criminal fraud, Siniscalchi's group retains 100% of the profits and you are instantly removed as trustee. You could be removed from your position and stripped of any profit-sharing. You sure about this?"

"Well, it's pretty standard procedure in these things, no?" I asked, "I mean, he is our partner. If we can't trust him, we shouldn't be involved with him in the first place."

"I get that, but we've only known this guy for what, nine months, a year maybe? That's a whole lot of trust."

"Look, are you doing anything illegal?"

"No."

"Are we stealing money from people?"

"No, of course not."

"Do we have anything to hide?"

"No, not at all."

"Then what do we have to worry about?"

I know what you're thinking, because I think about it every day of my life. An absolutely incredible lapse in judgment and foresight on my part. I just wasn't raised to think or anticipate the worst in people.

Especially people I knew and cared about for most of my adult life.

* * * * *

One Saturday afternoon in the summer of 1994, as the trust agreement with Jeff and Siniscalchi was thriving, I received a call from an old friend.

"Johnny D," he said, "How's it goin', man?"

It was Count. We stayed in touch every so often, but after an elbow injury forced him to retire from baseball in 1986, the past few years hadn't been good to John. 30 minutes of catching up on each other's lives lead into the true nature of his phone call.

"It's been a little rough around here, Johnny," Count told me, "Trying to get some things goin', it's not easy." There was a bit of silence on the line. I never made one of these calls and while they are uncomfortable on the receiving end, I imagined for an ex-jock – and let's face it, most professional athletes have been propped up by accolades and sometimes fame for most of their life, these type of calls are excruciating – I wanted to come up with a plan for them. Count was my dear friend. I knew his kids and Dory from back in the San Fran days - I would've done anything I could to help him.

"How about a job?" I offered.

"What, you think I'm Wall Street material?" Count joked.

"Well, what are you good at?" We both laughed loudly and knowingly in unison.

"All right, hot shot," I snickered, "What else you good at?"

"Horses," Count replied through expiring laughter, "I know horses."

"Horses, huh," I said, as I began flipping through my rolodex.

"What are you doin' this weekend?" I continued, staring at my travel agent's phone number.

* * * * *

"Oh, look at this," Count nodded, checking out my Porsche as I pulled up to the airport in San Diego, "Must be nice."

"Oh, stop," I replied, "I missed my car."

"Our car-"

"Yeah. Our car. It's my only luxury." We barely pulled out of the airport beltway when Count began his pitch.

"I got a good trainer," Count said, as we drove down the PCH toward my house. "Terry Knight, he's Bobby's cousin by the way, one of the best out there. He's up in Santa Anita. I can get a hold of a good bloodstock agent – can get us good horses for a good price out of France. Maybe Britain."

Count was always a fast-talker, but now he was challenging the speedometer in the car.

"What's a bloodstock agent again-"

"C'mon, Johnny, you know what a bloodstock agent is. It's like you, it's a broker-"

"I'm not a broker anymore, I'm an investment adviser-"

"Whatever, he's the guy that connects the horse buyers and the breeders."

"So he's the middle man-"

"-And nothing can be done without him. Johnny, I'm tellin' ya, there's money to be made in horse racing and I know horses. Just gotta know the right people. This is something we can do together, like the old days."

"Sounds interesting," I replied, "Anything I can do to help you and Dory."

"We could definitely use some help," Count added.

"How much help did you have in mind?" I asked.

"I need 10 grand. Have to take care of a few things around the house, you know, the girls. Get my head above water."

"Here's what I'm gonna do. I'll give you $10,000-"

"It's just a loan, Johnny-"

I knew better.

"I'll *give* you 10 grand, you take care of Dory and the girls, and if the situation makes sense, I'll hire you to run the investment for me. But no more cash advances-"

"Definitely."

* * * * *

We met with my partner Tom back at the house. Count walked us through the plan – how to find the horses, who to talk to, the cost of breeding, raising, stable fees. Tom was intrigued.

"Let's give it a shot," Tom nodded, "As long as we do this smart, we might make a few bucks."

I agreed to the plan. Once we walked Tom to his car in the driveway, Count turned to me as he left.

"You won't regret this, Johnny," Count said, throwing his arm around my shoulder.

* * * * *

I ended up paying Count $8000 a month. He stayed at my house at first until he found a place. Also leased him a car. He made all the contact phone calls. Count introduced me to the bloodstock agent. We traveled often to Santa Anita Racetrack outside Los Angeles. Between dashing back and forth from the betting window to the owners' boxes, Count was going a million miles a minute. We met just about everyone involved in the Southern California horse breeding community. Tom and I ended up conducting as much due diligence as possible. Ultimately, we bought interests in three horses about three weeks later – *Blue Burgee, Carloun* and *French Park*. Paid about $50,000 for French Park. We owned 50% of the horse with the bloodstock agent, who decided to partner with us on the investment.

Over the next three months, the horses ran a couple of times – two of them did really well. Carloun came in second at Santa Anita, winning us $20,000. We ran French Park in a stakes race. She placed third, won a little bit of money. This venture that began as a means of supporting my friend and his family was actually close to turning a profit at first.

The only problem was that Tom didn't get along well with Count. Lawyer's intuition, jealousy, I don't know. I was happy to be hanging out with my buddy again. I missed my baseball days, always found myself a bit nostalgic for the clubhouse, was glad Count was around me. You know, I would see Rollie Fingers every now and then. Had a fun dinner at least once a summer with Randy Jones and Marie, but I really didn't see many of the guys much. Count would pop into the D'Acquisto Financial Group offices to collect money to go pay stable expenses and stay for awhile. The two of us would recall tales from our crazier days. Upon Count leaving, Tom would watch him walk quickly toward the car.

"He's up to no good," Tom muttered. As much as I was thrilled to see my pal and old playmate, I didn't dismiss Tom's insights.

"What makes you say that?" I asked.

"Doesn't this all seem too easy to you? This whole horse business – the trainers, the bloodstock agents, the jockeys – he acts like the bloodstock agent's his long-lost brother. You're his long-lost brother."

"Well, that's what he set out to do, right?"

Tom shook his head slightly and tapped his finger on my desk.

"Somethin's up," he said, leaving my office.

It was time to pay closer attention to Count.

* * * * *

The working relationship between Jeff, Siniscalchi and DFG seemed fine. The overseas investments were for the most part, profitable, but soon I began receiving mixed signals. We would buy Swiss bank notes for the trust, have them verified by his account managers at Union Bank of Switzerland, Credit Suisse and Swiss Bank, then instructed not to deliver them. It was at the advent of email, so most messages were via voicemail or faxes. It became needlessly intricate and complicated. Almost as if signals were being mixed purposely. Seemingly out of nowhere, early in the summer of 1994, DFG was hit with a civil suit by Davide Siniscalchi in Chicago. Davide alledged that DFG withheld funds from the agreement and actually contacted the SEC that we were conducting a ponzi scheme. He filed the suit in Chicago, not San Diego.

"Shit," Tom sighed as he perused the document, "I was afraid of this."

"What?" He just shook his head as he handed me the document.

"What I was afraid of." I couldn't believe what I was reading. I helped make this man a decent return on his money, acted in good faith, and he was trying to ruin me.

"How can he do this?"

That was the beginning of the onslaught of the civil suit by the Securities and Exchange Commission. The SEC already had questions how I was able to afford a Major League Baseball team, as we were in the paper representing a group to buy the San Diego Padres. Never mind that I was barely more than a front man, the way George W. Bush was merely the face of the Texas Rangers purchase, or how George Steinbrenner basically owned less than 10% of the New York Yankees when he bought the team in 1972. Like it was offensive that an average player like me had to gall to even consider himself worthy of being a franchise owner. There must be something fishy going on, they assumed. It never occurred to the feds that perhaps my San Diego roots were more the impetus of the D'Acquisto ownership talk than deep pockets. I guess they just pay didn't enough attention. Or they had other motives. The end result, if all played out as hoped, was that my reputation would be ruined, I would be removed from the trust, my shares in the trust would be transfer to Davide's possession, which meant my share of a $22 million investment would be all his. Justice at work, right?

The thing was, I owned the trust. It was part of DFG. Now he had to deal with Tom Goodman as well, and off we went to Chicago to meet with the magistrate.

There were never any ill-gotten gains, I told the judge. It was so convoluted. I gave a deposition. We subpoenaed all the documentation from Jeff's bank, Lakeside Bank in Illinois. All the bank accounts connected to Jeff Kollar. We found a ton of money there. $2 million in notes; $4.4 million sitting there in cash. Oil Suez 256 contracts. Jeff and Davide made between $10-$22 million from the trust. I showed it to the judge, Ed Brobrick.

"They are claiming I took $7.1 million dollars," I stated, "I only received $6.8 million – here are the two documents. Sheraton Asset Mgt. $4.4 million and 2.2 million cash."

Judge Brobrick scanned the documents and said, "We're adjourning to my office."

"Your honor, they are trying to cut me out of the deal of the trust so they can split the money 50-50," I claimed, with Tom at my side.

He looked at them, "Is that what you're really trying to do?"

"Don't ask them that," I demanded, "We have the proof in our hands." Judge kept silent for a moment.

"This needs to be settled out of court," Judge Brobrick said, "$2 million dollars and you, John, have 48 hours to pay the money or else I'm gonna throw you in jail."

"But it's right there," I pointed at the documents, "There is no money. These guys have everything."

"I've made my decision," the judge responded without looking at me. I had to either agree to this or the judge was going throw me in a Chicago jail. Without a court date. Without an arrest warrant. I was up against something much bigger and much more sophisticated than I could imagine – or handle.

I sighed, "Fine, we'll agree to this." I thought that by signing off on it, the matter would be closed and I could get on with my life.

Leaving the courthouse in Chicago, I turned to Tom, "These guys are obviously working together."

"I don't know what they're trying to get from us," Tom replied, "We showed them the money was not in our possession. We can leave the state. It's not a federal issue."

"It is a federal issue," I shot back, "The judge is a federal magistrate."

"Well, it's a civil suit," Tom replied, "In a civil suit, there is no debtor's prison."

Once we returned to San Diego, Tom talked to their attorneys. They waived the jail threats. We went back and forth on the issue of the $2 million in damages.

"There is no money," Tom told their attorneys, "You guys have it all, and you know you have it all. Take the trust, take the entity, take everything that's left – we just want out and to move on."

Siniscalchi said he only received $220,000, yet in the deposition it showed he got $2.2 million, plus $4.4 million. I got $1.8 million. I sent $750,000 to Wolfgang Ladenburg and another $250,000 off to Dr. Peter Mozary – their investments plus profits. There's another $1 million dollars we paid out. There were no *"victims."* In this situation. Let me repeat that. THERE. WERE. NO. VICTIMS. This wasn't a Madoff thing where retired men who worked decades in a Maxwell House factory lost their pension savings, where widows lost their safety cushion.

There were no victims, there were no illegal promises to investors of monthly gains, there was no ponzi scheme, just a brilliant investor utilizing our nation's legal system to maneuver me out of a joint venture deal.

I will say, I should have taken whatever chips I had left and walked away from the table of high finance. I didn't, because I didn't do anything wrong. Why should I leave the business?

And yet, sometimes in life, "just because" is the best answer to why you should remove yourself from a potentially bad situation. *"Get out now."* Why? *"Just because." "Find another line of work."* Why? *"Just because." "Leave the high-stakes world of transactions and lawyers and corporate gamesmanship. Go have a mojito somewhere on the outside deck of a beach bar in La Jolla and enjoy the rest of your life."* Why? *"Just because."*

I still had yet to learn that lesson.

* * * * *

In the summer of 1994, DFG remained an entity and was still working with Jeff Kollar in the hopes of raising capital for his commodities algorithim. We came close with a number of investors, but they wanted to see some additional collateral on our books that we had enough money to effect the trades properly, which is completely understandable. We had contacted the Spanish financial institution Banco Santander about backing us with collateral to start-up the algorithim. Our contact at the bank, Pietro Pla, heard our pitch, was impressed with Jeff's presentation, his strategy and was eager to get involved. Tom and I conducted a conference call with Pietro.

"Who is the rest of your team at the bank?" we asked.

"I work alone," he replied, "My father is the CEO of the bank. I have my own division." This was good enough for us and we began the process and paperwork of creating an investment vehicle. Pietro was excited to get it going and offered to send us a check to show collateral to the other banks around Wall Street.

"That's fine," I said, "But please do not send anything to the bank until I have checked the documents." Pietro agreed and I had assumed the matter had been closed for the time being.

The following week, I received a call from our reps at Prudential Securities.

"Hey John," he said, "I've got something here I need to confirm with you. A representative from Banco Santander just sent you a check for $500 million dollars."

What???!?

"Excuse me," I replied, "We've been in discussions with them regarding an investment vehicle and they offered to spot us some collateral. Who did you speak to over there?"

"Well apparently, the check was sent from someone named Antonio Dos Reis and Rachel Grand."

"Who?"

"I'm assuming you know these people. Not every day someone decides to send a half a billion overseas without any documentation."

"I don't even know these people. My contact is Pietro Pla."

"When was the last time you spoke to Mr. Pla?"

"I dunno. Ten days ago, maybe."

"Well, we checked that out – apparently, Mr. Pla left the company early this week. No one is able to find him."

"I don't know who Rachel Grand or Antonio Dos Reis are. I've never met either of these people."

"Why don't you do this, John," he said to me, "How about you come to New York and we'll straighten this out."

"Well, I'm sure we can figure out the problem with me here, but, sure, I'll hop on a plane tomorrow and fix this." I hung up the phone and turned to Tom.

"That's really strange. Why would they send that over without any documentation?"

"You want me to go with you?" Tom offered.

"Why should you go? There's nothing illegal here. I think I can handle it."

* * * * *

I showed up two days later at Prudential's office. I entered the room where my broker was sitting with two men in suits.

"My name is Chip Wilson," the first man said, "I'm with the Secret Service, bank fraud division. We need to ask you some questions." They didn't arrest me right away, but we ended up heading downtown to the New York bureau of the Secret Service.

"How could you possibly think you could get away with a crime of this magnitude?" he said almost as soon as we sat down in the room.

"Excuse me," I asked angrily, "I never directed these people to send me that money."

"We spoke to Ms. Grand and Mr. Dos Reis. They said you did. And no one can find Pietro Pla. What do you know about these people?"

"I've never met them before." This went on for a couple of hours.

"Well, you're gonna need to stay in New York for a couple of days to clear up this 'misunderstanding.'"

They sent the note into Citibank to my account. They said I made that happen. They went ahead against my will and sent that into Citibank. Then I got a phone call from Prudential Securities.

I didn't like the agent's tone, as if he was assigning guilt right off the bat, almost as if he *wanted* me to have done this. Did I ask to bring my lawyer? Why would I, I didn't do anything wrong. Still a mistake. I should've brought someone with me. Soon, they brought in the documents which were sent to Citibank, in my care.

"We've checked the fingerprints," Chip said, "Yours are not on the document-"

"It's because I didn't send it." The fingerprints they found were from Rachel Grand and Antonio Dos Reis. Chip handed me the phone.

"You wanna cooperate?" he asked me.

"Of course, I do," I shot back, "That's why I'm here."

"Then call them and have them come to New York and settle this mess."

Remarkably, I was able to convince Rachel Grand and Antonio Dos Reis, whom I had never met, with the cooperation of Banco Santander, to travel to New York City and resolve this problem.

The following day, Rachel Grand and Antonio Dos Reis arrived at Prudential's offices. In a taped conversation, Rachel said, "We want to cut John out of the deal." The two of them were immediately arrested and taken away.

I flew home a couple days later.

* * * * *

A few months had passed and Count remained in California managing our horseracing interests. I used this as a diversion from the civil suit – got my mind off of the debacle. Our horse, French Park had just been placed to run in the annual Hollywood Turf Cup. We owned the horse in a 50-50 relationship with Hubert Guy, the bloodstock agent. The day of the race, Count showed up at my house as I was ready to go to Santa Anita Racetrack.

"Hey, let's head over to Del Mar OTB," he said as I was putting on my sport coat, "We'll put a bet down on the race over there."

"What, what are you talking about?" I replied, "We're going to watch our horse."

"Naw, don't worry about that. That stuff is for the beautiful people. Just you and me. We'll hang out down here."

"I don't understand , you said-"

"The trainer's a little funny. He's got a problem with you for some reason. I don't wanna get in his head before the horse posts. Let's just stay here."

"This is really fucked up, John-"

"C'mon, let's go." The dynamic of our relationship was such that I didn't give Count a whole lot of lip. I should've. We headed down to Del Mar OTB and straight to the cashier.

"French Park to win," Count said to the woman at the window. Count made a big bet for a guy making $8000 a month. French Park went off at 35-1. It was a stupid bet. Too stupid. Count liked to gamble, but he wasn't a dumb man. I bet a little, too.

The bell went off, French Park shot out of the gate as if on a mission.

"Son of a bitch, he's goin' wire-to-wire," I thought to myself. Corey Black, our jockey, had won the race the previous year, knew the track like the back of his hand and just let the horse do its own thing. French Park trotted swiftly around the track, around the clubhouse turn, in the mud, pulled away from the pack. French Park won by 30 lengths, simply blew the field away. The handicappers won a boat load. I walked out of Del Mar OTB a big winner.

So did John. Little did I know that before the race, Count, along with our partner, sold the horse to some NHL hockey player for $1.7 million. I never saw a dime of that money. Yeah, I made a smart bet, but winning 35-1 put a sour feeling in my stomach. Especially with the issues related to the firm. I had had it with everything. It seemed as though everyone was trying to pull a fast one on me. It was now time to completely clean the slate. Somehow, even my best friend used me. That night, I sat in bed staring at the TV, realizing that people only saw me as a walking ATM, not a partner, not an associate.

Not a friend.

The next day, I fired the employees of DFG, "Obviously, you see what I'm dealing with. I'm gonna have to let you all go." My brother-in law. Our comptroller, the ex-IRS man. The entire staff. "Tom, you're my attorney now. You know all the situations. You'll stick around and close the company properly."

Later that afternoon, I called Count.

"Go sell Blue Birdie. We're getting out of the business." So John drove to Santa Anita and met with this breeder we knew who expressed interest in the horse to work a deal. Count called me back couple hours later.

"He doesn't wanna pay $90,000 he'll pay $60,000."

"Fine," I replied, "We'll take $60,000."

Count called me back an hour later.

"This asshole's playing games. He knows it's a fire sale. He doesn't wanna pay me $60,000, he wants to pay me $50,000." I was starting to get pissed.

"What the fuck you doin', man?" I said, "Tell 'em no, we're selling it at $90k. Take it or leave it."

Another call an hour later. "He doesn't wanna do $90k. He'll do $30k cash and $10k check. Forty grand."

"That's not making any sense. I got other problems, just sell the fucker."

Another hour, another call. "He felt bad about the deal," Count said in a sympathetic voice. "He'll do it for $50k. 30 cash, 20 check."

I had enough. "That's cool. Sell the horse."

Count was at my front door later that night. He gave me the money, I gave him $5000 commission for selling the horse. As I poured us a couple drinks, Count shook his head quickly and got up to leave.

"Where ya goin'? It's late, let's just chill out here."

"Naw, I'm goin' to Vegas," Count said, grabbing his keys, "Gonna go meet some people at the MGM Grand."

"Hey," I said to him, "You make sure you take care of Dory."

Count got annoyed I brought them up.

"Thanks for your concern, but you let me worry about the girls, OK?"

"Do the right thing, man-"

"I hear ya. 'Later, JD."

Right then and there, Count bolted out of the house, into the SE 400 Lexus I leased him and took off for Vegas. I stewed on this for a few hours in my home office. Michelle came in to check on me.

"Everything all right?" she said, knowing I'm usually at my angriest when you don't hear my voice.

"I'm fine," I replied, "Go to bed, Honey. I'll be there in a little while." I didn't want to think that my best friend played me like this, using his family's needs as bait to get some quick cash. You ever get that feeling where you know the truth in your heart, and you don't wanna open the document, or read the email or ask the question that's going to confirm it and just change the way you perceive someone forever? That's how I felt when I called the breeder, just to "congratulate" him on his purchase of the horse.

"Nice trade, Lou," I laughed on the phone to him moments later, "Ya got me good."

"Hey Johnny," he replied in a friendly voice, "Whaddya talkin' about?"

"You know I'm having a tough time down here. I know business is business, but you got yourself a beautiful horse at bargain-basement prices."

"You think $90,000's a steal? What planet you livin' on?"

"Wait a second. You paid me ninety grand?"

"Yeah, that Count put up a hard bargain for that pony. Didn't you talk to him? Traffic can't be that bad at this hour."

I nearly threw up.

"Yeah, yeah he should be here soon. Thanks, Lou, you're a good man. Take care of the horse."

"You all right, Johnny?"

"I'm all right now. Thanks again." I hung up the phone and instantly called Count on his cell. When he answered, I could hear the ringing of dollar poker machines in the background, cheering voices of successful gamblers and the "*ching-ching*" of the slots, like everyone in the outside world was winning except for me. That only fueled my anger.

"John, you're fired."

Count was like, "Why am I fired?"

"You're fired because you ripped me off. Lou told me how he bought the horse for $90,000. You ripped me off for $40,000."

"You can't fire me? You owe me-"

"I owe you? Ya out of your mind-"

"Fuck you, man-"

"Know what, have fun, bring the car back with a full tank of gas, grab your shit and get out of my life."

"You'll pay for this, asshole." I hung up the phone.

My closest friendship in baseball – over. I loved him like a brother. Thought of him as my brother. People I eagerly engaged with to create companies, do things, to build things, build lives, were repeatedly hurting me. Even at this age, people were scamming me because I was a naïve surfer kid from San Diego, who only tried to help my best friend and his family in a time of need, and maybe I missed palling around with my buddy. Crazy as it sounds, it was like we were the badass Allman Brothers of baseball, traveling from town to town and rockin' them all.

Maybe I missed the cool kid I was from the '70s. I *missed* Fastball John. Missed him terribly. Seeing Count riding shotgun in my Porsche, listening to the Brothers and Sisters album, that I could perhaps travel in time, putting the spiritual band back together. Of course, it took me awhile to realize he was just a solo act.

Watching Count drive off to Vegas in my car, with my money, it was pretty clear what he did to me wasn't even a personal slight.

He was just a Ramblin' Man.

Strike Three

I decided I had enough. I took a sabbatical from the business and spent the next three months with Michelle and John Paul. My family took a trip to Palm Springs for a week in December of 1995. Once we returned home, emptied out the car, the phone rang a few times, I took the trash out and there they were at the front of my driveway in their unmarked Ford Taurus. Two police officers in plain clothes and Chip Wilson, the Secret Service agent from New York.

I was arrested for Securities Fraud.

* * * * *

No lawyer. No Miranda Rights. I never asked for an attorney and I fully cooperated because I knew I didn't do anything wrong. They drove me to MCC in downtown San Diego – everything processed in the parking garage. Again, I was grilled for four straight hours. Again, I told them I didn't know what was going on. Afterward, I was escorted into MCC San Diego awaiting arraignment bail. Finally, I made my phone call to Tom.

"I've been arrested," I told him. "Make arrangements for my bail." Michelle put up the house. I got bonded and released from

MCC in two days. TV cameras, news media. And life would never be the same.

The trial was set for June 1996 at the U.S. Southern District Court in New York City. I had no East Coast-based counsel. Tom made a request with the court to practice in New York, which was denied by the US attorney, on grounds that Tom was too valuable a witness to the "crime." The judge sided with her. I met with a local hot-shot defense lawyer in Manhattan. I still had a fair amount of money.

"You pay me $250,000 up front," he told me when we met at a Chock Full of Nuts coffee shop down on Wall Street a day later, "I'll get ya out of this." I was all set to cut the man a check and the prosecutor froze my accounts. I couldn't afford top-flight counsel. I was awarded a public defender, Neal Checkman.

"I can't believe you're in the middle of this," Neil said, perusing the court documents. "You're in a really tough spot here, and yet, from the looks of things, you really didn't do anything. Worse thing you could've done was accepting that deal in the Chicago deposition. You needed to fight that. They're gonna use that against you now." Soon, we discovered that Antonio Dos Reis, who worked for Banco Santander, cut a plea deal with the prosecutor. He was given 18 months in prison.

"Antonio took the deal," Neal said to me a couple days later. "He got 18 months. Maybe you should take the deal, too-"

"But I didn't do anything-"

"No, John, you didn't do anything. You didn't conduct the proper due diligence on these people, you didn't back away quickly enough when you realized this was turning into a bad situation, you didn't do anything. The amount of organizational incompetence here is staggering. You're an extremely personable, kind-hearted baseball player. You're not an international financier. But the prosecution is out for a pound of your flesh, and they're going to get it. The best I believe we can do is perhaps turn that pound into a couple of ounces. *Please* take the deal. You'll probably only get a year and a half, you'll serve nine months, and then this all goes away."

For once in my life, when it mattered most….*I didn't do as I was told.*

"I can't. I just can't."

"It's not like you're going to San Quentin. It'll be an easy nine months in a closed-off country club. Your name's already tarnished, but at least you'll be able to put all this behind you. If you press on, you'll provoke them. They'll think you're wasting the courts' time and taxpayers' resources, and they'll throw the book at you. It's your call."

"I can win this. *We* can win this."

Neal sighed. My lawyer knew exactly how this process would transpire, and like a smart manager, he asked me for the ball.

I told him get off my mound and we stayed in the game.

Neal worked with the U.S. attorney's office on the plea deal, but after a couple of back-and-forths, the prosecutor's office pulled the deal off the table.

We were going to trial.

* * * * *

The judge on the case was Robert L. Carter, a 93-year old civil rights lawyer who worked with Martin Luther King back in the

'60s. He wanted no part of this case and let the defense know it every step of the way. Judge Carter constantly overruled Neal, even threatened him with contempt of court at one point.

The prosecutor called Rachel Grand to the stand. She brought A-list dramatic skills, a limp, complaining of a bad back, even going so far as asking for a pillow. Rachel claimed that she was only acting on my behalf, even though the taped conversation at Prudential had her saying they wanted to "Cut John out of the deal."

Neal and I discussed our strategy. Should I take the stand? Should we call Tom to the stand? Ultimately, we never called Tom and I went on the stand. The prosecutor grilled me about the deposition in Chicago. Neal objected on the grounds that the civil case wasn't applicable – Judge Carter instantly overruled him. Admittedly, I lost my temper on the stand with both the prosecutor as well as the judge. I saw the hint of a smirk on the prosecutor's face. She wasn't there to ascertain justice. She was there to win a case and I didn't realize I was in the game of my life. She wanted a notch on her briefcase – I just wanted my world back. The prosecutor kept going back and back again to the civil case. Made it look like I was a repeat offender. Here were the three facts of the civil case and my arrest that I never articulated properly:

1.   The indentures of the trust stated that if someone sued me for fraud, I would be removed from the trust and Davide Siniscalchi would get the majority of the funds.

2.   I was sued for fraud by Davide Siniscalchi.

3.   The arresting secret service agent was a man named Chip Wilson – brother-in-law to Davide Siniscalchi.

Those are facts without comment.

* * * * *

In the end, the verdict was handed down in less than a day. On July 3ʳᵈ, 1996 – the day before a holiday weekend - Rachel Grand was acquitted on all counts. I was convicted on all counts. The judge asked me for a statement before sentencing. I said, "Your honor, how dare you-"

"I believe you are lying," Judge Carter shot back-

"If that's the case, then charge me with perjury. Why don't'cha charge me with perjury?"

"Mr. D'Acquisto, I would watch what you say-"

"You can't prove I'm lying because I'm not lying-"

"I hereby sentence you to no less than 63 months in prison." Michelle weeped in the front row behind Neal.

As I was led away, the words of Jimme Reese played in my head. I wasn't a money man. I was just a ball player.

And now I was a convict.

* * * * *

As bad as it was, Neal secured my freedom for another five months. I didn't go to prison right after the trial. While out on appeal, the court allowed me to work and raise a few dollars for my family's well-being. Michelle was supportive, but with the knowledge I would be away for awhile, we began to grow apart. I tried to bond with John Paul, but all of this was just too much for his nine-year old mind to ponder. I just made sure to let him know I loved him as much as I could.

It was soon December, 1996. I was going to jail.

* * * * *

Boron Federal Prison was an old air station in the California desert utilized by the government. Located close to Edwards Air Force Base, it housed about 500 or so prisoners who assembled parts for the military. I would be assigned a work clearance with a high-level security badge.

I was led to my cell, a 9-by-12 foot room. No bars or anything. Nice shelves, locker. Full-size bed, double mattress. Wasn't half-bad, actually, but it was still incarceration. I lay down, stared at the ceiling and tried to sleep. I had no more tears left – spent all those ashamed at how foolish I was to get involved with these people, upset at how much I would miss my son. The thoughts of John Paul and how I wouldn't be there to see him through the beginning of his teenage years, when a boy needs his old man most, kept me awake. I needed thoughts that would bring me joy and comfort. I searched through the pleasurable pictures in my mind, wishing I could close my eyes with a smile. Not even the sweet highlights of my baseball career could lull me to sleep. I rolled over and opened my overnight bag and reached for my walkman. We weren't allowed cassette tapes at Boron, but I managed to pick up a classic rock station signal relatively clear on the radio. The program director must've adored Bob Seger, cause it seemed as though I was humming a song about 1962 at least three, four times a week when I first arrived, reliving the deleted scenes of my personal life; Lisa, this brunette co-ed from Phoenix, who would finish every sentence she decided was important with a slightly unsure "*you know;*" the way Carol, that TWA stewardess in Chicago, propped her chin in her hand as she recanted off-the-wall flight stories from across the checkered tablecloth at some fancy Rush Street steakhouse; the ebullient greeting Joyce in St. Louis would throw my way as she met me in the lobby of the Gateway Hotel with her feathered hair bouncing in the air, held in check by aviator sunglasses atop her head; running through the cornfields of Decatur alongside Katie, when she would blink as the August Illinois sun would zap her hazel eyes just right; heh-heh, Tammy Blond back at the mall in Fresno, 1972, with her Pepsodent smile and her reassuring *"far out."*

Marlboro reds, the music and these memory angels kept me sane in my darkest hours.

I would need each and every one of them to get me through the next 1,825 nights during my timeout from polite society.

I remember, I remember, I remember…

Benched

"**S**tation 52, Squad 52, we have a rollover accident on 395, please respond?"

"Roger, responding, we're on our way!"

And so began my baptism by fire in early 1997.

As a member of the Boron Prison Fire Department, we only played AC/DC on the way home from a call, but it was in our heads as we barreled down the interstate to save trapped automobile passengers, extinguish gas trucks fallen by locked breaks and blown steel-belted radials. We worked in conjunction with the San Bernardino Fire Department. I had a walkie-talkie and pager by my side at all times. Boron sent us for EMT and fire-fighting certification. Performed CPR and time-of-death reports on more occasions than I care to remember. One time a gas truck veered across the interstate and lodged into the median. With my driving prowess and passions for all things on four wheels, soon I was the driver of the fire truck. We always had two trucks waiting. Most of the firefighters were US Customs agents, DEA dudes who went bad, border patrol guys. We were free roaming – we literally worked for the government. Most of the guys were in a special dorm right next to the firehouse. When I would hit the cybercom button, I would call the fire captain – who was an inmate as well. Our safety director.

Fred Alberts was the warden. Treated us like gold. Used to go to the warden's house – he lived nearby – and paint the garage, adjust the gutters, odd jobs. He'd make me a sandwich and we'd eat together.

The prison administrators were good to us actually, as long as you behaved yourself. They didn't worry about me, they knew I was the kind of guy who did as he was told.

A car accident on the railroad tracks between the crosshairs of 58 and Stronglan, toward Edwards. Car tried to cross the tracks – train hit the car. Couple people were dead at the scene. When we arrived, we got out, removed the bodies from the wreckage and I heard a faint cry. Wasn't in the car, but we heard it. I took off on foot into the desert and finally after about 15 yards, the cries became clearer and clearer. A baby was in the car seat in the bushes. Retrieved the child and brought her to child protective services to track down the nearest relative since the parents were killed instantly.

Jail or no jail, it was some of the most rewarding work of my life. One time, an ammonium nitrate truck blew a tire on the highway, its breaks locked, skidded as its tire caught the mile marker pole, puncturing the amoninum nitrate tank as well as the fuel tank – diesel fuel all over the place, nitrate spilling out and you had a fire. What's the combination? That's a bomb ready to go off.

So I got the call and as we left the prison, there were other emergency vehicles flying down both sides of the freeway. *Sam*, a law-enforcement agent who found himself on the wrong end of a shady drug deal at the border, rode beside me. When we arrived, the city firemen cautiously stood away from the truck, while directing us.

"Go put the fire out," the first firefighter said.

"What the hell's the matter with you guys?"

"That's ammonium nitrate – we're not goin' in," added another fireman, "We'll let you guys handle it."

So I looked at Sam, my captain, and I said, "You wanna do this?"

"Yeah, hell, let's do it," he shrugged.

Just the two of us. Stopped a few yards from the blazing vehicle; grabbed the extinguisher and put out the fire. I went over and plugged the tank. I grabbed a halogen and created a small reservior so all the fuel flowed into one spot and we began clean up. Sam and I walked back to the other guys waiting by their truck with smug grins.

"Oh, by the way, all secure." Then we were on the back of our fire truck smoking cigars when the rest of fire department showed up.

We received two to three calls a day, everything from 10-car pileups to hysterical grandmothers scared of rattlesnakes on their porches. We had about 200 homes on the base where the guards lived. We trained just about every day.

I missed my family, I missed my freedom, and no, it wasn't a country club. More like Hogan's Heroes, if you remember that '60's TV show. As long as you kept your nose clean, the warden treated us like human beings and appreciated all our hard work. Even a friendly woman who worked in the commissary would make me the occasional steak dinner on the sly. High-ranking officers at

Edwards Air Force Base would hear I was part of the fire department and on more than a handful of instances call me in for lobster lunches to hear baseball war stories. My first 18 months in prison were as comfortable as possible under the circumstances.

And then William Q. Hayes III decided he wanted to change my circumstances to further his career.

* * * * *

My attorney and ex-partner Tom Goodman was scheduled to meet with me at Boron. He arrived at the prison with an SEC attorney, Marianne Wisner. The warden called me into his office about an hour before the meeting.

"You know you don't have to give them anything, right?"

"What do you mean?"

"I don't know why they're coming here, but if you talk to them about anything, they are going to turn around and use it against ya."

"I don't know what to do."

The warden pushed the button to his intercom as he looked at me.

"I think I know," he said before getting his secretary's attention through the speaker, "Can you send Don in here?"

The warden provided me with his assistant, Don Campbell, who was also an attorney.

"Some people are coming here to speak to Johnny. I got a funny feeling about it. Why don't you sit in just in case they try to get cute with him."

Don turned to me.

"Is everything ok?"

"What else could they want?" I half-laughed, "I'm already here…right?"

* * * * *

I sat in a sparse office with Tom and the SEC attorney. I introduced Don to them. Tom offered a cautious hello to Don, then glanced slightly to Judith with a *"I didn't expect this"* look on his face. Really kind of weird that Tom was with her and wasn't really on my side. Even though Tom was still my attorney, it seemed odd that they arrived together and asked the questions sort of in sync.

"So go over the events surrounding the case in New York," Judith asked me.

"No, actually it was the civil case in Chicago," Tom corrected her.

"Oh, I'm sorry," Judith apologized.

Right then and there, I knew something was up.

"He doesn't have to answer that," Don interjected. Judith gave me a polite, yet frustrated leer.

"We're just having a conversation," Judith smiled.

"Then ask something else," Don replied.

This went back and forth for about 90 minutes. I said goodbye to Tom and the lawyer. Don and I watched them walk down the hall and leave the prison.

"I know nothing about your case," Don said as the two disappeared down a hallway, "But I don't think you've heard the last from them."

"I don't understand. What else can they do to me? I barely have any money. I'm already in jail."

Don piled his notepads into a briefcase and slammed it down.

"My guess is you're still a big deal in San Diego. Sometimes prosecutors *have* something and sometimes they *want* something. Nailing you again would make a nice trophy on some ambitious lawyer's mantelpiece. Go get some legal counsel – I'll keep my notes for when you need them. 'Cause you're gonna need 'em."

* * * * *

I woke up every morning in my bed at Boron wondering if this was the day someone from the San Diego Attorney General's office would return and break off another piece of my reputation – which was in tatters at this point anyway. I didn't expect the visitor who showed up couple weeks after my meeting with Tom and the SEC attorney.

"Hi John," Michelle greeted me in the visitors' room. John Paul and her aunt had come along as well. Michelle and I had been going through a great deal of conflict for the past few years due to the trials. The stress of living under this dark cloud had separated us. Either families remain tight or blow up because of legal troubles. We were barely holding it together. After spending 20 minutes talking with my son, Michelle's aunt led him outside to give us some privacy.

"What's going on?" Michelle asked me with worry in her voice, "Why are people asking questions again?"

"Who?" I replied, with a youch of anger, "Who approached you?"

Michelle's voice cracked. "People from the police. They wanted some documents in the house. I told them I didn't know what you had. They didn't believe me. They said if I didn't cooperate they were going to throw me in jail and take away John Paul-"

"They can't do that, they're just scaring you-"

"They did scare me. I can't live like this, I can't go through this again-"

"I'll get to the bottom of this-"

"From here?" Michelle half-joked, looking around the prison visitors' room, "You know I lost Dad during the last trial, I can't lose my son over this, he's my whole world, he means everything to me-"

"He's means everything to me, too-"

"You can't be there for him and he's the most important person in my world. We can't go on like this."

Even though I knew this day would come sooner rather than later, you're never prepared for it when it happens.

"You gave me a beautiful, beautiful boy," Michelle continued through tears, "And I'll always be thankful to you. But I gotta go. Please let me go."

I didn't want another divorce. I didn't want to lose my family. Michelle and I were having marital problems and things weren't great, but she was a smart woman and for awhile we were good together. I certainly didn't want to lose my son. Due in part to the public stress of the first trial, Michelle's father suffered a fatal heart attack. The health of my own parents' began to decline during this time as well. I didn't want the burden of my situation thrust upon anyone's shoulders any longer.

"Fine," I muttered, "You can go. They, uh, they treat me ok here. I'll deal with it."

"I'm sorry," Michelle weeped.

"Me, too." Michelle gave me a final hug as I walked her outside. I saw John Paul before they left the compound. Grabbed him and held him in my arms.

"It's gonna be awhile before I see you," I told John Paul, "You be good for Mom."

"I will," John Paul said. Even at nine, he had an idea of the seriousness of the visit.

I didn't have any idea how serious things would get.

* * * * *

Three days later, I was delivering goods to the Port Land Naval Base for UNICOR about an hour south of Boron. Traveling north on Interstate 5, I was listening to a news radio station when the headline hit.

"San Diego Pitcher John D'Acquisto has been indicted on 39 counts of securities fraud...."

I'm out on the road. This isn't like a ballplayer learning he's the centerpiece of a six-player trade while he's on vacation in Hawaii. No one said anything to me. How does the media get this information before I do? Usually, in baseball circles, beat guys receive tips from the front office about proposed deals, floating them in *"Baseball Notes"* columns as a trial balloon to gauge fan reactions before pulling the trigger on the swap. How does KCOP, the Union-Tribune or the Associated Press know about this before I do? I knew nothing about this happening. Why was this news *leaked*, as if someone in the prosecutor's office wanted the story believed and widespread?

If I wanted to, I could've taken that truck and hightailed it to Mexico, just to show you the incompetence of the San Diego Prosecutor's office at the time. Of course, I didn't. I went back to Boron.

Upon my return, the captain and warden came and got me, handcuffed me, led me to the stockade on the compound.

"Sorry, John," the warden said as the captain led me away.

The Captain, who was my friend, sat down with me in the stockcade.

"Johnny, what the hell's goin' on?"

"This has gotta be some sort of continuation of the trial."

"Is there something you're not telling me? They can't try you for the same thing."

"Tell that to the prosecutor's office."

"Well, I'm so sorry to do this, but we have to go by process. I gotta send ya to San Bernardino."

"San Bernardino? That place is a pit."

"I know. This is killing me to do this. Everyone likes you here. I hope you can figure out what the problem is and get your ass out of this mess."

So I was carted down to San Bernardino. Nothing at all like Boron. Hardcore gang-bangers, murderers, rapists. The real dregs of society. Close to maximum security. I found a San Diego-based defense attorney, Frank Veccionne. He visited me a day after I arrived in San Bernardino.

"Frank, you gotta get me outta here," I pleaded, "Look at my wrists." All cut up from the handcuffs. "There's 20 of us in an area the size of a child's bedroom." Bunk beds. Metal-based, little air mattresses – unbearable. It was like a Turkish prison. You couldn't even drink the water, it was full of sulfur. And your hair would start to fall out. You're talking completely inhumane treatment. The facilities didn't even purify your water to drink.

Frank sighed. "I need to read up more on the case, but from the looks of things, this smells really bad. The prosecutor wants to railroad you-"

"They've already railroaded me-"

"That's right. There's a serious double jeopardy violation here. It's like a local court trying a man for murder after he's been convicted in federal. The prosecutor is trying to navigate the wiggle room between your civil settlement and your conviction in New York for an easy, news-worthy conviction. It's shitty business and we're gonna beat 'em. Just keep your head down in here and gimme a little time."

"Thanks, Frank," I told him through the visitor's room telephone.

"Watch your back in here. I'll get you out soon."

I was left in San Bernardino for about 45 days. Finally, Frank was able to bring me in front of Judge Judith Keep in San Diego Federal Court. Frank explained my situation.

"Please approach the bench," Judge Keep told me. I stepped in front of the judge and showed her my wrists. A look of controlled anger came across her face as Frank walked her through my ordeal. Judge Keep turned to the prosecutor with a *"Are you kidding me"* expression as Frank suggested I be transferred to MCC, the local prison in San Diego.

"The defendant will be much safer here," Frank explained, "Mr. D'Acquisto doesn't belong in San Bernardino and the prosecutor *knows* he doesn't belong there."

"I'm allowing the transfer of the defendant to MCC," Judge Keep ordered, "This is absolutely unconscionable treatment. Dismissed."

MCC wasn't much better, but it wasn't the hellhole of San Bernardino. We weren't in cells, we were in open floors. We played cards. We could go outside where we'd work out and play basketball, but it was on top of the roof of the prison. There was no getting out. It was a smoky floor. There were gangs there, too, but I helped a few of them with their legal paperwork, so that was my protection. I was well-respected, well-liked. I knew prominent bankers, doctors and lawyers from San Diego that got themselves into trouble when the Great American Insurance debacle happened – a fair amount of executive VPs spent time there.

I felt safer in San Diego – my folks came to see me, my brother and sister, too. I felt slightly better about my situation that someone was looking out for me, because through the prosecutor's office and all the leaks to the media, someone was trying to bury me. With the transfer to San Bernadino, it was almost as if someone wanted to me to kill myself.

They didn't know me. I had been to this dance once before, believing the justice system was fair and true. I would be ready for the game this time. And they would throw everything they could at me to win.

Even my old friends.

* * * * *

About three months later, I discovered that the grand jury had a number of witnesses. Old colleagues of mine. Old acquaintances. And someone else.

My lawyer visited me at MCC for a consultation and updated me.

"First of all, the prosecution does not want you present for the trial," Frank explained.

"They can't do that-"

"I know, don't worry about that. We'll fight that and win." Frank kind of laughed, actually.

"Man, these people really want a piece of your ass, don't they?" I was not in the mood to hear jokes.

"What else did you find out?"

"Why did you buy a Mexican baseball team with investors' funds?"

"That was *my* money, I played there in the seventies. It's a nice business if you can buy it for the right price. I put down a $50,000 payment, but we couldn't raise the money and I got most of the deposit back. You got anything else?"

"Tell me about the horses-"

Now I was getting pissed.

"What does any of this have to do with the civil suit?" I said, very aggravated, "This was an investment Tom and I made to help my friend and his wife who were having money troubles-"

Frank kept going.

"What about the Porsche? Why did you buy the Porsche with investors' funds?"

"What?" I asked, taken aback, "How do you even know about the Porsche?"

"They're gonna bring it up, I have to ask you-"

"I've had a more expensive Mercedes for the last decade. I bought the car with my own money, I dunno, I was having troubles in my marriage, wanted something to make me feel good. The Porsche was my car when I played with the Padres and Giants. Why is that even relevant-"

Then it hit me.

"What?" Frank asked after a prolonged silence.

He always made snide remarks about my Porsche. He was furious that I fired him.

"Holy shit," I said in almost a whisper to Frank, "They're talking to Count."

"Who?"

"John Montefusco, my ex-teammate. He's the one who managed my horseracing investments."

I loved this man like blood. Count went before the Grand Jury, along with a number of former colleagues and acquaintances. The prosecutor reached out to nearly everyone I was associated with over the past decade in the hopes of building a case against me. I spent the rest of that afternoon conferring with Frank about my defense strategy.

"Do you have all the documents related to the civil suit?" Frank asked.

"I have everything back at my old home," I replied, "Everything that outlines my innocence. All the bank transfers, all the correspondence that the *judge wouldn't allow us to present* in the first case."

"You weren't allowed to present evidence in the first case?"

"No, the prosecution back in New York was allowed to cite the civil suit to gain a conviction but I wasn't allowed to use it to defend myself." Frank nodded and wrote down my old home address.

"We could call my old trader Jeff Kollar to the stand," I offered, "He'll be a wealth of information."

"I looked into that," Frank replied, "Can't. *He dropped dead of a heart attack six months ago.*"

"Damn," I replied, taken aback for a moment. Jeff was only 39 years old.

"I'll figure out the witness list. Let me work on this. The trial's in about two months. If you're telling the truth, and I believe you are, we're gonna beat this. I dunno if this gets you out or anything, it probably doesn't, but we're gonna keep you from extended prison time. They're gonna want a plea from you, you know, they're thinking the last thing you want is another conviction. We're gonna beat them." Then Frank showed me the letter.

"I've known John since he was a high school boy. He comes from a good family. He was well-respected among the coaches and his teammates. Knowing John for over 25 years, I can tell you, this crime is not at all in his makeup. I cannot for the life of me see John D'Acquisto committing this crime.

Sincerely,

Charles Francis Fox, manager, San Francisco Giants 1970-1974

There would be over 40 letters from former colleagues, acquaintances and respected members of the San Diego community who spoke on my behalf. I can't tell you how touched I was that Baseball reached out to support me in my time of need.

There were parts of the San Diego community that wanted me steam-rolled. There were also parts that wouldn't stand for it.

* * * * *

I was brought to Federal Court in San Diego a few months later. I handed Frank over 33,000 pages of documents and correspondence related to the D'Acquisto Financial Group. It spelled everything out. Judge Keep once again resided over the proceedings. Soon, the Judge asked for a list of witnesses. Frank and I submitted close to four pages of ex-colleagues, investors and brokers, traders, associates we were going to call to the witness stand in my defense.

"Can I see the list of witnesses the prosecution is prepared to call to the stand?" Judge Keep asked the prosecutor, Willian Q. Hayes. He stuttered a bit on his reply.

"The prosecution is prepared to present the case without any witnesses."

Judge Keep threw Hayes a double-take.

"Counsel, did I hear you just say you had no witnesses to present to this court?"

Turned out the people who spoke in front of the Grand Jury chose not to participate in the court trial. To the man's credit, Count chose not to get involved any further in my public lynching. Frank and I turned to each other. Frank, poker face in use, muttered a soft, curt, definitive, "Hmm."

"Nobody?" the Judge asked again.

"That is correct, Your Honor," Hayes replied. Judge Keep was furious.

"Baliff, place the defendant in holding," Judge Keep ordered, then pointed to the two lawyers, "You and you, in my chambers. *Now!*"

I sat in a holding pen for two hours, waiting, waiting, waiting with a U.S. marshall sitting across from me quietly.

"I never talk to prisoners because I think they're a bunch of fucking crooks," he finally said, "But I gotta tell ya, I've never seen any shit like this in my life. You're innocent, aren't ya?"

I couldn't say anyting to the Marshall. Just shrugged.

"I've never seen Judge Keep that ticked off." A few minutes later, Frank came back to get me.

"You should've heard her in there."

"Who, the Judge?" Frank nodded.

"'*This is dirty business going on,*' '*I don't want this in my courtroom.*' It was embarrassing."

"So what happened?"

Frank sighed. "You're not gonna get your day in court."

"Say that again?"

"This is going to a magistrate for a decision." Have you ever heard of that being done? Because we dumped so much evidence on the prosecutor, they couldn't properly develop their case. We had all this evidence. We humiliated the prosecutor.

"I think they're going to offer a deal," Frank continued. "What do you want to do?"

"Can we beat 'em?" Frank smiled.

"With the publicity we could generate with their heavy-handedness, maybe get you in front of some media, oh yeah. We can get beat 'em bad."

"Let me think about it," I said after a moment, "I've been through this before." Part of me just wanted this over and part of me was out for vengeance. These people, these public attorneys, they play with lives as a means of catapulting their careers. Awful people. That night I had it in my head to move forward and win, because I knew the prosecutor was just trying to run up the score on my life and I wanted to fight back. It might've gotten ugly, but I was itching for a brawl with these people. Especially when I knew I was gonna win.

"Johnny," the prison guard said to me, "You got a phone call. Sounds like an emergency."

I picked up the receiver. It was Fred, my brother.

"It's Pop," Fred said in a broken voice, "He had a stroke. He was at Saints working and then...Mom just called me from the hospital."

I was helpless. I couldn't run down to see my Dad. I just had to sit there and wait for bad news. My parents had gotten so stressed out from dealing with my legal troubles. You know, it's not just about what I'm going through. It's Mom heading to Safeway, pushing her cart up and down the aisles and familiar faces staring at her with gossipy gawking. It's Pop walking through the fish market – he may not hear the exact words of the whispers, but he knows they're there. I didn't want anymore of this on them. I called Frank the next day and told him the news.

"Johnny, I'm so sorry," Frank replied sincerely, "What can I do?"

"They offer a deal…take the deal."

"Why? We're going to win this-"

"I don't care. What are they gonna do, give me another five years? The days are just x's on a fuckin' calendar to me now. I don't want my parents and my family suffering anymore."

"We can beat them-"

"No. We'll take a deal if they offer it." Sure enough, two days later, Frank and I met with Hayes.

"We're dropping 38 counts of the indictment," he told us, "We're still charging you with misrepresentation."

I knew all along I was going to take the deal, but I wasn't about to make it easy on them.

"Why don't you drop 39?" I replied, "You know I didn't do this. You *know* that."

"Mr. D'Acquisto, we are prepared to accept your plea-"

"Look asshole, I'm gonna tell you something-"

"John, enough," Frank interjected.

"No, this man is ruining my reputation in the town I was born and raised to avoid embarrassment for him and his staff. This was all about you making points on my back to build your resume and you know it." The prosecutor sighed and didn't respond.

"What's the deal?" Frank asked him, ignoring me.

"Upon your acceptance and admission of guilt, you will be sentenced to another 53 months in prison to run concurrently with your current time in jail."

"What kind of deal is that," I asked.

"It means that the sentence runs back-to-back with your *current* sentence, correct?" Frank said to the prosecutor, as a manner of explaining to me.

"That is correct," Hayes responded, as Frank continued.

"It means while the defendant probably won't receive parole, assuming good behavior, he won't really serve anymore time than the current sentence. Perhaps even a little less. Is that correct?"

The prosecutor nodded as Frank kept talking.

"It means the prosecutor gets the win, gets the publicity, they don't look like the incompetent asses that they are, and we keep quiet about it, correct?"

The prosecutor nodded.

"This will be a sealed file."

"Sealed file," I exclaimed, "Fuck you, sealed file! If I take this all the way some heads are gonna roll down Broadway and Front Streets, that's why Judge Keep doesn't to be anywhere near this. How does someone not get their day in court to prove their innocence-"

"He'll take the deal," Frank replied, looking at me with a scolding expression.

I took the deal. At sentencing, Judge Keep, if you can believe this, asked me where I wanted to serve out the remainder of my sentence.

"Your Honor, if it pleases the court, I would like to return to Boron and resume my work as a fireman."

"Mr. D'Acquisto, I find that highly commendable. I order the U.S. Attorney to assign you to Boron Facility for the rest of your sentence."

And that was that. The prosecutor got his win. The newspapers got their story (*"Ex-Pitcher Convicted Again"*), the world thought I was going away until the year 2007, but I knew I would get a small portion of my life back within two years or so.

I had Frank Veccionne, a tireless attorney who helped me dig deep and find the truth to the story, with saving my life.

* * * * *

I returned to the Boron facility a couple months after the trial during the summer of 1999. The warden, Don Campbell, the captain, still a number of familiar faces. Still fought fires. Still blasted AC/DC on the ride back to the compound. It was a life of service, reasonable food with the occasional treat provided to me by the woman who worked in the commissary. I returned to school for environmental studies and further EMT certification. Our prison fire-fighting program was such a success we conducted demonstrations at facilities throughout California. About July 2000, it was announced that the Boron prison compound was closing and many of us would be sent to an outfit called Victorville, where we would assist in the construction and expansion of the prison. After close to 10 months, it was decided that Victorville would be a women's only facility and once again, I was on the move. It helped that the captain at the new Victorville was my friend from Boron. A few months later, the captain called me over as I was carrying cinderblocks across the camp one humid afternoon.

"I just got word about the transfer destinations," he said to me, "I'm recommending you go to Florence."

"Where the hell's that?"

"Colorado Springs." I shrugged.

"As good a place as any other, I guess."

"No, John, this 'll be good for you. They'll treat someone with your work ethic well." Off I went again. Seemed like I was swapped around like a proven bat at the August deadline, just in time for the stretch drive.

UNICOR hooked me up with a desk job at Florence, another minimum security outfit. Due to my decent computer skills, I received the head shipping operations position. I also drove a 53-footer when needed. I made deliveries to Cheyenne, Peterson Air Force Base – oh, I had a ball. Great job, making $250 a month, which was nice dough inside. All the cigarettes I wanted.

I was driving with my captain, getting gas outside the compound. I let my mind wander a bit as this sleek, Mercedes convertible pulled up beside us.

"Hey," the captain poked at me excitedly. A little too excitedly.

"Owww, what?"

"Do you know who that is?" I looked over.

Leaning against the Mercedes, he was six-foot-four, maybe six-five. Closely-shaved, grayish hair that obviously was golden blond at one time. Fu-manchu-like moustache.

Goose.

15 feet away from me and I couldn't say a word to him.

"That's The Goose! That's Goose Gossage. He lives in the area, you know. He's always at that bar around the corner from here. You know Goose, don'tcha?"

I turned to the Captain with a smile on my face.

"Maybe." The Captain caught on, or at least thought he did.

"Oh, yeah. That makes sense. Nice guy though, right?"

I knew the rules. As a prisoner, I was strictly forbidden from interacting with citizens while outside the facility on official business. I had six months left to go and I wasn't jeopardizing that to prove to a bunkmate that ballplayers still knew me. But that wasn't why I was smiling. Goose's appearance at that gas station might've been the rainbow I'd been praying for. Somewhere, somehow, the Baseball gods delivered me a message. *"See that guy beside that sweet Benz? That's you in six months. You're gonna be ok, Johnny."*

I didn't approach Goose on that bright, bright sunshiney day, but the message was clear as I looked straight ahead at the blue sky all around us.

The rain was almost gone.

At The End Of The Line

What's it like the day you leave prison? When you're not a habitual criminal and you *know* you're not going back, your mind locks off everything you saw, everything you felt and throws away the key. It never happened. Sure, you know there's going to be some random asshole that makes a remark or cracks a joke just to remind you, but for the rest of your waking hours, you function as if it was all a nightmare. It's the only way you can move forward. Those first few weeks, you walk in and out of stores, wondering if people looked at you differently. Every day was judgment day.

I came out with another divorce, another chapter of my family life under another roof. I looked for work – I wanted to be back in the game in the worst way, but it was 2002 now. Who among my contemporaries was left? Rickey Henderson was barely hanging on in Boston. Mike Morgan had the same situation in Arizona. Among the managers, Donny Baylor was on the verge of being fired in Chicago and my friend Bob Boone was having rough go of it as skipper of the Reds. Last thing they needed was a call from the past, asking about coaching gigs in Double A ball. Joe Torre was the king of New York, but I hadn't spoken to him in almost 20 years. Country Chuck Manuel was holding onto the Indians job by his fingernails and we hadn't crossed paths much since I dropped him off at the Sands Motel back in '73. All my close friends, the ones who hadn't retired or passed away, were in local TV broadcasting gigs or talking head stuff with ESPN. Besides, it wasn't really my style to contact a buddy out of the blue with my hand open. You can always feel it when you get that call or email, and it's never comfortable, especially when you're not a position of doling out charity. So a job in Major League Baseball was out for now.

What really killed me were the friends I reached out to upon release. There was an awkward silence on many of these calls, as if they were waiting for me to ask about a job, or even money. The oral sense of relief when they realized I was calling just to hear their voice hurt me a bit. I was never about money. I always took care of myself, my family and others.

I started working in construction, operating a crane for my friend Mike Samudio. The days were long, but after five years of incarceration, I could've pulled those levers all through the night, appreciating the freedom, the fresh air not contaminated by the refuse of incinerators, the knowledge that there was no legal curfew hanging over my existence. I was happy just to be alive.

I ended up getting a call from Mike Winn, an old buddy asking if I still played golf. He brought me on board to manage course operations for him at a local country club. Anything I could find that kept me outdoors, just a reminder that I was free. I appreciated every customer, every drink I enjoyed with a fan at the 19th hole, every swing I corrected. I loved the feeling that I left every member better off than when they met me.

That first party my family threw me upon my release was memorable. Fred was there, so many extended family members.

My sister Jeanette and her husband Nick held a wine tasting at the house – invited the family and all her friends. Was happy to see Jeannette's best friend, Sharon. I remembered working with her at the bank back in the '80s – her and my sister became close and had been pretty tight ever since. A five-foot-seven brunette with a shapely figure and a pretty face, we chatted a bit in between welcome home hugs and kisses from my family. The next night, Jeanette came over again for Sunday dinner.

"Johnny," my sister said as we cleared off the table for dessert, "I think Sharon kinda likes you. You two should meet up."

"Oh yeah?" I replied, "She's kinda cute. Smart, too."

"Just be a gentleman-"

"Well, I have been away awhile," I joked.

"You know what I mean," Jeanette shot back, elbowing my side, "Don't be a jock."

A few days later, Sharon and I had dinner at my place. We talked about the banking business – she had become a successful accountant since I first knew her. We talked about music, about San Diego, what I missed while I was gone. As she sat across the candlelit table in my dining room, describing her life before meeting my family, I realized I didn't miss dating, didn't necessarily miss women – *of course, I missed women* - but Lord knows, obviously I had more than my share through the years. What I missed was conversation with the *right* woman, the deep, back and forth that comes through mutual interest and desire to hear more about a person, not nominal curiosity that you know will end in someone's bedroom. That willingness to open your soul and tell another human being everything about you and how much you want to hear their thoughts, their dreams, their successes, their failures. And when the night ends early, you have that longing in your heart that makes you want to continue the dialogue as soon as politely possible.

I didn't ask for a second date and neither did she. Our expressions told us everything we needed to know.

"Good night," we said softly with a glance that demanded *"Call me soon."* I hadn't smiled that wide in a decade.

When I returned to my townhouse, there was a message on my machine from Jeannette.

"Sharon, you better not be there," the voicemail began with humor in her voice. That wasn't happening.

I always did what I was told.

I called my sister back, told her we had a nice time. No monkey business, just a mature, grownup dinner. "Maybe we'll do it again."

There was no maybe.

Those following weeks were filled with more dinners, movies, walks on the beach, sporting events – just as friends. Around the 10th or 11th time we were out together, a notion hit me, an idea this jock never considered in his whole life being around buddies and close-knit teammates, even though there was Onti my roomie through the minors, there was Count for a spell, there was Keith for a few months, there was Eric, Randy and Rollie in San Diego, they were great pals, but Holy shit, it wasn't like this.

I think I just found my best friend.

"I'm hosting Thanksgiving this year," I said to Sharon, "You know, breaking in the new townhouse. Mom, Dad, Fred, Jeanette and all the kids will be there. Why don't you join us?"

Sharon's eyes lit up at the sound of my invitation. Without saying a word, I knew I'd have to bring in an extra chair for the last Thursday in the month.

* * * * *

Mom's Italian stuffing. Jeannette's cranberry sauce. Kids stomping all over the living room of my new townhouse. The Detroit Lions getting beaten again by Brett Favre and the Packers. Warm, affectionate chaos going on around us and I shut it off like 20,000 screaming fans in a game at The 'Stick. Just Sharon and I talking.

"So what are you doing for Christmas?" she asked.

"Well, Christmas is my birthday," I replied, "But I'm not putting up lights or anything – you know, still not feeling very festive." Ever the sharp accountant, I could see Sharon calculating the personal data I just provided, weighing the emotional balance sheet of her thoughts at the moment, as a magnificent smile made its way across her face.

"I got a tree."

One week later, Jeannette brought over some extra bulbs and tinsel, and then I had a tree, too.

That night, I took Sharon to the The Hotel Del Cornado in San Diego, to watch the lighting of the 50 foot tree in the lobby, all the children ice skating with their families. A true holiday setting. We finished our visit with a drink at the hotel bar.

"I used to come to see this every year," Sharon said, her eyes poised on the hotel decorations, "It wasn't Christmas in my family until we saw this."

Once we got home, Sharon began trimming the tree in my living room. I poured us some wine.

"It's lookin' pretty good," I remarked, handing her a glass. We toasted our drinks, and her smile turned serious.

"I love you."

"What?"

"I love you so much," Sharon said. It had been, God, I don't know how long since a woman said that to me. 10 years? For the right woman? *Never?* I took a step back and walked toward my balcony, sliding the door.

"I love you too," I replied, though kinda quiet about it.

"You sure," Sharon said, with half a laugh. I needed some air, and it had nothing at all to do with my feelings for her, which were accelerating with every moment. I knew where this was headed. Smart, no-nonsense women like Sharon don't make statements like that unless they mean it. Sharon followed me out to the balcony.

"You ok with what I said?"

"Oh yeah. Oh yeah. I love you, but...."

"But, what?"

I married once out of youth. I married again out of loneliness.

"I've been married before. I'm not very good at it. I love you so much. How do I do this without fucking up?"

Sharon touched my heart with her confident smile. She held my hand, this woman, who knew everything about me, everything I had been through, and just basically told me with her eyes, *"This is not that. This is this. This is ok."* Never before had I fell for someone who I *liked* this much, never mind love, never mind attraction, liked. Like's huge. Like is what keeps it going. I didn't know exactly how to handle it, but I knew I never, ever wanted it to go away.

Sharon held my hand like a confidant, then hugged me like a friend. A best friend, as she presented her stance in no uncertain and logical terms.

"I love you, John. I loved you since the minute I saw you walk down the stairs at your parent's house. So what are you gonna do about it?"

It wasn't Mom telling me I had to get married.

It wasn't the crushing loneliness of the road convincing me to get married.

It wasn't a gorgeous girl wanting a baby convincing me to get married.

It wasn't someone who wanted my money, my name, my influence, my Rolodex.

It was someone who wanted *me*. Isn't it wonderful when you find someone who has everything necessary to prosper in this world but they want you, warts and all, *just because*?

I wasted some much love on friends that betrayed me, co-workers that nearly destroyed me, vicious people that stepped in between me and the world of baseball that I love so much. That relationship would still take some time to mend.

But in this moment before me, that night on the balcony, I gazed at the most glorious, precious gift God allowed to enter my life.

That night was almost 12 years ago.

My wife Sharon has decorated our tree every Christmas since.

Just A Song Before I Go

*"*H*i John, this is Mario Alioto. The Giants will be celebrating the last 50 years of the organization this season. We'll be breaking the ceremonies by position over the course of the year, so as to give as many players their moment with the fans. The team will provide you and your family round-trip tickets, lodging and $300 to cover incidentals for the weekend. Hope to see you there!"*

I received this email in late January 2008. I was walking the dog at the time when the message hit my blackberry.

"Hey Honey," I called out to Sharon, entering our home through the garage, "Take a look at this." Sharon's eyes lit up upon reading the email.

"Sounds like fun," she said, scanning the message, "They're flying us up, you'll get to see the fans, you said you missed that, you get to see your old teammates-" then she stopped.

"Oh."

"Yeah," I said. I get to see my old teammates.

* * * * *

I hadn't been to many major league functions those past six years. I married Sharon in 2004, a nice ceremony at the Stardust

Golf & Country Club in San Diego, relatively low-key. Our families, only a few close teammates. My old high school buddy Dave Gonzalez was there. Jerry Johnson, my ex-Giants teammate on the pitching staff, stopped by as well.

It was a beautiful ceremony at the club, and we settled in La Jolla for a couple years. In 2006, the San Diego Padres threw a homecoming for ex-players. Tony Gwynn was there, Randy was there, Rollie was there, too. Sharon and I attended. Enjoyed seeing old baseball war buddies at the reception. Then I entered into a room, where a few ex-Padres from the '80s I wasn't particularly close with chatted amongst themselves. One of them saw me in the corner of his eye and leaned into the group.

"Here comes Johnny D," he whispered loud enough for me to hear, "Watch your wallets." There was that *"Oh, you're bad,"* sort of playfully scolding laughter from the group. I didn't come here to hear that from my teammates. Not from *baseball.*

"I need some air," I said to Sharon, and walked outside for a cigarette.

I never thought someone from my Baseball family would take petty shots at me like that. baseball had always been my sanctuary from the bullshit of life.

"That was pretty rough, Bud," Randy said from behind me, following me out into the courtyard.

"He's lucky I don't go back there and deck him." I was furious.

"Aww, don't mind him," Randy said, "He's an asshole. Never could get anybody out, either."

"I'm tired of people acting like they know what happened, like I did something to hurt people."

"I know you didn't do it, Johnny. Some people are just mean to be mean. If it wasn't that, it'd be something else."

As usual, Randy made a bad situation better.

"C'mon back inside, JD." I dashed out my smoke and we returned to the party.

"Heh heh, you really wanna lay 'em out, don't cha?" Randy joked as we entered the open doorway.

"I do," I grinned. We shared a quick laugh, but nothing else happened. Still, that was only a couple years earlier and fresh in my mind. About 10 months later, Sharon and I moved to a town outside Phoenix. Not so much a fresh start as finding a place similar to San Diego, but with a much more comfortable cost of living. We've made a wonderful life together in Arizona.

* * * * *

All through dinner that evening, outside in the mild 90 degree heat, in the shadow of the Camelback Mountains, I started looking through a scrapbook my sister Jeannette kept for me from my playing days. I paged through team publicity shots and newspaper articles, box scores from my years in San Francisco.

So many incredible memories of the Bay Area – the restaurants, the bars, the clubs, the fans – oh, the fans. I missed the Giants fans like you wouldn't believe. The folks in San Diego always treated me like a family member, but San Francisco – you never forget your first. I spent a good 30 minutes with that scrapbook. Sharon poured us another glass of wine as the sun slipped behind the mountains.

"So you wanna go?" she asked me with a nudge. I looked down at the scrapbook one last time, finding a small UPI item from 1973 that sealed the deal for me.

"D'Acquisto Joins Satisfied Giants."

Four months later, Sharon helped me with my suitcase, stood before my eyes, drove us to the airport and onto the friendly skies of San Francisco.

* * * * *

My hip condition warning that kept me from serving in the Vietnam War became a full-fledged problem in the 2000s. I hadn't been on an airplane for many years. I was in a bit of discomfort on the flight to San Fran, sort of fussy, until I looked up at the person sitting across the aisle.

"Johnny D'Acquisto," he asked. I recognized the elderly gentleman with the inviting expression, then it hit me.

"Ray Sadecki," I exclaimed, "Great to see you, man! How are things?"

"Oh, getting old," Ray replied, settling into the aisle seat, "You know how it is. Where are you these days?"

"We're in the Sedona area. I see a few of the other guys around." Ray was a reliable number three starter for the Giants in the late '60s, but never lived down the fact that Stoneham traded Orlando Cepeda straight up for him, as the Baby Bull continued his Hall of Fame career after leaving the Bay Area. We were enjoying our conversation as this taller gentleman with an athletic build approached our seats.

"Are you guys going to the Giants thing?" he asked me, staring as if he couldn't quite place our faces.

"Why yes we are, Mark Davis," I grinned back, "John D'Acquisto."

"Johnny, hey," Mark replied with a *"Now I remember"* move of his hand, "How ya been?" Mark had been a promising southpaw starter for San Fran back in the early '80s until he was included in that blockbuster eight-player trade in '87 that brought Kevin Mitchell to the Giants.

The Giants' publicity department had thoughtfully booked all our plane tickets together. It was an enjoyable, two-hour flight down memory lane for the three of us, recounting our favorite Giants moments from our respective decades. None of us overlapped the other on the roster during our playing careers, so we shared stories about teammates that were new to each of us.

After we arrived safely, we all grabbed our luggage and headed toward the exit. I'll always remember the befuddled look on Sadecki's face.

"We got our stuff, now how the hell we supposed to get there?"

"I think they said there's a car waiting for us," Mark added. Sure enough, a man with a sign "Sadecki/D'Acquisto/Davis" was a few steps away. The three of us and our spouses piled into the stretch limo outside and headed for the reunion.

As we drove down Highway 101 toward the Marriott Courtyard, Sadecki leaned into me.

"I got cancer, ya know," Ray said quietly. Kind of out the blue. How do you respond to that, especially when it's someone you don't know all *that* well?

"You've always been a bulldog," I replied, "You still got a lot of innings left in that body."

Ray just laughed, "Stayin' in the game ain't the same as winnin'."

"I'll pray for you," I said sincerely, at sort of a loss for words.

* * * * *

The party began as soon as we entered the Marriott Courtyard. The faces hit me one after the other. John Antonelli. Tom Griffin. Donny Carrithers. Gaylord Perry. Dave Dravecky. Rags Righetti. Dave Rader. Jerry Johnson. Mike Sadek, my first catcher, was there with his kid, daughter-in law and grandchild. It was an absolute family affair. Deep hugs. Surprised expressions. Camera flashes. Smartphone clicks. We were brothers in arms. My Giants comrades began checking into the hotel in waves. Jim Barr. Milt May. Fred Breining. Every guy had a story to tell, family photos to share, a laugh to generate. I was having a drink with Donny Carrithers recounting our fishing trip in 1973 with Bobby Bonds when I offered to get a refill. Walking to the bar, I nodded and beckoned to at least five other Giants' pitchers and catchers, then I heard his voice.

"Hey, Johnny."

Count.

Wasn't quite sure how I would handle this. It had been over 12 years since we saw each other. The best of friends throughout most of our careers, until he betrayed me. In the back of my mind, I considered for four months how I would react if I saw him. I wondered if everyone was waiting to see how we would handle the meeting. Would I get in his face? Would I cause a scene? Would I let him know how much pain and agony his lying did to me, to my family, to my reputation?

"Hey Count," I replied without emotion. We must've stared at one another for close to a minute. Finally, I extended my hand.

"Whatever happened, happened. All in the past." Count and I shook hands.

"Thanks," Count said, "I'm sorry. For everything."

I nodded, still a wealth of conflicting emotions bubbling inside me.

"And now we move on." One of my earliest spring training teammates, John Cumberland, approached me with a hug. I didn't speak to Count again that afternoon.

Chemistry's a funny thing. Not just between a man and a woman, but buddies. You begin telling each other's jokes, you learn the other's likes/dislikes, almost to a point where they become your own. I spent most of that first day hanging out with Cumberland, reminiscing, what was, what could've been, all that stuff. He brought his grownup sons, John and Paul, showing off his kids to everyone. Later in the early evening, Cumberland tapped me on the shoulder, "What are we doing about dinner?"

"We have to go to the House of Prime Rib. Best piece of meat in town. We used to rip that place up back in the day."

"Johnny, House of Rib gets packed on a Saturday night," Cumberland explained, "There's no way we'll get a reservation."

I couldn't be reasoned with.

"We're goin' to the House of Prime Rib. We'll get a table." Well, the House of Prime Rib was packed solid and it did take finagling, but they accommodated the five of us, me, Sharon, Jerry Johnson, his wife and Cumberland. Here's the funny thing about chemistry. About 20 minutes into our meal, guess who stumbled out of the back room of the restaurant?

"Who let you guys in here?" Count laughed, walking through with Ed *"Ho-Ho"* Halicki, our old teammate and partner in the Porsche race. It was good to see Ho-Ho.

"Hey, John D," Ho-Ho greeted me in the same deep, sing-song voice from the old days. This was the best example of how close Count and I were at one time. Always on the same wavelength. They joined our table for 30 minutes or so, then left. The rest of us retreated to the outside bar at the Marriott for after-dinner drinks and then Cumberland's suite for even more cocktails once it was closing time. We got back to our room around four in the morning. You'd be surprised how much alcohol old athletes can put away.

Then again, maybe you wouldn't.

* * * * *

Five hours later – yes, five hours later - we were transported via trolley car to the stadium, greeted at this tent set up in Seals Plaza, a sectioned-off area of the parking lot of A T&T park for the welcome breakfast. Streamers everywhere, denoting the 50-year anniversary party. There wasn't a bright eye in the whole bunch. We were all hungover. 10 AM open bar, brunch buffet, but I actually turned to water and lots of it. There were moving speeches. Dave Dravecky, a fine pitcher who lost his arm to cancer, gave an incredible speech about surviving (and thriving) in the wake of a life-threatening disease. Giants' broadcasters and former players Mike Krukow and Duane Kuiper introduced the speakers. The greatest sight of the morning for me was seeing one of my best friends in of all baseball show up alongside his children and wife of 57 years.

"Hey there, Johnny," Roger Craig said, offering a warm hug as we saw each other.

"It's great to see you, Skip." Roger gave that wink and nod as he leaned in to speak softly.

"You and me had a hellvua run."

"We did," I nodded, "And I'll never forget it."

"I'm proud of you, Johnny."

"Thanks, Roger." I almost lost it there, and would have more opportunities for emotions to reveal themselves.

Couple hours later, it was time for the pre-game ceremony. The Giants had placed markers where each of us would stand, side by side, along the pitching mound as we were announced. We would walk onto the grass from an opening in right field corner, also known as "McCovey Cove." One by one, the pitchers and catchers were announced over the sound system, some players with historical achievements, some were simply on the team for x number of years. Finally, my moment came.

"He played for the Giants from 1973 to 1976 and won the NL Rookie Pitcher of the Year award in 1974, ladies and gentleman, John D'Acquisto."

To hear the fans, to see their faces, after everything that had happened to me, the marriages, the broken families, the incarceration, to be welcomed back into that baseball home, you couldn't see it from far away, but I was ready to cry. Few moments in my life touched me like this. And then the next player announced sent me over the edge.

Alvin Dark, my first manager in San Diego. As he stepped on his marker on the grass beside me, Al reached out his hand.

"Johnny," he said, "I was wrong about you. I was wrong about a lot of things. You're a good person. I'm sorry." I began to cry.

"You're a good person too, Al," I said back as we embraced.

I found a lot of things that weekend. My ability to forgive. My ability to accept another's sorrow. My undying love for the Bay Area. Most of all, I know now that, regardless of what cynical sportswriters and radio call-in jocks claim, the game of baseball sometimes *can* love you back.

Unconditionally.

* * * * *

So, is it a happy recap?

I think so. The greatest lesson in life that I never realized during my baseball career is what I give you now: as long as you are still alive, *keep playing*. I never stole money from anyone, not a dime. The managers of our nation thought otherwise, and suspended me for a few years. I could've given up, gone homeless, suicide, something drastic, but I kept playing. I got my life back together. I found the greatest love from the most wonderful person in the whole wide world. I stayed in the game. No one can keep you from playing except yourself. When Buzzie tried to ruin me in California, I allowed it to happen. When the Braves didn't call me up after three straight complete game victories, I let that business decision get in my head. When I didn't play for a manager that loved me, I allowed it to affect my performance. As an athlete in today's world, I guarantee if you play your game and you are great, someone will notice and no one will be able to hold you back.

There's so many people looking for you – you, the talented athlete - writers, bloggers, that kid stuck in accounting at a big six firm who stashes a minor leaguer in his fantasy keeper league, that dentist whose dream is to compile data and create baseball theories, they're dying to find you and they're looking every day, waiting to discover the next Greek God of walks, a pitcher who happens to have plus velocity, someone is going to find you. Just play your game, don't aim for the majors, just do what it is you were meant to do. *Just throw to the glove.* They will find you, and when they do, awwww, they're gonna virtually yell from the rafters of the internet, *"How can you not see what I see?"* And there's some intern from Brown analyzing the WAR of A-ball players for the big club working for pennies, reading every blog, every remark in a comment section, seeking that edge that's gonna catch the eye of the general manager, it's in his interest to find you. Never again believe that no one's watching – and this goes for all sports. No one who plays their game and succeeds will be left behind ever again. There's too many interested people seeking an edge, seeking a narrative. Your talent is their content, and no manager, no GM, no asshole coach can keep the data from seeping through to the interested parties.

They wanna find you. If you throw three complete games and get passed over, hang in there. Don't be like me. Don't let it affect your performance. Keith Law, Jim Callis, rifling through the data. They're all out there seeking that one kernel of potential, just for the moment to eloquently state, *"I called it."* If you have talent in life and someone is in your way, don't let them get in your head, just keep producing, keep working, keep going.

Keep.Playing.

The line score of my life, so far?

One good run, great hits, couple errors and an unearned walk.

Acknowledgements

When you undergo a literary project of this magnitude, you certainly need room for factual checks and balances. The last thing you want is leaving unforced errors behind that wouldn't occur with a bit of extra leg work. We would like to start things off by expressing our sincere gratitude to Sean Forman and all of his colleagues at Baseball-Reference.com. While I have certainly been blessed with quite a recall – to be sure, there's a few times in my life I'd much rather forget – the "B-REF" website was not only my virtual memory-checker but also reminded me of facts, figures and faces I hadn't thought of in years. Thank you so very much, Sean.

Another instrument in our fact-checking tool box was newspapers.com. It was quite a treat traveling through the yellowed pages of The Fresno Bee, the Arizona Republic, San Bernardino County Sun, pieces courtesy of UPI and the Associated Press, as well as the likes of The Decatur Daily Review, and the Phoenix Gazette, which are no longer with us. Also want to mention the San Bernardino beat reporter Jim Schulte, who really was Angels fans' eyes and ears back in 1981.

I would be remiss by not acknowledging Jim Furtado, Darren Viola and all the commenters at the Baseball Think Factory website. No one on the web has been a bigger advocate for the instreamsports.com athlete stories, and no one kept us as honest, either. The praise touched our hearts; the occasional criticism pushed us to improve our work with every post. It is, to me, the most intelligent group of baseball fans on the web. Thanks, folks.

We also would like to thank Jeff Polman, a fantastic artist and outstanding author in his own right, for the brainstorming sessions regarding the book cover. I know Dave had definitive ideas about the image we would convey and Jeff was generous with this time working through the process with us. Of course, I need to say thanks for my cousin Jimmy D'Aquisto, who was instrumental in the final artistic product as well.

We want to extend our gratitude to our proofreader, typesetter, formatting lead, Rosa Penn. Thanks so much for getting us to the finish line properly.

I never realized how supportive the sportswriters' community was until I decided to write a book. The great New York Yankees historian Marty Appel was very giving of his time, with providing street-smart advice on how to navigate the sometimes arbitrary avenues of the publishing world. It was his keen insights that led Dave and me to roll the dice on this project. Peter Golenbock also lent us an ear with words of encouragement and caution throughout the process. Embarking on what was truly a transcontinental project wasn't always easy, and I was fortunate to bounce ideas and thoughts off of my good friend Barry Bloom, who was always at the ready with intelligent perspectives into the process here in Arizona.

As much as we love what we've presented to you here, Dave and I were concerned about over-confidence clouding our judgment of the text. We sought feedback from a select group of close friends and acquaintances, not simply popular writers and bloggers but also folks who spend every day from September to June nit-picking every extra comma, every dangling participle. We would like to thank Scott Milslagle, a true baseball fanatic and school teacher, who took time from his large, lovely family and his coaching duties to give us the first read of the rough draft. Esteemed New York Mets writer Greg Prince gave of his time while finishing his excellent tome of the 2015 National League Champions, "Amazin' Again," to offer his thoughts on the completed manuscript. I know I'm speaking for Dave when I say there were many nights where Greg's simple sentences of enthusiastic support for the text pulled Dave from a state of extreme caution. Of course, I cannot forget the public vote of confidence we received from Rob Neyer, who generously offered his endorsement of the project. In addition, we would be remiss in not including the following people for their gift of time, advice, support and friendship from the very outset of my writing: Al Olson, Colin Greer, Ted Cogswell, Chris Case, Kevin Crane, Joe Bonomo, "Bakes," Samantha Moller, Bailey Walsh, Michael Ansaldo, Patrick Toth, Mike Holcomb, Bruce Markusen, Evan Schwartzberg and Mat Van Alstyne.

We also would like to thank our agent, Lyn Delliquari, who introduced us to the publishing community and worked as a tireless advocate for the finished product. More than simply our business representative, Lyn was the den mother to this book, always positive, always encouraging, always kept the ship moving forward.

I don't even know where to start about this man because without him there is no book. Dave introduced me to Dan Epstein a few years back – he served as something between a brilliant, conscientious editor and a literary big brother to "Fastball John." His notes upon reading the first draft were specific and insightful, offering a perspective that made the book so much better. I wish every first-time author had someone like Dan Epstein in their corner.

I have countless baseball brothers both long gone and still with us who fundamentally changed me for the better. At this time I would like to extend sincere thanks and appreciation to my buddies Eric "Ras" Rasmussen, Petey Falcone, Gaylord Perry, Kurt Bevacqua, Donnell Alexander and Randy Jones. Thanks for having my back every step of the way.

I also want to thank my family – my sister Jeannette who always made sure to keep an updated scrapbook of my career, my brother Fred who has been so much a part of the journey you've just read, my brother-in law Nick, my niece Cristina, my nephews Fredy and Derek. They all supported me through the ups and downs of a baseball career…and my life.

To my children Vanessa, Danica and John Paul; now you understand the circumstances of my life that were beyond my control. Not a single day goes by without thinking of each of you.

Lastly, to my beloved wife and best friend. Sharon, you stuck it out alongside me through the conversations and research into the early morning hours, the sleepless nights and late phone calls that kept you up for years in the process of writing this book. It all added to this tale and now you are a vital part of the story. I love you.

Index

ABOUT THE AUTHORS

John D'Acquisto was named National League Rookie Pitcher of the Year in 1974. John pitched in the major leagues for ten seasons, mostly for the San Francisco Giants and San Diego Padres. Named as one of the fastest pitchers ever, by Bill James, his fastball was recorded at 102.4 MPH. Currently, John works as a Field Timing Coordinator and Headset Replay Technician for MLB in Phoenix, Arizona, where he resides. John is also an accomplished artist licensed by MLB through Legendary Sports Prints and Artwork by John D'Acquisto.

Dave Jordan is the founder of Instream Sports, the first athlete-author website, home to the highly acclaimed first-person essays from many Hall of Fame and popular baseball and football players, praised by NBC Sports, Deadspin and SB Nation. He has also written, directed and produced films, including the SXSW festival hit "The Paper Mache Chase," starring Jim Gaffigan, Cynthia Nixon and Spalding Gray. He lives in New Jersey.

Made in the USA
Monee, IL
03 September 2021